The Future of Media

The Future of Media

Edited by Joanna Zylinska with Goldsmiths Media

Goldsmiths
Press

Goldsmiths
UNIVERSITY OF LONDON

Contents

THE FUTURE OF 'DIVERSITY' IN MEDIA

THE FUTURE OF FEMINISM

THE FUTURE OF QUEER MEDIA

THE FUTURE OF DANCE

THE FUTURE OF AUDIO

THE FUTURE OF ACTIVISM

THE FUTURE OF DIGITAL HUMANITARIANISM

Introduction: The Future of Media

Goldsmiths Media

This book is going to press at a time when speculations about the future – not just the future of media, be it 'traditional' or 'new', but also of the many other aspects of our socio-political life such as communication platforms, political frameworks or, indeed, the world itself – are rife with existential anxieties. We are in the middle of a global pandemic caused by the Covid-19 virus; the most vulnerable groups in our society are experiencing significant threats to their lives and livelihoods; the rise of populism, nationalism and totalitarianism across the globe is threatening to undermine the working of democracy; the post-Brexit UK is looking with uncertainty at its future relationship with the European Union; the university as a place of research, learning and encounter has been converted into an online service provider; while the ice extent on the Arctic is at a record low. Given the protracted timeline of the publication process, by the time this book reaches its readers some of the specific events of late 2020 and early 2021 will have no doubt receded into a distant memory, but their wider global underpinnings and consequences are likely to be with us for a long time: inequality, racism and sexism; the weakening of democracy; progressing automation and surveillance of life and labour; the health and mental health crisis; the looming climate catastrophe. It is against this horizon that the present collection is set.

Since media operate as one of the dominant forces through which we make sense of ourselves and the world, it seems apposite that a collection which investigates the future of media would adopt such a wide socio-political horizon. Avoiding a narrow technicist perspective, the authors see media as inherently shaped by cultural forces, while also being involved in the shaping of both culture and society. Yet as part of this inquiry due attention is also paid by many contributors to the specific technological developments in the present media landscape, from close analyses of specific genres and platforms through to accounts of their own work on and with media.

The idea for this book arose a couple of years ago, when the Department of Media, Communications and Cultural Studies at Goldsmiths, which is one of the oldest and largest departments offering this configuration of subjects in the world, decided to work on a shared project that would bring together our multiple approaches, positions and ways of working. We agreed that the 'future of media' theme should serve as an umbrella term for a more detailed exploration of various issues and questions, such as: Is the future of media to be primarily driven by ideas or by platforms? Is it to be led by academics or by the industry? By Silicon Valley or by China? By AI, by VR or by biotech? Under this umbrella we also wanted to explore the future of journalism as a profession and a way of being a media-making informed citizen. We wanted to look at the merging of media forms and formats, such as TV, film, photography and CGI, asking what media content, what platforms and what jobs this merging would bring about. Last but not least, we wanted to show how the university as one of the key places of media education and education *in* media literacy can be actively involved in shaping the future of media, and not just in commenting on it. In other words, we intended to reflect on, and demonstrate, how we can train better future media users *and* media workers.

The book is also a celebration – of the increasing vivacity and importance of the discipline of media studies in the modern world, and of our department, which in 2018 celebrated its 40th anniversary. What may at first glance seem like a narrow approach coming from one specific academic institution opens up onto the wider debates, approaches and issues that make up this particular node of media education located in the impoverished borough of New Cross in London, UK, yet connected to many other global (and local) forces, ideas, industries and bodies. These connections are visible in many of the contributions, where the voices of our collaborators, interlocutors, practitioners in the media industries – and, importantly, students – come to the fore.

Last but not least, the book is an experiment in collaborative modes of thinking and working in an academic institution, in multiple voices and by means of multiple approaches, at a time when scholars and students are increasingly being implored to compete against each other rather than act collectively. By making it freely available in the electronic version on an open-access basis, our goal is to enable access to the debate on the future of media to as wide a readership as possible. But *The Future of Media* is more than a book; the project is accompanied by a web platform presenting various media projects that are either explicitly discussed in the book or that have developed in parallel to it. Indeed, crossing the theory–practice divide, the divide between thinking about media and making media, has been one of our goals. With this, *The Future of Media* is also an invitation to all media scholars, students and industry practitioners to work together on trying to shape a better media future, for all of us – while simultaneously trying to work out the nature of this 'better'.

There are many possible routes through the book.

1. The linear route starts from a philosophical enquiry into thinking about the future in Chapter 1. This chapter makes it clear that in any interrogation of the future, and of the threats and promises it carries, we need to look at the past to understand that its remnants are always with us on an individual, social and global level. Chapters 2–8 then investigate the current, emergent and possible conditions of media. Each author offers a grounded analysis of a specific media issue or industry – and of the goals and possibilities for political and cultural change enabled (or perhaps disabled) by those industries. Chapters 9–10 add feminist and queer perspectives to the analysis and production of media. The book then turns towards a discussion of several creative media projects involving dance, motion capture and sound art (Chapters 11–13). In Chapters 14–16 the authors expand the scope of analysis to the wider socio-political context by focusing on activism, humanitarianism and urbanism. The closing chapters (17–18) offer a conceptual reflection on the very possibility of there being a future – of media, us and everything else – given the unfolding geo-political crises.

2. Some readers may decide to start their journey through the book by looking at specific media forms, practices and industries, e.g., journalism (Chapters 2–3), television (5), social media (7), publishing (8), film (10), VR and AR (11), audio (12–13), smartphones (14) or photography (17).

3. Others may wish to begin by looking at the socio-cultural issues that shape the media – and that shape us as media subjects, users and makers. As part of this route, they can read about media ownership (Chapters 2–3) and the job market for media professionals (6). They can look at the problem of abuse in and by the media, and at the accompanying problem of truth and post-truth (4). They can zoom in on issues of gender, sexuality and race – and on the openings and strictures around 'diversity', both in the media and in the wider world (7–10). Finally, they may want to look at the specific strategies of trying to make the world a better place via media, but also at the limitations of such attempts (1, 14–16).

4. It is also possible to start the book beyond its covers by exploring some of the practice projects presented on the accompanying website: www.golddust.org.uk/futureofmedia

Whichever route you as readers take, we hope to bring you not just into a conversation but also into a shared yet globally distributed project of making (better) media – and of making the world better, *with* media.

HOW TO TALK ABOUT THE FUTURE

1

The Future and the 'Poetry of the Past'

Gholam Khiabany

> Not all people exist in the same Now. They do so only externally, by virtue
> of the fact that they may all be seen today. But that does not mean that they
> are living at the same time with others.
>
> (Bloch 1977, 22)

I

Faith in progress remains strong and there is no shortage of images and imaginings
about amazing futures that lie ahead, futures that are offered and made possible
by technologies. As the timespan for introducing and marketing new products
and the latest technological innovations decreases, the academic rush to identify,
label and celebrate 'new phases' of progress and civilisation intensifies. The gap
between the third industrial revolution (1980s) and the latest, fourth, industrial
revolution was astonishingly short. And yet the path from the third to the fourth
industrial revolution in the field of media and cultural studies has been marked
with different stages, each of which are celebrated for their unique and hitherto
novel impact: Web 1.0, Web 2.0, Web 3.0, Web 4.0! Denis Smith points out that
in the 1980s there was no shortage of analyses that were predicting or announcing the imminent end of an era: the end of history, of organised capitalism, of
modernity, or even of Western civilisation (Smith 1990). Similar predictions were
offered about the future of media: the demise of political and economic elites
(Dyson 1998), the collapse of big media companies (Negroponte 1995), the death
of distance (Cairncross 1997), the end of centralised media (Rheingold 1993).

The new wave of technological innovations and developments, from AI to
big data, robotic, nano- and biotechnologies, to cloud computing and virtual
realities, is not just about imagining technologies and technological futures, but

also about imagining socio-cultural systems which are shaping technologies and which are being consolidated. The future of media as an emerging field of inquiry follows the sociology of the future and, as such, can learn from the theories, methodologies, agendas and contradictory movements and moments that have been explored, examined and critiqued. However, as fascinating and haunting as speculation about *the future* is, it is undeniable that remnants of *the past* have been haunting the imagination in recent years. Hidden from many academic accounts of technologically driven bright futures is the re-emergence of a darker past that is most starkly witnessed in the revitalisation of far-right neo-fascist movements. It is the far right which has been making the biggest strides all over the world and, in particular, in the belly of the beast – the USA. The result of the 2020 presidential election in the USA simply will not stop this regressive march.

The march of the far right is of course not limited to established liberal democracies. Right-wing militarism has returned to East Asia and in particular in the Philippines; the Bharatiya Janata Party (BJP) has successfully dominated the political scene in India; the 'appeal' of Putin's brand of authoritarianism extends beyond the border of Russia; Turkey's ruling Justice and Development Party, once regarded as an ideal model and a template for Muslim-majority countries, has plunged the country into darkness; and millennial Islamism has spread like wildfire in the wake of the defeat of the Arab uprisings of 2011–2012. The nonsynchronism of capitalism's development has always been recognised in variants of theories of 'uneven development.'

The darker side of Western modernity (Mignolo 2011) has been an essential factor for the production of surplus value, and the benefits of temporal differences between imperial powers and colonies have been immense for 'advanced' capitalism. For example, in his analysis of slavery, Marx argued that

> with the development of capitalist production during the period of manufacture, the public opinion of Europe lost its last remnant of shame and conscience … While the cotton industry introduced child-slavery into England, in the United States it gave the impulse for the transformation of the earlier, more or less patriarchal slavery into a system of commercial exploitation. In fact the veiled slavery of the new wage-labourers in Europe needed the unqualified slavery of the New World as its pedestal.
>
> (1976, 924–925)

Rosa Luxemburg also highlighted the significance of colonies for accumulation of capital. She argued that it is precisely on this stage that accumulation becomes more violent, and that aggression against colonies and rivals, not to mention war, genocide and looting, are committed without any attempt at concealment. 'Bourgeois liberal theory takes into account only the former aspect: the realm of "peaceful competition", the marvels of technology and pure commodity exchange; it separates it strictly from the other aspect: the realm of capital's blustering violence which is regarded as more or less incidental to foreign policy and quite independent of the economic sphere of capital' (1951, 452–453). For Marx the relationship between veiled and unqualified slavery, exploitation at national and international levels, was so intertwined that he wrote this memorable line about the dialectic of race and class: 'In the United States of America, every independent workers' movement was paralysed as long as slavery disfigured a part of the republic. Labour in a white skin cannot emancipate itself where it is branded in a black skin' (1976, 414).

If the temporal differences of capitalist development between the centre and periphery, 'advanced' and 'backward', 'first' and 'third' world, can explain the uneven development of capitalism in what is now indiscriminately labelled 'the global South', or the co-existence of advanced technologies with past modes of production and social relations, and the explosion of the far right into the political scenes of many countries in Asia, Latin America and Africa, then how can we explain the very visible (and in some cases triumphant) presence of capitalist prehistory in the USA and Europe?

II

In assessing factors contributing to the insurgence of right-wing parties and policies in particular, many commentators have rightly focused on issues of misogyny, racism and the devastating impact of austerity, the growing economic hardship and the staggering inequality that even the International Monetary Fund (IMF) and the World Bank appear to acknowledge. Another factor that is acknowledged is the role of social media, in particular its growing power as a political instrument and source of misinformation. And here we have another amazing paradox and a significant shift. We should not forget how the discussion about the role of digital technologies in the uprisings in Iran (2009) and the Arab world (2010–2011) was laden with optimism and the inevitability of change and progress. The fascination with the 'Facebook and Twitter revolution' was quickly replaced with fascination with the technologies of shock and awe of ISIS. Later an Iraqi journalist reported that 'the mobilisation techniques used in the Arab Spring, which brought thousands of demonstrators to a given place, were now being used to organise the new waves of migration' (Abdul-Ahad 2015). Such transformation is a sober reminder that there is nothing inevitable about the use of these tools.

These factors are all important but, as Victor Pickard (2016) suggested in his analysis of Trump's victory, the role of mainstream media requires particular attention. News media on both sides of the Atlantic not only failed to capture the changing political mood but effectively normalised and legitimatised candidates and politics that should not have been. According to Pickard (2016), 'in 2015, Trump received 327 minutes of nightly broadcast network news coverage, compared with Hillary Clinton's 121 minutes and Bernie Sanders' 20 minutes. The *New York Times* reported that Trump garnered nearly $2 billion in free media coverage during his primary campaign. Other estimates place it closer to $3 billion.'

There was also money to be made. Global Market Intelligence estimated that the three major cable news networks were set to make nearly $2 billion in ad revenues, and the three main business networks were set to add another $458 million in ad revenue from just the 2016 calendar year. The 2016 presidential election was the most profitable presidential election for mainstream media in the USA (Pickard 2016).

A similar pattern can be observed in the case of Brexit. The analysis of the campaign by researchers at Loughborough University (Deacon et al. 2016) shows that overall there was a greater volume (60 to 40%) of articles supporting 'Leave' over 'Remain'. But when these figures are weighted by newspapers sales, the advantage is far larger: 80% versus 20% in favour of 'Leave' (Deacon et al. 2016). And such coverage was also profitable for the British press. 'Lurid immigration front pages', as one *Daily Express* journalist put it, 'sell papers' (Donovan 2016).

The position of papers on the referendum or broadcasters (which have a duty of balance), however, camouflages the longevity of negative coverage of Europe and immigration in British media. Therefore, in assessing the role of British media it is crucial to go beyond the coverage of the EU campaign. For example, the surprise editorial line of *The Mail on Sunday* and *The Times* (both of which backed Remain) should not obscure the longstanding position of these papers on the EU or immigration. Another significant factor, clearly obvious during the referendum but a longstanding issue, is how newspapers set the agenda for broadcasters. The BBC in particular, mired in negotiations over its Charter review, tended to follow rather than lead during the campaign. The 'waning power of print media', in this particular case, indeed proved a false prophecy. We cannot begin to understand our sense of shock, disappointment and fear in recent years without understanding the historical routes and causes which have brought us here.

Recently the comparison between the 2008 financial crisis and the Great Depression of 1929–1939 has been extended to include a contrast between the contemporary forms of authoritarian politics and the emerging fascist movements in the 1920s and 1930s. The electoral breakthrough of far-right parties across Europe, Brexit and the victory of Donald Trump in 2016 are anything but a storm in a teacup. However, the problem with historical analogies is that they rob events of their distinct features in a historical mode of politics for the sake of 'simple repetition'. The alarmism which emerged in response to certain political developments and, in particular, to the election of Donald Trump for the most part ignores the fact that his victory was not an inevitable outcome of the current economic crisis. We should remember, after all, that the crisis in the USA between 1929 and 1939 led not to fascism but to the 'New Deal'. In addition, and at a time when established political norms are increasingly fragile, there are also huge opportunities for a renewal of politics and democracy. Witness the significant impact of the uprising in the USA in response to the murder of George Floyd.

It is also difficult to refer to the insurgency of this new 'common sense' as a singular movement. Concepts such as 'nationalism' and 'populism' have emerged and been employed by corporate media, journalists and academics to explain this particular phenomenon. Populism, which at some points used to refer to something specific in Latin America, is now vaguely employed to explain contradictory movements and political leanings, in some cases even antagonistic to each other, from Jeremy Corbyn to Nigel Farage, Bernie Sanders to Donald Trump, Syriza to Golden Dawn etc. At the time in which the impotence of the 'centre' has been exposed while it tries to revive itself and win back the legitimacy that it seems to have lost, the very concept of populism characterises opposing movements as if they were equally *against* the established elite and *for* the people. What the fig-leaves of populism hide is precisely the racism, sexism, homophobia and xenophobia of 'right-wing populists'. In addition, that the results of an election and referendum on both sides of the Atlantic were presented as the 'will of the people', and that 'the people' are defined as a stylised entity devoid of all subjectivities, is not novel. In the case of Brexit such framing of the result in terms of 'the people have spoken' conveniently brushed aside the fact that 62.5% of the British electorate (those who voted 'Remain' and those who abstained from referendum) didn't speak at all or in the same way. One of the ironies of what has been labelled as 'populism' is that it does not have the popular vote, either in Britain or in the USA. The narrative of absoluteness of 'popular sovereignty' and insisting that 'the people have spoken' was so dominant that even the politicians and commentators on the other side of the divide began to repeat it. It was therefore no surprise that when the British High Court (the very court that Brexit promised to liberate from Brussels) was asked to pass judgement on the process of triggering Article 50, one establishment newspaper, *The Daily Telegraph* (3 November 2016), framed it as 'The Judges vs. the People'. The next day another British newspaper, *The Daily Mail*, went even further and called the High Court judges 'Enemies of the people'. The Leave campaign, which had managed to list many foreign 'threats' undermining British independence and sovereignty, continued by adding more internal elites to the list of enemies of the people. In doing so the narrative of 'anti-establishment' was reinforced further by a different section of the elite. This top-down approach is bereft of any radical or popular transformative potential. The clash between two conceptions of democracy, on the one hand as a form of government and on the other as a form of social and political life (Rancière 2010), has led to what Fraser describes as a 'rejection of politics as usual' and a serious 'crisis of hegemony' (2019, 9).

The concept of 'nationalism' is no less troubling, for, as Aijaz Ahmad has pointed out,

> there really is no such a thing as nationalism, per se, with an identifiable, trans-historical essence, over and above particular historical practices and projects. At the deepest, most abstract level, nationalism is today the reflection, in thought, of the fact that nation-*states* either already exist in the world of material relations or are sought to be obtained in the future, as in the case of the Palestinians for example.
>
> (2018, 27)

Lumping together a wide range of developments, some very new and some decades old – such as xenophobic hysteria in British politics – is hardly helpful. What is novel is not racism but that it has been expanded and directed against Europe's own periphery. The integration of countries of Central and Eastern Europe with the global economy and the uneven severity with which they experienced the 2008 crisis not only have allowed for a degree of internalising their experience of xenophobia, but also for their attempts to outdo the European masters.

Another novelty, and by far the most important one, is that in contrast to the 1930s, in which the anti-fascist left was visibly present and strong, the current crisis has benefited the far right. That we have seen a spectacular rise of the far right in countries which were not hit hardest by the crisis (Denmark, Switzerland and Austria) is also important. This is not just to caution against simplistic economic explanations, but also to highlight that the remnants of the past and the yearning for a lost 'heritage' actually appear to be more visible in the most developed countries.

Covid-19 has highlighted and exacerbated many factors which paved the way for the rise of far right: the essential frailty of capitalism, the staggering inequalities, the precarious state of liberal democracy and the elevation of the state into a god-like creature which can control the lives and deaths of not only unwanted refugees but also its citizens. Under the deadly pressure of 'the small state', the 'big society', if it can breathe, does so with great difficulty. That there is an extreme concentration of global wealth in the hands of the few is well known. According to Oxfam (2020), in 2019, 2,153 billionaires had more wealth than 4.6 billion people; the richest 22 men in the world own more wealth than all the women in Africa. Nearly half the world is trying to survive on $5.50 a day or less. An earlier report by International Labour Organization (ILO; 2011) had suggested that 1.53 billion workers (more than 50% of the global workforce) were in precarious employment. The picture is even bleaker post-pandemic. According to the latest report by the ILO, 80% of the global workforce of 3.3 billion have been affected by full or partial workplace closures. The ILO (2020) estimated the decline in global working hours in the second quarter of 2020 as equivalent to 495 million full-time jobs. In the USA alone, as over 200,000 people have died in one year (more than the US death tolls from World War I, World War II and the Vietnam War combined) and 50 million have lost their jobs, it was reported that '[t]he collective wealth of the billionaire class increased from $2.95tn to $3.8tn. That works out to gains of $141bn a month, or $4.7bn a day' (Neat 2020). By July 2020, Jeff Bezos' personal fortune had risen by $73.2 billion since the start of the crisis to a record $186.2 billion, a staggering increase of 65%. In the same period the estimated fortune of Bill Gates grew by 19% to $116 billion. While the tech giants presented themselves as the solution to the crisis, Covid-19 seems to have been a solution to their prayers. Microsoft and Amazon valuations have surpassed $1 trillion, Google (Alphabet) is close to the trillion-dollar figure, Facebook is valued in the region of $700 billion and Apple is now the first company to reach a $2-trillion valuation.

The fortune of digital companies has moved to the opposite of the state of democracy. In March 2020, research by openDemocracy revealed that parliaments in 13 countries were partially or fully suspended, leaving more than 500 million people unrepresented (Provost et al. 2020). Around the world, addressing the current crisis was managed not through investment in healthcare but through punishment. In Kenya the police were beating and killing people. In India migrant workers were beaten and sprayed with chemicals and thousands of workers – old, young and children – were forced to walk hundreds of miles to return home to self-isolate. In the Philippines, poor people who had violated the curfew were put in dog cages, and in Paraguay people were beaten and threatened with tasers. A new policy passed by Hungary's parliament is allowing Prime Minister Viktor Orbán to rule by decree and in the Philippines and Thailand a state of emergency had been declared (Ratcliffe 2020). Governments are preparing for the protests that are sure to come when the devastating impact of job losses and poverty become even more visible. Such assaults on the demo-cratic rights of citizens, carried out in the name of protecting them, is already part of the strategy of political establishments around the world for tackling the crisis. In the calmer political climate of Britain, the human rights organisation Liberty had labelled new emergency laws introduced as part of the government's response to Covid-19 as the 'biggest restriction of our freedom in a generation' (Liberty 2020). Liz Fekete has rightly warned us that history 'teaches us that inhumane police practices are quick to establish but hard to dismantle with long-term consequences for policing by consent within a democratic order' (2020). The angel of history (Benjamin 1968) is looking at the catastrophe that is piling wreckage upon wreckage. The shock we feel now only sounds unique if we assume that the authoritarian shifts in recent times are some kind of transgres-sion of the 'law of history'.

III

The epigraph from Ernst Bloch that opens this chapter firmly locates the debate about nonsynchronicity, the existence of the past in the present and the presence of something which appears out of time and out of sync with Now. The sense of shock and bewilderment resulting from Brexit and Trump's victory in 2016 and our grieving over the gradual death of liberal democracy (Brown 2005), and, we might add, shame and decency, more than anything else is an expression of disbelief about the rise of the undead. How could these things happen in the twenty-first century? Bloch's work provides an intelligent description of a crucial period in European history, the rise of fascism. In examining the myths and aspirations that the Nazis appropriated and the classes that were most receptive to them, he highlights the historical context and issues that remain pertinent. Bloch's sober and highly critical assessment is a reminder that the history of capitalist Europe has not been a forward march of liberty, democracy and rationality; it has, in the form of fascism, generated and exercised systemic violence not only against non-Europeans but also against large sections of its own population. The sense of shock and bewilderment being expressed at extreme capitalism is not novel. What sets Bloch's assessment of fascism apart is his attempt at going beyond the simple economist interpretation of fascism to identify the deeper historical roots of fascism. That important part of Europe's modern past, in the absence of a revolutionary break, appears to be its possible future.

Significant in Bloch's theory of fascism was the ideological element or, as Oskar Negt (1976) calls it, the problem of propaganda. Bloch suggests that such ideologies, even though they are brought to the surface by socio-economic crises, are embedded in a much deeper and older source and heritage. It is not just the crisis itself, but the fact that the 'workers are no longer alone with themselves and the bosses. Many earlier forces, from quite a different Below, are beginning to slip between' (1977, 22); the peasants' old form of production relations, 'of their customs and of their calendar life in the cycle of an unchanged nature counteracts urbanization and binds them to reaction, a re-action which is founded on nonsynchronism. Even the sobriety of the peasants is old and sceptical, not enlightened, and their alert sense of property (for the soil, for a debt-free farm) is more rooted in things than the capitalist' (1977, 24); an 'immiserated middle class wants to return to prewar conditions when it was better off' (1977, 25). The crisis, the absence of a self-assured liberal state, the complicity of liberal intelligentsia, the desperation of a large section of the population bring the 'undisposed of the past' to the fore. Listen to angry, disillusioned and badly informed voters in capitalism's heartland and Bloch's observation still rings true: 'In spite of radio and newspapers, there are couples living in the village for whom Egypt is still the land where princes pulled the baby Moses from the river, not the land of the Suez Canal; it is still viewed from the Bible and the Children of Israel, rather than from the pharaoh' (1977, 25). One of course could change 'in spite of radio and newspapers' to 'because of radio and newspapers'.

The central argument in Bloch's analysis is the persistence of a problematic character of a past, the '*declining remnants* and, above all, uncompleted *past*, which has not yet been "sublated" by capitalism' (1977, 31). The less radical economic and political transformation of Germany, compared to England or even France, had allowed the survival of older social forces and relations alongside a weak bourgeoisie. This, for Bloch, had turned Germany into a 'classic land of nonsynchronism'. 'Nonsynchronism' became manifest in the attitudes of large sections of the population, who, in the moment of crisis, seized upon the myths and 'heritage' that were exploited by the Nazis. It is through this concept which Bloch explores the appeal of Nazi mystification and propaganda to youth, peasantry and immiserated middle classes. 'As an existing remnant of earlier times in the present it is objectively nonsynchronous. The subjectively nonsynchronous, having been for a long time merely embittered, appears today as pent-up anger' (1977, 31). Fascism for Bloch is a 'swindle of fulfilment'. The past is beautified when the last inkling of fulfilment has vanished. But capital also uses 'that which is nonsynchronously contrary, if not indeed disparate, as a distraction from its own strictly present-day contradictions; it uses the antagonism of a still living past as a means of separation and struggle against the future that is dialectically giving birth to itself in the capitalist antagonisms' (1977, 32). Anson Rabinbach rightly notes that:

> The contradiction between these temporal dimensions demands what Bloch calls 'the obligation to its dialectic', a recognition of complexity which not only focuses on the synchronous, but on the non-synchronous, the multi-temporal and multi-layered contradictions within a single present. For Bloch it is precisely this sedimentation of social experience that creates the intense desire for a resurrection of the past among those groups most susceptible to fascist propaganda. For Marxism the problem is that fascist ideology is not simply an instrument of deception but 'a fragment of an old and romantic antagonism to capitalism, derived from deprivations in contemporary life, with a longing for a vague "other"'.
>
> (1977, 7)

IV

According to Rabinach (1977, 5), Bloch's take on fascism as an incomplete past and a swindle of fulfilment represented his double exile – from fascism and from

Stalinism, which was unable to comprehend fascism for what it was. Bloch's analysis of the power of fascism as cultural synthesis came to be seen as a transgression from Marxism and as such was not embraced in the Moscow camp. However, Bloch takes his cue from Marx and indeed borrows heavily from Marx's writing on the weight of the dead on present generations. In the preface to the first edition of *Capital*, Marx pays attention to what a few decades later Bloch called nonsynchronism.

> [W]e suffer not only from the development of capitalist production, but also from the incompleteness of that development. Alongside the modern evils, we are oppressed by a whole series of inherited evils, arising from the passive survival of archaic and outmoded modes of production, with their accompanying train of anachronistic social and political relations. We suffer not only from the living, but from the dead. *Le mort saisit le vif*!
>
> (1976, 91)

In *The Communist Manifesto*, Marx and Engels write that workers at the time were not fighting their enemies, but enemies of their enemies, 'the remnants of absolute monarchy, the landowners, the non-industrial bourgeois, the petty bourgeois' (Marx and Engels 1955, 18). The burden of the past on capitalist Now is also stressed by comparing capitalism with communism; whereas 'in bourgeois society ... the past dominates the present', under communism 'the present dominates the past (Marx 2000, 257). Marx repeats the same point in *The Eighteenth Brumaire of Louis Bonaparte*.

> The social revolution of the nineteenth century cannot take its poetry from the past but only from the future. It cannot begin with itself before it has stripped away all superstition about the past. The former revolutions required recollections of past world history in order to smother their own content. The revolution of the nineteenth century must let the dead bury their dead in order to arrive at its own content. There the phrase went beyond the content – here the content goes beyond the phrase.
>
> (Marx 2000, 331)

Given the shifting temporality of capitalism, the weight of the dead on the present generation is a recurrent theme in Marx. The struggle for today and for the future is conditioned by the past. If people make their own history but not under the condition of their own choosing, it is likely that circumstances in which they have found themselves will be inherited from the dead.

Synchronous contradictions and the presence of a still-living past under capitalism were also noted by Rosa Luxemburg. In her 1912 speech 'Women's Suffrage
and Class Struggle' she argues that in 'advanced capitalist, highly industrialized,
twentieth-century Germany, in the age of electricity and airplanes, the absence of
women's political rights is as much a reactionary remnant of the dead past as the
reign by Divine Right on the throne' (2004, 239). These phenomena, she suggests,
have become the most important tools in the hands of the capitalist ruling class. It
was the defeat of the German Revolution of 1918 and the triumph of the remnants
of the dead past in the Now which paved the way for fascism.

Marx's allusion to the nonsynchronous development of capitalism is also
investigated by Leon Trotsky. His concept of the 'uneven and combined development' of capitalism not only captures the essence of Marx's concern over the
burden of the dead against the living, but also offers a fruitful and sophisticated
analysis of the unity of the world economy and the interdependence of what
Luxemburg sees as the two aspects of capital accumulation: the realm of
'peaceful' competition and the violence of war and the lootings of colonies. In
the first volume of *The History of the Russian Revolution*, he writes: 'From the
universal law of unevenness thus derives another law which, for want of a better
name, we may call the law of combined development – by which we mean a
drawing together of different stages of the journey, a combining of separate steps,
an amalgam of archaic with more contemporary form' (Trotsky 2008, 4).

Even though the concept has been used to focus on the unit of the nation
state, the relationship between the imperial powers and developing nations and
studying the dynamics of the presence of older modes of productions elsewhere,
it is highly relevant in understanding not only the combination of advancement
and backwardness in China or India, but also the persistence of archaic forms of
social relations in advanced economies that are characterised by complex interdependencies at the global level on the one hand and exercising hegemony over
the oppressed on the other. This is what Trotsky had to say about the USA: 'It
is considered unquestionable that technology and science undermine super-
stition. But the class character of society sets substantial limits here too. Take
America. There, church sermons are broadcast by radio, which means that the
radio is serving as a means of spreading prejudices' (1973, 257). The uneven and
combined development approach allows us to move beyond the binary of social
versus geographical.

The undeniable unevenness of not only the life chances but also the systemic
unevenness in production and social reproduction at the heart of advanced

capitalism urges us to take Marx's concerns over the deadly weight of the past, and Bloch's intelligent and critical take on that, very seriously. As we mourn over the gradual death of liberal democracy (Fenton and Titley 2015) and wonder about the *future*, it is essential to delve into the fervour and anger which drive millions of people into 'democratically' voting against their own interests and future, the root causes of such anger and energy and the heritage which they call upon. At the heart of the recent developments lies an emotional, and partly hysterical, upheaval of moral indignation, revulsion and fury, which has been ignored for decades and generations. Nonsynchronous development can produce nonsynchronous revolt. The evolutionist and mechanical understanding of historical development, as ever, is unlikely to comprehend the contradictions that have engulfed modern societies. It is no wonder that academics, mesmerised by technological progress and armed with meticulously put together facts, tables and figures, have failed to see the revolutionary and regressive movements and moments even when they were right in the middle of them. The rise and regeneration of the archaic meanings that were assumed to have been fully repressed or assigned to the dustbin of history is indeed a significant cause for concern, not least for media studies. At a time in which what Habermas has called the public sphere seems in total disarray, a realm of our social life in which citizens are guaranteed access and can achieve public opinion through rational and critical debate, it is crucial to repeat Eberhard Knödler-Bunte and Russell Berman's pertinent and penetrating question: 'Why did he [Habermas] exclude a discussion of the institutions and phenomena of the fascist public sphere, and what are the implications for an analysis of late capitalist and proletarian public?' (1977, 42).

To this we might add and ask: How is it that the far right is able to exploit the sentiments arising from contradictions between older and more modern forms of living and production? And how can we explain the coexistence of the paralysis of political imaginations and the imaginative fantasies about technological futures? What Bloch's theory of nonsynchronism does wonderfully is issue an invitation to not only explore 'the fertile and productive soil' from which fascism emerged, but also to be concerned with 'them as an unclaimed radical heritage passed by the Left in its abstract critique of the illusory and "false consciousness"' (Rabinbach 1977, 11). It is precisely on this latter point that Bloch's analysis differs from Marx's. We have to take the spirit of the past seriously. One cannot dream about the future without 'poetry from the past'. The far right only directs the anger 'against symptoms, not against the exploitation' (Bloch 1977, 35). Walter Benjamin articulates this succinctly in his essay on the work of art.

Fascism attempts to organize the newly created proletarian masses without affecting the property structure which the masses strive to eliminate. Fascism sees its salvation in giving these masses not their right, but instead a chance to express themselves. The masses have a right to change property relations; Fascism seeks to give them an expression while preserving property. The logical result of Fascism is the introduction of aesthetics into political life. The violation of the masses, whom Fascism, with its Führer cult, forces to their knees, has its counterpart in the violation of an apparatus which is pressed into the production of ritual values.

(1968, 241)

Throughout modern history various social movements and revolts have appeared which tried to go beyond the existing limit. Their history has been denied, repressed, marginalised and not taught. Their history is part of what Benjamin referred to as the tradition of the oppressed. The weight of history in that sense is what should and can drive us forward, for there will be no redemption if we do not take seriously the claims and sufferings of the victims of history.

References

Abdul-Ahad, G. 2015. 'Some Tips for the Long-Distance Traveller'. *London Review of Books*, 8 October. Available at: www.lrb.co.uk/the-paper/v37/n19/ghaith-abdul-ahad/some-tips-for-the-long-distance-traveller.

Ahmad, A. 2018. 'Extreme Capitalism and the "National Question"'. In *The World Turned Upside Down?: Socialist Register 2019*, edited by L. Panitch and G. Albo. London: Merlin Press, 26–49.

Benjamin, W. 1968. *Illuminations*. New York: Schocken Books.

Bloch, E. 1977. 'Nonsynchronism and the Obligation to its Dialectics', M. Ritter, trans. *New German Critique*, 11: 22–38.

Brown, W. 2005. 'Neoliberalism and the End of Liberal Democracy'. In *Edgework: Critical Essays on Knowledge and Politics*. Princeton, NJ: Princeton University Press.

Cairncross, F. 1997. *The Death of Distance: How the Communications Revolution Will Change Our Lives*. London: Orion.

Deacon, D., D. Wring, E. Harmer, J. Stanyer and J. Downey. 2016. 'Hard Evidence: Analysis Shows Extent of Press Bias towards Brexit'. *The Conversation*, 16 June. Available at: https://theconversation.com/hard-evidence-analysis-shows-extent-of-press-bias-towards-brexit-61106.

Donovan, P. 2016. 'Pointing the Finger'. *British Journalism Review*, 27(3): 9–11.

Dyson, E. 1998. *Release 2.0: A Design for Living in the Digital Age*. New York: Broadway.

Fekete, L. 2020. 'Is the "War on Covid-19" Morphing into a War on the Poor?' Institute of Race Relations, 9 April. Available at: www.irr.org.uk/news/is-the-war-on-covid-19-morphing-into-a-war-on-the-poor/.

Fenton, N. and G. Titley. 2015. 'Mourning and Longing: Media Studies Learning to Let Go of Liberal Democracy'. *European Journal of Communication*, 30(5): 554–570.

Fraser, N. 2019. *The Old Is Dying and the New Cannot Be Born*. London: Verso.

ILO. 2011. 'ILO Global Employment Trends 2011'. Available at: www.ilo.org/global/about-the-ilo/newsroom/news/WCMS_150581/lang--en/index.htm.

ILO. 2020. *ILO Monitor: COVID-19 and the World of Work*, 6th edn. Geneva. Available at: www.ilo.org/wcmsp5/groups/public/@dgreports/@dcomm/documents/briefingnote/wcms_755910.pdf.

Knödler-Bunte, E. and R. Berman. 1977. 'Fascism as a Depoliticized Mass Movement'. *New German Critique*, 11: 39–48.

Liberty. 2020. 'New Law is Biggest Restriction on Our Freedom in a Generation'. 26 March. Available at: www.libertyhumanrights.org.uk/issue/new-law-is-biggest-restriction-on-our-freedom-in-a-generation/.

Luxemburg, R. 1951. *The Accumulation of Capital*. Translated by A. Schwarzschild. London: Routledge & Kegan Paul.

Luxemburg, R. 2004. 'Women's Suffrage and Class Struggle'. In *The Rosa Luxemburg Reader*, edited by P. Hudis and K. Anderson. New York: Monthly Review Press, 237–242.

Marx, K. 1976. *Capital: A Critique of Political Economy*, Vol. 1. London: Penguin.

Marx, K. 2000. *Karl Marx: Selected Writings*, edited by D. McLellan. Oxford: Oxford University Press.

Marx, K. and F. Engels. 1955. *The Communist Manifesto* with selections from *The Eighteenth Brumaire of Louis Bonaparte* and *Capital* by Karl Marx, edited by S. H. Beer. New York: Appleton-Century-Crofts, Inc.

Mignolo, W. 2011. *The Darker Side of Western Modernity: Global Futures, Decolonial Option*. Durham, NC and London: Duke University Press.

Neat, R. 2020. 'Wealth of US Billionaires Rises by Nearly a Third during Pandemic'. *The Guardian*, 17 September. Available at: www.theguardian.com/business/2020/sep/17/wealth-of-us-billionaires-rises-by-nearly-a-third-during-pandemic.

Negroponte, N. 1995. *Being Digital*. London: Hodder & Stoughton.

Negt, O. 1976. 'The Non-Synchronous Heritage and the Problem of Propaganda'. *New German Critique*, 9: 46–70.

Oxfam. 2020. *Time to Care: Unpaid and Underpaid Care Work and the Global Inequality Crisis*. Oxford. Available at: https://oxfamilibrary.openrepository.com/bitstream/handle/10546/620928/bp-time-to-care-inequality-200120-en.pdf.

Pickard, V. 2016. 'Yellow Journalism, Orange President'. *Jacobin*, 25 December. Available at: www.jacobinmag.com/2016/11/media-advertising-news-radio-trump-tv/.

Provost, C., N. Archer and L. Nambiru. 2020. 'Alarm as 2 Billion People Have Parliaments Shut or Limited by Covid-19'. openDemocracy, 8 April. Available at: www.opendemocracy.net/en/5050/alarm-two-billion-people-have-parliaments-suspended-or-limited-covid-19/.

Rabinbach, A. 1977. 'Unclaimed Heritage: Ernst Bloch's Heritage of Our Times and the Theory of Fascism'. *New German Critique*, 11: 5–21.

Rancière, J. 2010. *Dissensus: On Politics and Aesthetics*. London: Bloomsbury.

Ratcliffe, R. 2020. 'Teargas, Beatings and Bleach: The Most Extreme Covid-19 Lockdown Controls around the World'. *The Guardian*, 1 April. Available at: www.theguardian.com/global-development/2020/apr/01/extreme-coronavirus-lockdown-controls-raise-fears-for-worlds-poorest.

Rheingold, H. 1993. *The Virtual Community: Finding Connection in a Computerized World*. Boston, MA: Addison-Wesley Longman Publishing Co., Inc.

Smith, D. 1990. *Capitalist Democracy on Trial: The Transatlantic Debate from Tocqueville to the Present*. London: Routledge.

Trotsky, L. 1973. *Problems of Everyday Life: Creating the Foundations for a New Society in Revolutionary Russia*. New York: Pathfinder Books.

Trotsky, L. 2008. *History of the Russian Revolution*. Translated by M. Eastman. Chicago, IL: Haymarket Books.

THE FUTURE OF MEDIA REFORM

2

Media Reform and the Politics of Hope

Natalie Fenton and Des Freedman

Media Power after Covid-19

This chapter offers a critique of contemporary dynamics of media power and their likely direction of travel given current geo-political realities and uncertainties. It then shifts gear to imagine other possible media futures with new ways of coordinating and producing media as part of a more general 'politics of hope'. The chapter includes both critical reflections on media ownership, journalism and content, and empirical research drawn from the authors' involvement in the Media Reform Coalition, an advocacy network that campaigns for increased accountability and diversity in and independence of the media.

As we write, Covid-19 has, of course, thrown the media – along with virtually every other sector of society – into chaos. It has unsettled its business models as advertising revenue has fallen but increased appetite for its content as the need for information and entertainment has increased; it has dramatised the need for high-quality news and pervasive distraction in the present but also posed some fundamental questions about how our media have responded to the pandemic and what kind of media systems would be best able to offer up the representations and scrutiny that are required in the future. The virus has destabilised neoliberal assumptions – such as the idea that the state should play a minimal role in funding or coordinating the media – because the scale of the advertising crisis has forced public subsidies for newspapers onto the agenda given that the media have been redefined as 'essential services'. Huge audiences are turning to traditional broadcast and news services that were widely seen as being in decline while social media, often greeted as the harbinger of a bright, participatory media future, are trusted less than more established sources of content (Ofcom 2020). Whatever view we have about the performance of our respective media organisations, Covid-19 has served to crystallise debates about who is best served by the existing distribution of media power and how we need to reconceptualise our media systems so that they operate in the public interest.

This chapter argues that media power constitutes a central way in which social norms are proposed and policed by elite interests and that it is a regulatory force committed to upholding a status quo based on private property and the rule of capital. While it is not immune from the contradictions and tensions that are to be found in all societies – indeed, the most effective forms of media power are precisely those that provide limited expressions of discontent within a more general embrace of existing social relations – its loyalty is to a capitalist logic in which it is deeply embedded. Tech owners, newspaper editors, senior broadcasters, advertising executives, regulators and policymakers are all partners – even if, at times, warring ones – in the management of media markets and systems across the globe. Their power is vested in economic and political control of communications landscapes – a dominance that is scarcely comparable to the far more limited opportunities for individuals to deploy their own symbolic resources.

Yet the cry from media moguls and some media theorists is that this is an outdated picture of a consolidated and concerted media power, one that perhaps fitted the monopoly conditions of a former analogue century but certainly not the heterogeneous character of the digital present. Media power is now said to be more fragmented, dispersed, opaque, complex and polycentric in the light of digital transformations, the falling cost of entry to media production and distribution, the decline of traditional media and the more general dissipation of expertise and authority. Media are no longer 'sticky' but 'spreadable' (Jenkins et al. 2013) and analysis of media power should be liberated from its functionalist and conspiratorial associations with top-down forms of control. According to one influential theorist, media power should be understood 'in a non-reductive and multifaceted sense, as the use of resources, of varying kinds, that ... enable individuals or collectivities to pursue their values and interests' (Chadwick 2017, 21).

That media power can now be seen as productive and *not* disabling owes much to the legacy of Michel Foucault and his proposition, developed throughout the 1970s, that power is not always 'prohibitive' but resolutely constitutive of human subjectivity. In one very famous expression, he declares the following: 'We must cease once and for all to describe the effects of power in negative terms: it "excludes", it "represses", it "censors", it "abstracts", it "masks", it "conceals". In fact power produces; it produces realities; it produces domains of objects and rituals of truth' (Foucault 1977, 174). Foucault isn't arguing that power is simply a benevolent or equalising force but he is anxious to disentangle power from a single source of domination – such as class or wealth – and instead to paint it as a far more amorphous, if ubiquitous, phenomenon. Power is now to be understood as a 'machine in which everyone is caught, those who exercise power just as much as those over whom it is exercised' (1980, 156). In a decisive shift away from power being the tangible property of a specific social group, Foucault encourages us to think in terms of 'capillary power', 'biopower', 'pastoral power' and 'panoptic power' – all of which highlight the role of dispersed and self-policing individuals in the production and reproduction of power (Foucault 2002).

Despite the ongoing resistance emanating from critical political economists of the media and stubborn Marxists, the idea that power seeps, drains and circulates effortlessly throughout society – that it operates without an overarching class dynamic – remains pervasive (e.g., Zuboff 2019). While this approach has expanded our vocabulary and highlighted experiences perhaps marginalised by more singular perspectives, it has also sidetracked our politics by encouraging us to look away from those sites in which power remains highly concentrated. These include the state, which continues to shape the dynamics of the communications landscape, and capitalist firms which exert an increasingly tight grip over sectoral media markets, as well as influencers (from presidents to commentators to celebrities), whose voices are amplified by gatekeepers hungry for traffic. In this situation, the most effective metaphor for media power is no longer Foucault's panopticon but the watch tower, not the network but the hierarchy, not entrepreneurial pebbles but industrial boulders, not the long tail but the blockbuster.

This points to a context in which we face the challenge of a renewed *executive power* where elite groups deploy their resources – their access to capital, their political influence and their ideological congruence – to dominate contemporary media systems. Here we find tax-avoiding corporations and offshore billionaires; data brokers and infrastructure empires; market-friendly politicians and captive regulators; complacent commentators and establishment editors. These are the neoliberal vanguards who preside over media and communications in defence of a status quo that suits their material interests.

Executive Media Power on Trial

The hope that patterns of concentrated power in legacy press and broadcasting markets would not be replicated in digital conditions has long since evaporated.

Now there are regular warnings about the dangers of an oligopolistic tech sector that, thanks to lax (or non-existent) regulation and an avaricious DNA, is accruing massive amounts of power and undermining the conditions for a deliberative democracy. Facebook, as Siva Vaidhyanathan (2018) argues, is both a 'pleasure machine' and a 'surveillance machine', a 'protest machine' and a 'disinformation machine', that is structurally fixated on hovering up personal data and circulating content no matter its accuracy or consequence. Together with Google, it is expected to account for just under 65% of all digital advertising in the UK and 59% in the USA by 2021. Google alone earns more from advertising than the ad revenue of China and the UK combined; indeed, Google's ad revenue is larger than that of any ad market in the world with the exception of the USA (Richter 2019). We are truly in an age of 'digital dominance' manifested by growing public concern with 'user autonomy, user agency and the power of platforms to impact the decision-making of consumers and citizens through profiling, information control, and behavioural nudges' (Moore and Tambini 2018, 398).

Yet the size and impact of these digital behemoths should not distract us from the continuing presence and impact of legacy media that are re-consolidating precisely in order to face up to digital challenges and that, as we have already argued, played a particularly crucial role during the coronavirus pandemic. Today's global media giants include not only the FAANG (Facebook, Amazon, Apple, Netflix and Alphabet/Google) companies (together with their Chinese counterparts Alibaba and Tencent) but household names from across the world including Sony, Disney, Comcast, Bertelsmann, Televisa and Prisa. In the USA, where Disney controls more than 40% of the Hollywood box office and accounts for some 30% of all primetime scripted broadcast programmes, a wave of mergers is taking place to better allow 'traditional' media to compete in digital media markets (Nicolaou 2019). In Brazil, Grupo Globo is dominant across all media sectors and boasts that it reaches over 100 million Brazilians, some 50% of the population, every day. In Argentina, just four conglomerates have nearly half of total audience share across television, radio, print and online with the Clarin Group alone accounting for 25% of consumption. Media markets across the globe are characterised by oligopolistic structures and cartel-like behaviour.

Public policy, however, is increasingly gripped by the threat of digital disinformation (or 'fake news' about, for example, the origins of Covid-19 or unproven ways to treat the virus) and the need, above all, to regulate and to 'rein in' out-of-control tech platforms; it is far less absorbed by concentrated media power inside newspaper and broadcast markets. Indeed, the conception appears to be that, particularly in relation to news given its importance to the democratic process, legacy media need *additional* protections from digital intermediaries in the shape of new subsidies and tax breaks. This ignores the fact that the online dominance of a handful of established news organisations is reproducing and intensifying existing patterns of agenda-setting power that continue to exert a substantial influence over media and political culture. Given the roles of Fox in mobilising support for Donald Trump, of Globo in amplifying the insurgent voice of Brazilian president Jair Bolsonaro and the UK's tabloid newspapers in constantly urging their readers to 'BeLeave in Britain' ahead of the referendum on EU membership, it is premature to write off the impact of legacy media. As Tony Gallagher, former editor of the *Sun* (a UK tabloid newspaper), noted immediately after the referendum result: 'So much for the waning power of print media' (Martinson 2016). Traditional news outlets are leveraging their influence into the online world so that we now have 'a *shared* dominance of digital agendas by a relatively small number of institutional megaphones, be they platform monopolies, aggregators, or major conventional news organizations' (Schlosberg 2018, 209).

In the UK, levels of concentration of press power are actually increasing. In 2015, three companies controlled 71% of national newspaper readership; by the end of 2018, the same three companies – Rupert Murdoch's News UK, DMG Media (publisher of the *Mail* titles) and Reach (publisher of the *Mirror* titles) – accounted for 83% of the national audience. By themselves, News UK and DMG, strong supporters of the Conservative Party and purveyors of anti-immigrant and anti-welfarist agendas, dominate over 60% of the market share of national newspapers. Despite drops in circulation of their leading daily titles of approximately 25% since 2015, they continue to have a prominent presence in online spaces where the *Sun* and *Daily Mail* alone account for nearly 40% of total daily offline and online UK newsbrand reach (Media Reform Coalition 2019b). This also guarantees them continuing attention from politicians and, evidence suggests, from broadcasters. For example, one study of intermedia agenda-setting during the 2015 UK general election found that television news, while bound by impartiality regulations, nevertheless 'pursued a similar agenda to UK newspapers during the election campaign and followed their lead on some of the major stories'. More than half of all BBC stories on election policy issues had previously been published in newspapers, a figure that rose to nearly two-thirds of stories on Sky News, controlled at the time by Rupert Murdoch's 21st Century Fox (Cushion et al. 2018, 178).

As previously noted, digital markets were initially conceptualised as representing the death knell of the blockbuster economy and its replacement by a 'long tail' where *niche* replaces *hit* as its overarching logic. The problem is that the evidence, at least in relation to news and information markets, does not bear out this optimism; niche products may have far more of an edge than they used to but they remain overshadowed by the size and influence of dominant sources and mainstream media. For example, after examining some 7.5 million tweets about the 2015 refugee crisis, researchers concluded that 'power, understood as visibility and ability to set the agenda through hashtags mentions and RTs, is concentrated in some accounts and hashtags that include well-established actors who already enjoy power and visibility both on and off Twitter' (Siapera 2018, n.p.). The power to frame the issue of migration – as with so many other issues – still remains in the hands of elite politicians, mainstream media and well-resourced lobbyists.

We can see this unequal share of voice inside the UK news landscape. While the left-wing digital native news site the Canary attracted a very creditable 817,000 UK visits in January 2019, this is less than 1% of the traffic to *The Guardian*, with nearly 104 million visits. During the 2017 UK general election campaign period, the Canary outperformed the *Daily Mail* online when it came to Facebook shares of articles on the two main party leaders. Yet its actual reach was, over the same period, a tiny fraction of the *Mail*'s (1% versus 36%). And in the month the election was called, page views of the *Daily Mail* website outnumbered those of the Canary by a factor of more than 700. Similarly, the right-wing outlet Westmonster saw 614,000 visits to its site in January 2019, approximately 0.6% of that of the *Daily Mail*, with 102 million visits. Indeed, none of the top ten news websites in the UK (measured by reach) are new start-ups; all of them are legacy newspapers or broadcasters, with the BBC, *Sun*, *Daily Mail*, *The Guardian* and *The Telegraph* occupying the top five positions (Ofcom 2018).

What does the media's concentrated power mean for journalism's analysis of pressing societal problems and for the public's right to be informed about the full range of approaches that is required to address these problems? It means that there is a disincentive to ask tough questions about power when media organisations are intertwined in multiple ways with the networks of privilege and influence they are supposed to hold to account. So, for example, despite some impressive examples of critical reporting on the UK government's handling of the coronavirus in relation to testing and tracing and the provision of personal protective equipment (PPE), there was a failure immediately and systematically to interrogate government responses and instead a propensity to amplify the official statements in government press briefings. Of course, even a global pandemic does not magically transcend pre-existing political loyalties, so there was far more criticism in liberal US cable news networks of Donald Trump's leadership than there was of the UK government's attempt to manage the crisis.

It means that frameworks and solutions that run counter to established positions are likely to be discredited or marginalised. Consider the impact of economics coverage that 'began from the 1980s to prioritise sources from the financial sector and business community as well as "pro-business" officials, to the detriment of voices from labour and other sections of society' (Basu 2018, 24). It was not so much that the media 'failed' to predict the 2008 banking crisis but that, as we have already suggested, they helped celebrate the financial instruments and deregulatory landscapes that ultimately paved the way for the crisis. Coverage in the British media in the aftermath of the crisis didn't just fail to consider possible alternatives but instead repeatedly highlighted the dangers of a growing deficit with a specific focus on the need for cuts in public spending. Berry, who has carried out detailed research in this area, argues that 'pro-growth policies or levying wealth, property or transaction taxes were invisible as public policy options' while the press, in particular, was crucial in 'establishing key strands of audience belief that helped justify the implementation of austerity policies' (Berry 2019, 277).

It means that major media outlets are complicit in fostering trivial narratives about the environment that undermine the possibility of urgent debate that can lead to decisive action. All too often news bulletins show pictures of revellers enjoying the hot weather in parks and on beaches when, in reality, the underlying story ought to be about the fact that 18 of the 19 warmest years on record have all been in this millennium. A study by Media Matters found that of 127 stories on network news covering the 2017 heatwave in the USA, only one referred to climate change; the same organisation researched TV coverage of Hurricane Harvey the same year and found that two of the main US news networks, ABC and NBC, failed to mention climate change at all in their reports (Al Jazeera 2018). When the UN's Intergovernmental Panel on Climate Change produced a report in 2019 showing how greenhouse gas emissions, deforestation and intensive farming are jeopardising the future of agricultural land, Media Matters revealed that only 7 out of 20 newspapers in the main agricultural states mentioned the report on their front page while none of the main Sunday TV news programmes referred to it at all (Media Matters 2019).

It means that where radical political alternatives are proposed, they are likely to be shot down by the mainstream media. When Jeremy Corbyn was elected as leader of the Labour Party in the UK in 2015 on a radical, anti-austerity and anti-imperialist platform, the media's reaction was immediately to go on the offensive; 60% of all coverage in his first week as leader was overtly negative, with only 13% of stories containing positive messages. Subsequent studies of press coverage tended to confirm this initial judgement. In July 2016, researchers at the London School of Economics assessed over 800 articles in eight leading newspapers. They found that the majority of coverage was either 'critical' or overtly 'antagonistic' and argued that the press had moved from a 'watchdog' to an 'attack dog' role that was aimed at delegitimising the Labour leader because of his willingness to challenge the political establishment. Broadcasters, expected to respect 'due impartiality', were less obviously partisan but they nevertheless happily reproduced memes about Corbyn's 'unelectability', his alleged links to terrorists and his reluctance to send millions of people to their death by pressing the nuclear button. This combination of vilification and misrepresentation was intensified in the 2019 general election and contributed to Labour's defeat and to Corbyn's resignation as Labour leader (Jackson et al. 2019).

Part of the problem is that the restricted scope of mainstream coverage is due to the media's own lack of diversity. For example, research by the Sutton Trust found that the news media is one of the most elitist sectors of British society, with a substantial overrepresentation of people with a privileged educational background. While just 7% of the UK population is schooled privately, 44% of newspaper columnists, 43% of the top 100 senior journalists, editors and presenters and 29% of BBC executives went to 'independent' schools; 44% of columnists, 36% of the 'News Media 100' and 31% of BBC executives attended either Oxford or Cambridge, hardly proportionate to the less than 1% of the UK population who studied there. The researchers identified a 'disconnect' between journalists and publics which leads to an agenda-setting that reflects the news media's own priorities and class situation, and diminishes those experiences with which they are less familiar (Sutton Trust 2019).

Considering the Alternatives

We need, therefore, to promote a different kind of media as a fundamental feature of a different kind of social system (Fenton et al. 2020). Fortunately, the rising tide of racism and authoritarianism coincides and clashes with an appetite for collectivist approaches and an embrace of social justice. Despair and defeatism about current trends of polarisation and illiberalism are matched by a growing enthusiasm for more radical and progressive solutions. Genuine alternatives, however, need to be located in newly imagined political strategies such as those put forward by the UK Labour Party prior to the 2019 general election, based on a series of policies aimed at democratising ownership of the British economy (Labour Party 2018). These ranged from nationalisation, to worker ownership funds, to boosting support for the cooperative sector. They are useful starting points with some significant repercussions for the media and tech sectors. But if we are to reimagine our media futures, this will require not just alternative strategies and policies but also an alternative politics. Such a critique begins from a concern with the problems a capitalist economy has left us with: burgeoning inequality and poverty, global warming, the biospheric damage from a dominant economic system powered by fossil fuels and predicated on endless consumption and growth that concentrates economic and political power in the hands of oligarchs and autocrats. To change this direction of travel requires political and economic alternatives to this system that are just and inclusive, ecologically wise and socially regenerative, shifting economic and political power back to communities and democratic institutions.

Conceiving of a media that supports a newly imagined democratic political economy means conceiving of a world not simply post-Covid but also post-capitalism. It means breaking away from a market economy to something that looks more like a citizen's economy or a solidarity economy. Taking account of the key elements of democracy and ownership, what might this look like in terms of the media? We can point to three key normative criteria that are required if we are to begin to articulate an alternative politics and apply it to the media (adapted from Fraser 2018). To be truly transformational, all three criteria must be met.

Wholesale Egalitarianism

Egalitarianism refers to both external structural factors relating to the broader environment that media organisations function within and to internal structural factors relating to the workforce and working practices of the organisations themselves. The principle of egalitarianism clearly runs counter to the concentration of media ownership endemic across the globe, with the tech giants now the largest oligopolies the world has ever seen. Limiting concentration of media ownership is vital but only takes us so far. It may relax the stranglehold of power that certain media corporations exert but it does not necessarily alter the neoliberal nature of the system they operate within. So it is also crucial to enable, support and sustain forms of media ownership that are *not for profit* and are fully independent of commercial pressures and government preferences, are organised cooperatively and democratically, and are responsive to the needs of the communities they serve rather than at the behest of the market. The principle here is for new models of ownership that redistribute and circulate wealth rather than extract it.

In a context in which mainstream media industries are largely bastions of privilege for political and economic elites, and operate with fierce hierarchies resistant to change, publicly owned media organisations may appear to be a viable solution. For example, public service media such as the BBC are often seen as the best redress for a contemporary journalism marked by hyperpartisanship and hypercommercialism, with the ability to offer journalism independent of the state or market, inclusive of diverse voices and with space for more critical coverage. But, as Freedman (2018, 206) argues, the BBC 'is a compromised version of a potentially noble ideal: far too implicated in and attached to existing elite networks of power to be able to offer an effective challenge to them'. As noted above, despite its claims of impartiality and independence, the BBC has always sided with the elite and been in thrall to those in power. Over the last three decades, the BBC's independence has been steadily eroded and its programme-making increasingly commercialised.

Broadcasting in the UK was originally regulated according to public service principles. That model has been increasingly marginalised as the BBC has become more and more subject to a market-based regulation. Currently, BBC activities have to be balanced with consideration for competition through 'public value' tests. They are also subjected to 'market impact assessments' by Ofcom, the UK's communications regulator, which has been criticised for privileging consumer interests over those of citizens. Severe funding cuts, particularly in recent years, have also caused the BBC's editorial culture to become more conservative and risk-averse. Mills (2016) and the Media Reform Coalition (2019a) argue that adequate, secure public funding that is independent of governmental control is the pathway to real political independence and insulation from the market-based approach that has eroded the BBC's public service ethos. Rather than returning to the top-down, statist model on which the BBC was founded, to fulfil its public service promise the BBC must become a modern, democratised public platform and network, fully representative of its audiences and completely independent.

Another relevant model of democratic ownership is the cooperative: an autonomous association of people who have come together voluntarily to meet their common economic, social and cultural needs and aspirations through a jointly owned and democratically controlled enterprise. Cooperatives are based on values of self-responsibility, democracy, equality, equity and solidarity. As such, they aim to eschew gender, social, racial, political or religious discrimination and pursue equity through things like education and training. Cooperatives work for sustainable community development through policies approved by members. They are concerned with the nurturing of people and communities and democratic self-rule. Cooperative ownership has been argued to increase employment stability and increase productivity levels by discouraging an approach based on short-termism for shareholder return and the use of low-wage labour (Davies et al. 2014). As cooperatives are collectively owned and controlled, they are also more democratic and responsive to internal demands for more egalitarian employment and working practices. There is no employer and employee but a membership of worker-owners that are no longer solely answerable to capital; rather, the idea is that capital serves the cooperative that is democratically organised and governed.

Egalitarianism means getting rid of inequalities and so is also related to the internal plurality of media organisations. An egalitarian media will recognise ways in which media have held certain people back – Black people, old people, disabled people, working-class people – and will seek to counter those forms of discrimination by taking special measures to compensate for the social and economic inequalities of unjust social structures in full recognition of the different yet connected structural conditions of class, racial and hetero-patriarchal domination. The majority of mainstream media organisations are alarmingly lacking in diversity in output and in the workforce. An increasingly casualised workforce also impacts disproportionately on those from lower-income families, women, minority groups and those with disabilities. Egalitarianism would require a major power shift in the general media landscape away from capital-hungry commercial media organisations and also in how power is shared within media organisations themselves – a shift that recognises egalitarianism not just as an economic concern but a social and political one too.

Substantively Meaningful Democracy

Just as a strong egalitarianism in the media goes beyond plurality of media own-ership, so a substantively meaningful democracy goes beyond liberal versions of democracy with their emphasis on individual rights and jurisprudence to recon-nect with a democratic tradition premised on equality, participation and popular sovereignty. In practice this will also involve a strong sense of localism and community-managed resources (including local media), run sustainably with mechanisms to progress equality and to prevent anyone taking unfair advantage. This fits most comfortably with the notion of 'subversive commoning' proposed by Birkinbine (2018). If we see the media as part of a shared public informa-tion and communications resource necessary for a healthy functioning democ-racy – and a form of public utility – then we have to shift from viewing them as primarily competitive corporate entities to seeing them as shared resources that can be co-owned and/or co-governed by the users and media workers according to their own rules and norms as part of the commons. This relates to physical spaces that are shared or pooled; the co-production of the resource; the means of maintaining that resource; as well as the mode of governance – how decisions are made collaboratively through collective problem-solving to distribute and use the resource (Fenton et al. 2010).

Cooperatives, as discussed above, are democratic organisations controlled by members who jointly participate in setting policies and making decisions. Media coops are on the rise. The global newsletter published by Cooperatives Active in Industry Services (CICOPA) reported that in 2017 there had been a 27% increase in coops in the field of information and communications around the world, with many emerging in response to the need to preserve pluralism, escape commer-cial and state pressures and ensure independent journalism. Most of these are worker cooperatives with democratic governance at their core and the majority operate in Europe. Many face issues of lack of finance, regulatory complexity, tax and administrative burdens but, nonetheless, they are increasing in number. Part of the growth is due to the emergence of platform cooperatives where users and/ or workers ultimately own and control the platforms based on principles of eco-nomic fairness, training and democratic participation in the running of online businesses (Scholz and Schneider 2016).

In Cairo the online news cooperative Mada was born out of the crisis in 2013 (when mass protests across Egypt demanding the resignation of the president ended in a coup d'état) and formed by a group of journalists who had lost their jobs and were worried about the future for independent journalism in Egypt. They describe their journalism as the kind that constantly challenges, raises questions and proposes different possibilities. They operate an open and ongoing editorial conversation on the ethics of their journalism, especially with regard to protecting the rights of the oppressed and the vulnerable, and preserving the privacy of sources. In the UK, *The Bristol Cable* is changing the face of local journalism as a grassroots community-led media cooperative. It prints a free quarterly magazine with a circulation of 30,000 copies and publishes investigative and community-led journalism regularly online. It also delivers free media training equipping local people with the skills to report on issues that are important to them. It is funded by over 2,000 members, each paying a small monthly fee (who all have a say and own an equal share in the coop), by foundation support and crowdfunding. Income is also generated from advertising in the print edition regulated by an ethical advertising charter determined by members. Each year its members vote on the annual budget, the overall focus for content and who sits on the board of directors. They insist on democratic decision-making throughout the organisation. Media coops like *The Bristol Cable* are trying to figure out what workplace democracy could be in the media industry – from who gets to do what jobs, to who makes decisions on content and resource distribution.

Financial and Environmental Sustainability

Media institutions across the globe are facing multiple crises: of funding, trust, representation, accountability and legitimacy. In many of the countries that make up capitalism's core, the newspaper and magazine industry is in serious decline as large digital intermediaries gobble up the majority of advertising revenue. Much of the debate about the sustainability of the news industry circulates around debates relating to this 'broken business model'. Local news in particular is increasingly under threat. In the UK, the majority of the population (57.9%) is no longer served by a local daily newspaper (Media Reform Coalition 2017). To retain high levels of profitability, media corporations have closed or merged titles and cut jobs, often moving journalists long distances away from the communities they serve and no longer being able to provide content of relevance to them. In short, a profit-driven response means media become ever more unsustainable.

However, if we shift our perspective from one of media as a source of profit to media as a resource for the public good, then the question of financial sustainability becomes a rather different one: a means to pay journalists a decent living wage in good working conditions to deliver journalism in the public interest rather than maximise shareholder profitability. *The Bristol Cable* most closely fits the description of a multi-stakeholder cooperative (MSC) whose membership includes both the workers and readers. MSCs offer a means of financial sustainability through membership payments. *The New Internationalist*, a magazine dedicated to human rights, politics and social justice, describes itself as one of the largest media cooperatives in the world. Founded in 1973, it became a workers coop in 1992 and then an MSC in 2017. By 2019, it had over 3,600 investor members who have a say in how the magazine develops. Becoming an MSC has given it long-term financial sustainability and enabled it to do more investigative and long-form journalism. *The Ferret*, based in Scotland, is also a cooperative run by its members and funded by subscriptions, donations, paid-for stories or material and grants and gains its following from being democratic and having a clear public purpose.

Infrastructural support for media plurality needs to go further than simply recognising the necessity of guaranteeing citizens' access to a wide range of diverse information and debate for a flourishing democracy. To be fully sustainable we need to put citizens at the centre of democratic media governance too. An approach based on the commons is aimed at strengthening the collective solidarity of workers and offering mutual life support to all inhabitants. A media *commons* is by definition sustainable.

Conclusion

This chapter has attempted to make the case for structural changes to the media by reflecting on extensive academic research into the multiple ways in which our media and communications systems fall short of providing citizens with accurate, diverse and representative media that is capable of informing and nourishing the kind of inclusive public debate that is the lifeblood of functioning democracies. But this book is concerned with addressing media futures and so we are also concerned with social change. We have outlined some key principles on which change should be premised: wholesale egalitarianism, meaningful democracy and financial and environmental sustainability that situates media futures in a broader, visionary and emancipatory politics for social, political and economic transformation. Without reforms that can realise these principles, our media will become ever more concentrated in fewer hands, more susceptible to market pressures and distorted by commercial priorities, less diverse and less able to fulfil the potential of digital platforms for public purposes.

Critically, we need to imagine media systems that prioritise the value of the public over profit and collaboration over competitiveness – and to develop economies that go beyond capital. Operationally, this means that we have to formulate mechanisms of inclusive citizen participation and democratic control of the spaces we inhabit. Rethinking and rebuilding our media worlds according to these principles will require enormous energy and enthusiasm. We will have to learn from other social struggles and solidarity movements that sought to advance economic equality, civil rights and social justice but we do so on the basis that there can be no meaningful democracy without media reform.

References

Al Jazeera. 2018. 'Why Media Need to Turn Up the Temperature on Climate Change'. 22 October. Available at: www.aljazeera.com/programmes/listeningpost/2018/10/media-turn-temperature-climate-change-181020140721880.html.

Basu, L. 2018. *Media Amnesia: Rewriting the Economic Crisis*. London: Pluto.

Berry, M. 2019. *The Media, The Public and the Great Financial Crisis*. London: Palgrave Macmillan.

Birkinbine, B. 2018. 'Commons Praxis: Towards a Critical Political Economy of the Digital Commons'. *tripleC*, 16(1): 290–305.

Chadwick, A. 2017. *The Hybrid Media System: Politics and Power*, 2nd edn. Oxford: Oxford University Press.

Cushion, S., A. Kilby, R. Thomas, M. Morani and R. Sambrook. 2018. 'Newspapers, Impartiality and Television News'. *Journalism Studies*, 19(2): 162–181.

Davies, R., A. Haldane, M. Nielsen and S. Pezzini. 2014. 'Measuring the Costs of Short-Termism'. *Journal of Financial Stability*, 12: 16–25.

Fenton, N., D. Freedman, J. Schlosberg and L. Dencik. 2020. *The Media Manifesto*. Cambridge: Polity.

Fenton, N., M. Metykova, J. Schlosberg and D. Freedman. 2010. *Meeting the News Needs of Local Communities*. London: The Media Trust.

Foucault, M. 1977. *Discipline and Punish: The Birth of The Prison*. London: Vintage.

Foucault, M. 1980. *Power/Knowledge: Selected Interviews and Other Writings*. London: Pantheon.

Foucault, M. 2002. *Power, vol. 3 of the Essential Works of Foucault*. London: Penguin.

Fraser, N. and R. Jaeggi, 2018. *Capitalism: A Conversation in Critical Theory*. Cambridge: Polity.

Freedman, D. 2018. '"Public Service" and the Journalism Crisis: Is the BBC the Answer?'. *Television & New Media*, 20(3): 203–218.

Jackson, D., E. Thorsen, D. Lillekar and N. Weidhase (eds). 2019. *Election Analysis 2019*. Bournemouth: Centre for Comparative Politics and Media Research. Available at: www.electionanalysis.uk.

Jenkins, H., S. Ford and J. Green. 2013. *Spreadable Media: Creating Value and Meaning in a Networked Culture*. New York: New York University Press.

Labour Party. 2018. *Alternative Models of Ownership*. Available at: https://labour.org.uk/wp-content/uploads/2017/10/Alternative-Models-of-Ownership.pdf.

Martinson, J. 2016. 'Did the Mail and Sun Help Swing the UK towards Brexit?' *The Guardian*, 24 June. Available at: www.theguardian.com/media/2016/jun/24/mail-sun-uk-brexit-newspapers.

Moore, M. and D. Tambini. 2018. 'Conclusion'. In *Digital Dominance*, edited by M. Moore and D. Tambini, 396–408. Oxford: Oxford University Press.

Media Reform Coalition. 2017. *Mapping Changes in Local News: More Bad News for Democracy*. Available at: www.mediareform.org.uk/wp-content/uploads/2017/12/mapping-changes-in-local-news-2015-2017-interactive-research-report-march-2017.pdf.

Media Reform Coalition. 2019. *Media Manifesto 2019*. Available at: www.mediareform.org.uk/blog/media-manifesto-2019.

Media Reform Coalition. 2019. *Who Owns the UK Media?* Available at www.mediareform.org.uk/wp-content/uploads/2019/03/FINALonline2.pdf.

Mills, T. 2016. *The BBC: Myth of a Public Service*. London: Verso.

Nicolaou, A. 2019. 'A Second Wave of Media M&A is Coming'. *Financial Times*, 7 August. Available at: www.ft.com/content/9629af48-b8b3-11e9-8a88-aa6628ac896c.

Ofcom. 2018. *News Consumption in the UK*. Available at: www.ofcom.org.uk/__data/assets/pdf_file/0024/116529/news-consumption-2018.pdf.

Ofcom. 2020. *Covid-19 News and Information: Consumption and Attitudes*. Available at: www.ofcom.org.uk/__data/assets/pdf_file/0031/193747/covid-19-news-consumption-week-one-findings.pdf.

Richter, F. 2019. 'Infographic: The Incredible Size of Google's Advertising Business'. *International Business Times*, 22 August. Available at: www.ibtimes.com/ infographic-incredible-size-googles-advertising-business-2816856.

Scholz, T. and N. Schneider. 2016. *Ours to Hack and to Own: The Rise of Platform Cooperativism*. New York: OR Books.

Schlosberg, J. 2018. 'Digital Agenda Setting: Re-Examining the Role of Platform Monopolies'. In *Digital Dominance*, edited by M. Moore and D. Tambini, 202–218. Oxford: Oxford University Press.

Siapera, E., M. Boudourides and S. Lenis. 2018 'Refugees and Network Publics on Twitter: Networked Framing, Affect and Capture'. *Social Media & Society*. https://doi.org/ 10.1177/2056305118764437.

Sutton Trust. 2019. *Elitist Britain*. Available at: www.suttontrust.com/research-paper/ elitist-britain-2019/.

Vaidhanathan, S. 2018. *Anti-Social Media*. Oxford: Oxford University Press.

Zuboff, S. 2019. *The Age of Surveillance Capitalism*. London: Profile.

THE FUTURE OF JOURNALISM

3

An End to Futility: A Modest Proposal

James Curran

Introduction

There is a deeply engrained fantasy that technology will always fix things. Any proposal for media reform should not involve the state, it is argued, because this will undermine freedom of expression. There is always a more agreeable alternative that entails no risk: technological liberation. This approach draws on fervent libertarianism. It found an eloquent voice in Silicon Valley prophets who proclaimed that the virtual world of the internet – 'cyberspace' – is free, egalitarian, interactive, self-expressive and global. This virtual world, they declared, is superior to the physical world, and will redeem it.[1] All that is needed is for the state to stay out of the way, and allow the internet to save the universe unimpeded. As the Grateful Dead lyricist John Perry Barlow wrote in 'A Declaration of the Independence of Cyberspace': 'Governments of the Industrial World, you weary giants of flesh and steel, I come from Cyberspace, the new home of Mind. On behalf of the future, I ask you of the past to leave us alone. You are not welcome among us. You have no sovereignty where we gather' (Barlow 1996).

Former members of the Revolutionary Communist Party are the nearest counterpart to this millenarian anti-statist tradition in Britain. They regularly proclaim the power of science to build a better world provided it is unfettered by the capitalist state. This has led them to attack proposals for more regulation of biotechnology (including genetic modification). Some have gone further and disputed climate change 'orthodoxy' with its agenda of state intervention. For example, Claire Fox, a former co-publisher of the magazine *Living Marxism* (now defunct), dismisses Extinction Rebellion as 'anti-progress, anti-development' (Anderson 2019).

These outriders of libertarianism can be politically mobile. John Perry Barlow was a former Republican (and campaign organiser for the Republican politician Dick Cheney) who drifted to the hippy left at peace with corporate power. Claire Fox, a former Trotskyist activist, became a UKIP MEP, and is now a baroness. But despite their political wanderings, they have been consistent in believing in the emancipatory power of science and technology, and in opposing an enlargement of the role of the state (at least, as presently constituted).

Their views are merely an extreme version of mainstream thought. The dominant political creed from the 1980s onwards has been neoliberalism: the belief that reducing the influence of the state on the economy – through privatisation and deregulation – will build a more prosperous society. This approach won growing support within the economics profession, think tanks, public bureaucracies, governments and the leadership of opposition parties. Coming from the right, it gained adherents across the political spectrum, even in the Rhineland and Nordic heartlands of social democracy. Although its ascendancy was weakened by the 2008 crash and the 2020 pandemic, it remains a powerful intellectual force.

If anti-statism became more widespread in the later twentieth century, a belief in the role of science and technology as a force for progress has long been with us. Indeed, it is the metanarrative of modernity. Historians like to deride Whig history – and its belief in the advance of reason and science as the midwife of progress – proclaiming it to be a relic of the Victorian age. But like the undead, the Whig historical narrative of progress lingers on. This is for a very good reason; science and technology have in fact contributed to greater prosperity, longer life and better health.

These two traditions – suspicion of the state and reverence for technology – have given rise to repeated bouts of delusion every time a new media technology comes along. On each occasion, it is proclaimed that a new dawn has arrived in which the ills of the media will be remedied. State-sponsored media reform is deemed redundant. Yet, prophecies of technological redemption often prove to be empty.

It is worth recalling five past moments of delusion. They suggest that a more effective approach than 'techno-olatory' (to invent a new word) is needed.

Four Moments of Delusion

In the 1980s, a wish-fulfilment fantasy was woven around the camcorder, a portable video camera which incorporated a videocassette recorder. It was relatively cheap and easy to use. At last, it was proclaimed, ordinary people had the tech-nology to create their own programmes, making possible the creation of an alter-native television sector under democratic control. The camcorder would breathe new life into the struggling video movement that had emerged in the later 1960s. It would enable new forms of collaborative work between professionals and amateurs, which would be relevant and true to people's experience. The tech-nology would, in the words of one group, 'bring people together to speak and listen to each other and help build and support strong communities' (Viewpoint Community Media (Swindon) n.d.). The excitement engendered by the new tech-nology was conveyed by the names that groups awarded themselves, such as the 'Camcorder Guerillas', a collective based in Scotland (Coyer et al. 2007, 198).

In the event, some humorous family videos were shown on commercial tele-vision. Moving testimonies were recorded, and shown to small audiences in com-munity centres (and are now a rich source for social historians). But the people's television revolution never materialised.

The second delusive moment occurred when new-generation commercial cable TV was launched in Britain in 1983. Wise heads predicted that it would lead to an entertainment-led information revolution. Cable TV would provide not only 'film-on-request' but adult education programmes which, according to the *Times Educational Supplement* (28 October 1983), would have an impact comparable to the advent of the public library. Advanced cable TV would supply numerous channels for minorities including the deaf and elderly. And it would supply innovative off-air services such as home visits by the doctor. None of these developments materialised. Instead cable TV showed mostly tired repeat programmes, and was adopted by just 1% of homes in the UK by 1989 (Goldberg et al. 1998, 10).

The third delusive moment occurred in Fleet Street in the mid-1980s. The conventional wisdom was that the introduction of computer-aided print tech-nology would inaugurate a newspaper revolution by enormously reducing costs. Ian Aitken, political editor of *The Guardian*, wrote that it would enable the emer-gence of 'entirely new newspapers representing all points of view', while *The Observer* journalists Robert Tayler and Steve Vines declared that it would break 'the tyranny of the mass circulation press' (Aitken 1985; Vines and Taylor 1985). A number of new national newspapers were launched in the late 1980s. With one exception, they all failed. *The Independent* (including its Sunday edition) alone survived but ceased to be independent when it became the property of a Russian oligarch. It subsequently became a website-only publication (though a later offshoot, the *i* newspaper, still exists). The main impact of the 'print revolution' was to enable newspapers to become fatter, and for print workers to be sacked. It also aided for a time the development of alternative community newspapers, although most of these folded by 1990.

The fourth delusive moment began in the mid-1990s, and was the most bizarre of all. It repeated the fables spun around cable TV the decade before but applied them to interactive digital television, called at the time 'iTV'. The same promises were made – video-on-demand, home visits from the doctor, programmes for the elderly, mass adult education – but this time round there was more emphasis on viewer power. Readers of the British press were told that they would be able to vote on key issues, choose the story line for a drama, compile dream schedules of programmes from around the world and instruct their TV sets to scan and select news on topics they were interested in (Curran and Seaton 2018). The key to all this viewer power was the red button.

Most of these much-trumpeted new features of interactive TV sets did not materialise. 'Red button interactivity' was widely judged to be a huge disappointment. Market research carried out in Britain, reported in *New Media Age* (27 April 2006), revealed that the majority of viewers never used any of the modest red button facilities (such as betting on a horse) that were available.

The Grand Delusion

The grand delusion was different because it was played out not at a particular 'moment' but for the best part of two decades. The fantasy was that the internet would bring about a renaissance of journalism.

A legion of citizen journalists and digital-born websites, it was hoped, would sweep away press barons and newspaper chains. The internet would be 'journalism's ultimate liberation', proclaimed Philip Elmer-Dewitt (1994), because 'anyone with a computer and a modem can be his own reporter, editor and publisher – spreading news and views to millions of readers AROUND the world'. The era of capitalist domination of the press, according to the distinguished media historian John Nerone (2009, 355), was over. 'The biggest thing to lament about the death of the old order', he declared, 'is that it is not there for us to piss on any more.'

The second claim was that journalism would be reborn in a better form as a collaborative project involving both professionals and amateurs, based on diverse forms of media ownership. The 'old economic model of journalism,' declared Yochai Benkler (2006), would give way to a 'new social model.'

In fact, the old order of journalism was not swept away. In most countries, large legacy media organisations dominate the most-visited websites. In 2020, they controlled eight out of the ten most-visited news websites in the UK, nine out of ten in Australia and seven out of ten in the United States – a pattern reproduced elsewhere (Reuters Institute 2020).

Large legacy news organisations also extended their reach through social media. Studies show that legacy media content was prominent in political discussion on Twitter in 2017 elections in France and Germany and prominent also on Facebook in the 2019 general election in India (Majó-Vázquez et al. 2019; Majó-Vázquez et al. 2017a, 2017b). In the UK, legacy media also dominate the news followed through the four leading social media – Facebook, Twitter, Instagram and Snapchat – although they did not monopolise all the top spots in 2018 (Ofcom 2018).

The dream of reinventing journalism through civic involvement also turned sour. There were occasional professional-amateur experiments like the South Korean website OhmyNews, which had short-lived success (Kim and Hamilton 2006). But these were few and far between. More typical was the US TV network NBC, which abandoned an attempt to involve citizen journalists in a professional-amateur partnership after six years (Elvestad and Phillips 2018). There were reasons for this failure. To judge from a seven-nation study, most people have no desire to be amateur journalists (Boczkowski and Mitchelstein 2013). This lack of enthusiasm is matched by that of journalists who are already inundated with information, and are under enormous deadline pressure. They are not sure how reliable and independent their would-be amateur partners are. So they have tended to resist time-consuming experiments of working with non-professionals, confining them to the role of sources.

What has been achieved is the worst of all possible worlds. Traditional newspaper chains have not been ousted by exciting web start-ups. These chains still dominate but they have been undermined by the migration of press advertising to Facebook, Google and websites like Craigslist. British newspaper advertising revenue more than halved between 2007 and 2017, as did that of American newspapers between 2003 and 2015 (Department for Digital, Culture, Media and Sport 2019; Pickard 2020). As a consequence newspapers closed, editorial budgets were slashed and journalists were sacked. US newspaper publishers shrunk their workforces by over half between 2001 and 2016 (Pickard 2020), whereas their

British counterparts reduced the number of journalists they directly employed by 26% (Department for Digital, Culture, Media and Sport 2019). This has resulted in news deserts where local affairs are no longer properly reported, ghost local newspapers which are run in effect from regional news hubs and, above all, more superficial, PR-dependent journalism.

In short, legacy news media have not been dethroned. But newspapers have haemorrhaged revenue, depleting their quality and coverage. As a consequence, the recent period has marked the decline rather than renaissance of journalism.

Causes of Delusion

There are multiple causes of these repeated bouts of delusion. It is not just that some progressives have sought a technological solution to media shortcomings, conditioned by their libertarianism and awe of new technology. It is not even that they have clutched at straws because they did not want state involvement. The explanation is more complicated than this, and has something to do with the difficult-to-predict nature of technological innovation. Interactive TV eventually brought a version of 'video-on-demand' through Netflix, Amazon Prime and other subscription on-demand services (SVODs). But this happened decades later than predicted, partly in a different form, delivered not through a red button but a handset.

Similarly, the future of journalism has turned out to be, in a sense, non-journalism. There has been an efflorescence of self-expression about our common social processes in the form of tweets, posts and social media sharing. But while this has been profoundly democratising, there is still a need for good traditional journalism.

There are other explanations too, of which perhaps the most important is a frequent lack of understanding of business. Most national papers that were launched full of hope in the later 1980s ran out of money – in the case of *Today* and *News on Sunday* within weeks (Goodhart and Wintour 1986; Chippendale and Horrie 1990). The community video movement was doomed from the outset because it lacked access to adequate distribution and to the capital needed to mount professionally processed, compelling documentaries. The anticipated rise of digital-born news websites did not happen on the scale that was anticipated due to their undercapitalisation and the power of oligopoly.

It is worth taking a closer look at this last phenomenon because it illustrates how important money – not just technology – is in media creation. Legacy media largely saw off the digital start-up challenge by adopting a classic anti-competitive strategy. They mostly gave away their online content free, cross-subsidised by their print or programme operations. This put digital-born rivals in a double bind. If they matched this free offer, their run-in costs would soar. They would have to build up, over an extended, loss-making period, a user base large enough to break even from advertising alone – something that most failed to do. But if they charged a subscription fee, they would deter would-be users who are used to getting their online news free. No alternative commercial model – including micro-payments and crowdsourcing – emerged that worked.

This is why digital-born news websites have made only limited headway. A small number have managed to break through and become commercially viable. This includes, notably, Buzzfeed (though it is now in financial difficulties) and Huffpost, which was swallowed by a media conglomerate. There is a second stratum of sites (such as Yahoo News and MSN) which are parasitic content aggregators, though some originate a small amount of their own news. The third stratum consists of sites with rich patrons: like Breitbart News, established with right-wing millionaire support, and openDemocracy, endowed by progressive foundations. The fourth stratum consists of sites confined to marginalised, low-cost ghettoes. A successful example is the Canary, which had more monthly visitors in 2018 than any other digital-born political website in the UK. Yet it operates on a shoestring, and has less than 1% of the combined online and offline audience of the *Sun*, which embodies everything that it opposes (Media Reform Coalition 2019, 7 and 12, tables 4 and 8).

The fifth category consists of failures. Some start-ups died within months. Others briefly soared, generating much academic excitement, only to disappoint. An example of the latter is the Independent Media Center (usually known as Indymedia) which was widely viewed as inspirational (e.g., Platon and Deuze 2003). It was launched in 1999 on the eve of the anti-globalisation protests in Seattle and had built by 2006 a network of around 150 publishing collectives in six continents. Yet by 2014, only 22 functioning centres were left and its audience had drastically shrunk (Bunz 2015). Like other projects of its kind, its trajectory followed the rise and decline of the social movement to which it was linked – in this case, the social justice movement.

What Money Can Buy

Just as the European aristocracy subsidised the arts (notably music) in the eighteenth century, so the American plutocracy subsidise some contemporary media with a public purpose. This is one of the ways they pay less tax, and it also avoids the hazard, as they see it, of state involvement in the media. It is worth registering what additional funding – whatever the source – can achieve.

The Sandlers, a rich banking family, have bankrolled ProPublica, an online newsroom in New York. Other charitable trusts such as Carnegie and Atlantic Philanthropies have also backed the project. ProPublica draws on the rich tradition of investigative reporting in the USA. It is led by veteran journalists but also employs young talent. It is an impressive organisation which has won three Pulitzer Prizes for news reporting. It has secured a large audience by working with leading media organisations on specific projects.

Its output is, broadly speaking, centrist but it includes some progressive journalism. One notable example of its output is 'Machine Bias', an analysis of the software supplied by a private company which is used by judges across America when passing sentence. The software results in black people being incarcerated more often than white people for committing similar crimes on the basis of flawed risk assessments. This is because its algorithm (informed by responses to a lengthy questionnaire) predicts future criminality in ways that are racially biased and demonstrably false. Of those who were labelled high-risk but did not reoffend, 50% were African American and 23% were white. In the case of those who were assessed as lower-risk but did reoffend, 48% were white and 28% Black. ProPublica's statistical analysis, backed up by other evidence, was given a dramatic focus through reports about particular individuals (Angwin et al. 2016). This investigation was carried out by a team of four people with a background in computer science as well as journalism. In the context of the Black Lives Matter movement, it provides a timely insight into how institutional racism actually works.

To produce journalism of this quality requires not just skill and intelligence but also time and money. It is a reminder of what is increasingly lacking in our financially strapped press.

British Digital Corporation

In Europe we have stopped relying on the rich to do good works through private philanthropy. It seems preferable for the democratic state – rather than the aristocracy – to determine the public good. This is why it was decided in Britain that Parliament should define the shape of broadcasting in the 1920s. It adopted the then-innovative idea that radio should be organised as a public service, with its own source of funding but with objectives defined in a public charter.

It is time that we consider how the gains of digitisation can be harvested for the public good. Digitisation enables media interoperability and lowers costs. James Harding, the former editor *of The Times*, has suggested the idea of a British Digital Corporation (BDC). Jeremy Corbyn, then leader of the Labour Party, endorsed this proposal in a public lecture (Corbyn 2018). Yet, the form which this new body should take remains elusive. Essentially, we have a good name but little more. Below I set out some ideas about how the concept could be developed.

The key to any realistic proposal is its funding. The idea of the licence fee – in effect a hypothecated tax – has been central to the success and longevity of the BBC. The obvious source of new finance are the immensely profitable tech giants which are parasitic oligopolies sucking revenue from the media industries. A tax should be levied on revenue from online advertising, appearing in the UK, of companies (like Facebook, YouTube and Google) with more than a 20% share of online search and social networking markets.

A recurrent defect of past media subsidy schemes is lack of access to distribution. This can be addressed by requiring all UK public service broadcasters – that is, both publicly owned and fully regulated commercial broadcasters (BBC, ITV, Channels 4 and 5) – to commission a set proportion of their qualifying content from programmes funded by the BDC. This will prevent its marginalisation.

The role of the BDC would be to create and fund an *independent media sector* producing output with a public purpose. This would include anything from film, TV programmes, websites and print publications to videogames. This independent sector should operate alongside the commercial and public service media sectors.

The projects eligible for funding could include the following. Each category serves a public purpose:

- a newsroom of skilled investigative journalists (like ProPublica)
- 'state of the nation' drama, both of the left and the right
- community journalism, especially in areas where there are 'news deserts'
- children's programmes and documentaries – two categories of programming that have experienced a sharp drop of public funding sustained over a number of years despite the important part they play in the life of the community
- national news websites that extend the political diversity of the media

- media job creation in de-industrialised areas, such as in videogame production, a sector in which the UK is increasingly successful
- television programmes that are innovative, distinctive or enable different
  groups in society to engage in a collective dialogue
- media companies which give their workers a say in decision-making
- media enterprises that extend the diversity of employment in the creative
  industries
- the development of innovative digital media technology

The directors of the British Digital Corporation would be selected by an independent appointments panel. They would be appointed on the basis of relevant
experience and expertise, taking account of the diverse political, regional and
demographic make-up of the nation. In addition, a specified number of directors
would be elected by workers in the creative industries.

The great advantage of the BBC (which should be defended through reform)
is that it achieves economies of scale, has accumulated expertise, a clearly defined
public purpose, a large following and is the main reason why the UK is a leading
international producer of TV programmes. But given its anchorage to the political
class, and its increasingly centralised and market-oriented corporate culture, the
BBC needs to be shaken up by competition from a more innovative and autonomous rival better reflecting the diversity of British society. The BDC resembles in
this respect the original conception of Channel 4 but extends this concept to all
digital media.

The creation of a British Digital Corporation will not be easy in the context of
Brexit Britain. It will be strongly opposed by the US government in bilateral trade
negotiations. It will mean taxing large US communications corporations on their
UK operations in a form that is difficult to evade. And it will generate a subsidy for
the UK creative media industry that will be judged unfair competition – the same
reason why a trade lobby in the USA has in the past pressed for the abolition of
the BBC's licence fee. The BDC is something that a future UK government will
have to fight for. This means that the concept needs to be debated, refined and to
win support from a broad spectrum of opinion. The fact that it originates from a
Conservative (Harding) backed by a socialist (Corbyn) is a good start.

Sometimes it takes time for an idea to pick up impetus, be refined and win
support. It took years for the conception of Channel 4 (originally conceived as
the Open Broadcasting Authority) to bubble up, be reworked and win favour.
But in the end, it was proposed by a Labour government and adopted by a

right-wing Conservative government. A similar process is needed for us to determine how best to reform the media without relying on the magical elixir of new technology.[2]

References

Aitken, I. 1985. 'Whose Back against the Wall?' *The Guardian*, 25 November 1985.

Anderson, C. 2019. 'Brexit Party MP Blasts Labour MP on Climate Change as He Calls Greta Thunberg a "Hero"'. *Daily Express*, 15 October 2019. Available at: www.express.co.uk/news/uk/1191022/brexit-party-brexit-news-claire-fox-extinction-rebellion-video-bbc-politics-live-no-deal.

Angwin, J., J. Larson, S. Mattu and L. Kirchner. 2016. 'Machine Bias'. *ProPublica*, 23 May. Available at: www.propublica.org/article/machine-bias-risk-assessments-in-criminal-sentencing.

Barlow, J. P. 1996. 'A Declaration of the Independence of Cyberspace'. Electronic Frontier Foundation, 8 February. Available at: www.eff.org/cyberspace-independence.

Benkler, Y. 2006. *The Wealth of Networks*. New Haven, CT: Yale University Press.

Boczkowski, P. and E. Mitchelstein. 2013. *The News Gap*. Cambridge, MA: MIT Press.

Bunz, M. 2015. 'How to Speak the Truth on Social Media: An Inquiry into Post-Dialectical Information Environments'. In *Routledge Companion to Social Media and Politics*, edited by A. Bruns, G. Engli, E. Skogerbo, A. Larsson and C. Christensen. Abingdon: Routledge, 137-150.

Chippendale, P. and C. Horrie. 1990. *Disaster! The Rise and Fall of the News on Sunday*. London: Sphere.

Corbyn, J. 2018. 'Alternative MacTaggart Lecture'. Labour Party, 23 August. Available: https://labour.org.uk/press/full-text-jeremy-corbyns-2018-alternative-mactaggart-lecture/.

Curran, J. and J. Seaton. 2018. *Power Without Responsibility*, 8th edn. Abingdon: Routledge.

Curran, J., N. Fenton and D. Freedman. 2016. *Misunderstanding the Internet*, 2nd edn. Abingdon: Routledge.

Department for Digital, Culture, Media and Sport. 2019. *Cairncross Review: A Sustainable Future for Journalism*. Available at: www.gov.uk/government/publications/the-cairncross-review-a-sustainable-future-for-journalism.

Elmer-Dewitt, P. 1994. 'Battle for the Soul of the Internet'. *Time*, 25 July, 50–56.

Elvestad, E. and A. Phillips. 2018. *Misunderstanding News Audiences*. Abingdon: Routledge.

Goldberg, D., T. Prosser and S. Verhulst. 1998. *Regulating the Media*. Oxford: Clarendon Press.

Goodhart, D. and P. Wintour. 1986. *Eddie Shah and the Newspaper Revolution*. London: Coronet.

Kim, E.-G. and J. Hamilton. 2006. 'Capitulation to Capital? OhmyNews as Alternative Media'. *Media, Culture and Society*, 28(4): 541–560.

Morozov, E. 2011. *The Net Delusion*. London: Allen Lane.

Nerone, J. 2009. 'The Death and Rebirth of Working-class Journalism'. *Journalism* 10(3): 353–355.

Reuters Institute. 2020. *Digital News Report*. Available at: www.google.com/search?client=firefox-b-d&q=digital+news+report+2020.

Taylor, R. and S. Vines. 1985. 'Farewell to Fleet Street'. *The Observer*, 5 January 1985.

Majó-Vázquez, S., F. Simon and R. Nielsen. 2017a. *Digital-Born and Legacy News Media on Twitter During the German Federal Election*. Reuters Institute, University of Oxford. Available at: https://reutersinstitute.politics.ox.ac.uk/sites/default/files/2017-10/20171030_RISJ_German_Factsheet_.pdf.

Majó-Vázquez, S., J. Zhao and R. Nielsen. 2017b. *The Digital-Born and Legacy News Media on Twitter during the French Presidential Elections*. Reuters Institute, University of Oxford. Available at: https://reutersinstitute.politics.ox.ac.uk/sites/default/files/2017-07/Maj%C3%B3-V%C3%A1zquez%20-%20The%20Digital-Born%20and%20Legacy%20News%20Media%20on%20Twitter.pdf.

Majó-Vázquez, S., S. Mukerjee, T. Neyazi and R. Nielsen. 2019. *Online Audience Engagement with Legacy and Digital-Born News Media in the 2019 Indian Elections*. Reuters Institute, University of Oxford. Available at: www.digitalnewsreport.org/publications/2019/factsheet-online-audience-engagement-legacy-digital-born-news-media-2019-indian-elections/.

Media Reform Coalition. 2019. *Who Owns the UK Media*? Online edition 2. Available at: www.mediareform.org.uk/who-owns-the-uk-media.

Ofcom. 2018. *News Consumption in the UK*. Available at: www.ofcom.org.uk/__data/assets/pdf_file/0024/116529/news-consumption-2018.pdf.

Pickard, V. 2020. *Democracy Without Journalism*? New York: Oxford University Press.

Platon, S. and M. Deuze. 2003. 'Indymedia Journalism: A Radical Way of Making, Selecting and Sharing News?' *Journalism*, 4(3): 336–355.

Viewpoint Community Media (Swindon). n.d. *About Community Media*. Available at: https://viewpointcommunitymedia.org.uk/.

THE FUTURE OF TRUTH

4

Future Faking, Post-Truth and Affective Media

Lisa Blackman

Introduction

The Covid-19 pandemic has brought into sharp focus relatively hidden aspects of domestic abuse, with rates rising exponentially into a global epidemic itself. At the same time, there is widespread agreement that we are living in a post-truth age in which we no longer know whether media messages we receive are 'true'. Even if they aren't true, they might *feel* true or have what Foucault (1980) called truth-effects. This is one of the paradoxes of post-truth, which highlights the role of covert and coercive forms of power in shaping perception, attention, feeling, emotion, understanding and behaviour. Post-truth discloses the close relationship between truth, coercion and consensus, revealing that truth-effects can be the object of manipulation and power struggles (Bufacchi 2020; Oliver 2020; Giraud 2017). Manipulation of media and social media became big news after the exposure of the Cambridge Analytica scandal, where users' Facebook data was harvested by Cambridge Analytica to be used in political advertising. The breach of 80 million users' personal data, without their knowledge or consent, allowed Cambridge Analytica to build psychological profiles of users who were covertly targeted through computational marketing techniques. This event drew attention to the weaponising of 'psychological warfare tools' in the attempt to manipulate publics (Wylie 2019, 5). As Venturini and Rogers (2019, 532) have argued, 'the 2016 US presidential election will be remembered for the scandal surrounding Cambridge Analytica ... a marketing firm that illegitimately acquired data on millions of Facebook ... users and used them to contribute to Trump's campaign'. Strategic disinformation is part and parcel of media and other forms of power.

But this sense of scandal and public outcry in relation to the effects of covert forms of emotional and psychological manipulation should not be limited to the media or to particular strategies used by governments and political consulting firms. It is a key aspect of distorted communication from abusers in some forms of domestic abuse, namely coercive control and narcissistic abuse. Coercive control and narcissistic abuse share similar logics, affects, techniques and relations to those found in post-truth media and government strategies. They are forms of non-physical abuse that are exercised through covert psychological and emotional techniques, and a range of deceptive strategies that destabilise facts and fabricate distorted realities. Coercive control has been described as a form of malevolent conduct based on deception and deceit that misdirects attention and *makes* sense based on lies and twisted forms of reality distortion. These techniques enmesh the victim with the abuser by creating 'invisible chains', or a trap that makes it very difficult to leave (Stark and Hester 2019). These practices have entered the mainstream in communication and practices well suited to social media and mediatised politics. Their ubiquity in political communications and across social media are normalising communication once only discussed in self-help manuals, workshops, blogs and memoirs, primarily written for victims and survivors of abuse.

In different ways the common communication and behavioural patterns under discussion work through a range of reality-distorting techniques and strategies of disinformation and misinformation, based on fakery, trickery, deception and twisted forms of storytelling. They destabilise facts and manufacture consent through the production of an *indeterminacy* of feeling (confusion, chaos, panic, fear, cognitive dissonance) using devious and covert means. This includes practices such as ghosting, gaslighting, trolling, staging, baiting, charm offensives, deception, deflection, backtracking, blame-shifting, confabulation, boundary violations, guilt-mongering, misinformation, disinformation, stonewalling and an adversarial attitude of righteous indignation. This is an affective tone cultivated through the perpetrator's sense of injustice when exposed or held to account that reveals their commitment to their own lies, or a deceptive commitment to stating absolute fiction as fact.

The post-truth era is one primarily characterised as an 'affective politics' that has an 'increasingly visible emotionality' (Boler and Davis 2018, 75), driven by the 'power of feelings' (Davies 2018). Feelings and emotions are seen to be transforming democracies 'in ways that cannot be ignored or reversed' (Davies 2018, xvii). Boler and Davis go further by stating that we are witnessing the 'affective weaponization of communications technologies ... used to mobilize and capture affect and emotion' (2020, 1). However, what are overlooked in some commentaries that ascribe newness to the role of feelings in politics are the very long traditions of work that have valued the power of feelings as important sources of knowledge about power, oppression and governance. This includes feminist, Black and queer scholarship on public feeling and emotion (Gunaratnam and Lewis 2001; Cvetkovich 2012), as well as reclamations of suggestion as an important modality of communication found within the interdisciplinary field of affect studies (see Blackman 2012; Borch 2019, Gibbs 2010). As we will see, this world, although understood as new, shares features with longer histories of strategic deception and misinformation that have been part of media since their inception (see Blackman 2007; Corner 2017). We might decry or reject these strategies as undermining democracies, even leading to 'fake democracies' in their challenge to the ideal of rational deliberative communication. This is primarily seen as the index and measure of liberal democracies (see Fenton 2018). I will argue, however, that there are important continuities between the past, present and future of media that we might miss if we adopt this position.

This includes taking seriously the role of coercion and covert forms of power in shaping public opinion, belief, feeling, emotion and understanding – what Boler and Davis (2020) call propaganda by other means. These connections have been severed within the public sphere, unmoored from their close genealogy with all forms of abuse and coercive forms of power that historically have been associated with fascism or communism, but that we are less likely to accept as being part of democratic forms of power. I have referred to these forms of power as *affective* as they primarily work through the orchestration of feelings, emotions, nervous states, moods and atmospheres. They modulate the indeterminacy of borders, boundaries and thresholds between self and other, fact and fiction, present and absent, past and present, emotion and reason, human and technical, public and private, trust and doubt, integrity and dishonesty, for example, and often operate at the edges of consciousness rather than through rational deliberation (see Blackman 2012; 2019a; 2019b). They have an association with nineteenth-century theories of suggestion and contagion that have historically been pathologised and rejected from theories of democratic power within the public sphere, displaced onto the working classes, colonial subjects, women, children and people with different sexualities who have been understood as 'overly suggestible' and as lacking the 'power of reason' (see Blackman and Walkerdine 2001).

Extending some of these debates in relation to the future of media, I will examine how forms of coercive power traverse domains (non-physical abuse and political communications) that mobilise post-truth as a strategy of deception. This focus allows the possibility of moving beyond the simple oppositions of truth and falsehood towards an understanding of how what has been glossed as post-truth actually works, with profound consequences for the understanding of the sociality and polity in our contemporary present. There are various explanations put forward to understand post-truth and its significance, including declining belief in the value of expertise, the militarisation of politics (including a war of attrition), globalisation, entitlement and a lack of investment in the rules of public life (Davis 2019). What is missing but haunts these analyses is the link between post-truth and experiences of non-physical abuse that challenge what has been described as an 'incident and injury' approach, which categorises and recognises domestic abuse through discrete acts of physical assault or violence. This approach misses abuse that is exercised through the manufacture of coercive atmospheres, and through the use of covert tactics of emotional and psychological control and exploitation. The tactics and strategies of deceit and disinformation share a common genealogy linking thought reform, psychological military techniques, non-physical abuse, and the art and science of manipulation, with the use of emotion as a technique of governance (Blackman and Walkerdine 2001).

One contemporary example of the disavowed link between post-truth politics and abuse comes through in political commentaries on Brexit in UK politics. The academic and commentator Will Davies has coined the term the 'Berlusconifying' of British politics in relation to Brexit and the leadership strategies of Boris Johnson.[1] This term is used to identify the collapse of the separation between politics, business interests and the media and its effects on political campaigning. What Aeron Davis (2019) has called a 'new normal' of lies, which includes deception, betrayal, ruthlessness, incoherence, sabotaging, attack and counter-attack, is changing the frame of politics. However, Silvio Berlusconi, the former Italian prime minister (for four terms), was also shrouded in controversy for various alleged sex scandals with young women and girls. The new normal of politics are contexts marked by an industrial-scale and overwhelming normalisation of languages and practices associated with known perpetrators of abuse.

The two political figures that have condensed some of what is of issue are Donald Trump and Boris Johnson, although other world leaders have exhibited marked tendencies towards such practices. Trump and Johnson have both been accused of abuse and sexual misconduct, of being reckless and opportunistic (see Davis 2018), of being pathological liars, of being manipulative and calculating (fake news), of normalising racist practices, language and behaviour[2] and of inaugurating and enacting forms of power associated with sociopathy, showing the close links between pathocracies and democracies (Lobaczewski 2007), which is registering as a new form of authoritarianism (also see Venn 2020). As some commentators have suggested, what is glossed as a 'post-truth era' is one where psychological forms of manipulation associated with narcissistic abuse and coercive control are profoundly shaping politics and social relations (see Andronici 2019; Sweet 2019; Sarkis 2018;[3] Stern 2018). These practices have come to the foreground in the 'new normal' of politics in many countries, including the USA, the UK, India, Turkey, Mexico, Russia, the Philippines and Brazil.

In order to explore some of these arguments I will focus on an array of practices, many that will be familiar to most readers, that appear in tactics and strategies of manipulation and wilful deception associated with non-physical forms of abuse. They appear in digital practices of communication linked to abuse, harassment and bullying, and increasingly within political communication strategies of misinformation and strategic deception associated with post-truth politics. I will explore the *broken genealogy* that connects these strategies of deception and reality-distortion that traverse the media, government and mental health, particularly within contexts linked to the rise of populisms and right-wing authoritarianisms. My argument will join many commentaries that are grappling with what has happened to politics and the new forms of mediatisation, including fake news, lying and other forms of deception that have entered and significantly changed the media frame. The chapter will discuss the implications of these connections for politics, and particularly the mediatisation of politics, for our online relationships and embodied experiences of digital relations, often discussed in relation to the affordances of different platforms and infrastructures, and how we can best protect ourselves from the many ways in which abuse appears in our lives across different contexts and settings – what I am calling the affective and social lives of abuse.

An Ecosystem of Abuse

Ghosting is a practice estimated to affect millennials more than any other age group and refers to the sudden disappearance of somebody, often on social media, where all communication is stopped. Referred to as a 'unilateral ceasing communication' (LeFebvre 2017, 230), it describes the sudden ending of dating or romantic relationships often through the medium of dating apps without explanation or dialogue, but can also refer to technologically mediated contact and connection across social media where you might be censored, ostracised or find your views or feelings rejected without notice (see LeFebvre et al. 2019). The person disappears from your life or your social media networks, where you might find you have been 'unfriended', been given restricted access or blocked from somebody's profile or social media timeline (sometimes referred to as a 'social media blackout') in what can feel like a very cold, ruthless way. It is an extension of being completely ignored or given the silent treatment that can be exercised across digital platforms in devastating ways. As well as indifference, ghosting can also be done with a calculated intent to bully somebody through a form of disengagement that can be hurtful, aggressive, vicious, damaging and offensive, enacted through the medium of a resounding silence. It can leave you feeling alienated, distressed, isolated, confused, abandoned, rejected and so on. 'Ghosting differs from other relationship dissolution strategies insofar as it takes place without the ghosted mate immediately knowing what has happened, who is left to manage and understand what the partner's lack of communication means and is unable to close the relationship' (Navarro et al. 2020).

During the Covid-19 pandemic there were warnings made across entertainment and news media in relation to the practice of *zombie-ing*, a close kin of ghosting, where people who have previously ghosted you might return or be resurrected from the dead. You can be haunted through practices of presence and absence with contacts appearing and disappearing in ways that can unnerve and unsettle. Other practices associated with perpetrators of abuse that have been extended and become part of an array of digital practices and communications, linked to manipulation and coercive forms of control, include trolling and baiting. *Trolling* and *baiting* are closely related practices that are rife across social media and in digital forms of communication. Trolling has been described as a deliberate strategy of trying to get a rise, or 'bait' somebody for a reaction, through posting inflammatory or controversial comments, often under the cloak of anonymity, and through enacting a form of bullying and harassment. Trolling contributes to 'uncivil discourse' and to what has been described as the *affective* nature of communication on the internet, referring to the visible emotionality of what takes place, challenging the idea of communication as primarily rational and deliberative (the so-called 'power of reason'), as has been assumed within theories of the public sphere influenced by Jürgen Habermas in his book *The Structure of Transformation of the Public Sphere* (1962).

Mediality

Theories of the public sphere have been subject to queer, Black and feminist critique, drawing attention to who is excluded from such an ideal, and whether communication and our investments and commitments to ideals, beliefs and opinions are ever purely rational. There have been many revisions to this concept, including arguments which have advanced ideas of Black and subaltern public spheres (Squires 2002), feminist public spheres (Fraser 1990), ideas of the counter-public drawing from queer theory (Berlant and Warner 1998) and affective publics (Papacharissi 2014, 2016). The latter works across the aforementioned critiques to explore how our investments and attachments to beliefs, ideologies, opinions and politics are also affective, that is, shaped through emotion, feeling, mood, atmosphere, nervous states and intensities that become co-assembled and conjoined as shared processes. The important focus is on how feelings or desire for connection and disconnection, what Papacharissi (2016) terms 'bonds of sentiment', can be amplified, mobilised and mediated, and the role different forms of media can play as framing devices for shaping these affective desires. This might include television, film, radio, photography, but also hashtags, reader comments and communities that come together across different digital platforms, including Twitter, Facebook, Reddit, Quora, Weibo, TikTok and other forums and platforms. This includes those that gather through friendship communities, specific interests and shared experiences and, as we have seen, alliances and allegiances forged through abusive practices, hate and victim-blaming, each public having a distinctive *mediality*, that is, the general influence, form, content and affect(s) generated by the affordances of different media as they enable, support, shape and become shared processes of *making* sense.

As Papacharissi has argued, 'mediality shapes the texture of these publics and affect becomes the drive that keeps them going. The circumstances that drive each of these public formations are different, but it is a public display of affect that unites, identifies, or disconnects them' (2016, 2). Papacharissi likens processes of mediality to different storytelling structures, which work primarily through affect, feeling, emotion and sentiment, or at least affect is the primary register, force and intensity that drives attachments to different ideas, opinions, beliefs, tastes and politics. Drawing on Raymond Williams' (1977) concept of 'structures of feeling', she argues that 'structures of feeling are both rendered and reorganised by the soft and networked architectures of online media' (2016, 5).

The term 'structure of feeling' is 'a specific structure of particular linkages, particular emphases and suppressions, and, in what are often its most recognizable forms, particular deep starting-points and conclusions' (Williams 1977, 134). These linkages exist at the edge of semantic availability or can only be seen retrospectively or from a different vantage point. These patterns are differentiated in different contexts, which gave Williams a potent way of talking about class differences in feeling, including fear and shame. Although it is an ill-defined concept, for many media and affect theorists it provides a useful way of exploring the background of feeling related to context, history, milieu and setting that is available, or might become available, to consciousness. It has links to Black scholarship exploring how long cultures of systematic racism shape somatic feeling – what the Black feminist Hortense Spillers (1987) called the 'flesh'. Structures of feeling exist at the edges of consciousness or semantic availability, and are a potential driver of different actions and reactions – the processes and mobilising power that might bind and bring people together as a collective or part of a commons: *#BlackLivesMatter*.

We can consider the aforementioned processes in relation to the practice of trolling and to consider what kind of mediality trolls enact. Trolls are often described as mean, nasty, hateful people who are looking to disrupt discussion and take pleasure in offending others (see Cheng et al. 2017). In these more psychologised explanations, the troll refers to a person who deliberately posts inflammatory, controversial, shocking comments, exploiting user-generated content and the capacity to co-create meaning, feeling and understanding to upset people and create discord. They do this to provoke negative emotions and feelings rather than considered debate and dialogue, and to deflect attention from their own actions and to blame others (usually the victim). Trolling has been described as a form of harassment or baiting that the person engages in primarily for his or her own gain or enjoyment. They have fun or even experience sadistic pleasure at someone else's expense.

We know that trolling is both a human and non-human practice, where automated bots (trollbots) extend trolling practices without (human) feeling, enabling them to break into more and more networks, often avoiding detection. They have a close kinship to fake news and political campaigns on social media that circulate lies, untruths and disinformation. Trolling, lying and baiting underpin new forms of algorithmic power that shape and manipulate belief and feeling through orchestrating social media feeds and political commentary. Trolls weaponise forms of emotional and psychological manipulation, remediating already-existing structures of inequality and power, including racism, sexism and transphobia. In their more socially sanctioned form, these forms of covert and deceptive tactics might appear as soft power, priming and nudge theory, or theories of behavioural conditioning (see Blackman 2019a).

Disinformation

The troll can also be a useful heuristic device to identify a common set of disinformation tactics characteristic of a particular political strategy or persona. Trump is regularly described, for example, as both a liar and a troll, or in some cases the world's greatest troll, an epic troll, or even a 'world champion troll'.[4] During his presidency he was positioned as the troll in the White House circumventing White House convention through his curveball Twitter posts, becoming the figurehead and helping to build and mobilise a wider political trolling community for 'sustained disruption', such as in the online community that organised through the subreddit */r/The Donald* (see Flores-Saviaga et al. 2018, 82). This community extended across different forms of media and platforms in order to scale up and do maximum damage to Trump's opponents (particularly Hillary Clinton) during the 2016 presidential campaign. Their trolling tactics included PR trolling, using forms of perception management, harassment, firehose trolling (flooding social media with divisive propaganda), satire trolling, creating satirical media including hashtags and memes to mock and ridicule Clinton. All of these related forms of trolling were used to amplify messages from other sources and connect them together as part of an ecosystem of political abuse. This included:

> Netflix boycotts after Netflix promoted TV shows opposing their political views ... orchestrated one-star Amazon reviews for Megyn Kelly's book ... Members of T D also organized the 'Great Meme War' to harass Trump's detractors and flood the Internet with pro-Trump, anti-Hillary Clinton propaganda ... Participants of T D also actively promoted the use of satirical hashtags, such as #DraftOurDaughters to troll Hillary Clinton's initiative about supporting women to register for the military draft ... or #ShariaOurDaughters to take Islam ideologies to an absurd extreme ...
>
> (Cited in Flores-Saviaga et al. 2018, 82)

As well as psychological understandings of the troll as a mean, nasty person, in the above examples we can see how the troll is also a social figure who embodies a mediality that exacerbates and weaponises an already existing fabric and infrastructure of strategic deception and coercion that is built into the internet and digital platforms. As Hal Berghel and Daniel Berleant (2017) have argued, trolling has become synonymous with or even inseparable from social media and digital practices, and some of the reasons for this take us back to much older histories of strategic deception and misinformation that are embedded within platform infrastructures, as we will go on to explore. Trolling can be contagious, attracting others and leading to 'flame wars' and 'doxxing', which are all practices carried out with malicious intent to do harm to, harass, intimidate and injure others. The contagiousness of trolling amplifies what has been called 'networked virality' (Sampson 2012), demonstrating how the networked structures of digital media amplify and extend relationships and connections that can infect others across time and space, increasing and intensifying already-existing 'social, cultural, political and economic contagions' (Sampson 2012, 1). As Sampson suggests, networked virality increases the speed, reach and spread of fads, fashions, political rumours, gossip, scandals, hype, conspiracy theories, for example, cascading and infiltrating like viruses throughout populations.

Trolling is a good example of a practice of 'contagious relationality' that exploits, extends and remediates racism, sexism, transphobia and other forms of discrimination and victim-blaming (encounters shaped through already-existing discriminatory cultures and practices), taking them into, and contaminating, public forums, attempting to close down opposition, silence activists and other critics, conjoining bodily feelings shaped through long histories of oppression, including racism, colonialism, white supremacy, slavery, misogyny and patriarchy, with a volatile mixing and remixing of emotion, affects, feelings, atmospheres and moods. In other words, rather than engage in debate, trolls *bait* for reactions, deliberately provoking their targets through attack and counter-attack, orchestrating hate, fear, shame, guilt, humiliation, paranoia, anger, confusion, chaos, panic, hostility and other negative affects to unsettle and destabilise perception. Interestingly, one strategy to deal with trolls is to 'ghost them', that is, not to give them a reaction or feed them, treating them with indifference and silence. In this example we can see how ghosting, baiting and trolling are all interrelated strategies of manipulation and coercive control that are part of an ecosystem of abuse and harassment that traverses and is mobilised, augmented and modulated in online communication. They are all common practices in narcissistic abuse as described and experienced by survivor communities (see Arabi 2016; Hart and Hart 2018).

Online Abuse

We know that online abuse is a huge problem, not only for public figures, journalists, celebrities and politicians but also for people who seek to draw attention to the very structures and conditions, such as systemic racism, sexism, misogyny, homophobia, xenophobia and transphobia, which enable the problem. A good example of this is the controversy surrounding a book published by the activist and psychologist Jessica Taylor, *Why Women are Blamed for Everything: Exploring Victim Blaming of Women Subjected to Violence and Trauma* (2020). After publication she was bombarded with thousands of comments illustrating the very issue of victim-blaming that she is writing about. Examples of the misogynist abuse that she received on Twitter and Facebook, including rape and death threats, and having her personal computer hacked attracted the attention of the news media, who discussed the organised nature of the trolling, including 'the "alt-right", men's rights activists, incel (invol- untary celibates) and Mgtow (men going their own way) movements'.[5] This is one example of a structural endemic problem that is turned against and individualised in relation to an activist who is identifying the structural nature of the problem.

In a revealing analysis of 70 million *Guardian* reader comments left on the newspaper website, it was found that Black and ethnic minorities and female journalists attracted significantly more abuse than their white male counterparts, for example, with journalists describing the chilling effects of these 'below the line' comments (see Gardiner 2018). Whether it is journalists writing about racism and sexism, or attracting more abuse because of who they are, the issues reveal how abusive strategies are normalised and enabled through communica- tion practices, such as readers' comments, opened up to encourage interaction, commentary and user-generated content, but leaving behind a trail, a trace and afterlives of offense, hostility and hatred towards others. Although many of the comments are blocked or moderated, they leave an archive of haunted data that exists as a dynamic presence, exerting influence through the cultivation of ugly feelings and negative affects (Blackman 2019a; Ngai 2007). Victims are left to deal with the affects and effects of these comments through their own safeguarding practices – 'don't read the comments!' or 'don't react' – with little to nothing to protect them from the actions of perpetrators. With smear campaigns, which are also a related part of this ecosystem of abuse, we know that lies and smears of somebody's reputation or character can stick and do harm regardless of whether the comments have any veracity. They can have 'truth effects', demonstrating clearly the close relationships between coercive forms of power, the production of feeling, including nervous states, anxieties and depression, and the exercise of racism and sexism.

Platform Infrastructures of Strategic Disinformation

In their illuminating article written from the perspective of computer scientists, and from an information-theoretical approach, Hal Berghel and Daniel Berleant (2017) argue that we need a 'taxonomy of trolling' to really understand how embedded trolling is within the software architectures of the internet and digital platforms. Indeed, in the example of the subreddit */r/The Donald* we explored how this political trolling community employed a variety of trolling tactics and practices, creating and circulating disinformation across different media, to exert influence in ways that are more difficult to detect and counter due to their deceptive and covert nature. Berghel and Berleant differentiate disinformation from misinformation through the concept of *wilful intent*. Misinformation is a general problem with 'fake news' as there is an abundance of information and sources that circulate across digital platforms that are difficult to verify. However, *dis*information is done with the *calculated intent* to deceive and conceal one's actions and represents a more insidious form of lying and reality-distortion. As Berghel and Berleant highlight, 'Disinformation techniques and content vary with the purpose, targeted demographic, medium, and social networking platform' (2017, 44).

These tactics of wilful intent to deceive and destabilise have much in common with practices associated with coercive control and narcissistic abuse, as well as with longer histories of strategic deception and disinformation. They all deploy a common and shared range of reality-distorting techniques that destabilise distinctions between truth and falsehood, reason and emotion, self and other, private and public, fact and opinion, personal and political, seriousness and satire. The aim is to construct and enlist support for a particular twisted version of reality that often positions the perpetrator as the victim and likens political campaigning to a sport, competition or game enacted with impunity. Donald Trump is perhaps the best example of a former world leader who extends these tactics into politics, deflecting from the injurious consequences of his actions. As with the taxonomy of trolling that Berghel and Berleant call for, the connections also reveal the complex and differentiated strategies and practices of lying, deception and deceit that underpin the range of communication tactics that come together within the context of post-truth, for example.

Berghel and Berleant (see 2017, 45) make an important related argument about the affordances of the internet and platform infrastructures in enabling and extending these communication tactics. Their argument adds weight to what Papacharissi has called the soft and networked architectures of online media and their role in shaping different forms of mediality. Going back to the history of the development of the web, Berghel and Berleant argue that web-enabled communication is structured by a:

> fundamental flaw in the notional roots of the modern Internet-enabled Web. Those roots are typified by, for example, Paul Otlet's Mundaneum system, implemented in 1910 to collect and categorize all of the world's important knowledge (www.mundaneum.org/en); H.G. Wells's notion of a World Brain, outlined in a 1938 collection of essays and addresses with that title; and Vannevar Bush's Memex system, described in his influential 1945 article 'As We May Think' ... the 21st century's spin on Bush's vision might progressively become 'As We May Deceive.'
>
> (2017, 45)

The use of what is called 'associative indexing and browser history-like "paths" not unlike the use of hypertext to organize the Web' (Berghel and Berleant 2017, 45) reveals an imaginary that helped to visualise the internet. This architecture assumed the reliability and validity of information revealing a structural and systemic commitment to 'neutrality', providing fertile ground for disinformation to become normalised and for racism and sexism to become ingrained in algorithmic forms of power (see Noble 2018; also see Chun 2016). Safiya Noble's concept of algorithms of oppression reveals how platform infrastructures carry and reproduce existing cultures and practices of oppression and inequalities. This issue, which is revealed through algorithms such as the Google PageRank, unveils the politics of page rankings and the measures and criteria which govern and enable particular associative links rather than others. Berghel and Berleant's arguments add weight to Bernhard Rieder's (2012) genealogical approach to software studies. His focus is on exploring the conditions of possibility for Google's automated logic of page ranking to take form, what he calls its 'conceptual *a priori*'. Rieder cogently analyses how software programmers have drawn on and materialised a particular ontology of the network, which is derived in part from sociometry, enacted by a specific algorithm known as Lawrence Page's PageRank.

Sociometry is a broad area of study which purports to analyse and, importantly, visualise the psychological characteristics of populations, linked to Kurt Lewin's topographical approach to psychology. As Rieder argues, the concept of the network, central to these theories, staged connections and links based on status, authority and influence. These concepts were put to work in particular ways where calculations of social status and social *power* were made from sociometric data, rather than other kinds of connections and influences, such as *inequality* and *marginalisation*, for example. The conceptions of social influence that this enacted provided the normative model for various metrics of ranking to be performed. These are based primarily on relations of prestige, hierarchy and power rather than other measures that become foreclosed, disavowed and hidden. The Google PageRank algorithm therefore makes commitments to certain conceptions of the social that are reproduced in the different regimes of visibility and perception, which govern different digital platforms (see Blackman 2016). Rather than simply issues of data reliability and source authentication (fake news), we can see how strategies of disinformation and deception are integral to associative indexing and hypertext, leaving behind a trail of haunted data (Blackman 2019a).

Conclusion: Affective Media

Different media have now become so entangled with who and what we are that it is difficult to make a separation between media and society (see Kember and Zylinska 2012). Mark Deuze has coined the term 'media life' to argue that 'who you are, what you do, and what all of this means to you does not exist outside of media. Media are to us as water is to fish' (2012, x). Deuze gives numerous examples of how media are organising and re-organising politics, celebrity and science, where people, he suggests, might perform themselves in terms of media – a politician imagining him or herself as a photograph, soundbite, tweet or speech. We know politicians are increasingly required to be media-savvy and to imagine how their image, actions and tweets, for example, might be put to work in particular rhetorical ways. Politicians are more literate with the use of different medial concepts such as dramatisation, cutting, framing, staging, liveness, premediation and preemption (see Blackman 2018).

What we might give less attention to are how these medial practices have a close yet disavowed relationship with abuse tactics, and have been extended through post-truth tactics, such as gaslighting and other forms of fakery, staging and trickery. I will finish this chapter outlining a popular example of an abuse tactic that has become associated with post-truth mediatised politics. It is an insidious tactic that can seriously destabilise perception and is linked to narcissistic abuse (see Stern 2018), has become a term to talk about racial microagressions (see Gomez 2015),[6] is rooted in social inequalities (Sweet 2019) and provides an entry-point to analysing the affective and social lives of abuse. Gaslighting was one of the buzzwords in 2018 identifying the toxicity of some post-truth political contexts. Gaslighting refers to the intent or capacity to manipulate (a person) by psychological means into questioning his or her own sanity. In other contexts gaslighting and related tactics are more explicitly framed as forms of *psychological warfare* that are injurious, corrosive, insidious and difficult to detect, measure and isolate, due to their covert nature.

The term 'gaslighting' was regularly used to identify the rewriting of history that has occurred on an almost daily basis during the pandemic, where, for example, former President Trump's previous comments to the press and on social media and decisions about the pandemic were *confabulated*, such that reality was fabricated, distorted and falsified. These confabulations, whether done with calculated intent to lie and mislead or being the result of disordered thinking, became shared in various satirical videos, memes and GIFs. This includes videos using comedic cataloguing and editing of these 'errors', such as in the very funny video shared on NowThisPolitics titled, 'Trump's not a Doctor but he plays one on TV'.[7] As well as an affective economy of disbelief, what we find across social media is an archive of public feeling expressed through astonishment, humour, confusion, anger, rage and the real fear and danger of various of Trump's convictions. As with abusive dynamics it was very difficult for those close to him to challenge him without becoming the target of his rage and retaliation for any perceived slight or criticism. In the case of his conviction about disinfectant being a potential solution to the coronavirus by being injected into the lungs, Trump's statement became a 'media event', being picked up by news and broadcast media expressing the incredulity of audiences. Trump retaliated through a tone of righteous indignation by saying he was being *sarcastic*, shifting the blame onto audiences and cancelling his daily pandemic briefing by saying he was goading the media, while also accusing them of being hostile to him, what was described as a 'just-joking defence'.

This is one recognisable example of a tactic associated with narcissistic abuse and coercive control that extends post-truth into our hearts and minds in damaging ways. A chilling example of the interrelationship of gaslighting, deflection, blame-shifting, baiting and staging is the image of Trump stood in front of a church brandishing a Bible to pose for photographs. Prior to this he had ordered police in riot gear to fire teargas and rubber bullets against peaceful protestors marking their outrage at the killing of a Black man, George Floyd, by a white police officer. Walking a path from the White House, he stood posing for photographs, without acknowledging the protest, commenting upon his prior actions or offering leadership, but rather chose to engage in an abhorrent use of gaslighting by saying, 'We have a great country, the greatest country in the world.'[8]

This chapter has only focused on examples of those tactics that are more easily identifiable and popularised. However, there are a range of other, lesser-known techniques of reality distortion that are shaping a political and affective economy of lies and strategic deception. There are also counter-media of disbelief, those that actively oppose post-truth claims, often through their own forms of satirical media. These issues are the subject of a forthcoming book, *Abuse Assemblages: Power, Post Truth and Strategic Deception*, of which this chapter is a preliminary introduction to how we might approach the future of media when we accept that strategic disinformation is part and parcel of media and other forms of power.

References

Andronici, J. 2019. 'This is the Most Dangerous Moment in Donald Trump's Cycle of Abuse'. *Ms*, 14 October. Available at: https://msmagazine.com/2019/10/14/this-is-the-most-dangerous-moment-in-donald-trumps-cycle-of-abuse/.

Arabi, S. 2016. *Becoming the Narcissist's Nightmare: How to Devalue and Discard the Narcissist While Supplying Yourself*. New York: SCW Archer Publishing.

Berghel, H. and D. Berleant. 2017. 'The Online Trolling Ecosystem'. *Computer*, August: 44–51.

Berlant, L. and M. Warner. 1998. 'Sex in Public'. *Critical Inquiry*, 24(2): 547–566.

Blackman, L. 2007. 'Reinventing Psychological Matters: The Importance of the Suggestive Realm of Tarde's Ontology'. *Economy and Society*, 36(4): 574–596.

Blackman, L. 2012. *Immaterial Bodies: Affect, Embodiment, Mediation*. Los Angeles, CA, London and New Delhi: Sage/TCS Book series.

Blackman, L. 2016. 'Social Media and the Politics of Small Data: Post Publication Peer Review and Academic Value'. *Theory, Culture & Society*, 3(4): 3–26.

Blackman, L. 2018. 'Affect and Mediation'. In *Affect in Relation: Families, Places, Technologies*, edited by B. Rottger-Rossler and J. Slaby. London and New York: Routledge, 221–240.

Blackman, L. 2019a. *Haunted Data: Affect, Transmedia, Weird Science*. London and New York: Bloomsbury Publishing.

Blackman, L. 2019b. 'Suggestion, Affect, Speculative Science'. In *Imitation, Contagion, Suggestion: On Mimesis and Society*, edited by C. Borch. London and New York: Routledge, 221–228.

Blackman, L. and V. Walkerdine. 2001. *Mass Hysteria: Critical Psychology and Media Studies*. Basingstoke and New York: Palgrave.

Boler, M. and E. Davis. 2018. 'The Affective Politics of the "Post-truth Era": Feeling Rules and Networked Subjectivity'. *Emotion, Space and Society*, 27: 75–85.

Boler, M. and E. Davis. 2020. *Affective Politics of Digital Media: Propaganda by Other Means*. London and New York: Routledge.

Borch, C. 2019. *Imitation, Contagion, Suggestion: On Mimesis and Society*. London and New York: Routledge.

Bufacchi, V. 2020. 'Truth, Lies and Tweets: A Consensus Theory of Post-Truth'. *Philosophy and Social Criticism*: 1–15. DOI: 10.1177/0191453719896382.

Cheng, J., M. Bernstein, C. Danescu-Niculescu-Mizil and J. Leskovec. 2017. 'Anyone Can Become a Troll: Causes of Trolling Behavior in Online Discussions'. *CSCW: Proceedings of the Conference on Computer-Supported Cooperative Work. Conference on Computer-Supported Cooperative Work*: 1217–1230. https://doi.org/10.1145/2998181.2998213.

Chun, W. 2016. *Updating to Remain the Same: Habitual New Media*. Cambridge, MA: MIT Press.

Corner, J. 2017. 'Fake News, Post-Truth and Media-Political Change'. *Media, Culture & Society*, 39(7): 1100–1107.

Cvetkovich, A. 2012. *Depression: A Public Feeling*. Durham, NC: Duke University Press.

Davies, W. 2018. *Nervous States: How Feeling Took Over the World*. London and New York: Vintage.

Davis, A. 2019. *Political Communication: A New Introduction for Crisis Times*. London and New York: Polity.

Deuze, M. 2012. *Media Life*. Cambridge: Polity.

Fenton, N. 2018. 'Fake Democracy: The Limits of Public Sphere Theory'. *Javnost – The Public*, 25: 1–2, 28–34.

Flores-Saviaga, C., B. Keegan and S. Savage. 2018. 'Mobilizing the Trump Train: Understanding Collective Action in a Political Trolling Community'. *Proceedings of the Twelfth International AAAI Conference on Web and Social Media* (ICWSM 2018): 82–91.

Foucault, M. 1980. *Power Knowledge: Selected Interviews and Other Writings 1972–1977*. London and New York: Vintage Books.

Fraser, N. 1990. 'Rethinking the Public Sphere: A Contribution to the Critique of Actually Existing Democracy'. *Social Text*, 25/26: 56–80.

Gardiner, B. 2018. '"It's a Terrible Way to Go to Work": What 70 Million Readers' Comments on the Guardian Revealed about Hostility to Women and Minorities Online'. *Feminist Media Studies*, 18(4): 592–608.

Gibbs, A. 2010. 'Sympathy, Synchrony, and Mimetic Communication'. In *The Affect Theory Reader*, edited by G. Seigworth and M. Gregg. London and Durham, NC: Duke University Press, 186–205.

Giraud, E. 2017. 'Post-Truth is a Feminist Issue'. Discover Society, 4 October. Available at: https://discoversociety.org/2017/10/04/post-truth-is-a-feminist-issue/.

Gomez, J. M. 2015. 'Microaggressions and the Enduring Mental Health Disparity: Black Americans at Risk for Institutional Betrayal'. *Journal of Black Psychology*, 41(2): 121–143.

Gunaratnam, Y. and G. Lewis. 2001. 'Racialising Emotional Labour and Emotionalising Racialised Labour: Anger, Fear and Shame in Social Welfare'. *Journal of Social Work Practice*, 15(2): 131–148.

Habermas, J. 1962. *The Structural Transformation of the Public Sphere: An Inquiry into a Category of Bourgeois Society*. Cambridge, MA: MIT Press.

Hart, L. and R. Hart. 2018. *Operation Lighthouse: Reflections on Our Family's Devastating Story of Coercive Control and Domestic Violence*. London: CoCoAwareness Ltd.

Kember, S. and J. Zylinska. 2012. *After New Media. Mediation as a Vital Process*. Cambridge, MA: MIT Press.

Koessler, R. B., T. Kohut. and L. Campbell. 2019. 'When Your Boo Becomes a Ghost: The Association Between Breakup Strategy and Breakup Role in Experiences of Relationship Dissolution'. *Collabra: Psychology*, 5(1): 29.

LeFebvre, L. E. 2017. 'Phantom Lovers: Ghosting as a Relationship Dissolution Strategy in the Technological Age'. In *The Impact of Social Media in Modern Romantic Relationships*, edited by Narissra M. Punyanunt-Carter and Jason S. Wrench. New York: Lexington Books, 219–235.

LeFebvre, L. E., M. Allen, R. D. Rasner, S. Garstad, A. Wilms and C. Parrish. 2019. 'Ghosting in Emerging Adults' Romantic Relationships: The Digital Dissolution Disappearance Strategy'. *Imagination, Cognition and Personality*, 39(2): 125–150.

Lobaczewski, A. 2007. *Political Ponerology: A Science on the Nature of Evil Adjusted for Political Purposes*. New York: Red Pill Press.

Navarro, R., E. Larrañaga, S. Yubero and B. Víllora. 2020. 'Psychological Correlates of Ghosting and Breadcrumbing Experiences: A Preliminary Study among Adults'. *International Journal of Environmental Research and Public Health*, 17(3): 1116.

Ngai, S. 2007. *Ugly Feelings*. Cambridge, MA: Harvard University Press.

Noble, S. 2018. *Algorithms of Oppression: How Search Engines Reinforce Racism*. New York: New York University Press.

Oliver, M. 2020. 'Infrastructure and the Post-Truth Era? Is Trump Twitter's Fault?' *Postdigital Science and Education*, 2: 17–38.

Papacharissi, Z. 2014. *Affective Publics: Sentiment, Technology and Politics*. Oxford: Oxford University Press.

Papacharissi, Z. 2016. 'Affective Publics and Structures of Storytelling: Sentiment, Events and Mediality'. *Information, Communication & Society*, 19(3): 307–324.

Rieder. B. 2012. 'What Is in PageRank? A Historical and Conceptual Investigation of a Recursive Status Index'. *Computational Culture*, 2 (28 September 2012). http://computationalculture.net/what_is_in_pagerank/.

Sampson, T. 2012. *Virality: Contagion Theory in the Age of Networks*. Minneapolis, MN: University of Minnesota Press.

Sarkis, S. 2018. 'Donald Trump is a classic gaslighter in an abusive relationship with America', *USA Today* (10 March). https://eu.usatoday.com/story/opinion/2018/10/03/trump-classic-gaslighter-abusive-relationship-america-column/1445050002/

Spillers, H. 1987. 'Mama's Baby, Papa's Maybe: An American Grammar Book'. *Diacritics* (Culture and Countermemory: The 'American' Connection), 17(2): 64–81.

Squires, C. 2002. 'Rethinking the *Black Public Sphere*: An Alternative Vocabulary for Multiple *Public Spheres*'. *Communication Theory*, 12(4): 446–468.

Stark, E. and M. Hester. 2019. 'Coercive Control: Update and Review'. *Violence Against Women*, 25(1): 81–104.

Stern, R. 2018. *The Gaslight Effect*. New York: Harmony Books.

Sweet, P. 2019. 'The Sociology of Gaslighting'. *American Sociological Review*, 84(5): 851–875.

Taylor, J. 2020. *Why Women are Blamed for Everything: Exploring Victim Blaming of Women Subjected to Violence and Trauma*. London: Constable.

Venn, C. 2020. 'Affective Field and Political Subjectivities in the Shadow of Neo-Fascism'. *Subjectivity*, 13: 89–114.

Venturini, T. and R. Rogers. 2019. ' "API-Based Research" or How Can Digital Sociology and Journalism Studies Learn from the Facebook and Cambridge Analytica Data Breach'. *Digital Journalism*, 7(4): 532–540.

Williams, R. 1977. *Marxism and Literature*. Oxford: Oxford University Press.

Wylie, C. 2019. *MindF*ck: Inside Cambridge Analytica's Plot to Break the World*. New York: Profile Books.

THE FUTURE OF TELEVISION

5

How Will the Future Cope With(out) Television?

David Morley

An Archaeological View

One of the characters in Eli Griffiths' novel *The Crossing Places* (2016) suggests that if you wanted to make a record of your home so that an archaeologist of the future would better understand how you had lived, the most important thing would be to show the way in which the chairs in your sitting room had been arranged. As she says, the diagram would demonstrate that the single most important object in the living room of the twentieth-century home was the rectangular screen in the corner, as it evidently functioned as some kind of totemic object around which the chairs were clustered. Within the field of popular television itself, this observation finds an echo in a remark made by the character 'Joey' in *Friends*, when he meets a young woman who surprises him by announcing that she has no television at home. In genuine puzzlement, Joey responds by asking her 'So what does your furniture point at?'. Here we begin to see the ways in which technological forms and particular domestic lifestyles are commonly intertwined at the most fundamental level.

Television's Funerary Rites?

For some time now, there has been debate about how soon the impending death of television will come. The problem with that starting point for debate is that it presumes that we already know what television is. If, indeed, we already knew what its essential properties are, our task would simply be that of measuring any future change against this fixed and naturalised standard of what television has come to be (see Spigel 2004). But while one particular form of broadcast television, featuring characteristic genres and styles, came to dominate much of domestic life in the Western world throughout the last half of the twentieth century ('TV' – as we know it), we would be mistaken to imagine that was its predestined form and natural role. Indeed, Judith Keilbach and Markus Stauff (2013) argue that television has always been in a process of transformation and that to see it as existing in a state of indeterminacy is far more appropriate than to see it as fixed by any essential quality.

The basic point here about how best to conceptualise the 'age of television' is rather similar to Gramsci's notion that any form of hegemonic dominance within a particular field of activity, whether political or technological, is always a succession of unstable equilibria, rather than a fixed state which only occasionally undergoes the experience of transformation. To put it another way, that is to say that television – in the particular forms that we have come to know it – did not necessarily have to end up as it did, but rather has always been a product of circumstantial and temporary adjustments and flexibilities.

The obvious starting point here is Raymond Williams' argument about how television (like any other medium) has been shaped by the social, institutional and political contexts within which it has developed (Williams 1974). However, I want to go rather further than that, to argue that it has never been entirely clear what television is. (A particular mode of signification, characterised by distinctive genres? A specific form of broadcasting? A particular mechanism for the electronic distribution of images? A machine in the corner of the most comfortable room in the house? A crucial element of suburban lifestyles? Or perhaps all of these things?) If we take that point seriously, then the particular form in which television came to dominate domestic life in the late twentieth century – massively familiar to many of us as it is – is revealed as merely one, by no means inevitable, staging point in the long, and still continuing, development of the medium. Thus, it is but a part of the convoluted history of how television has been reimagined in a whole variety of different ways at different stages of its development. Nor is this simply a matter of television's internal history: it has been almost continually redesigned so as to respond to, take advantage of and compete with simultaneous developments taking place in other media.

To exemplify these points, I will take Stuart Hall's (1975) discussion of the nature of television as a medium, in a paper written for UNESCO at a moment in the medium's development when Marshall McLuhan's (1966) technologically determinist arguments were at their most influential. One of the key developments of the period was the technical transformation of the medium produced by the coming of colour. In this context, Hall argues that the development of colour television by the BBC in the UK in the 1960s cannot be understood as simply a matter of technical history. Rather, he claims, it has to be seen as a part of the economic and institutional drive for British television to produce a marketable product for sale to other national networks abroad (and especially in the USA) while simultaneously boosting its prestige as a national organisation deserving of continuing governmental support at home (Hall 1975).

His basic argument is that we must attend to the complex ways in which technical, aesthetic, professional, institutional and economic levels of determination interpenetrate. In the particular case of television, he insists that we recognise how it is embedded in socio-economic structures and institutions, political and ideological configurations which establish parameters to – and determinations of – its history, and which 'bear back upon the screen and the image itself – its production, distribution and reception – through the relevant internal practices' (see also Hall 1972). He recognises that any medium has certain technical qualities but insists that these are not fixed. Thus, he argues, in considering matters of medium specificity, it would be foolish to speak of anything more than the technical limits of a medium at a certain determinate stage of its development. While the technical properties of a medium may impose constraints, these are always compounded by other, socio-economic and cultural, levels of determination. The way in which media are embedded in these complex structures has a reciprocal effect on which aspects of a technology will be developed and which neglected. Thus the technical nature of a medium has itself to be seen as a determinate function of the socio-economic and institutional networks into which it is inserted.

Television Histories: The Medium that Nearly Failed

In order to further develop these points, let me now turn back to the early history of television, long before the point at which it achieved its late-twentieth-century domestic hegemony. My premise here is that incorporating the medium within a more historicised framework will also enable us to better understand its potential future. My approach here considers television (like any other technology) as having evolved (or been invented) in order to solve particular, context-bound problems. In this case, one of those problems was how to deliver low-cost entertainment to cater to the leisure requirements of the newly suburbanised domestic households of the USA and other affluent Western industrial societies in the post-1945 period. The present-day parallel would perhaps be to consider our own smartphones and other individualised media delivery systems as coping devices, invented to deal with the specific problems of navigating our way through the complexities of our post-Fordist societies. In these casualised labour markets, in which there are no more jobs for life or fixed social structures, but only an eternally shifting landscape of individuals, we are all now required to operate as entrepreneurial selves, constantly networking our contacts so as to optimise our socio-economic prospects – and our smartphones are the devices needed to juggle all our varying and contradictory commitments.

Looking backwards from a contemporary perspective, it is easy to presume that television's success was somehow inevitable or predestined. However, the medium's early history shows that in its commercial form, as initially developed in the USA, it narrowly escaped being abandoned as a total failure. In focusing my argument on this particular case, I am conscious that I risk seeming to take a relatively narrowly focused Anglo-American perspective on the medium. Later I will deconstruct the assumptions underlying this approach by looking at how television has developed in other areas – but in the first instance, we need to be clear just how very influential the particular North American commercial model was, worldwide, over a long period.

One of the ways in which television has often been defined (most notably by John Ellis, 1982) is by contrast to the cinema, these media being effectively distinguished by their different forms of textual organisation, which presume different forms of attention from their spectators, generated by their respective (public/private) contexts of consumption. What is interesting here is that when television was first invented, it was in fact directly *modelled* as being a kind of mini-cinema. However, this was premised on the idea that television could achieve the same kind of rapt attention from its audience that cinema can usually presume. The problem was that in practice, this model just didn't work and for a while it seemed that television would not prove to be a viable medium, as it seemed too hard to integrate it into the daily patterns of domestic life.

The assumption behind the idea that television had to be modelled on a cinematic mode of focused viewing was that it required complete and unfaltering visual attention because if the eyes were to wander, programme continuity would be lost. But consuming television in a domestic home simply does not allow (except in special circumstances) for that kind of attentiveness as, within that space, the television is competing with all the complexities of family life going on around it.

Thus, early experiments with television modelled as mini-cinema produced very disappointing results, indicating that it might never get more than a small percentage of the desired audiences – and was therefore not viable as a mass medium. In particular, the issue was that the companies setting up broadcast commercial television in the USA were dependent on the prospect of advertising revenues from manufacturers wanting to sell their products to viewers. Their focus was on the housewife as the family's principal consumer, and on whether she would be able to spare the time to watch television given her many domestic duties. If she was unable to give television her constant attention, then, so far as advertisers were concerned, television was simply not going to be an attractive medium.

The solution to this problem, which persists to this day, was the redesign of television programming not on the model of mini-cinema, requiring close visual attention, but as a sound-driven 'show and tell' medium. Thus, to a large extent television became a form of 'radio with pictures', with the narrative mainly carried by the soundtrack and the visuals playing a subordinate, merely illustrative, role. With this modified form of mode of address to its audience, television no longer required full attention. Most importantly, from the point of view of the advertisers, the housewife could now follow the programme from the soundtrack (which could be relied on to 'cue' her in when something exciting was going to happen on screen), while getting on with her domestic duties – and thus television became an economically viable medium.

Mixtures, Repeats and Symbioses

This example alerts us to the necessity of thinking of how each medium is often caught up in a set of competitive responses and adaptations to developments in the media which surround it. Any one medium routinely cannibalises elements from others – a process which we can see all around us today. Looking back, we can see how in the 1950s there was considerable anxiety within the cinema industry that it would be killed off, losing its audience to the new medium of television. What the cinema did, by way of response, was to invent forms of spectacular, technicolour, Big Screen viewing, providing a form of full-colour splendour with which television could not compete. In response, in more recent years television has transformed itself into a medium with larger and larger screens, which are better able to compete with the spectacles which cinema can provide. That technical development has subsequently spawned new modes of panoramic programming on television (nature/travel documentaries, landscape porn etc.) which can take advantage of these new technical capabilities. Most recently the cinema has responded to these new aspects of what television can do by developing greater emphasis on the quality of its own soundtracks (e.g., Dolby 'Surround Sound' at an increasingly higher volume) as a key dramatic feature of the cinematic experience, especially in action movies. In turn, television has now responded with the invention of the 'sound bar' to enhance television's own capacity to provide a high class of audio experience.

To return to the question of medium specificity, there was a long period when the phenomenon of 'Flow' was defined as central to the television experience – best characterised by the development of forms of scheduling designed to hold the viewer to a given channel. This of course was completely antithetical to the initial model of broadcasting as developed in the UK by Lord Reith, who insisted that there must always be a moment of silence between any two radio programmes as part of the schedule, precisely so as to dissuade people from just listening to whatever came next.

Today we see encomia to the death of the (supposedly) passive forms of broadcast television consumption, in favour of the more individually curated modes of active viewing held to be characteristic of the podcast era. However, one might well argue that the marketing of box sets and the encouragement of 'binge viewing', along with the algorithms developed by institutions like YouTube to suggest what else you might 'like', based on your viewing history, can best be seen as the reincarnation, in new technical dimensions, of what used to be the skills of the television scheduler.

The debates and moral panics about any given technology often take a repetitive form. Today's parental anxieties about the need to restrict the quantity of children's overall 'screen time' per week are an obvious rerun of earlier anxieties about whether too much television (or, later, too many video nasties) were likely to be deleterious to children's socialisation (see Spigel 1992 on the crisis in American family life provoked by the entry of television to the home in the 1950s). Moreover, contrary to the suppositions of those arguing that digital media are so distinctive as to constitute a Year Zero from which media and communication studies must start anew, abandoning the 'outdated' wisdoms of the analogue age, many old theories apply very well to new media (see Gauntlett 2000). Thus the 'Two-Step Flow' theories first developed by Elihu Katz and Paul Lazarsfeld (1955) still provide the best model for explaining why people today like to get their news from social media and why they are most influenced by news that comes to them via a trusted gatekeeper/source – whether from a family/friend network or an 'influencer' in a public sphericule of like-minded people (see Hilbert et al. 2017).

The Dawning of the New Days

At the heart of the currently hegemonic version of the story of fundamental change in our media cultures is the idea that the age of the Bad Screen of broadcast television – and its passive, mass audiences – is being replaced by the Good Screens of the newly interactive age of personalised computer-aided communications, as we move from the era of the old-fashioned consumer to that of the 'prosumer' (Jenkins 2006; Toffler 1973). However, if we focus in detail on the question of what is actually happening to television, matters are more complicated than that. To offer a historical comparison, in the UK in the 1980s it was widely argued that the arrival of multiple television sets would entirely transform household media consumption. In fact, it turned out that even when some people simultaneously watched televisions in separate rooms, they quite often watched the same programme and talked about it together afterwards – hence, insofar as the consumption process is not simply limited to the moments spent in front of the screen, they still consumed television within their social relations. Furthermore, at other times, they still gathered together on the sofa, ritualistically, to watch favourite programmes 'as a family' (see Silverstone et al. 1991).

For many years now predictions of the total transformation of viewing culture have been regularly advanced, telling us that the age of broadcast television and its couch potatoes is over (if such phantoms ever existed) and is being replaced by new forms of supposedly more interactive communications. However, despite predictions to the contrary, we still do not seem to have reached the long-predicted moment when the majority of users cross over from a viewing environment where content is consumed through a linear schedule to one where it is mainly consumed through search and on-demand procedures. When you look at the empirical data, it turns out that television viewing in the UK can better be seen as slowly evolving so as to incorporate a variety of new modes of consumption. This is so, not least, because of the continuing attractions of shared group viewing of live broadcast television. Naturally enough, when asked about the prospect, many people enthuse about the increased choices offered by on-demand viewing but, nonetheless, it turns out that in practice they return again and again to a few favourite channels and shows – because in fact, beyond that, they suffer from choice fatigue.

Evolutionary changes are certainly occurring, and websites now offer a popular supplement for viewers to follow up on programmes that have interested them. As I walk about my own neighbourhood of an evening, I can see, through their lounge windows, an increasing number of my neighbours watching (or, perhaps, listening to) the main television set in their lounges, while sprawled on their sofas with their laptops and smartphones open. But just how different is this from the older habit of watching television while leafing through a magazine or newspaper?

Predictions that social networking would kill television had proved distinctly premature, and television programmes (along with the national press) continue to set the daily agenda for much social media discussion. People do increasingly use networks like Facebook and Twitter while viewing, but these new platforms are proving to often be a complement, rather than a competitor, to television. One of the reasons for the continued popularity of broadcast television concerns the pleasures of 'TV talk', whether conducted face to face around the office water cooler the next day, or virtually, in real time. As the German media theorist Claus Dieter Rath once put it, with television, the motivation is often not so much to view the contents as to be among those who have viewed them, and who can thus share the pleasures of discussing them (Rath 1988).

The discourse of digital nativism presumes that younger people will necessarily be more adventurous in their media consumption habits, not least because they are presumed to be more technologically competent than their elders. However, some years ago now, research on Taiwanese audiences showed that even those who, as teenagers or young adults, are very adventurous in their media use may fall back into rather more conventional modes of media consumption at a later stage in their lifecycle, when they are married with children and thus have less disposable leisure time for innovative forms of leisure (Yu 2009). The common presumption that the current behaviour of a specific generation of the affluent segments of advanced industrial societies offers us a valuable glimpse into the future of how majority audiences worldwide will consume media in the future turns out to be ill-founded – and not even, necessarily, a good predictor of their own future behaviour. Banal matters such as household structure and stage in the lifecycle, long recognised in the conventional field of leisure studies but still ignored in most debates surrounding 'new media', are still a powerful influence on media consumption.

These developments rarely run a straightforward course. Indeed, in a classic example of an unforeseen effect of technological progress, the development of highly expensive, very sophisticated, large-screen televisions has, at times, reversed the trend towards the fragmentation of viewing in the UK. Few households can afford more than one set with the highest-definition viewing quality. Thus, for some types of viewing, the most up-to-date set, in the household's most comfortable room, is still preferred and that set is thus re-enshrined in the central position which it had before the advent of multi-set households (see Morley and Silverstone 1990).

Indeed, it seems that we should perhaps look to a future in which big channels will still exist and traditional forms of broadcast television will develop symbiotic modes of relationship with the newly emerging alternatives to them. Evidently, significant changes in the media landscape are afoot, as television programmes are increasingly removed from the structure of television schedules and embedded in the new matrix of interfaces, hyperlinks and databases (see Curtin 2009). Further, television itself is now rather less of a site-specific technological form and is available across multiple platforms. However, it is as well to remember that as we rapidly domesticate them, the digital media become increasingly more ordinary and taken-for-granted, just as television itself has been for most of its history. Television has already responded to the threat posed by the new media by finding ways to colonise the emerging digital world. Further, the hybridity of digital media, far from being an entirely new development, only underscores the validity of Raymond Williams' identification of television itself as always having been a hybrid of earlier media forms (see Bennett 2011, 10, 15, 7).

Furthermore, these developments do not necessarily represent a one-way street. The crisis in domestic life all over the word created by the Covid-19 crisis and the subsequent immobilisation of social activity during the 'lockdowns' of that period have had the result, among other things, of massively boosting the viewing figures for the main broadcast television channels.[1] The point here is not simply that in such moments of crisis, fragmentation and social isolation the consolation of being part of a broader community than that of the fellow fans of your favourite programmes becomes all the more appealing – as, indeed, does the sense of ontological security provided by feeling that you are a part of a national audience, along with your fellow citizens.[2] The further issue here is what the various dimensions of these Covid-related crises reveal about the fragility of the assumptions on which the patterns of both virtual and physical mobility that had emerged in the early years of the twenty-first century were based. It would be quite foolish to imagine that there will be any easy return to that particular mode of normality – and in the 'new normals' of coming years, television may well be among the many things whose importance (re)gains a substantial boost.

Television's Varying Prospects...

I will now turn, as promised earlier, to the question of the Eur-Amcentric nature of the dominant perspectives developed with television studies thus far. There can be no singular, linear history of television, even at the simplest level. For instance, while television in many countries in the rich industrialised Western world began as a domestic medium which only escaped the home in the relatively recent past (as documented in the work of scholars such as Anna McCarthy 2001), in other places, such as Japan, television began in public spaces and was only subsequently incorporated into the domestic sphere (Yoshimi 1999).

Arvind Rajagopal has argued that to understand the career of television outside the West, one must recognise the fact that 'if the liberal bourgeois public sphere can be said to characterise the "norm" of modern culture, dominated by narratives of the rational secular development of individuals', in other places in the contemporary world, one is nonetheless forcefully confronted with 'deeply embedded pre-modern narratives of community – narratives whose relevance continues to be felt, even in a modernising society' (Rajagopal 2000, 294, 302; see also Rajagopal 2001). In a parallel sense, Kuan-Hsing Chen usefully draws on Partha Chatterjee's analysis of how India's subaltern classes operate according to a different logic than that of the political space created by the colonial powers. Chen calls this a *minjian* space which cannot be absorbed within the terms of Western modernity, but which, while incorporating traditional concerns and often expressing itself in mythical terminology, is nonetheless also an alternative form of modernity – once that concept is detached from its Western origins (Chen 2010, 216; Chatterjee 1986).

A similar perspective has been developed within media studies by Graeme Turner and Jinna Tay, exploring the new dynamics of the 'post-broadcast' era, with specific reference to its global variations (Turner and Tay 2009). The key point here is that, the commonality of its technology notwithstanding, the development of digital media is always shaped conjuncturally, by contingent, local factors, concerning socio-cultural, political and industrial conditions. Thus, we must resist models of a uniform worldwide digital future which are based on the very particular experience of television in the USA or Europe. Indeed, precisely because 'television involves such varying forms, platforms and contents, in its different national and regional locations', it is increasingly implausible for one particular set national experience to be regarded as representative of developments worldwide (Turner 2011, 32). Furthermore, as indicated earlier, it would be particularly imprudent to regard the behaviour of a small number of early adopters of digital technologies, from a restricted set of social backgrounds in affluent countries, as reliable indicators of all future international trends. To this extent, we must also avoid any evolutionary presumption that there is one single future trajectory for digital media, independent of location (see Pertierra and Turner 2013).

The increasing convergence of recent trends in Western media markets has perhaps encouraged Western scholars to underestimate the contingency of the relations between television, nation and culture to which they are accustomed. Turner and Tay thus argue for the need to recontextualise the default settings of Anglo-American Television Studies so as to better recognise the continuing effectivity of local, national and regional histories. This also involves recognising the variety of platforms, formats and distinctive cultural forms currently in play in different geo-linguistic markets. Above all, we must recognise that not all of them are developing in the same direction – let alone at the same rates – as the Western media on which most of our theoretical models are based. We should not assume that variations from the Eur-American template currently displayed in other regions represent merely historical lags, as a result of their simply being at earlier stages in one universal process of development. To argue thus would be to replicate the worst errors of the simplistic modernisation theory (see Rostow 1953) which dominated Western social science in the post-World War II period and which was, regrettably, revived by Francis Fukuyama (1992) and his followers, when they mistook the fall of the Berlin Wall for the end of History.

To say this is also to recognise that, while we know what 'TV' was in the classical era of broadcasting and we know that, in some places, that story no longer applies, for at least some part of its erstwhile audience, we do not yet know what it is going to be in the twenty-first century – and we should resist any siren calls to extrapolate a universalised answer from our contemporary Western experiences. This is also to recognise that, empirically speaking, the assumed truths of media studies only pertain to media operating within very particular types of socio-cultural, legal and economic frameworks and we must be sensitive to how particular locales produce different media cultures and technological forms (see Larkin 2008). In the worlds of the media, as elsewhere, we must attend to geographical, regional and spatial variability. In this sense, 'spatialising' media theory means recognising its multiplicity and its openness. In the conventional story of modernity, there is only one story to tell, as 'modernisation' is presumed to be capable of only one (predetermined) outcome. As Massey (2005) observes, the recognition of regional or spatial multiplicities is a precondition for the recognition of temporal openness, so as to literally 'make space' for other stories of the future.

The Contextually Specific Forms and Modalities of Television

As we have seen, for quite some time now, television scholars have been announcing the death of television in its conventional form and its supersession by 'social media' and algorithmically led streaming shows, or what has variously been described as the platforms and portals of online or internet-distributed television (Johnson 2019; Lotz 2017, 2018). However, as Joke Hermes and Annette Hill observe, television has lately been experiencing a new heyday, after a time when critics had definitively consigned it to the history books as merely a 'legacy medium' (Hermes and Hill, forthcoming). As they point out (and as I indicated earlier), although television as a medium had been declared more or less dead by the beginning of the millennium, under the particular conditions more recently produced by the coronavirus crisis, television has become once more 'a vital resource for solace, daydreaming, social ritual, knowledge and storytelling.' If John Fiske and John Hartley (1974) once described television as the 'bard of our times', then John Ellis goes further, using a psychoanalytic analogy. Ellis (2002, 2020) suggests that television is not simply a storyteller but also, in the newly 'normalised' conditions of crisis, a vital means via which to monitor and 'work through' our anxieties.

   In the conditions of 'lockdown' created by the Covid pandemic people have thus turned again towards television and the conditions of the crisis have reconsolidated television's earlier position as master storyteller and as a platform for cultural citizenship.[3] In these conditions, the particular affordances of the medium (both affective and material) have allowed it to once again provide its viewers with a sense of ontological security (Giddens 1991). This has been reflected especially in the medium's capacity to generate the feeling of virtual community – or, indeed, being 'alone together' – which is television's signature achievement. The forms of reassurance which broadcast television can offer are all the more critical in a period, such as the Covid crisis, in which societies are riddled with existential anxieties. Thus, in that moment, television has once again come to perform, for many people, the valuable function of virtually 'undoing' the social distancing which has so problematically undermined the previously established and familiar forms of material geography and social life (see Hermes and Hill 2020; Hill 2019). This recent experience thus offers us a valuable lesson, which we would do well to remember the next time we are tempted to imagine that the future of any medium will be to develop in a predictable and unidirectional manner towards a readily foreseeable future.

References

Bennett, J. 2011. 'Introduction'. In *Television as Digital Media*, edited by J. Bennett and N. Strange, 1–30. Raleigh and Durham, NC: Duke University Press.

Chatterjee, P. 1986. *Nationalist Thought and the Colonial World*. London: Zed Books.

Chen, K. H. 2010. *Asia as Method: Towards Deimperialisation*. Raleigh and Durham, NC: Duke University Press.

Curtin, M. 2009. 'Matrix Media'. In *Television Studies After TV*, edited by G. Turner and J. Tay, 9–20. London: Routledge.

Ellis, J. 1982. *Visible Fictions*. London: Methuen.

Ellis, J. 2002. 'Television as Working Through'. In *Television and Common Knowledge*, edited by J. Gripsrud, 65–80. London: Routledge.

Ellis, J. 2020. 'What Do We Need in a Crisis? Broadcast Television!' Blog post, 24 April. Available at: https://cstonline.net/what-do-we-need-in-a-crisis-broadcast-tv-by-john-ellis/.

Fiske, J. and J. Hartley. 1974. *Reading Television*. London: Methuen.

Fukuyama, F. 1992. *The End of History and The Last Man*. Harmondsworth: Penguin.

Gauntlet, D. 2000. *Web.Studies: Rewiring Media Studies for a Digital Age*. London: Arnold.

Giddens, A. 1991. *Introduction to Sociology*. Harmondsworth: Penguin.

Griffiths, E. 2016. *The Crossing Places*. London: Quercus Books.

Hall, S. 1972. 'The External/Internal Dialectic in Broadcasting – Television's Double-Bind'. CCCS Occasional Papers #4, University of Birmingham.

Hall, S. 1975. 'Television as a Medium and its Relation to Culture'. CCCS Occasional Papers #34, University of Birmingham.

Hermes, J. and A. Hill. 2020. 'Television's Undoing of Social Distancing'. *European Journal of Cultural Studies*, 23(4): 655–661.

Hilbert, M., J. Vasquez, D. Halpern, S. Valenzuela and E. Arrigiada. 2017. 'One Step, Two Step Network Step? Complementary Perspectives on Communication Flows in Twittered Citizen Protests'. *Social Science Computer Review*. http://escholarship.org/uc/item/0nn4p7mv.

Hill, A. 2019. *Media Experiences*. London: Routledge.

Jenkins, H. 2006. *Convergence Culture*. New York: New York University Press.

Johnson, C. 2019. *Online Television*. London: Routledge.

Katz, E. and P. Lazarsfeld. 1955. *Personal Influence: The Part Played by People in the Flow of Mass Communications*. New York: Free Press.

Keilbach, J. and M. Stauff. 2013. 'When Old Media Never Stopped Being New – Television's History As an Ongoing Experiment'. In *After the Break*, edited by M. de Valk and J. Teurlings, 79–98. Amsterdam: Amsterdam University Press.

Larkin, B. 2008. *Signal and Noise: Media, Infrastructure and Urban Culture in Nigeria*. Raleigh and Durham, NC: Duke University Press.

Lotz, A. 2017. *Portals: A Treatise on Internet-Distributed Television*. Ann Arbor, MI: Michigan Publishing, University of Michigan Library.

Lotz, A. 2018. *We Now Disrupt This Broadcast: How Cable Transformed Television and the Internet Revolutionised it All*. Cambridge, MA: MIT Press.

McCarthy, A. 2001. *Ambient Television*. Durham, NC: Duke University Press.

McLuhan, M. 1966. *Understanding Media*. Harmondsworth: Penguin.

Massey, D. 2005. *For Space*. London: Sage.

Morley, D. and R. Silverstone. 1990. 'Domestic Communications: Technologies and Meanings'. *Media, Culture and Society*, 12(1): 31–55.

Pertierra, A. C. and G. Turner. 2013. *Locating Television: Zones of Consumption*. London: Routledge.

Rajagopal, A. 2000. 'Mediating Modernity: Theorising Reception in a non-Western Society'. In *De-Westernising Media Studies*, edited by J. Curran, and M. Park, 441–469. London: Routledge.

Rajagopal, A. 2001. *Politics After Television: Hindu Nationalism and the Reshaping of the Public in India*. Cambridge: Cambridge University Press.

Rath, C. D. 1988. 'Live/Life: Television as a Generator of Events in Everyday Life'. In *Television and Its Audience*, edited by P. Drummond and R. Patterson, 199–205. London: BFI.

Rostow, W. W. 1953. *The Stages of Economic Growth: A Non-Communist Model*. Oxford: Oxford University Press.

Silverstone, R., E. Hirsch and D. Morley. 1991. 'Listening to a Long Conversation: An Ethnographic Approach to ICTs in the Home'. *Cultural Studies*, 5(2): 204–227.

Spigel, L. 1992. *Make Room for TV*. Chicago, IL: University of Chicago Press.

Spigel, L. 2004. 'Introduction'. In *Television After TV*, edited by L. Spigel and J. Olsson, 1–34. Raleigh, NC: Duke University Press.

Toffler, A. 1973. *FutureShock*. New York: Pan Books.

Turner, G. 2011. 'Convergence and Divergence: The International Experience of Digital Television'. In *Television as Digital Media*, edited by J. Bennett and N. Strange, 31–52. Raleigh and Durham, NC: Duke University Press.

Turner, G. and J. Tay. 2009. *Television Studies After TV*. London: Routledge.

Williams, R. 1974. *Television: Technology and Cultural Form*. Harmondsworth: Penguin Books.

Yoshimi, S. 1999. 'Made in Japan'. *Media, Culture and Society*, 21(2): 149–171.

Yu, G.-C. 2009. *Multi-Platform Film Viewing: Taipei Audiences and Generational Variation*, PhD thesis, Goldsmiths College, University of London.

THE FUTURE OF MEDIA WORK

6

Our Platformised Future

Clea Bourne

The Logics of Media Work

Well-known media occupations such as journalism, public relations (PR) and advertising have evolved with *professional logics*, which kept them separate yet interconnected. In many regions, journalism was governed by a professional logic of impartiality, PR guarded organisational reputation, while advertising aligned itself closely with creativity and innovation. While these professional logics were subject to exceptions in everyday practice, they bolstered professional identity. Various theoretical lenses have been used to explore interactions between these professions. Notably, tensions between journalism and the promotional professions are often examined through the lens of information subsidies (Gandy 1982; Verčič and Colić 2016). From this perspective, advertising and PR subsidise journalism and editorial processes by supplying paid content (advertising and sponsorship) and earned content (corporate announcements, features, pitched story ideas, images and video).

However, the information subsidies lens generally disguises what journalists and promotional workers have in common. While they may regard each other with suspicion, journalists, PR and advertising professionals are mutually governed by *media logic*. Some now argue that media logic has itself evolved into algorithmic logic (Klinger and Svensson 2018), as journalism, advertising, PR and other media professions now find their expertise increasingly disarticulated and systematically devalued by digital platforms. Indeed, digital platforms are rapidly reorganising all forms of media work. Some traditional media roles have either been hybridised or superseded by newer forms of media expertise such as data trading, content strategy, digital marketing, UI/UX (user interface/experience) design and social media management. These newer media specialisms have come about in response to digital platformisation and accompanying digital workflows necessitated by data collection, codification and curation (Beer 2019; Ottovordemgentschenfelde 2017).

While the impact of digital platforms and platformisation has been at the forefront of academic and industry debates, there has to date been little attempt to understand the *collective* impact of platformisation on traditional media professions such as journalism, advertising, media production and public relations. This is despite the rise of algorithmic logic superseding any previous media logics governing all these professions (Klinger and Svensson 2018). Contemporary media content now operates more logistically than it does narratively or representationally, as content attracts and organises digital users, places and things across time and space (Andrejevic et al. 2015, 381). A collective approach to platformisation and its accompanying algorithmic logic is crucial because, as I will argue in this chapter, platformisation is now intertwining previously separate media occupations in a way that erases much-cherished professional boundaries.

This chapter will consider the platformised future of media work affecting all media and communication professions, both old and new. First, I will map the contours of digital platforms, before outlining their jurisdictional battle with media publishers – specifically the print and electronic media – where journalists, editors and media producers are employed. Next, I will explore a similar battle between platforms and the global advertising and marketing industries, where advertising, marketing, branding, PR and media buying professionals are employed. I will then shift the discussion to the challenges facing individual media workers and the impact of datafication on their professional aspirations and pursuits.

By exploring the shifting sands of media work the chapter will ask: Where do the professional boundaries lie in the platformised future of media work? And who controls the shifting nature of these boundaries? I will conclude by suggesting that, as traditional media work is being collectively commoditised and devalued by digital platforms, collective rather than separate approaches are needed to secure the future of media work.

Digital Platforms

Digital platforms have emerged as a new means of production in the wider global economy by extracting, circulating and controlling vast amounts of data as an economic, social and political asset. The metaphorical term 'platform' describes an infrastructure which enables two or more groups to interact, combining big data, cloud and mobile telephony together as an increasingly competitive weapon (Gillespie 2010; Srnicek 2017). Digital platforms position themselves as intermediaries bringing together different users, customers, advertisers, service providers, producers, suppliers and even physical objects (Srnicek 2017, 43). What they really intermediate is not media content per se, but data flows, by continuously and unrestrainedly measuring audiences, ranking preferences and applying predictive analytics to track, extract, curate, circulate and control vast amounts of data (Beer 2019; Srnicek 2017; Miège 2019).

Platforms now have billions of users around the world, achieving this dominance by providing mostly free content to drive user traffic, rendering platforms more valuable to corporate partners, publishers and advertisers. The USA and China now dominate the world's digital platforms. Of the world's ten most valuable brands ranked by *Forbes* magazine in 2020, the top five were platforms – Apple, Google, Microsoft, Amazon and Facebook (Swant 2020). Many of China's most valuable companies are platforms too, including search engine Baidu, Tencent (owner of WeChat and QQ), the Alibaba group (owner of Alibaba, Alipay and Taobao) and up-and-comer ByteDance (owner of TikTok).

While there are many ways to categorise digital platforms, media workers are most likely to interact with these platforms via four categories (Watts 2020). The first category is social media platforms, including Facebook, Instagram and WeChat. The second is knowledge-sharing platforms for team working, file sharing and data management, such as Slack or Monday.com. The third category is media sharing platforms, such as YouTube, Spotify and TikTok. Finally, there are service-oriented platforms like Amazon, Uber and Airbnb. Many digital platforms engage in aggressive digital marketing and media practices to support their brand visibility and competitive positioning. As a consequence, while social media platforms have sociality baked into their funding model, other kinds of platforms now incorporate 'social' qualities too.

Because data is *the* raw material produced by digital platforms, just like any traditional industry, these digital platforms require more raw material in order to expand (Manokha 2018). This is why the *modus operandi* of all digital platforms is continuous information gathering on ever more users and objects, via ever more platform activities, so as to generate ever more data. As Dave Beer (2019, 1) argues, the salient question then becomes 'who has the power to speak with that data?'. Crucial to answering this question, says Beer, 'is an understanding of the new types of knowledge that are emerging along with an understanding of how that knowledge achieves authority, credibility and legitimacy'. Beer's work explores the field of data science as a rapidly expanding professional project focused on providing data insights. As Beer points out, it is not the data collected by digital platforms that is itself powerful but the resulting data insights through which 'hidden' value can be unearthed for organisational agendas – whether commercial, political or societal. As an emerging profession, data science has asserted its data power while simultaneously encroaching on several areas of digital media and marketing expertise, by producing the insights needed to understand what drives customers and audiences. The focus of this chapter is to apprehend *which* media professions most closely approximate the data power now enjoyed by the emerging data science profession.

While Beer focuses on the professional legitimacy acquired through data insight, Leicht (2016) contends that the professions of the future are the ones most associated with interpreting, making or creating markets. To this end, it already seems clear that the successful media professions of the future are the ones best able to create and interpret platformised markets by determining, designing and constructing strategies for capturing and sequestering data, and converting this data into various forms of value (Ruckenstein and Granroth 2020; Fourcade and Healy 2017; Nadler and McGuigan 2018). However, future media workers cannot all be strategists; the vast majority are likely to be tacticians, involved in daily data-driven tasks that may look like traditional media work, but that will exist only to support a larger 'data gaze' (Beer 2019).

Platforms versus Publishers

The future of media work will also be shaped by battles now waging between old and new media power. The first of these battles pits digital platforms against traditional media publishers. Media publishers include many well-known brands – broadcasters such as the BBC and ITV, news media such as *The Sunday Times, The Economist* and the *Daily Mail*, and multimedia publishers such as Bauer Media, which owns a stable of periodical publications such as *Grazia, Empire, Heat* and *Closer* magazines, as well as its radio stations Kiss FM, Magic FM, Absolute Radio and others.

These media publishers historically derived much of their power, profitability and significance from controlling old media technologies and channels (Nielsen and Ganter 2018). However, the digital platform business model disarticulates publishers' power by matching producers and consumers of news, information and entertainment, and closing the gap between them, offering cheap, targeted online advertising to producers in turn for large volumes of mostly free, shareable media content delivered to consumers.

Digital platforms have always pitched their role to traditional media publishers as a collaborative one, in which platforms and publishers co-create value (boyd 2014; Jenkins et al. 2013). Over time, platforms have disarticulated processes which allowed media publishers to retain any leverage in their platform enterprise. For instance, several platforms now require media publishers to co-produce content using the platform's specialised, proprietary editorial tools (Rein and Venturini 2018). These tools, initially pitched as a way to drive traffic and referrals to publishers, increasingly allowed people to access news and feature stories within the platform rather than going to the publisher's website or app (Nielsen and Ganter 2018). The effect is a 'walled garden' in which the platform captures the users' data, which can then be monetised (Rein and Venturini 2018).

This leaves media publishers to act as little more than traffic drivers, shunting content towards platforms to generate advertising revenue (Rein and Venturini 2018). The largest media publishers can invest seriously in driving traffic. Platforms subvert publishers' efforts to dominate user traffic by regularly tweaking platform algorithms to control what media content is seen where. To combat this, publishers need in-house data teams constantly tracking and analysing a platform's algorithms. *Financial Times*, for example, has a large team focused on analytics and engagement; the audience engagement team sits in the newsroom, working directly with journalists (Southern 2016). Smaller media publishers are less well-resourced than *Financial Times*, and simultaneously more reliant on digital platforms. A change to a platform's algorithm can send a smaller publisher's content plummeting down a platform's viewer ranking, a practice that has already spelled the death of smaller publishers' operations.

Meanwhile, Google now owns a piece of every part of the media ecosystem: ad-serving systems, television-targeting capabilities as well as its own news products (Wodinsky 2020). Google will reportedly take an even bigger cut from stories that might show up in Google's search engine, with only 51% going back to the publisher in question (Wodinsky 2020). Studies of value co-creation on digital platforms now clearly indicate that all co-created value on digital platforms is more beneficial to platform owners than it is to any of the companies accessing platform services (Haile and Altmann 2016). Regulation could address this imbalance. In 2021, Australia introduced a new media code designed to force platforms to pay for news and bargain with news publishers. Google complied, but Facebook responded by briefly banning Australian news from its platform, before reaching a deal with the Australian government. Some commentators believe that if the Australian government had 'held its nerve' it would have created the first opening for rival social media companies in the Australian market for almost two decades (Meagher 2021).

Platforms versus Adland

Media publishers are not the only major players whose expertise has been disarticulated by digital platforms. The same has happened to global advertising and marketing empires. Digital platforms, in closing the gap between production and consumption, have squeezed the very space traditionally controlled by advertising, marketing and PR. Facebook, Google and other digital platforms have systematically targeted every kind of advertiser, from global brands to small-to-medium-sized businesses to self-employed influencers, offering access to (potentially) billions of users via packaged advertising services. Facebook and Google have quickly become the largest advertising companies in the world, accounting for nearly 70% of digital advertising spend in the UK (Goetzen 2020). Facebook has further broadened the scope of its advertising activities into marketing as well, hailing its Marketing API (MAPI) as a platform for marketing research and development, and related services (Helmond et al. 2019).

Even those promotional media roles which owe their existence to digital platforms, such as programmatic advertisers that buy and sell digital advertising content and space, face an uncertain future as digital platforms protect their walled gardens. Programmatic advertising specialists use technologies and logics to personalise price, information, news and entertainment. These technologies, including the banner ad, the interactive link and the cookie, defined an entire decade of online advertising (Turow and Draper 2012). Cookie-matching enabled advertisers to buy the right to reach a consumer whom other companies had previously tracked around the web (Turow and Draper 2012).

Digital platforms established structural norms of working with advertisers and marketers just as they had with media publishers and, just as with media publishers, platforms then changed the terms and conditions. In 2020, Google announced it would stop using third-party cookies, the pieces of code that track what a user or their device does across different websites, helping companies figure out when to serve an ad. Other platforms have followed suit, throwing programmatic advertising professionals into disarray. The demise of the third-party cookie further cements power asymmetries between platforms and the advertising industry, since platforms continue to collect masses of first-party data within their walled gardens. Brand owners and advertising agencies with enough resources have responded by investing in cloud-based data management stacks to consolidate their own first-party data with other data sources (Vaccaro et al. 2019, 90).

Equally, brands and promotional agencies with the deepest pockets are best able to respond to other realities of a media market ruled by digital platforms. WPP, the world's largest advertising company, is in a position to buy expertise needed to boost its data power. In 2021, the advertising giant bought DTI Digital, a Brazilian software engineering company, to boost its expertise in data collection, app development and e-commerce (WPP 2021). Other large firms are exploring how to accelerate their flow of digital content. Edelman, the world's largest independent PR firm, has launched a production house to focus on data-driven content. Edelman's international network of studios and production operations is the latest in a series of moves by the PR titan to compete with advertising giants for digital content spend (Marszalek 2021). Large advertising, marketing and PR departments and agencies can also afford to experiment with new algorithmic logics. For instance, the Clubhouse audio app, which launched in 2020, expanded the algorithmic logic of platforms by boosting the popularity of live conversation during the Covid pandemic. Clubhouse was ad-free at launch, yet brands such as Pernod Ricard were able to establish visibility with Clubhouse users by staging a week of sponsored conversations with social media influencers during US Black History Month (McCoy and Joseph 2021). While large companies can invest to compete, the digital divide has become a real issue for smaller brands and promotional agencies, as it has for individual media professionals, whom I discuss in the next section.

Implications for Media Workers

Having briefly explored the battles waging between digital platforms and various media stakeholders, I now reflect on the future of media work, where an individual's labour is primarily, even solely, defined as the production of value through data. There is no question that future media and communications professionals need practical skills to navigate digital platforms and their persuasion architecture. What remains unclear at the time of writing is which set of media and communications specialisms will acquire greater professional status, and which fields of expertise will come to dominate our popular understanding of 'media work'. The race is now on to determine which media professions will be indispensable to their client organisations as media work becomes further integrated into data-driven culture.

Where once we understood media work by its traditional media channels (broadcast versus print) or by the nature of media output (paid advertising content versus earned PR content), the future of media work may be bifurcated by upstream versus downstream activities within data flows (Dimitrov 2018). Upstream, we find media professions that control the *wholesaling of data strategy and insight*. This group now incorporates data scientists, who design and test experiments using statistics, calculus and linear algebra; data analysts, who implement strategy around data; audience strategists, tasked with protecting and growing value of collective audiences; and digital knowledge managers, who control data integrity for the organisation, its brands, products, people, locations and services (Baer 2017; Liffreing 2018). Some of these data-driven media roles will become more recognisable and permanent, while others will merge into parallel upstream responsibilities in data strategy and management.

Recasting Content Creation

Downstream, meanwhile, is the large cluster of traditional media professionals involved in *retailing digital content* (Dimitrov 2018), notably journalists, media relations practitioners, copywriters, film and video producers, photographers and advertising creatives. The declining status of traditional media work taking place 'downstream' of data flows is a matter of some concern. Downstream, media activity is collectively described as 'content creation'. This catch-all phrase incorporates expert activity by professionals who spent many years perfecting their skills in news and feature writing, investigative coverage, film and video production, magazine publishing, speechwriting, copywriting, blogging, vlogging, photography, graphic design and animation.

Nevertheless, in a platformised media world, 'content', no matter how complex, painstakingly conceived, richly textured or aesthetically beautiful, becomes simply a digital object combining creative content with metadata. Metadata consists of hidden, descriptive material generated behind the scenes to tag content as it traverses digital spaces. This original metadata then combines with accumulated metadata from likes, comments and reactions generated by platform users (Dushay 2002). Inevitably, occupational shorthand has taken over; media workers' content is no longer approached as content but simply as metadata (Andrejevic et al. 2015). Ultimately, media content itself becomes commoditised and devalued, because the real value lies in the metadata and the experience it delivers as the digital content 'comes alive' on a digital platform through sharing and manipulation (Dushay 2002). This experiential 'liveness' attached to media content is what generates advertising revenues and captures additional consumer data for future predictive customer profiling, analysis and data strategy (Bilton 2019).

Media workers not only face deskilling of their content creation in favour of metadata; they must also contend with platformised approaches to professional storytelling. Digital platforms require a relentless flow of malleable 'spreadable' content (Jenkins et al. 2013). Journalists, advertising and PR professionals alike have found their storytelling skills have now shifted from professional expertise to that of co-created projects with non-specialists and amateurs. The media professional is instead encouraged to become the story owner, building a 'story system' outward through co-creation with third-party media partners, as well as consumers who must be lured into adapting or responding to the original content, at minimal cost to the digital platform (Bilton 2019; Lowengard 2019).

It is now apparent to many traditional media workers that the skills they once honed in producing media content to inform, educate or entertain no longer hold the same professional status. Media and advertising bosses (and their shareholders) have all grown more focused on the traffic generated by media content than on any long-term informational, societal or aesthetic value that content might reap. Furthermore, media professionals increasingly compete with everyday citizens who are platform users, and who, through sheer numbers, can produce far more content, much more quickly, than most media professionals – who must follow normative rules and organisational guidelines.

I end this chapter by returning to the assertion made at the start: that interprofessional tensions and struggles have largely shaped our understanding of the relationship between various media professionals operating on different sides of an old-world media divide. Today there is a new media divide in which digital platforms dictate the lives and prospects of all professional media stakeholders.

The direction of travel suggests that the future of media work may be best secured through recognising shared interests among all media workers whose professional efforts may be designed and packaged to 'sell', but who ultimately play an important role in how we inform and develop society and the human condition.

References

Andrejevic, M., A. Hearn and H. Kennedy. 2015 'Cultural Studies of Data Mining: Introduction'. *European Journal of Cultural Studies*, 18(4–5): 379–394.

Baer, J. 2017. '2 Key Marketing Jobs that Did Not Exist Last Year'. Convince & Convert blog, 8 November. Available at: www.convinceandconvert.com/baer-facts/marketing-jobs-that-did-not-exist-last-year/.

Beer, D. 2019. *The Data Gaze: Capitalism, Power and Perception*. London: Sage Publications.

Bilton, C. 2019. 'The Disappearing Product and the New Intermediaries'. In *Making Media: Production, Practices, and Professions*, edited by M. Deuze and M. Prenger, 99–109. Amsterdam: Amsterdam University Press.

boyd, d. 2014. *It's Complicated: The Social Lives of Networked Teens*. New Haven, CT: Yale University Press.

Dimitrov, R. 2019. *Strategic Silence: Public Relations and Indirect Communication*. Abingdon: Routledge.

Dushay, N. 2002. 'Localizing Experience of Digital Content via Structural Metadata'. *Proceedings of the 2nd ACM/IEEE-CS Joint Conference on Digital Libraries*, July, 244–252.

Fourcade, M. and K. Healy. 2017. 'Seeing Like a Market'. *Socio-Economic Review*, 15(1): 9–29.

Gandy, O. H. 1982. 'Beyond Agenda Setting: Information Subsidies and Public Policy'. *Public Relations Review*, 29: 99–124.

Gillespie, T. 2010. 'The Politics of "Platforms"'. *New Media & Society*, 12(3): 347–364.

Goetzen, N. 2020. 'The Duopoly's Share of the UK Ad Market Will Dip Below 66%'. eMarketer, 19 August. Available at www.emarketer.com/content/google-facebook-share-of-uk-ad-market-will-dip-below-66-percent.

Haile, N. and J. Altmann. 2016. 'Value Creation in Software Service Platforms'. *Future Generation Computer Systems*, 55: 495–509.

Helmond, A., D. B. Nieborg and F. N. van der Vlist. 2019. 'Facebook's Evolution: Development of a Platform-as-Infrastructure'. *Internet Histories*, 3(2): 123–146.

Jenkins, H., S. Ford and H. Green. 2013. *Spreadable Media*. New York: New York University Press.

Klinger, U. and J. Svensson. 2018. 'The End of Media Logics? On Algorithms and Agency'. *New Media & Society*, 20(12): 4653–4670.

Leicht, K. T. 2016. 'Market Fundamentalism, Cultural Fragmentation, Post-modern Skepticism, and the Future of Professional Work'. *Journal of Professions and Organization*, 3(1): 103–117.

Liffreing, I. 2018. 'Confessions of a Data Scientist: Marketers Don't Know What They're Asking For', Digiday, 19 November. Available at: https://digiday.com/marketing/confessions-data-scientist-marketers-dont-know-theyre-asking/.

Lowengard, M. 2019. 'Confessions of a Content Marketer'. Institutional Investor, 4 March. Available at: www.institutionalinvestor.com/article/b1czwm4ktgdmbp/Confessions-of-a-Content-Marketer.

Manokha, I. 2018. 'Surveillance: The DNA of Platform Capital – The Case of Cambridge Analytica Put into Perspective'. *Theory & Event*, 21(4): 891–913.

Marszalek, D. 2021. 'Edelman Targets Ad Agencies with Production Studios Launch'. PRovoke, 17 February. Available at: www.provokemedia.com/latest/article/edelman-targets-ad-agencies-with-production-studio-launch.

McCoy, K. and S. Joseph. 2021. '"Because it's So New and Fresh": It Took a Minute, but Brands Are in the Clubhouse App'. Digiday, 22 February. Available at: https://digiday.com/media/brands-are-in-the-clubhouse-app/.

Meagher, J. 2021. 'Australia's Move to Tame Facebook and Google is Just the Start of a Global Battle'. *The Guardian*, 24 February. Available at: www.theguardian.com/commentisfree/2021/feb/24/australia-facebook-google-global-battle-governments-journalism.

Miège, B. 2019. 'Cultural and Creative Industries and the Political Economy of Communication'. In *Making Media: Production, Practices, and Professions*, edited by M. Deuze and M. Prenger, 73–83. Amsterdam: Amsterdam University Press.

Nadler, A. and L. McGuigan. 2018. 'An Impulse to Exploit: The Behavioural Turn in Data-driven Marketing'. *Critical Studies in Media Communication*, 35(2): 151–165.

Nielsen, R. K. and S. A. Ganter. 2018. 'Dealing with Digital Intermediaries: A Case Study of the Relations Between Publishers and Platforms'. *New Media & Society*, 20(4):1600–1617.

Ottovordemgentschenfelde, S. 2017. 'Organizational, Professional, Personal: An Exploratory Study of Political Journalists and their Hybrid Brand on Twitter'. *Journalism*, 18(1): 64–80.

Rein, K. and T. Venturini. 2018. 'Ploughing Digital Landscapes: How Facebook Influences the Evolution of Live Video Streaming'. *New Media & Society*, 20(9): 3359–3380.

Ruckenstein, M. and J. Granroth. 2020. 'Algorithms, Advertising and the Intimacy of Surveillance'. *Journal of Cultural Economy*, 13(1): 12–24.

Southern, L. 2016. 'The Financial Times Has a 30-Person Data Team for Edit and Marketing'. Digiday, 4 February. Available at: https://digiday.com/media/lessons-financial-times-data-maturity/.

Srnicek, N. 2017. *Platform Capitalism*. London: Polity.

Swant, M. 2020. 'The World's Most Valuable Brands'. *Forbes*, 27 July. Available at: www.forbes.com/the-worlds-most-valuable-brands/#15a45052119c

Turow, J. and N. Draper. 2012. 'Advertising's New Ecosystem'. In *Routledge Handbook of Surveillance Studies*, edited by K. Ball, K. D. Haggerty and D. Lyon, 133–140. London: Routledge.

Vaccaro, A., S. Mager and N. Groff. 2019. *Beyond Marketing: Experience Reimagined*. London: Deloitte MCS Limited.

Verčič, A. T. and V. Colić. 2016. 'Journalists and Public Relations Specialists: A Coorientational Analysis'. *Public Relations Review*, 42(4): 522–529.

Watts, S. 2020. 'Digital Platforms: A Brief Introduction'. BMC Exchange: The Business of IT Blog, 8 July. Available at: www.bmc.com/blogs/digital-platforms/.

WPP. 2021. 'WPP Acquires Leading Brazilian Digital Innovation and Software Engineering Company DTI Digital'. WPP, 10 February. Available at: www.wpp.com/news/2021/02/wpp-acquires-leading-brazilian-digital-innovation-and--software-engineering-company-dti-digital.

Wodinsky, S. 2020. 'Google to Journalists: Shut Up and Take the Money'. Gizmodo, 2 October. Available at: https://gizmodo.com/google-to-journalists-shut-up-and-take-the-money-1845239982.

THE FUTURE OF SOCIAL MEDIA

7

The Celebrity Selfie: Gender, Race and 'New' Old Ways of Seeing

Milly Williamson

Introduction

This chapter will take as its starting point John Berger's pioneering suggestion that every image embodies a way of seeing, in order to examine what the ubiquitous celebrity selfie can tell us about our ways of seeing today. Berger's *Ways of Seeing* (1972) has been deeply influential – it has been credited with opening very many minds by revealing the role that image making plays in reproducing inequality, and offering a lens with which to view the world afresh. I read it as an undergraduate in the late 1980s and, like so many us, I felt as if it had been written especially for me. As a young woman in the lad culture of the 1980s, when women were being told that equality had been achieved, it spoke to my experiences of concealed but palpable unequal gender expectations and treatment. The book spoke for all of us who wanted to question the hidden norms that seemed to structure our lives. It was as if Berger had turned on a light in the darkness.

However, the book, and the television series it is based on, have faced some criticism in the news media for being too general or too crude, for painting 400 years of art history with too broad a brush stroke (Livingstone 2017). The clarity with which Berger explained the complicity of the European art tradition from the 1500s to the 1900s with the politics of capitalism, gender and racial oppressions and colonialism was an exceptionally challenging and radical proposal. But as Michael McNay reminds us in his obituary of John Berger from January 2017, it was considered by Norbert Lynton to be simply 'lying about art in order to make political points'. While stepping back from such bald accusations, McNay nonetheless suggests that Berger's 'Marxist dialectic' forced him 'into uncomfortable contortions' (McNay 2017). That the book can generate such sentiments forty-five years after it was published is a testament to its power to demystify art and culture, to expose the ways of seeing of dominant groups and of the art establishment and it seems to me that, even if it is imperfect, it speaks for the oppressed and against the powers that subjugate us, as I will argue below.

For all of the attention is has received, *Ways of Seeing* has generated very little recent academic discussion in media and cultural studies, and seems to have fallen out of fashion. There has been little appraisal of what Berger's insights might lead us into seeing today (or tomorrow), or how we might fill in the gaps of his 'broad brush strokes' in the context of a media and cultural landscape that looks so different to the early 1970s. This chapter hopes to contribute to a contemporary discussion of ways of seeing in the new spaces of social media in which it is estimated that 93 million selfies are posted every day (Meyer 2018). The selfies that are most viewed and circulated on social media are celebrity selfies, many of whom have tens of millions of followers.[1] How can we make sense of the social and cultural meanings of this immense new form of image making, what forms do these selfies take and what light can Berger's approach shed?

Berger explains that what we are seeing when we look at a painting or a photograph is not a mere record of a time and place, but rather the painter or photographer's way of seeing. In the case of photography, we are not seeing a mere mechanical reproduction of reality – we are seeing the photographer's choice of subject, its framing and lighting; with the selfie, we are seeing the selection of the self as subject and the photographer's choice to frame the self in one way rather than another. Of course, our perception of the image is conditioned by our own way of seeing too, forged in social, cultural, political and economic histories, as well as in learnt assumptions of beauty and other aesthetic considerations, and in the politics of gender and race, and their binary structures of thinking.

For Berger, relations of seeing in the West are deeply unequal, typified in the European art tradition of paintings of nudes, where generally white recumbent women are displayed for a presumed white male onlooker, whose gaze is constructed as controlling the objectified female image. Has the selfie altered those relations of seeing? For, unlike the posed photographic portrait, fashion shoot, paparazzi shot or even the family snaps of the past, the selfie seems to unify subject and object, where the subject and the photographer seem to be one. Does that control of image production, made easy with the advent of digital photography and the convergence of information and communication technology, alter these relations of looking? Berger's suggestion, influenced by Walter Benjamin (2008 [1935]), is that the camera disrupted European Renaissance art conventions which had long emphasised stasis and stability, due to the convention of 'perspective', which was centred on the individual viewer – making the single eye (a white male European eye) the centre of the visible world. In contrast, the camera demonstrated mobility and destroyed the idea that images are timeless or that meanings are fixed, while the very reproducibility of the photographic image destroyed its uniqueness. For Berger, this inaugurated important new ways of seeing. But Berger was not a technological determinist and did not suggest that how we see is only or primarily shaped by our media technology. Instead, he argued that gendered ways of seeing in the twentieth century were so historically embedded into the relations of power and of looking that the conventions of the oil painting nude transferred into new forms of image making such as the still and moving photographic image.

This chapter will examine the celebrity nude selfies on social media to examine whether, in this widespread new form of image production, we are observing new empowered female ways of seeing, as some suggest (Cashmore 2019), or the reproduction of old gendered ways of seeing in new media forms and technologies. There is a variety of different forms of celebrity selfies, but this chapter will concentrate on a growing genre of celebrity images that are posed as selfies – predominantly female celebrities posing nude or semi-nude, smartphone in hand, caught in the act of taking a selfie by a photographer/viewer outside of the frame. This chapter will pay particular attention to this version of the nude celebrity selfie to consider what this specific arrangement reveals about the gendered social relations of seeing of our times and looking into the future. The chapter begins by revisiting key aspects of Berger's analysis of ways of seeing, and then moves on to examine in detail a number of posed nude celebrity selfies to raise questions about these widely circulating images.

The Nude versus the Naked

Berger tells us that the conventions of the nude painting reveal the crux of gender relations from late medieval/early modern period to the late twentieth century, when he was writing. What these conventions reveal are the unequal positions men and women occupy socially and culturally, and they express the different ways in which men and women understand themselves personally in the world. He argues that men are considered in relation to action, that is, a man's presence in the world is exterior to him – it is seen in what he is capable of doing. In contrast, a woman's presence is interior – a woman must continually watch herself as 'she is almost continually accompanied by her own image of herself' (1972, 46). Being born into a man's world, a woman must adapt, but at the cost of splitting herself in two. Her sense of herself and her identity as a woman 'is as *surveyor* and *surveyed*' (1972, 46). Women must survey every aspect of themselves for how they appear to others, because, argues Berger, men survey women before deciding how to treat them. To gain some control over this process, women internalise this surveillance so that a woman's actions are not for her own sake, but to show how she would like to be treated. Berger famously writes that 'men act and women appear. Men look at women. Women watch themselves being looked at. This determines not only most relations between men and women but also the relation of women to themselves. The surveyor of woman in herself is male: the surveyed female. Thus, she turns herself into an object – and most particularly an object of vision: a sight' (1972, 47).

Berger further argues that the nude subject of the European oil painting reveals the criteria and conventions by which (white) women have been seen and have been judged as 'sights'. He suggests, for instance, that there is considerable difference between being depicted as naked and being depicted as nude. Being *naked* is to be oneself, whereas the female *nude* of the European art tradition is to be seen naked by others, to have one's image possessed by another, not to be oneself, to be put on display. Berger argues that to be on display in this way is 'to have the surface of one's own skin, the hairs of one's own body, turned into a disguise which, in that situation, can never be discarded. The nude is condemned to never being naked. Nudity is a form of dress' (50).

These passages are not initially easy to take – the suggestion that as women we are not entirely in control of how we see ourselves and our own bodies and that we are forced by social circumstances to participate in the construction of ourselves as objects seems to diminish the role of our agency as humans. This is a problem that has been central to feminist theory for many decades – where does the balance lie between the determining power of structural oppression and our ability to act in the world and challenge domination? Many feminist theorists have turned to Foucault's work on the body in *Discipline and Punish* (1975) to challenge dominant ways of seeing that insist that human biology determines gender difference. Instead feminists have used the work of Foucault to argue that the body is not a simple biological category but is produced through power relations and is therefore cultural rather than natural (McNay 2000). However, the tension between structure and agency is evident in Foucault's work too – *Discipline and Punish* focuses on 'technologies of domination', which posit a 'docile body' limiting the potential for self-determination, while his later work such as *The Use of Pleasure: The Care of The Self* (1990) posits 'technologies of subjectification', which are understood as practices through which individuals may actively fashion their own identities. In my view, this tension between being a subject with agency and being subjectified by dominant social norms is never resolved in Foucault's thought, despite the crucial efforts by some to rethink the structure/agency dichotomy found in his work (McNay 2000).

The issue of the relationship between structural domination and agency (or our ability to act) continues to be a central problem for feminist thought and the politics of liberation; how can we act in circumstances that we have not chosen and which shape us, and how can we change those circumstances? I would like to suggest that denying or minimising the power of our circumstances inhibits rather than progresses a politics of liberation (but so too does a suggestion that domination is inescapable or that resistance is futile). Berger offers a crucial insight into understanding how binary ideological structures and ways of seeing impact on the self, the fundamental to-be-looked-at-ness that most women have felt and the sense of self-surveillance that results. The question remains about how we can overcome our split selves; is it an individual act of will or do we begin the process of changing ourselves in the struggle to change our circumstances and our world?

It is important to remember that, although Berger did not directly address race in his analysis of the nude (he addresses the colonial gaze in a separate chapter of his book), the ways of seeing revealed in the image of the nude are also racialised ways of seeing in which the ideal of feminine 'to be looked-at-ness' is white European – and the surveying and judging male gaze is also white European. The modern period created differences between the construction (and idealisation) of the white female body (and sexuality) as passive, coy and restrained and the colonial and black female body as overly sexual and atavistic. This binary structure of seeing, while it essentialises all women as bodies, permits violence on black and brown bodies and the projection of culturally taboo male sexual fantasy upon those bodies. We can see this in the case of Sarah Baartmann (Saartje Baartman), an African woman who was exhibited in England in the early nineteenth century (when scientific racism came to prominence) in order to display her 'prominent buttocks, which were imagined to be a sign of her overdeveloped sexuality' (Doerksen 1997, 139). Significantly, she was labelled the 'Hottentot Venus', which alludes to both the name for female wax anatomical models of the time (implying the dissectability of her body) and to Baartmann's racial difference. When Baartmann died at the age of 25, her body was indeed dissected, and her buttocks and external genitalia were removed and donated to the Musée de l'Homme in Paris, where they continued to be displayed until 2002. This way of seeing Baartmann depended on dehumanising her, considering her to be 'savage' and 'excessively sexual', strong echoes of which remain with us today in mainstream constructions of black and brown femininity.

Although scientific racism (which produced the dehumanising way of seeing Baartmann) did not exist prior to the modern period (Hochman 2019), and race scholars cannot agree about the origins of race as a concept (Devisse 2010; Heng 2011; Hochman 2019), there is emerging consensus that groups were 'racialised' in the late medieval to the early modern period in Europe and that racialised ways of seeing groups of humans were well established by the zenith of Renaissance painting at the end of the sixteenth century (Hochman 2019; Heng 2018). Relations of looking, then, built over centuries, not only reveal gender inequities, but also the dominant Western view that white bodies and white identities are the accepted centre of culture and form culturally conditioned ways of seeing, presenting as neutral and natural what is privileged and constructed (Hall 1992; Dyer 1997). This raises the question of how the whiteness of the heritage nude interacts with the aesthetics of today's celebrity selfie nude; is the legacy of gendered whiteness transferred into new media image making?

Berger's approach seems to offer a way of revealing the deep and overlapping binary structures of thinking in the modern period, so that even for those of us who try to eschew the binaries that structure gender, race and heteronormative ways of seeing, wider culture produces unequal ways of seeing – and ways of seeing ourselves that are situated within them. The central question remains: How can we resist these ways of seeing and is it only an individual effort or must there be strong collective energy in the remaking of ourselves?

Social Media Celebrity, Gender and Power

Some suggest we have moved beyond the power hierarchies revealed in these gendered ways of seeing. Berger wrote *Ways of Seeing* in 1972, when the second-wave women's movement was still young, and there are those who would argue (Cashmore 2019; Wolf 2016) that women now can control their own images, including sexualised images. Social media are seen to have given women the means of image production and allowed them to sidestep traditional media hierarchies, agenda setters and gatekeepers (see Turner 2010 for a critical discussion of this issue). Some contemporary commentators (Wolf 2016) argue that we can see current versions of empowerment in the way that female social media celebrities flaunt their bodies in 'naked defiance of cultural norms' (Cashmore 2019, 32). Ellis Cashmore argues that women 'create objects around or from their own bodies and assert ... their right to circulate these as freely as they wish' (2019, 32). There are echoes here of Foucault's 'technologies of subjectification', but absent is any serious assessment of the countervailing technologies of domination. Digitisation has empowered these female celebrities, he suggests, because it allows them to circumvent traditional media. Rehearsing the feminist debates around postfeminism, Cashmore asks if social media icon Kim Kardashian is complicit in the continued reduction of women's value to sex. Or is she a gender-rule-breaking, postfeminist icon who, standing on the shoulders of Madonna, courts scandal by exposing herself of her own free will, and thereby takes 'ownership' of her sexuality and body? He very much falls down on the side of the latter – she is 'playing others who think they are playing you' (2019, 47).

Quite apart from the widespread criticism of the overly celebratory view of new media found in this perspective (Curran et al. 2012; Barbrook and Cameron 1996; Turner 2006), this asset-utilisation idea of female empowerment, even were it satisfactory in its own terms, does not escape Berger's central point that the social relations of looking constrain woman to turn herself into an object; no matter how she profits from that way of seeing, her split understanding of herself cannot be discarded – these are our cultural norms, not a break with them. In a well-known photograph of Kim Kardashian in which she is posing nude in front of her bathroom mirror, gazing at her own image in an iPhone while stroking her neck (@kimkardashian, Twitter, 7 March 2016), Kardashian arouses a sense of a viewer looking in at her sexualised body and her awareness that she is being looked at in this way – indeed, inviting it. This is a way of looking and seeing women that has been in place for centuries, as we shall see. While among his many hyperbolic claims Cashmore does fleetingly admit that women's position in the overall structure has not significantly altered, he suggests that our recent freedoms and protections mean that the position for women is not so bad: 'Why should women not want to show off their bodies? What's wrong with desiring the attention of others? Aren't women who flaunt themselves as ostentatiously as they can in order to provoke envy, admiration, defiance and sexual arousal just exercising *agency*...' (2019, 33). This suggestion that women choose to remain within the oppression of patriarchy reproduces the very power relations of dominant ways of seeing that Berger so insightfully lays bare – that women are judged as body visions, and our lives and our sexualities are circumscribed by these ways of seeing, even while we are accused of willingly participating in turning ourselves into sights.

There is no question that Kim Kardashian is now one of the most recognised women in the world, amassing a fortune from her visibility on social media and reality television. She and her sister, Kylie Jenner, are two of the highest-paid social media influencers/celebrities (ranked fourth and first respectively).[2] But has she really challenged dominant ideas about woman-as-body? Recall that Kim Kardashian initially came to notoriety in 2007, when a sex tape made by her then boyfriend, R&B singer Ray J, was leaked to pornography studio Vivid Entertainment, which released it under the title *Kim Kardashian Superstar*. In the video she performs female sexuality within traditional white norms of passivity, while at the same time the video focuses on her buttocks in a manner that plays into conventions of black and brown female sexuality as excessive and exotic. This performance of what Priscilla Peña Ovalle identifies as 'racial mobility' (2011, 7) has been a feature of Kardashian's social media and reality TV body-persona ever since. Alexandra Sastre argues that Kim Kardashian leverages her Armenian heritage (which is legally designated as Caucasian in the USA) in order to oscillate between privileged normative whiteness and 'authentic' exotic blackness in a manner that reinforces and essentialises both (Sastre 2014).

Kardashian has built her personal brand on her white but ethnically signified buttocks and indeed has produced a public performance of her body that invites speculation – it is a body, and a butt, to be looked at and talked about. Displacing the gaze onto her buttocks reinforces a colonial gaze, but one that Kardashian, because she is actually white, benefits from without suffering the burden of racial oppression. Thus, Cashmore's claims that Kim Kardashian (and her fans' adulation of her) changes 'our understanding of gender, sex, race, consumption, privacy, fame and even ourselves' (2019, 11) ring rather hollow. Kardashian's public image reinforces dominant values in each of these areas. As Susie Orbach puts it, the body is the 'arena in which women have been allowed to express themselves' (1978, 23). While some women may amass fortunes by publicly participating in, and monetising, these ways of seeing, this does not fundamentally alter them for society as a whole or for society's understanding of woman or her understanding of herself, and while we may all be captured in patriarchy, our racialised treatment within it differs, and the vast majority of women do not share in the wealth or the accoutrements of fame of the privileged few.

In addition, the idea that these public displays of female intimacy are new and ground-breaking is equally misleading. The history of female fame from early modernity to the present day has been predicated precisely on sexualised and racialised public performances of intimacy. Women's public existence has for centuries depended upon collapsing the distinction between public and private (Williamson 2016). For example, actresses in seventeenth-century Restoration theatre (the first group of women in Europe to be famous outside the aristocracy) were primarily defined in relation to their sexuality and sexual availability. Theatre managers realised that blurring the line between public image and intimate knowledge could heighten an actress' marketability and they often encouraged actresses to reveal their intimate selves on stage. Actresses would often deliver prologues and epilogues with enticing secrets and male spectators often paid a fee to visit them backstage in the hope of gaining sexual favours (Nussbaum 2005). It made 'sense' for Restoration actresses to participate in this 'illusion of public intimacy' in order to increase their fame and popularity, so they deliberately tried to merge their theatrical persona with their private, sexualised selves (Wanko 2003). This rather undermines the idea that it is trailblazing and radical for women to use sexuality and public intimacy to gain fame and money – it is a practice hundreds of years old in the West and it reinforced the ideas of women-as-body and women-as-sight at precisely a time when women were entering the public realm as never before, restricting the possibilities for public women in ways which have followed us down the centuries. Once contained within definitions of sexuality, women actors found it almost impossible to escape these meanings. And so, this is simultaneously the beginning of 'public woman' and her being captured by sexualised and body-oriented ways of seeing, no matter what her performed public persona.

The History of the Nude

It is not insignificant that these sexualised meanings of public women gained prominence in European culture where images of women in the high art tradition were those of often submissive white female nudes on display for (white European) male sexual pleasure. Berger points out these *are* peculiarly European ways of portraying women and human sexuality. In early Indian, Persian, African and pre-Colombian art traditions, female nakedness is not supine and submissive as it is in the European art tradition. Berger suggests that in these traditions where the theme of a work was sexuality, 'they were likely to show active sexual love between two people, the woman as active as the man' (1972, 53). While this seems to centre heteronormative sexuality, it is at least active on the part of the woman.

In contrast, Berger offers an important discussion of the transformation of the pictorial depictions of the first female nude, Eve, from medieval times to early Renaissance painting. Medieval paintings often told the story of Adam and Eve as a pictorial narrative, rather like a strip cartoon, depicting Adam and Eve eating the apple and the subsequent loss of innocence (explained in Genesis as *becoming aware* of their nakedness). Renaissance paintings did away with the sense of narrative to focus on a single moment – the moment of awareness as shame. Berger points out that in Genesis, after eating the apple, Adam and Eve become aware of their nakedness only because they *see each other differently* – in other words 'nakedness was created in the eye of the beholder' (1972, 48). He also points out that it is the woman who is blamed and who is punished by being made subservient to the man: 'In relation to the woman, the man becomes the agent of God' (1972, 49). Renaissance painting transformed the depiction of shame, which is no longer seen in relation to each other, 'but in relation to another, the spectator' (1972, 40), and Berger argues that this shame gradually becomes a form of display 'when the tradition of painting became more secular, other themes offered the opportunity of painting nudes. But in all of them there remains the implication that the subject (a woman) is aware of being seen by a spectator' (1972, 50).

Those who celebrate the nude celebrity selfie as a form of female empowerment do not address the power relations of women internalising social surveillance as self-surveillance, nor do they consider the impact this has for the whole of society. They also do not consider the deep-seated psycho-social consequences of adjusting to that reality, in attempting to wrest some control by trying to perform historically racialised and sexualised versions of femaleness and, quite literally in the case of the selfie, seeming to be the agent of that image production, watching oneself do so and circulating it.

The Celebrity Nude Selfie

The nude selfie is a celebrity staple on social media sites (particularly Instagram) which seems to reveal the transfer of these deeply embedded ways of seeing onto new media forms. And while some male celebrities post nude selfies, the overwhelming majority come from female celebrities, which, because of the politics of looking, are deeply gendered; the male nude does not possess the same conventions of submission or of surveying himself being watched. The male nude is often placed standing in a waterfall or under a shower; his gaze is not usually directed out at the viewer, but up into the water or to the side, as if he is immersed in the experience, rather than displaying an awareness of the viewer watching him – he is more naked than nude, despite the invitation to look inherent in the image. This is not to suggest that there is no visual pleasure for the viewer, but that the relations of looking are different, for he is not offering up his sexuality and is depicted as simply being unaware of being surveyed. In addition, male nude images also emphasise active masculinity with a ubiquitous display of hard bodies and rippling muscles.

In contrast, the far more frequent female celebrity nude selfies display soft bodies posed in the conventions of being-looked-at derived from the female nude of the Renaissance art tradition, where white female bodies are displayed in ways that are refined and restrained as well as being sexually available. Berger explains that our ways of seeing the nude are not confined to art – there are also nude photographs and poses. But, he suggests, 'what is true is that the nude is always conventionalised – and the authority for its conventions derives from a certain tradition of art' (1972, 53). Berger describes the Renaissance nude as a 'sexual provocation' (1972, 54) in which the woman's body is arranged to display it to an unknown man looking into the picture at the woman's body. In a painting of Venus by Titian (about 1506–1576) we see that her sexual provocation lies in her recumbent pose and the way that she looks out at the unseen spectator with a coy and sexually inviting expression, her hand placed on her pubic area. This awareness of the gaze of the beholder is for Berger the central convention in Renaissance nude paintings that reveals our long history of unequal ways of seeing. We can observe these conventions operating in many female celebrity selfies. For instance, in a highly circulating nude image of Miley Cyrus (@mileycyrus, Twitter, 4 May 2019), we find her body arranged in a reclining, traditionally submissive position. Her arm partially covers and partially reveals one breast, her pose is a form of dress which partly reveals and partly conceals. Her shoulder in the foreground is lifted slightly in a gesture intended to charm the unknown viewer, with the curve of one buttock on display, aiming at the sexuality of the image. Because the display of her breast and buttocks is not explicit, and neither are large or 'excessive', the image conforms to a classy – or rather classed – version of nudity. These are the conventions found in the magazine *Playboy*, which positions itself as tasteful and intelligent, rather than the more explicit and pornographic images found in *Penthouse* or *Hustler*. Passivity, 'classiness' and inexplicit framing come together to situate Cyrus within the white European nude tradition; Cyrus looks out at a viewer with half-open eyes, aware that she is being looked at, with an expression that hints at sexual invitation. She is posed to demonstrate her awareness of the viewer looking at her and the image is intended to appeal to the presumed male viewer's sexuality, rather than being to do with her own sexuality. In this picture Cyrus is a nude rather than naked. 'She is not naked as she is / She is naked as the spectator sees her' (Berger 1972, 50).

Of course, like many social media images that are designated as 'selfies', this is not really a selfie, for this is not a photo that Cyrus took of herself. But it is part of social media selfie culture where Cyrus and other celebrities post and share nude images of themselves – this image featured in *Seventeen* magazine in a piece on nude selfies (*Seventeen* Editors, 2020). It is important, but the subject of another study, to consider how these ways of seeing are inculcated in the next generation as magazines aimed at young teens reproduce them as the norm and such images are circulated many hundreds of thousands of times.

Another trope of the Renaissance nude is the woman in a bath. Berger discusses the painting 'Susanna and the Elders' (Tintoretto, 1518–1594), where men are spying on the woman taking a bath. The pleasure in this looking is as a voyeur, peering in at a naked woman, a public display of the private and intimate self. But she isn't naked, she is clothed in her nudity. Susannah is looking back at us looking at her – she is a nude because she is positioned as undressed in the eye of the beholder and is aware of that surveying gaze. We saw in the previous image Cyrus looking directly at the viewer watching her, transforming her nakedness into the clothing of nudity. In a famous social media post (@kendalljenner, Twitter, 20 June 2019), Kendall Jenner is taking a selfie in the bath, but she is not really taking a bath, for the bath is empty. Instead she is posing nude in a bath. She is also not really taking a selfie; she is posing as if she was taking a selfie for the camera outside of the frame, drawing attention to the artifice of pose. When considering the significance of the emergence of the selfie, it is important to recognise that very many selfies are not actually selfies at all. There is a whole new genre of shared images that are *posed* as selfies, but which have been taken by a photographer who is not the subject of the image. The politics of seeing here and the meaning of the cameraphone in these images is important.

Jenner is looking out of the frame, with eyes very slightly and demurely averted, where the viewer watches her take a picture of herself. Like Cyrus, she too is posed with an awareness of displaying semi-revealed nudeness, of revealing herself as a sight. Like Cyrus, her pose is decorous and 'tasteful', conforming to passive and restrained white female sexuality.

But it is also important that this image is not a selfie but a portrait of a selfie – it adds a further layer of signification. Judging from the position of the cameraphone, that selfie, if it exists, would be a close-up of the side of her face. Instead, this image is entirely framed for the spectator, where the presence of the cameraphone adds a further layer to the relations of looking because it acts as a kind of mirror – the woman is looking at herself in her cameraphone in just the way she might gaze at herself in the mirror. In the conventions of nude paintings, a mirror signifies vanity – for, looking at herself in a mirror, the woman joins the spectators of herself. The screen of the digital cameraphone is a contemporary version of the mirror, whose real function, argues Berger, was always 'to make the woman connive in treating herself as, first and foremost, a sight' (1972, 51). Just as the woman who looks at herself in a mirror is condemned for vanity, so too does the presence of the cameraphone in the frame condemn the woman holding it. However, in Renaissance painting, it was a male painter whose moralistic framing was clearly hypocritical – the painter condemned the woman whose nudity he was producing for his own pleasure. In the case of the celebrity nude 'selfie', the fact that it is a woman seemingly taking a picture of herself (even though we know it is not) allows the spokesmen of patriarchal culture to condemn it as banal narcissism and/or to indulge in its sexual visual pleasures free of guilt on the grounds that, as she is doing it herself, it must be an act of empowerment (Riviere 2015). What remains unacknowledged and hidden from sight is that the gendered relations of seeing are left intact – ways of seeing which insist that woman is a body-vision and then condemn her for it.

Another aspect of the female celebrity nude selfie is the almost universal absence of body hair. Hair on the female body has been unacceptable since ancient times (Williams, 2006). The female body is expected to be smooth and hairless; body hair for women is 'surrounded by shame, disgust, and censure' (Lesnik-Oberstein 2006, 2) – it is, according to Karín Lesnik-Oberstein, 'the last taboo' (2006, 2). Joan Ferrante argues that 'superfluous' hair is considered to blur the 'boundaries that separate woman from man' (Ferrante 1988, 222), while Carolyn D. Williams suggests it is often depicted as 'a warning of perversion or unfeminine rebellion against patriarchal rule' (Williams 2006, 104). Berger points out that the European art conventions tended not to paint hair on a woman's body because hair is associated with adult male sexual power and passion. Berger writes, 'This picture [Venus] is made to appeal to *his* sexuality. (Here and in the European tradition generally, the convention of not painting hair on a woman's body helps toward the same end. Hair is associated with sexual power, with passion. The woman's sexual passion needs to be minimized so that the spectator may feel he has the monopoly of such passion.) Women are there to feed an appetite, not to have one of their own' (Berger 1972, 54–55).

Daniela Caselli, one of the few scholars to address Berger (as a literary and not a media scholar), considers this to be an 'extraordinary' statement because the meaning of body hair is made parenthetically. She argues that his discussion is left undeveloped and 'begs the question of how exactly body hair, femininity and "sexual power" interact' (Caselli 2006, 21). Despite this criticism, she goes on to expand on Berger's insight through an analysis of female body hair across a range of literary texts to suggest that even in texts that offer critiques of femininity and masculinity, representations of hairy women are firmly situated in the male/female binary by either signifying disgust or designating some women as 'pseudo-male' (not appropriately feminine). Absence of body hair for women, then, is a significant means of signalling 'proper' femininity (banishing any hint of masculinity with its connotations of power and action), of reinforcing the constructed boundary between men and women and of signifying restrained female sexuality.

Bella Hadid posts very many nude and semi-nude selfies, which use lighting techniques to emphasise the smooth hairlessness of her skin. In one particularly striking posed selfie (@bellahadid, Instagram, 4 December 2019), sunlight falls across the top of her thigh and part of her buttock (which is small and 'docile' in the Foucauldian sense), highlighting its smooth texture. This combines with a recumbent position with partially exposed breasts and 'tasteful' arrangement to produce Hadid's body in conformity to classed and white European standards of femininity. The slight covering of the body in clothes ensures that this image cannot be mistaken for the banality of nakedness, and reminds us that this pose is about sexual gratification, just not hers. As in the Kardashian/Jenner images, she holds a cameraphone, so that this is not actually a selfie, but a portrait of a selfie. Here again, the camera acts as a mirror, reminding us, with condemnation, that women are implicated in turning ourselves into objects, while inviting the viewer to look, but absolving him of responsibility for the sexual pleasures and fantasies projected there. The conformity to European norms of femininity is significant because Hadid is actually Palestinian American and is proud of her heritage. She is a vocal advocate of Palestinian rights and vociferously rebuked Instagram for removing her post of her father's Palestinian passport, insisting that 'you can't erase history by silencing people'. This highlights the complexities around the issues of structure and agency raised earlier – it is hard to be an outspoken Palestinian in a world in which most of the powerful nations deny one's existence, but Hadid *acts* – she is agentic on this matter; it seems that it is harder still, however, to step outside of white European and patriarchal norms of femininity, or to overcome the deep structures of seeing that position woman as a surveyor of herself. Berger writes that the woman 'has to survey everything she is and everything she does because how she appears, and ultimately how she appears to men, is of crucial importance for what is normally thought of as success in her life. Her sense of being herself is supplanted by a sense of being appreciated as herself by another' (1972, 46).

While very many celebrity nude selfies conform to the 'tasteful' and restrained conventions of the European art tradition, there are some that instead refer to the pornographic. Berger comments that in breaking from the European tradition, avant-garde artists of the early twentieth century had little to replace its idealism but in 'the realism of the prostitute' (1972, 63). Is it possible for those celebrities whose poses are not situated within the art tradition to overcome that dichotomy? Let's examine a well-known selfie of Tana Mongeau in a semi-masturbatory pose on her knees, her right hand clutching her buttock, wearing skimpy lingerie with tongue out (@tanamongeau, Instagram, 9 October 2017). It is important to note that Mongeau is openly bisexual, was in a high-profile (and much-talked-about) relationship with Bella Thorne and that her sexuality confounds the binaries around sexuality. Can we take this image as an active refutation of passive female sexuality and a celebration of female gratification? Is Mongeau refusing to enact a restrained and upper-middle-class nude pose? At one level it obviously conforms to soft porn conventions found in magazines like *Penthouse* and adult television channels which usually feature models with buttocks raised and breasts thrust forward, often in masturbatory poses. However, Mongeau seems to be signalling to the viewer that there is an irony in the pose. She includes her socks (and jokes about them in the post), showing an awareness of what the codes for this kind of image are and that she can have 'fun' and break them. She seems to be signifying that she is in control of the image production. However, while she presents her pose as pleasing herself, she is inevitably pleasing an external viewer and is aware that she is doing so.

With tongue out, exotic underwear and the suggestion that she is fingering her backside, Mongeau cannot, as an individual act of will, overthrow the meanings embedded in these long-standing ways of seeing by conforming to them. The tongue-out selfie, which is widespread among celebrities and ordinary women alike, and which suggests fellatio, anchors the meaning of woman, and her visible understanding of herself, as an object of male sexual pleasure.

Celebrity transwomen also face these inescapable looking relations despite disrupting a male/female binary based on sex. We will investigate this claim through Lavern Cox's nude selfies. Cox is credited with being the first openly transgender actress and she came to fame in her role as Sophia Bruset in *Orange is the New Black* (Netflix), in a ground-breaking role as the first transgender woman on television to play a transgender woman. She is also a woman of African American heritage. Cox is a trans and LGBTQ+ advocate and has played an important role in bringing trans issues and demands into the public sphere. However, like Hadid, her political commitment to making visible identities that are shunned by mainstream culture has not automatically enabled her to escape our gendered ways of seeing. Berger argues that our essential way of seeing women has not changed, despite the dispersal of the image of women across emerging media technologies. He suggests that women continue to be depicted 'in a quite different way from men – not because the feminine is different to the masculine – but because the "ideal" spectator is assumed to be [a man] and the image of a woman is designed to flatter him' (1972, 64).

In a widely circulating image in the press (@lavernecox, Instagram, 19 May 2017), Lavern Cox, like Kylie Jenner and Bella Hadid, is posing as if she is taking a selfie, but the camera taking the portrait is out of the frame. She holds a cameraphone (steeped in the signification of the mirror and vanity) and looks out at the spectator, lips parted in anticipation, with a partial breast and buttock exposed, a towel modestly covering her pubic area. This image conforms to each of the conventions that we have identified that take their legitimacy from the European art tradition; in this image, Cox, as is the case in other female celebrity nude selfies, is aware of her to-be-looked-at-ness and faces the same charges of vanity, display and complicity, which titillates the male spectator, while laying the locus of discussions about the politics of looking in patriarchy back on the terrain of her female body. Her body is hairless, her curves are visible but restrained and it is difficult to identify her African American ethnicity in this particular image, for the image conforms to white European conventions of the Renaissance nude art tradition. As women, escaping these ways of understanding ourselves is extremely difficult; our political commitments, our enthusiasm, achievements and skills, our actions in the world, our experiences, our very lives are situated within unequal relations, where the pressure not just to conform to idealised (and sexualised, body-based) norms of feminine beauty, but to understand ourselves in these terms and to judge ourselves (and other women) in relation to those norms seems almost inescapable.

Inevitably, therefore, there will be women who decide to play the cards that were dealt to them, to situate themselves in the 'capitalist realism' (Fisher 2009) of commentators such as Cashmore, to try to monetise the structures of their oppression, accepting that there are no alternatives, and often to proclaim as freely chosen these socially produced but internalised ways of seeing.

Final Thoughts

For Cashmore and other 'realists', any critique of the existing relations of power is doomed. Such critique reminds him of the Ghost Dance practised by First Nations and Indigenous peoples of America – 'a ritual practiced by an American Indian cult in the late nineteenth century, the followers of which believed that the dance would drive away white people and restore the traditional way of life ... Like the ill-fated Ghost Dancers, critics of celebrity culture have discovered that ... their caveats are useless' (2019, 178). Celebrity culture here stands in for consumer capitalism, with a strong suggestion, in his flippant and insulting reference to the genocidal treatment of Indigenous peoples of North America and the stealing of their land, that gender essentialism in social media celebrity culture is simply inevitable, an unavoidable change and may even signify progress. Racist capitalist patriarchy thrives on the hopelessness engendered by this way of seeing; it reifies the present and darkens any dreams for the future and visions of freedom.

Celebrity culture, of which the social media celebrity selfie is now a mainstay, plays a role in that reification. It reproduces racialised and gendered hierarchies while reinforcing the commercial, economic and symbolic power of capitalist cultural production and, throughout its history, it has functioned to increase commercial control over the cultural sphere and has assimilated and disciplined a vast array of bodies and identities in the process (Williamson 2016). But the power of dominant ways of seeing is never complete and the cultures and histories that produce them are contradictory and subject to change. The symbolic meaning of the nude celebrity selfie helps to reify gender and to individualise our experiences. But celebrity selfies and their connotations also belong to a wider culture in which symbolic meanings *are* contested, where celebrities themselves, even while performing normative racialised and gendered identities, also have ethnic, class and gender belongings that potentially reject the dominant ways of seeing and offer alternative ways of being human. These alternative ways of seeing have been the basis for many of the emancipatory projects of the twenty-first century. Celebrities may be vocal on these issues, but these movements do not emanate from celebrity culture. Instead, some celebrities are influenced by these movements – movements that are built on the solidarity and collective politics of many millions of ordinary people. We can change our ways of seeing, and we can change ourselves, but this can only be a collective endeavour, which must have solidarity between men and women, black and white, gay, straight and trans at its heart, because *all of us* have to change our ways of seeing and ourselves – not just the oppressed – and this can only be effective as part of our project to make the world anew.

References

Barbrook, R. and A. Cameron. 1996. 'The Californian Ideology'. *Science as Culture*, 6(1): 44–72.

Benjamin, W. 2008 [1935]. *Art in the Age of Mechanical Reproduction*. London: Penguin.

Berger, J. 1972. *Ways of Seeing*. London: Penguin.

Caselli, D. 2006. '"The Wives of Geniuses I Have Sat ith": Body Hair, Genius and Modernity', In *The Last Taboo: Women and Body Hair*, edited by K. Lesnik-Oberstein, 18–47. Manchester: Manchester University Press.

Cashmore, E. 2019. *Kardashian Kulture: How Celebrities Changed Life in the 21ˢᵗ Century*. Bingley: Emerald Publishing.

Curran, J., N. Fenton and D. Freedman. 2012. *Misunderstanding the Internet*. London: Routledge.

Devisse, J. 2010 [1979]. *The Image of the Black in Western Art, Volume II: From the Early Christian Era to the "Age of Discovery", Part 1: From the Demonic Threat to the Incarnation of Sainthood*, new edn. Trans. William G. Ryan. New York: William Morrow. Reissued with an introduction by Paul Kaplan and a preface by David Bindman and Henry Louis Gates. Cambridge, MA: Belknap Press of Harvard University Press.

Doerksen, T. A. 1997. 'Deadly Kisses: Vampirism, Colonialism and the Gendering of Horror'. In *The Fantastic Vampire: Studies in the Children of the Night: Selected Essays from the Eighteenth International Conference on the Fantastic in the Arts*, edited by J. C. Holte, 127–139. Westport, CT and London: Greenwood Press.

Dyer, R. 1997. *White: Essays on Race and Culture*. London: Routledge.

Ferrante, J. 1988. 'Biomedical Versus Cultural Constructions of Abnormality: The Case of Idiopathic Hirsuitism in the United States'. *Culture, Medicine and Psychiatry*, 12: 219–238.

Fisher, M. 2009. *Capitalist Realism: Is There No Alternative?* Winchester: Zero Books.

Foucault, M. 1975. *Discipline and Punish: The Birth of the Prison*. London: Penguin Modern Classics.

Foucault, M. 1990. *The Uses of Pleasure: The Care of the Self*. London: Vintage.

Hall, S. 1992. 'Race, Culture and Communications: Looking Backward and Forward at Cultural Studies'. *Rethinking Marxism*, 5(1): 10–18.

Heng, G. 2011. 'The Invention of Race in the European Middle Ages 1: Race Studies, Modernity and Middle Ages'. *Literature Compass*, 8(5): 315–331.

Heng, G. 2018. *The Invention of Race in the European Middle Ages*. New York: Cambridge University Press.

Hochman, A. 2019. 'Racialization: A Defence of the Concept'. *Ethnic and Racial Studies*, 42(8): 1245–1262.

Lesnik-Oberstien, K. (ed.). 2006. *The Last Taboo: Women and Body Hair*. Manchester: Manchester University Press.

Livingstone, J. 2017. 'Beyond John Berger's Ways of Seeing'. *The New Republic*, 4 January 2017. Available at: https://newrepublic.com/article/139615/beyond-john-bergers-ways-seeing.

McNay, M. 2017. 'John Berger Obituary'. *The Guardian*, 2 January. Available at: www.theguardian.com/books/2017/jan/02/john-berger-obituary.

McNay, L. 2000. *Gender and Agency*. Cambridge: Polity.

Meyer, P. 2018. 'The Selfie Generation'. *hq: News for Hamden and Quinnipac*, 9 December. Available at: www.hqpress.org/blog-2/2018/11/20/the-selfie-generation#:~:text=On%20 average%2C%2093%20million%20selfies,to%20instagram%20every%2010%20seconds.

Nussbaum, F. 2005. 'Actresses and the Economics of Celebrity 1700–1800'. In *Theatre and Celebrity in Britain. 1660–2000*, edited by M. Luckhurst and J. Moody, 148–168. Basingstoke: Palgrave Macmillan.

Orbach, S. 1978. *Fat is a Feminist Issue*. London: Random House.

Ovalle Peña, P. 2011. *Dance and the Hollywood Latina: Race, Sex and Stardom*. New Brunswick, NJ: Rutgers University Press.

Turner, F. 2006. *From Counter Culture to Cyber Culture: Stewart Brand, the Whole Earth Network, and the Rise of Digital Utopianism.* Chicago, IL and London: The University of Chicago Press.

Riviere, S. 2015. 'The Kardashian Sisters are the True Heirs to the Brontes'. *The Telegraph*, 5 May. Available at: www.telegraph.co.uk/culture/books/11584309/Kim-Kardashian-is-a-feminist-artist-for-our-time.html.

Sastre, A. 2014. 'Hottentot in the Age of Reality TV: Sexuality, Race and Kim Kardashian's Visible Body', *Celebrity Studies*, 5(1–2): 127–137.

Seventeen Editors. 2020. '70+ Times Celebs Shared Their Nudes on Instagram'. *Seventeen*, 21 April. Available at: www.seventeen.com/celebrity/g20867874/celebrity-nude-pictures-instagram/.

Turner, G. 2010. *Ordinary People and the Media.* London: Sage.

Wanko, C. 2003. *Roles of Authority: Thespian Biography and Celebrity in Eighteenth-Century Britain.* Lubbock, TX: Texas Tech University Press.

Williams, C. D. 2006. '"That Wonderful Phænomenon": Female Body Hair and the English Literary Tradition'. In *The Last Taboo: Women and Body Hair*, edited by K. Lesnik-Oberstein, 103–125. Manchester: Manchester University Press.

Williamson, M. 2016. *Celebrity: Capitalism and the Making of Fame.* Cambridge: Polity.

Wolf, N. 2016. 'Emily Ratajkowski's Naked Ambition'. *Harpers Baazar*, August. Available at: http://bit.ly/2ucx0NS.

THE FUTURE OF 'DIVERSITY' IN MEDIA

8
Rethinking 'Diversity' in Publishing

Anamik Saha and Sandra van Lente

Introduction

This current moment of racial capitalism (Leong 2012; Melamed 2015; Bhattacharyya 2018) has produced an interesting contradiction when it comes to media. While we have seen the rise of right-wing/far-right populism in seemingly 'liberal' nation states, the ascendency of which has been based on explicitly racist and anti-immigrant rhetoric, media corporations – whether public or private – seem obsessed with 'diversity'. This applies to attempts to make their workforces more diverse, based on the recognition that racial and ethnic groups in particular have been historically excluded from media. It also includes attempts to make media content more diverse, in order to attract more diverse audiences (or, indeed, markets). Again, this emphasis on diversity seems to go against the grain of what is going on politically in those nations. In light of the pretty blatantly racist pronouncements of our democratically elected political leaders, such a focus at least appears to be a progressive force that gives us hope for the future of media.

However, to what extent does the discourse of diversity really attend to the structural inequalities that racialised groups continue to face in creative and cultural industries? Critiques of 'diversity' (Ahmed 2012; Gray 2016; Nwonka and Malik 2018) have shown how initiatives that aim to increase diversity in media, whether in production or content, are tokenistic, performative and in fact serve an ideological function, only appearing to meet the demand of racial and ethnic groups while keeping racial hierarchies intact (Saha 2018). Moreover, to what extent is racism embedded in the very logics of industrial cultural production, a situation which leads to the reproduction of racial and ethnic stereotypes in the media? This, we argue, is the most urgent issue with regard to race, racism and media, and something that the current diversity paradigm does not properly address. In light of this critique, 'diversity', we argue, needs to be *rethought* – if not radically reconceptualised – in order to properly undo the structures of racism that shape media and cultural production.

What follows is an extract from our report *Rethinking 'Diversity' in Publishing* (Goldsmiths Press, June 2020),[1] one of the first in-depth academic studies into diversity in the publishing industry. The purpose of this research was to examine the dynamics of race in an industry where the issue of diversity is high on the agenda. UK publishing, perhaps more than any other creative industry, recognises that it has a serious problem with its own lack of racial/ethnic diversity. Publishing remains an overwhelmingly white and middle-class industry, and this is reflected in the books that it publishes. Despite the successes of authors of colour, from Malorie Blackman to Zadie Smith, writers from minority backgrounds nonetheless struggle to get their books published or reach certain audiences. Indeed, from our research we found that publishers experience anxieties when publishing writers of colour. The purpose of this research was to unpack these anxieties and identify the particular challenges that publishers face (or believe they will face) when working with authors from racial/ethnic minority backgrounds. It was also to consider the opportunities that such authors are encountering; in this moment of 'diversity', there certainly seems to exist a heightened demand for new talent from racial and ethnic minority backgrounds. In other words, the aim of the research was to delve deeply into the publishing process and see how it affects writers of colour.

The research was based on in-depth interviews, each lasting an hour on average, with people who work at each stage of publishing. This included agents, publishers, editors, people who work in marketing, design, publicity and sales and booksellers. We also interviewed authors and festival organisers. Overall we interviewed 113 people, 66 of whom were white and 47 'BAME',[2] all from different levels of seniority. All the big publishing houses were included, as well as independent publishers. The purpose of each interview was to get an insight into how each respondent approaches their role, particularly in relation to the books of writers of colour.

To reiterate, the aim of the chapter is to go beyond the mere question of whether the publishing industry is sufficiently diverse and examine more closely the obstacles that writers of colour face. The chapter is split into three sections that examine key stages of the publishing process, namely acquisition, promotion and sales. Each section demonstrates how writers of colour are disadvantaged within these stages. While the focus of the chapter is on publishing, we argue that the same broad dynamics exist across the creative and cultural industries. We also argue that meaningfully tackling the future of diversity in media depends upon undoing and rethinking the assumptions, logics and processes that shape each key stage of industrial cultural production when it comes to the creative work of racial and ethnic groups.

Finding and Acquiring Writers of Colour

Acquisition is the first gate that can block the entry of writers of colour – disproportionately, we argue, compared to their white, middle-class counterparts. Moreover, we found that for those writers who do make it through, it is often because they have been moulded (or have moulded themselves) to fit in a way that conforms with the worldview of the predominantly white, middle-class editorship.

While the acquisition process technically refers to the process of when a publisher acquires an author, we broaden the term to include the discovery of writers by agents. Nearly all of the editors we interviewed stated that they rely on agents to find authors, with many saying that an author without an agent is unlikely to be acquired. The opacity of the process, however, holds working-class and 'BAME' writers back. A common narrative that we encountered from publishers and agents, both 'BAME' and white, was that having an awareness of the agenting process is based on privilege. This raises the issue of class, and how it gets reproduced at the agenting stage of production. As an experienced white woman author told us:

> I think the first hurdle's getting an agent, and I think agents are overwhelmingly white, middle-class, very *Guardian*-reading, liberal by and large, and that's the first hurdle and that's the hard one. They are not people who spend their lives dealing with difference.

Aggravating the problem further, the majority of agents we spoke to use the same routes to find authors. This includes scouting on creative writing courses, networking events, recommendations from other agents/writers, literary prizes/competitions and via open submissions. When we asked agents specifically about writers of colour, they all agreed that they would like more 'diverse' writers, but discovering such writers was generally presented as a major challenge for agents. On the other hand, literature development organisations that develop a pipeline of highly skilled marginalised authors are often not included in the process.

Also, agents claimed that they did not track the race or ethnicity of the submissions and could not tell from a manuscript. Interviewees suspected that people of colour might not be interested in writing and assumed financial (need to earn more money) and cultural (don't see this as an option) obstacles. A 'BAME' respondent[3] retorted: 'this idea that we're not interested and that it's always about money, is just so offensive.'

The publishing industry over the past few years has seen a number of writing competitions and writing schemes that target writers of colour. Having spoken to the people behind them it was clear that there was no shortage of submissions, suggesting that *there is* a pool of writers from marginalised backgrounds that is still being untapped. And those agents and publishers who are more proactive invest a lot of time and effort: 'It's a long process, I've sown plenty of seeds and I'm hoping that eventually some of those will come to fruition, but it takes a long time, and that stuff doesn't just come to you organically all the time' ('BAME' respondent).

After focusing on the agenting process, we wanted to explore how and which type of writers of colour are signed by publishers. One of the findings from the *Writing the Future* (2015) report was that writers from minority backgrounds feel steered into reproducing racial and ethnic stereotypes. While publishers did not admit to this, what became clear from our interviews is the strategy of replicating past successes. As one 'BAME' writer put it to us, publishers 'don't want the next big thing. They want the next big thing to be just like the last big thing, only slightly tweaked.' This comment was deliberately facetious, but many other editors made a similar point, that publishers want *the same, but different*, especially in commercial fiction. It is in this way that familiar tropes around racial and ethnic difference are reproduced.

Conforming to White Expectations

Many of the 'BAME' respondents we spoke to felt that in order to get a publishing deal they had to fulfil certain expectations of what white, middle-class editors want.

> [A] lot of white editors were like 'We thought you were giving us this immigrant narrative, but you're not, and so we're not going to pursue it.' ... I think there's a particular narrative that they're at ease with, and they know how to

grapple with politically, and they know how they want to publish it in a particular way.

('BAME' respondent)

Several responses led to the conclusion that the stories of writers of colour needed to conform to the worldview of the white, middle-class editors who have particular expectations over what kind of stories are supposedly authentic to these writers – or 'relatable'. We observed a fear that the core (white) audience will not be able to relate to stories by writers from racial and ethnic minorities.

What we found interesting about a number of replies are the different euphemisms that editors use to explain their fears over the relatability – or, more accurately, *marketability* – of books by writers of colour: 'It didn't resonate with me'; 'I don't know if I can place this book'. When it comes to writers of colour, publishers struggle to imagine an audience for such books, or, more precisely, audiences beyond the supposed 'core' audience. One of our key findings is that publishers do not know how to engage the communities that those authors belong to.

We find that writers of colour are stuck between a rock and a hard place. On the one hand there is an expectation of what stories such authors are able to write about (usually relating to the author's racial or ethnic identity in some way), but there is also a fear that such stories might appear too niche.

The Art of Comping

In addition to the perceived risk related to the core target audience, books by writers of colour were also seen as a riskier investment if publishing staff had nothing to compare them to. *Comping* – the process of finding comparative titles in order to predict sales – is at the core of commercial publishing. Comparative titles are usually brought up by the commissioning editors in their acquisition meeting pitches and in sales, while marketing and other staff bring in their own comps.

One issue that was raised was whether to compare writers of colour to other writers of colour or to white writers. While some respondents were critical of 'forcing a white comparison', some writers of colour would appreciate being compared in this way, rather than have their book compared to one by another author based solely on a shared racial/ethnic background. Associated with this was a fear of being pigeonholed and thus marginalised.

Linked to this is the lack of data that exists for authors of colour, which affects how they are comped. As one senior white woman editor said to us, the lack of such data 'could disadvantage [authors of colour] if there's not good comparisons in the marketplace'. A 'BAME' respondent agrees that a lack of data can 'hold authors of colour back':

> [F]inding a comparison can prove incredibly difficult, or the comparisons might not necessarily have the numbers the editor or sales might want, so it might mean that a book isn't published, cos there isn't a comparison to go with it.

Several people referred to a *chicken-and-egg* situation; the reason that we do not see more authors of colour published is because we have not seen enough commercially successful authors of colour.

Another related aspect is that, essentially, writers of colour are being comped in relation to data that comes from a single readership: the white, middle-class audience. And we argue that a lack of data around untapped audiences – especially 'BAME' ones – is holding back writers of colour. To reiterate, we do not believe that there is a right or wrong way to comp a writer of colour. Rather, we want to draw attention to how the question of whether to compare a writer of colour to a white or non-white author is even a question in the first place. As one 'BAME' respondent said to us, when it comes to 'non-diverse' books (that is, books by white authors), 'there just seems to be more freedom in what you can do'. Data, perceived as objective and neutral, is used creatively to back up the editor's own agenda. And comping is a creative practice, but a constraining one when it comes to writers of colour.

"If It's Good, We'll Publish It": 'Quality' and Meritocracy

While all our respondents agreed that the publishing industry could do more when it comes to publishing writers of colour (particularly in case of commercial fiction), there was also a fear of tokenism. Tokenism refers to a situation when writers of colour are published in order to tick a 'diversity' box. While all of our respondents agreed that they would like to publish more 'diversely', some expressed a concern that this this would lead to a lower quality of books being published. However, when pressed, many of the publishers we spoke to – across both literary and commercial fiction – conceded that not everything they published was necessarily of the highest 'quality'. Instead, they might see a book/writer as being 'commercial', but this very rarely applies to writers of colour for reasons that shall be explored throughout this chapter. In general, though, we found that that it is the fear of compromising quality that is essentially holding back writers of colour.

In this regard we want to challenge what publishers mean by 'quality'. 'If it's good, we'll publish it' is a comment we would hear throughout the research. But to what extent is this notion of 'good' really that universal? In an industry that is dominated by the white middle classes, many of whom attended Russell Group universities, their notions of 'quality' are shaped by a very particular experience and education, based on a canon that in recent times has been questioned for its Eurocentric view of the world. While some publishers may contest this, what we would suggest is that the real challenge to diversity is less about the fear of diminished quality and more about the publishing industry's sense of its own audience. The publishers we spoke to admitted to publishing books they do not always love but know that there is an audience for. Thus, the discourse around how a particular writer of colour may lack 'quality' can also be read as not believing that the core, white, middle-class audience will see *value* in this book – and as showing that the publisher lacks confidence or the inclination to reach wider audiences.

Underpinning the narrative on quality is a broader issue relating to merit-ocracy. Frequently we encountered comments that are basically premised on publishing as a meritocracy – that everyone has the chance to be published if their work is of a high enough quality. It follows that 'diversity', when it is understood as giving special affordances to writers of colour, is seen as potentially undermining the publishing industry's meritocratic foundations. Thus publishers want to pub-lish more 'diversely' but are held back from taking proactive, *affirmative* measures to address this issue as it might be seen as giving writers of colour an unfair advan-tage over white writers (expressed in terms of publishers not wanting to com-promise quality). We argue that in order for publishers to publish more diversely, they need to challenge their own assumptions about whether publishing truly is a meritocracy. The monocultural nature of the industry, the books published and the audiences catered for suggest that, despite its best intentions, publishing is not the level playing field that it might claim to be.

Summary

The main challenges for writers of colour in this early stage of publishing are com-placency and limited assumptions about readers. Agents and publishers often use the same sources to find authors, and literature development organisations that produce a pipeline of new writers are not seen. Comping can be a creative practice but is often restrictive when it comes to writers of colour. It boils down to the limited ideas publishers have about their audiences. Ultimately, if publishers want to discover more writers of colour, they need to widen their perception of who their audiences are. This is a recurring theme we also saw in the packaging and promotion of books, and in bookselling.

Packaging and Promoting Writers of Colour

Our study finds that publishers and booksellers do not have the resources, know-how or, indeed, the inclination to reach wider audiences beyond the white middle classes. We have also found out that 'BAME' and working-class audiences are undervalued by publishers, both economically and culturally. This in turn affects the acquisition, promotion and selling of writers of colour.

When we interviewed people who work on the promotion of a book – including jacket design, marketing and publicity – it became apparent that they all shared a common understanding of their 'core' audience: explicitly middle-class, implicitly white. In other words, publishers have a very narrow sense of who their audience is, and if a writer of colour is not seen as having value to this very specific group then they are less likely to get published. It follows that writers of colour who do get acquired are packaged and promoted in a way that is made to appeal to a white, middle-class audience.

Who Is the Audience?

Our main finding is that – with particular reference to the major publishing houses – writers of colour are marketed in a way that appeals specifically to the core publishing audience – as a respondent in sales put it to us, 'a sort of 50-something middle-class to upper-middle-class white woman who reads a lot because she has time, and she has resources to spend on books'. She was often sardonically referred to in our interviews as *Susan* or *Suzie*. The understanding of the core book-buying audience as middle-class became very clear in our interviews. When we asked a senior marketing manager if he had ever used a social grade category other than 'AB' when defining the potential market for a particular book, he replied: 'never, you would never start there, even if that might be your ultimate audience.' An engagement with minority audiences is seen as an additional aspect, rather than the core marketing activity.

What concern us here are the implications for writers of colour of the fact that the target audience consists of white, middle-class women. One 'BAME' respondent told us how they once observed editors asking for changes to a manuscript by a writer of colour that basically amounted to it being 'translated for a white reader'. As they put it, 'not every book is being written for a white reader', and sometimes the writer in question is 'writing [for] their own community'. The question, then, is to what extent are publishers able to reach – or *invested in reaching* – these communities?

Exoticisation or Whitewashing? Cover Design and Marketing Topics

Publishers' focus on a very particular white, middle-class audience leads to the presentation of the books by writers of colour in very particular ways that either downplay or reject strong racial signifiers through fear of making the book too niche, or represent their difference in a softly *exoticised* way (such as the use of ethnic fabrics) that would appeal to a liberal, white, middle-class sensibility. In particular in commercial fiction, we found that there remains a fear that featuring a racial or ethnic minority character on the cover could lead to diminished sales – to the extent that black or brown characters literally get whitened on covers.

Also, we observed a tendency to push books with protagonists from marginalised communities to literary fiction – in design as well as in the overall communication strategy. This again can have implications for sales numbers (usually lower in literary fiction compared to more commercial genres) and can feed into the narrative that 'BAME' books are commercially less successful.

In addition, the focus on this one audience and its alleged preferences in combination with the abovementioned practices creates 'expectations for [writers of colour] to write a certain type of book', as a 'BAME' respondent commented, in order to fit into these kinds of marketing categorisations. This limits the opportunities for writers of colour who want to talk beyond their experience and racial or ethnic identity. While a writer of colour might choose to talk about their marginalised experience, such a burden prevents authors of colour from speaking about broader issues or interests. A 'BAME' respondent stated that such an attitude can end up 'exoticizing people', as authors of colour find themselves having to *perform* their racial and ethnic identities in ways that conform to mainstream white, liberal views in order to get media exposure. They add, 'the industry says it wants to diversify, but it's on its own terms'.

Lack of Creativity

Our interviews revealed a lack of creativity when it comes to the selection of media for promotional and marketing activities. Communication departments still rely on traditional media channels, e.g., national newspapers and BBC Radio 4, which are used by a narrow segment of the population. Some white respondents expressed hope that the coverage would cross over into other segments and communities, but we observed a high level of complacency. Based on the understanding that getting big book sales relies upon obtaining national press coverage, the sole focus on what one publicity manager described as 'traditional media' can disadvantage writers of colour. A 'BAME' respondent described how 'mainstream media' is also targeted for books by writers of colour,

> because that's what Waterstones, and that's what the independents, and that's what Amazon understands. They only understand mainstream [media] that has quite a white-middle class audience. Because that's their customer base.

What we find particularly interesting about this quote is its reference to booksellers. Publicity here is less about reaching audiences and more about winning over booksellers. In other words, publicity managers need to focus on media that the booksellers recognise and see as valuable.

Lack of Awareness

When we spoke to 'BAME' respondents in particular, there was a strong sense that publishers do not do enough to engage more diverse audiences. We identified several ways in which this was expressed, for example, in the words of this 'BAME' respondent: 'I think just the lack of relationship and the lack of willingness to build a sense of community with people who aren't white is really present'.

We found that publishers undervalue 'non-mainstream' media and don't seem to know the relevant magazines, blogs and influencers that target communities that have been neglected by mainstream media. These outlets are perceived as niche. Publishers see engaging with such media as a supplement to, rather than as the core of, their marketing campaigns.

Interestingly, new media are gaining much cultural (and commercial) significance beyond their core audience. *gal-dem* and *Black Ballad* were mentioned first and foremost by younger publishers. It was felt that the big publishers in particular are failing to engage with this new generation of digital media even though they present unique opportunities for engaging particular audiences. As one 'BAME' respondent put it, these platforms are 'perfect opportunities where you can put books by people of colour ... but they're not being targeted.'

Indeed, in our interviews with white people who work in press and publicity we got a sense that they do not know what media channels to target for writers of colour. As one respondent conceded: 'I don't know if we know as much about black media.' This raises the issue of recruitment and the value of making promotional teams more diverse.

Resources

Limited resources pose another challenge. The 'BAME' respondent below describes how, despite their aspiration to do so, they are unable to reach underrepresented audiences through a lack of resources.

> I would say that is my biggest challenge. I can have every ambition to find new audiences and diversify their reading, etc. But at the end of the day, who is actually going to do that and how is that going to happen and who is going to help you make that happen?

What this respondent refers to is how they feel they do not have the resources – in terms of money or people power – to reach the communities that writers of colour belong to. With the best will in the world, this person feels that finding 'new audiences' is beyond the means of publishers, that this is the 'reality'. But regardless of the question of funding (and the £1.67 billion turnover of the industry in 2019 suggests that there is some money somewhere), the more pressing question is: Do publishers, as a whole, have the inclination to reach new audiences? Do they find *value* in such audiences? During our research, respondents persuaded us that they do care about engaging new communities for readers. But to achieve this, publishers need to understand that they need to go beyond the traditional channels.

Burdening 'BAME' Staff

One major issue regarded the expectation placed on 'BAME' publishers to undertake the labour of reaching more diverse audiences. We found a variety of responses in this regard. Some 'BAME' respondents were happy to perform this role.

> I feel like I have a responsibility to do so, because if I don't, I just know that these groups will not be approached. And I just know that in acquisitions or in board rooms or in meetings when I'm not there, I know that certain things would be said that are false and untrue.

Others found it demeaning and tokenistic.

> I feel like being asked to fix diversity as the one diverse person infuriating, but then when I do try and fix it and you don't listen to me, then that's just tokenism.

While hiring more people who belong to communities not traditionally targeted by publishing can bring new, fresh perspectives to the promotion of books, it should be made explicit in the job description if candidates are hired for this purpose. Then it's up to the candidates to decide whether they want to work under those circumstances. Also, these roles must be supported properly, otherwise it represents nothing more than tokenism.

Summary

To reiterate, one of our key findings is that the publishing industry is set up to cater for just one – white, middle-class – audience. Writers of colour are essentially promoted to appeal to this core audience, which can lead to their exoticisation and marginalisation. Fundamentally, publishers need to challenge their assumptions about minority audiences, including the belief that they are not interested in books. While we should be careful not to define racial and ethnic groups as homogeneous, publishers need to recognise that such audiences have been profoundly neglected. There is huge commercial potential in these audiences but reaching them entails publishers realising their cultural value as well as economic potential.

Selling Books by Writers of Colour

Market Concentration and the Lack of Decision-Makers

With 202,078 print books published in 2019 (Nielsen), publishers are competing for the attention of readers as well as for shelf space and bookshop support. Independent booksellers aside, most book-buying on the retail side is centralised in the UK and the buying power is in the hands of very few people. While the particular bookshops can decide what they want to stock from the central warehouse, outlets like supermarkets don't have any room for regional differentiation. As a senior white book-buyer stated, 'that level of complexity would just kill the whole system, it's just a big machine for moving books through fast and efficiently'.

The comparatively tiny number of book-buyers and the monoculturalism of the decision-makers pose an obstacle to the backing of books by 'BAME' authors, especially when assumptions about book-buyers are so narrow. As one 'BAME' respondent suspects: 'I think that because at the top level, it's quite a homogeneous group of people who kind of are the decision-makers, who sanction it, that they'll have a little bit of it'. Thus, even though there is a commercial argument, retailers don't see the opportunity and/or are content with having a token number of 'BAME' authors stocked.

In addition to the impact on what is stocked, the decision-makers in retail also have an impact on book cover design. Again, the decision-making power lies in a few hands.

> [W]e're aiming to get into Waterstones or the supermarkets and a lot of a book's [sales] success will depend on whether they get those slots or not. We have had instances where we've shown a cover to Waterstones and the Waterstones buyer didn't like it, so, we then have to change it basically, otherwise it's not going to get into the shops.
>
> (Design – senior, white female respondent)

The centralised nature of book-buying, combined with the commercial pressure booksellers reported, can lead to a concentration on a very limited range of books, i.e., books by authors who already have a positive track record or books that publishers and booksellers feel confident they know the audience for – thus perpetuating the status quo of representation.

Supermarkets

Supermarkets have the potential to reach customers in every location and social category, but they stock only a limited selection of books, i.e., bestselling titles with a great track record which are dominated by established white authors. Adding to this problem is that publishers need supermarkets because of the large volume they can sell once they choose a title. So it becomes self-perpetuating; supermarkets want to see high sales numbers before they stock a book and if they don't stock a book, it is really hard for it to reach such a wide audience.

If books by 'BAME' authors are considered 'too niche' for supermarkets and/or get packaged as literary fiction where sales figures are generally lower, conclusions might be drawn that 'BAME' books have less commercial appeal. One 'BAME' respondent calls for 'more championing of authors of colour in commercial spaces' and emphasises that as 'more authors of colour get funnelled more into literary spaces', one side effect is that 'you don't get to see huge numbers'. It becomes a perpetuating system, in particular if 'BAME' books are comped with other 'BAME' books with lower sales numbers, which again makes supermarkets less likely to stock them.

> The supermarkets are the most traditional of all the retailers out there in terms of being – not resistant to change but the commercial side of it is really the only thing that they're interested in. And so, taking risks is just not in their vocab. ... it's the Catch 22 that authors, if they're not stocked in supermarkets, aren't going to sell shitloads, which is so infuriating.
>
> (Sales – senior, white female respondent)

Online Retail

One significant gap in our research is online retail. While we did make contact with a major online retailer, we were disappointed that they declined to participate in the research. From what other respondents shared, the work with Amazon is perceived as an opportunity as well as a challenge due to ever-changing parameters, opaque processes and the fact that the company only shares a fraction of its data. As one salesperson (white female) said: 'it is a never-ending beast: Amazon will change their parameters around stuff at a drop's notice, that will completely change our metadata and how we organise stuff'.

While some respondents spoke about opportunities in digital sales channels and formats, they also emphasised that a certain level of visibility must be attained first. The main obstacle here seems to be rooted in the assumption that 'BAME' books are a riskier investment and thus often receive less publicity and marketing budget, as described in the previous section.

At the same time, direct communication with (and sales to) audiences via digital channels can avoid some of the challenges in sales/retail, as the following 'BAME' respondent explains.

> I think the digital space now gives us a great opportunity to really experiment and try new things, because we can now target more audiences. We've got the tools to do that and start through data these social media companies supply now. We can identify who is the target market, what's their behaviour and how do we connect with them ... we can start talking to them, start engaging with them, without worrying about a buyer at Tesco or a buyer at Asda.

Lack of Insight and Engagement

In sales and retail, we encountered once more the perception that books by writers of colour are seen as niche. And if the one person responsible for all buying decisions has a limited idea of their audience, writers of colour face huge obstacles. The following quote came from the editor of a book that featured a person of colour on the cover.

> There was one supermarket who told our sales director that their demographic was white working-class and therefore they saw no reason to support the book.
>
> (Editorial – senior, white male respondent)

Interestingly, the booksellers we interviewed claimed not to track the ethnicity of their customers, so the assumptions were revealed to be just that: assumptions. On the retail side, obtaining more data about the audiences' socio-economic and ethnic backgrounds might be a first step in approaching a wider audience.

On the sales side, concerns were raised that sales reps, the link between publishers and bookshops, might not be as much on-board with the diversity schemes as one would hope. One senior white woman in sales described sales reps as 'predominantly older white people' and added, 'I think perhaps it's more difficult for them to adjust to some of the initiatives that are coming through than it might be for some of my other colleagues'. And a senior white bookseller (male) called sales reps a 'slightly slow-changing breed' and expressed concern that they, the 'gatekeepers of a lot of bookstores ... are not being fed the reason why this is all important'.

White Spaces?

One challenge that brick-and-mortar bookshops face is that they can feel exclusive to non-white, non-middle-class people. Our respondents suspected the following reasons for this: what booksellers stock (i.e., highbrow books or books with predominantly white, middle-class protagonists); how the shop is designed; the location; and the staff of the bookshops (i.e., white, middle-class). Independent booksellers in particular could benefit from reflecting on how their spaces might feel exclusionary to certain demographics. Those respondents who had the closest ties with the communities they served beyond the selling of books managed to attract the most diverse audience.

When looking at booksellers, one cannot help but notice that most are white. An attitude issue was brought to our attention by a 'BAME' respondent who shared: 'I was the only person of colour in the bookshop. A colleague also referred to me once as the token and would send every person of colour my way for recommendations'. The white bookseller claimed that 'they didn't know how to recommend to people of colour', once again putting the burden on 'BAME' staff and refusing to interact with customers outside their own race/experience.

While the selection of stocked books might lead to the effect of a wider audience, independent booksellers face particular challenges when it comes to pricing. Independent booksellers reported that stocking, e.g., commercial crime fiction does not make any sense for them because of the high discounts that bigger retailers can pass on to their customers. So, in turn, the stock of the affected independent booksellers might make the shop feel less accessible; 'the highbrow-ness is another barrier for people to coming in. It's not class or money', said a 'BAME' respondent, referring in particular to how some commercial fiction is priced so low at the bigger retailers that a small independent bookseller selling at RRP (recommended retail price) cannot compete. Another white female bookseller added: 'We don't bother stocking 90% of what a supermarket does. Because they have silly prices'.

Summary

The dominance of a few retailers and the decision-making by very few people, combined with the reliance on data that is not as objective as it is often being portrayed, is seen as a major obstacle for writers of colour. In particular where so much power lies in so few hands, a more diverse team can be game-changing. The whiteness of sales, book-buying and retail spaces and personnel, or rather their unconscious bias, raises concerns as well. And while digital channels can be a way to bypass exclusive spaces and gatekeepers, more investment in publicity is needed to make 'BAME' authors and their books visible at the same time. In addition, retailers – as well as agents and publishers – need to radically rethink who they see as their audience.

Conclusion

Our research found that *writers of colour are disadvantaged during each key stage of the publishing process.* The key findings can be summed up as follows.

1. Publishers have a very narrow sense of their audience. The idea of the core reader as a white, middle-class, older woman remains dominant. There also remain suspicions over whether racial and ethnic minorities read at all, or at least to the same extent. As such we find that the core publishing industry is set up essentially to cater for this one white reader. While this does not rule out opportunities for writers from minority backgrounds, until the publishing industry diversifies its audience, writers of colour will always be 'othered'.

2. There is ambiguity around 'diversity' as *both* a moral and economic imperative. In our interviews respondents articulated strong moral/ethical and commercial cases for why the industry needs to publish more 'diversely'. However, we are not convinced that publishers really believe in the economic value of diversity. Or, more precisely, they are not convinced

that their core audience is fully interested in books by writers of colour. And as the traditional market remains very lucrative (according to Nielsen Total Consumer Market (TCM) data, the turnover for print books in 2019 was £1.67 billion), we don't believe that there is a genuine *inclination* to engage new – and more *diverse* – audiences.

3.   While publishers would like to publish more writers of colour, they believe it is too commercially risky to do so. Publishing, like all forms of cultural production, is an inherently unpredictable business. Because of the intense competition within publishing – according to Nielsen there were 202,078 print books published in the UK in 2019 – we find it mostly produces risk-averse behaviours, rather than risk-taking ones. Against this backdrop, writers of colour become seen as a particularly dangerous investment, which, as we have shown, affects not only their acquisition but how they are promoted and sold.

The fundamental challenge that publishers face when addressing diversity is the supposed dichotomy between the commercial and the cultural. All the publishers we spoke to recognise the strong cultural value of their work. Respondents gave us a very genuine sense that they care about the books they publish, in terms of how those books can enrich people's lives and what they can contribute to society. In this way, respondents spoke of publishing as almost providing a public service. But they also recognise that they are fundamentally a business and need to sell books. Indeed, sometimes they spoke of how commercial pressures prevents them from doing some of the work with writers of colour that they would love to do. But is this a given? As suggested, the main problem for publishers is that the publishing industry is geared up to cater for one (admittedly lucrative) segment of a much bigger audience. We argue that it is only when publishers rethink 'diversity', in a way that goes beyond the question of workforce composition and instead focuses on catering for the full diversity of the nation, that we will see more writers of colour published, and published well. Our hope is that the findings will encourage publishers to challenge their assumptions and reflect on their practice – and that they will help make the industry a space where writers from all backgrounds can flourish.

References

Ahmed, S. 2012. *On Being Included: Racism and Diversity in Institutional Life*. Durham, NC and London: Duke University Press.

Bhattacharyya, G. 2018. *Rethinking Racial Capitalism: Questions of Reproduction and Survival*. London: Rowman & Littlefield International.

Gray, H. 2016. 'Precarious Diversity: Representation and Demography'. In *Precarious Creativity*, edited by M. Curtin and K. Sanson, 241–253. Oakland, CA: University of California Press.

Leong, N. 2012. 'Racial Capitalism'. *Harvard Law Review*, 126 (8): 2153–2225.

Melamed, J. 2015. 'Racial Capitalism'. *Critical Ethnic Studies*, 1(1): 76–85.

Nwonka, C. J. and S. Malik. 2018. 'Cultural Discourses and Practices of Institutionalised Diversity in the UK Film Sector: "Just Get Something Black Made"'. *The Sociological Review*, 66 (6): 1111–1127.

Saha, A. 2018. *Race and the Cultural Industries*. Cambridge: Polity.

THE FUTURE OF FEMINISM

9

Exit Wounds of Feminist Theory

Sarah Cefai

The question of the 'future of feminism' calls on the reader to consider how feminism originates and then transforms. Academia is one such context for feminism's originary transformation. The future of feminism at stake in academic feminist knowledge is reason enough for the role of feminist theory to be hotly contested. The work presented in this chapter is the outcome of a longstanding enquiry into how the relationship between feminism and feeling shapes and is shaped by the institutionalisation of feminism in feminist theoretical knowledge. If the chapter has a working hypothesis, it's that the felt register of writing as a mode of feminist theory might complement the feminist poststructuralist theories that largely omitted the subject of feeling from their accounts of power, subjectivity and knowledge.

'Exit Wounds of Feminist Theory' asks how feminist theory, as affective and subjective zoning, creates the vulnerabilities of its bodies (of its writers, of its knowledges, its communities) and imperfectly defends them. Historically, writing has cultivated a 'heightened awareness of personal physical boundaries and a sense of those boundaries as the vessel of one's self' (Carson 1986, 44). If '[s]elves are crucial to writers' (1986, 41), the contemporary moment gives the obverse formulation more airplay; at stake in writing is the self and, by extension, the conventions that defend against non-sovereignty (dependency, that which threatens to overwhelm, the innervating outside). If '[w]hat is managed in an emotional experience is not an emotion but the self in the feeling that is being felt' (Denzin 1984, 50), writing is connected to feeling in the play between writing and the self. To go down into the silence and inarticulateness 'there in the deep structure' (hooks 1996, 49) is to travel down into the writing, to where what is at stake is felt, to the edging of a self, and feminist theory itself, into and out of existence. To this end, the exit wound offers an image of feminist thought that foregrounds the terms of recognition that seed feminist knowledge.

Julietta Singh describes 'the body archive' as an 'assembly of history's traces deposited in me' (2018a, 29). Here, I plumb the body archive of feminist theory by assembling its 'found exits'. Foregrounding the elsewhere, the feminist scene of exile might offer a force for assembly, which Verónica Gago defines as the *'concrete place where words cannot be detached from the body'* (2020, 161, emphasis in original). This image of feminist thought hopes to 'engender "thinking" in thought' (Deleuze 1994, 147), in feminist philosophy and politics, including the ways in which feminism is lived and understood as 'a living thing' (Wiegman 2010, 80). 'In the end', writes Singh, 'we are not bounded, contained subjects, but ones filled up with foreign feelings and vibes that linger and circulate in space, that enter us as we move through our lives. We likewise leave traces of ourselves and our own affective states (which are never really just our own) behind us when we go' (2018a, 31). 'Exit Wounds of Feminist Theory' was written with these traces, in the flight from bruised intentions. Intention means not only (1) a thing intended, and (2) conceptions formed by directing the mind towards an object, but also (3) the healing process of a wound (OED 2020).

***

All the Way Down

Go all the way down. Sink below the turbulent waters. Get under those tangled currents. Go to where the water runs still. 'That's what Sara Ahmed does', he adds. Bar talk. That was years ago now, before I stepped into her exit wound. Feminist theory is full of exit wounds – stories of leaving and being left; feminist historical aftermaths; 'feminism besides itself' (Elam and Wiegman 1995).

Sure, academic departments are bigger than the legacy of particular individuals, but places and fields of study are spun out of individual stories. They are sedimented with fleshy memories – 'atmospheres', as Ahmed herself put it (2008). Fields of knowledge and academic careers are enmeshed social realities. Consider this too as Ahmed's point; where a culture is 'built around (or to enable) abuse and harassment', the predicaments of individuals are entangled in that 'institutional culture' (2016). Individual legacies demonstrate what is possible, or necessary, in relations of power and knowledge. In other terms, there is a 'crucial difference between a field's discourse of the political and the operations of the political that constitute it' (Wiegman 2012, 17).

By her own account, Ahmed resigned from her position to protest and remove herself from a culture of harassment. Her act of leaving 'broke a seal' in the concealment of academic power: 'academics exercise power often by concealing that power' (2016). Her unsealing of concealment was also an act of amplification: one exit wound amplifying the exit wounds of others. Sound waves gain amplitude in the body of an instrument, exchanging energies of their own accord. In the body of an institution, language is an instrument of power – a performative concealment. In the body of a language, the metaphor amplifies what cannot be indexically described or spoken. In the language of feminist theory, metaphors institute modes of relation as critical entities of transformation (they are 'seal breaking').

When Gloria Anzaldúa says, 'I am my language' (2007, 81), she says, language is *a skin of feeling*, broken and forged in the exit wounds of colonialism.

> 1,950 mile-long open wound / dividing a *pueblo*, a culture, / running down the length of my body, / staking fence rods in my flesh, / splits me splits me / *me raja me raja*
>
> This is my home / this thin edge of / barbwire
>
> But the skin of the earth is seamless …
>
> The US-Mexican border *es una herida abierta* where the Third World grates against the first and bleeds
>
> (2007, 24–25)

Written in the skin of feeling, the exit wounds of feminist theory run all the way down. Go all the way down with the concept. All the way down with feeling. Ruminate on ruination. What if feminism and feminist philosophy are made in exile, out of broken feeling?

'It is because there is a direct connection between the forces and features of the earth and those that produce the body, it is because the earth is already directly inscribed contrapuntally in the body,' says Elizabeth Grosz, 'that the body can sing the earth and all its features, which both mark these features as theirs to preserve and look after, but also mark their debt to and affinity with the earth and its particular qualities' (2008, 49).[1] A molten interior is exposed on the earth's surface in just a handful of places. In Hawaii, lava tubes bleed out into the ocean. The sun is inscribed contrapuntally in the earth. A liquid sun in an exit wound universe.

The 'identification of female identity with a sort of planetary exile' has been 'a topos of feminist studies,' says Rosi Braidotti (1994, 21), since Virginia Woolf wrote: 'As a woman I have no country, as a woman I want no country, as a woman my country is the whole world' (1938 [1978], 44, cited in Braidotti 1994, 21). The question of where, how and to whom we belong might reveal our place on the outside, where the 'very longing to belong embarrasses its taken for granted nature' (Probyn 1996, 9). We might be shamed in our 'knowledge of the impossibility of ever really and truly belonging' (Probyn 1996, 8). Coupled with and felt out by structures of desire, belonging solicits our attention only to proliferate in unexpected ways and places, always marking the complex, contradictory, (extra) ordinary, intrinsic and enduring ways that we are compelled by others – by other worlds, by the interval of otherness within ourselves. Transformed by a desire, one set of terms for belonging gets sublimated or complicated by another. Desire can be relinquished, orchestrated, politicised. Equally, we usually hold fast to whatever attaches us, to our place in the world.

Judith Butler comments on the 'loyalty and aggression' that Luce Irigaray expresses towards those who taught her (Cheah et al. 1998, 19) [1]. It is through her conflict with/in the field of study that Irigaray opens up a radical practice of 'critical mimesis' [2]. As a woman, Butler says, Irigaray was 'explicitly excluded or explicitly demeaned' from within the philosophers' texts, but 'she would read them anyway' (19) [1]. So described, the closeness of Irigaray's reading can be understood in Gayatri Spivak's terms as the intimate act of translation, 'in the closest places of the self' (1993, 180). The planetary exile of feminist philosophy begins here, in the intimacy of reading from within a relation of power and its affective forces – adoration, aggression, 'eros' (Carson 1986). The mimetic concept of the feminine as a textual method of theorising sexual (in) difference is an intimate act of (dis)inheriting – phallocentrism is jettisoned from within that closest place [2]. We might conceive of the feminine thus as the exit wound of Western philosophy. Sexual difference is constructed out of the negations of Western epistemology; out of the fallout of its own sexual indifference [1+2].

We might say that:

[1] exit wounds of feminist theory are the material, symbolic, psychic, affective, ecological, historical, and other *contextual circumstances* of feminist theory; and

[2] exit wounds of feminist theory are the *concepts and affects* that feminist theory puts into the world.

Wounds in Exile

In the symbolic order of Western culture femininity is a wound (Cheah et al. 1998, 24). Moreover, Western theory is littered with wounds. They cluster especially in origin stories. Let's note, citing Donna Haraway, what Sigmund Freud saw as the 'three great historical wounds to the primary narcissism of the self-centred subject' (2008, 11).

1. The Copernican wound removed Earth itself, man's home world, from the centre of the cosmos, opening the cosmos to a universe of inhumane, nonteleological times and spaces. Science made that decentring cut.
2. The Darwinian wound put *Homo sapiens* firmly in the world of other critters, all trying to make an earthly living. Science inflicted that cruel cut too.
3. The Freudian wound posited an unconscious that undid the primacy of conscious processes, including the reason that comforted Man with his unique excellence. Science seems to hold that blade too.

To these, she adds the following.

4. The informatic or cyborgian wound that infolds organic and techno-logical flesh, melding the Great Divide of nature and society, nonhuman and human.

This time it is the blades of critical immanent theory that make the cut. These 'wounds to self-certainty' (Haraway 2008, 12) are the necessary correlates to a subject who 'tries to hold panic at bay by the fantasy of human exceptionalism' (Haraway 2008, 11).

The ontology of human exceptionalism relays back to the gradual separation of the human from the natural world. As Joanna Zylinska reminds us, 'the tragic world view' that accompanies this separation is a compensatory philosophy that expresses man's inability to come to terms with the very finitude of life with which he is preoccupied. In Zylinska's example, human exceptionalism underpins the apocalyptic narrative of the Anthropocene, yielding a 'temporarily wounded yet ultimately redeemed Man, who can conquer time and space by rising above the geological mess he has created' (Zylinska 2018). The 'planetary relocation' promised by the Anthropocene's figure of the 'exit man' recycles the tragic exceptionalism of colonialism. Man's Anthropocene is beset by the 'onto-pathology' of the settler-colonial subject whose possessive ontology is predicated upon the very indifference to (dis)possession it prefigures (Nicolacopoulos and Vassilacopoulos 2014, 15).

Rather than make this split subjectivity commensurate with women's liberation, the cut of feminist philosophy proposes an inverse relation between human exceptionalism and its own ontology of relating. 'Cutting is a feminist aesthetic proper to the project of female unbecoming', is how Jack Halberstam (2011, 135) put it. '[E]xiled from subjectivities founded on and through mastery', the itinerant feminist seeks out 'a radical dwelling in and with dehumanization through the narrative excesses and insufficiencies of the "good" human' (Singh 2018b, 4). That is, s/he undoes their subjectivation and what appears to be taken for granted in the present. 'I also like the pastoral of self-loss on behalf of a nonrepetition of the world as it presents itself', reflects Lauren Berlant (2009, 684). Feminist pedagogy encounters the question of what falls away over time; how the feminist subject is cut as both person and field of knowledge; how to track the differences made by feminist movement; how to register and harness the intensities and vibrations of feminisms that transport worlds.

Feminist theory made itself 'smart' by rejecting socially and biologically determinate narratives that not only oppress women (Wilson 2015, 30) but exemplify the stupidity and violence of an illusory 'unity, mastery, [and] self-transparence' (Braidotti 1994, 12). Feminism claims an alternate subjectivity, but what about the mastery of its discourse? How does feminist mastery relate to the negativity 'intrinsic (rather than antagonistic) to sociality and subjectivity' (Wilson 2015, 6)? Despite the self-referentiality of a feminism 'increasingly anxious about itself' (Elam and Wiegman 1995, 2), feminist theory seems to rarely admit its aggressive investments in 'the subject' (Huffer 2016). All-too-true tropes of 'female antagonism' and 'generational envy' (Ngai 2005) crowd out other stories. Paying 'more attention to the destructive and damaging aspects of politics that cannot be repurposed to good ends' (Wilson 2015, 6) calls on us to adjust the optimism of feminist theory to emergent modes on the periphery of the 'good' human. On the periphery, 'a text's contradictions, ruptures, and non-coherences could be more important to a reading than its apparent seamlessness' (Brinkema 2014, 42, discussing Roland Barthes). Excess is surely feminist philosophy's primal scene. Just look at how Haraway's more-than-feminist discourse rolls like a tumbleweed, picking up dust and critters, scrambling form and content, methodology and philosophy. Composed of images that are loaded with sensation, the feminist

cyborg conducts immaterial forces through the milieu of its allegory. The speculative, textual and technological figuration of the cyborg bears witness to the *still-
unfolding event of feminist philosophy*.

The Intimacy of Feminist Epistemology

The history of the present of feminist theory reflects what might be called the
'sociology of feminist knowledge' or the 'epistemological turn' in feminist
thinking. Problems of knowledge pivotal to the Second Wave – 'a monolithic
social movement ... in fact made up of many tiny, unevenly connected groups'
(McKinney 2020, 8) – were translated into theoretical problems with disciplinary
prerogatives.

Feminist thought, social relations and affects entered the disciplines that in
turn entered feminism. The articulation of the crisis of the legitimacy of feminism
as a crisis of epistemic position is a manifestation of this translation. However,
as Linda Zerilli notes (discussing Hannah Arendt), politics can't be reduced
to 'the contest of better arguments' (2005, 3). Rather, politics come out of 'our
deep sense of necessity in human affairs' (2005, 3). This necessity suggests more
socially embedded and multiply indeterminate points of origin compared with,
say, the utility of feminist concepts vis-à-vis the problems of jurisprudence.
Insofar as social bonds also stem from an indeterminate necessity, feminist politics and sociality are symbiotic. This is why feminism can be described as 'a living
thing' (Wiegman 2010, 80). So, while feminist concepts are in evidence according
to the sociological facts that they help frame (such as violence against women),
the necessity of feminist politics is also felt out 'in the images and figures that
generate belief' (Zerilli 2005, 10). This can be a good thing, if we consider how
the examples of 'feminist achievement, once plotted as a future destination' have
produced 'disappointment in the emergency of a present of which it could never
have conceived' (Wiegman 2010, 81).

'Translation', urged Spivak, 'is the most intimate act of reading' (1993, 180).
'The translator earns permission to transgress from the trace of the other – before
memory – in the closet places of the self'. Feminist theory is an institutional culture
of knowledge, social structure and language, lived with its own desire that, like all
desires, 'evades us in the very act of propelling us forth' (Braidotti 1994, 14). The
nomadic language of poststructuralist feminist philosophy can be experienced
intimately as one's 'own way of being' (Braidotti 1994, 12). We find the intimacy

of feminist theory in the act of its translation if, as Spivak put it, we sometimes prefer 'to speak in it about intimate things' (4, 180). To speak in the language of feminist theory is to transgress from the trace of the other in the self, from the relation between desire and difference, from the ways in which language has been lived by others. From this trace, feminist theory provides a holding space for the intimacy of 'opening up the world that has been disclosed to us through language' (Zerilli 2005, 9).

In the course of an interview Elizabeth Povinelli relays her admission that she has 'kind of stubbornly refused to say how [her] work relates to feminism' (Povinelli and DiFruscia 2012, 80). By way of an explanation, she says: 'when I think about what organizes, disorganizes and distributes power and difference then I am led to a set of more intractable issues, below a certain field of visibility as defined by identity categories. And these issues cut across liberal forms of intimacies, the market and politics'. Rather than view this position as manifesting the exhaustion of feminist concepts, we might think of it as an expression of *the necessity of feminist politics* – evidence of the way in which feminist concepts are not limited to the epistemological guidance of an established feminist theory or perspective (i.e., the application of feminist concepts *as* feminist concepts), but proper to the emergent character of the political (in Michel Foucault's terms, to the question of 'how to live otherwise'). The feminist concept belongs to a feminist theory that belongs to a feminist politics – a site of emergence, which means related to what is recognisably feminist but also not overdertermined by it. In the USA and beyond, the pedagogical 'yearning for definitive theories of women's oppression and for prescriptivism in feminist theory' (Zerilli 2012, n.p.) is pegged to the promise of feminist knowledge despite the challenges of its institutionalisation. Feminism traffics the longing to belong but also conjunctural forces steadfast in their repurposing of whatever it is that feminism brings into the world.

An immanent view would tend to the varieties of feminist thought, including ones that aren't recognisably feminist as such; to feminist concepts that are antecedent, larval, not-yet-thought, '*incorporeals*, potentials, latencies' (Grosz 2011, 78). In an international or 'globalised' feminist classroom, this is an important pedagogical point. National, technological and cultural imperialisms traverse the classroom but do not extinguish the common ground felt out by students, that offers a different order of 'thought' from that which is openly deliberated. We might yet think of feminist concepts as felt out by a structure of feeling that registers the 'constitutive differences within what we might call the force field of feminism' (Wiegman 2010, 84).

The interventions of twentieth-century feminists cannot be repeated: the inaugural critiques of sexual (in)difference, objectivity, the mind–body dualism and the specific yet broad spectrum interjections of feminist poststructuralism and intersectionality were crystalline. We learn so much of what we need to from this earlier moment, and yet there is still so much we need to learn. Feminist concepts aren't taxonomic according to the determinations of institutionalised knowledge, but must 'innovate' new meanings if they are in some way to speak to the present: 'you have to get it from the times rather than just from the text' (The Brooklyn Rail 2020). The task of translation is one of staying with this desire to learn from a historical moment without (re)producing its mastery.

Another way to phrase this is, insofar as feminist concepts place us in between languages, in the space-times of linguistic histories, and therefore in the political, they foreground 'the affective level as the resting point' of feminist theory. Braidotti interprets this as an abandonment of the 'triumphant cogito' in exchange for a 'trust in traces' (1994, 14). 'This is not idle fantasy', wrote Audre Lorde, 'but a disciplined attention to the true meaning of "it feels right to me"' (1984, 37). Here, concepts make themselves known *as the condition of possibility for feeling*; the feminist concept is not primarily an interpretive back-formation, but an intuition that aligns feeling to a sensibility ('it feels *right*' / 'it *feels* right'). A feminist concept can be 'already felt' (Lorde 1984, 36). Following Trinh T. Minh-ha, we might say that feeling takes form in the language of feminist theory *intransitively*.

> To write is to become. Not to become a writer (or a poet), but to become, intransitively. Not when writing adopts established keynotes or policy, but when it traces for itself lines of evasion.
>
> (1989, 18–19)

The immanent and social character of feminist worldbuilding is not sublimated by the dialectical terms of knowledge, of making a 'better argument' (Zerilli 2005). The metaphor, the theoretical text, the classroom debate are each made possible by and are sustaining of *feminist intransitive affect*. With Gago, we might reconceive the excess of feminist theory as *feminist potencia* – a 'desiring capacity' where desire is 'the force that drives what is perceived as possible, collectively and in each body' (2020, 3).

Your Contingent Foundations Are My Exit Wounds

Emotion has long been the terrain of feminist politics. Feminist consciousness raising hones in on the control that 'phallist' men exercise by determining the terms in which women interpret and therefore come to experience what gets felt as real through their own 'refusal to experience women as persons' (Frye 1983, 47). The patriarchal denigration of emotion produces and at the same time dismisses subjugated realities. Feminist theory also recognises emotion as a mobilising force within feminism and as a condition of possibility of feminist knowledge (e.g., Jaggar 1989; Spellman 1989). Simone de Beauvoir linked the hierarchical opposition between reason and emotion to sex (in the Anglo-American discourse, more often now 'gender'); the ability of certain men to dominate relied upon the gendering of the universal powers of abstraction masculine/male. In turn, the ideological construct of woman was a means to '[s]hut [women] up'/'[s]hut up [women]' 'in the sphere of the relative' (1997 [1949], 652). That is, via that unstable nexus of sex and/or gender, attachment is emotionally and psychically differentiated: 'The word *love* has by no means the same sense for both sexes' (1997 [1949], 652). This differentiation has been a key concern for feminism all the way through feminist philosophy and psychoanalysis, from Nancy Chodorow to Lauren Berlant. It was Betty Friedan's *The Feminine Mystique* that 'captured the early feminist imaginary' through its expression of and resolution to women's suffering (Zerilli 2012). As Zerilli synopsises, 'Friedan's feminist message was: Get out of the house and get a job. (Or, more precisely, Get a cleaning lady so that you can get out and get a job)'. Comparatively, Beauvoir was far more ambivalent, 'deeply sceptical of any such pragmatic approach to the vicissitudes of feminine subjectivity'.

Such feminist reflections on emotional subjectivity, on 'what feels right to me' (Lorde 1984, 37), invoke the politics of experience. Emphasis on the psychic, ideological and discursive terms of experience – including the experience of the critic – has often overlooked the significance of feeling to how such terms take effect. For instance, while in many ways Joan Scott's (1992) defence of poststructuralist feminism against 'the evidence of "experience"' (1992, 24) couldn't be more pertinent to contemporary feminist debates, her critique of experience 'conceived through a metaphor of visibility or in any other way that takes meaning as transparent' (1992, 25) was an insufficient means of locating feminist politics in the field of experience, i.e., the subsumption of discourse within the political. As a postgraduate student of gender studies, I wondered why, in spite of such faithful readings of Foucault by Scott and her contemporaries, no one seemed very interested to observe feeling as 'the truth of the self'.[2] Surely, the repeat experience of an asymmetrical emotion was a 'truth effect' of gender normatively conceived? Surely, what singularised 'confession' as a flashpoint in subjectivation was people's capacity to emote in a relation of power, revealing in turn the investment of power in an emotion? Surely, any feminist theory of representation, subjectivity and power is impoverished by a lack of a theory of feeling? Wasn't a feminist poststructuralist philosophy of subjectivity without a theory of feeling a contradiction in terms?[3]

Emotion might have been denigrated by those feminist theorists claiming rationality for women – the denigration of feeling 'emotional' at a certain moment might have made feminism 'smart', to use Wilson's (2015) term. However, just because feeling made a 'bad' object choice for a feminist theorist doesn't mean it doesn't come to pass. What was decided in the poststructuralist feminist moment in particular was not only the substantive content of how questions of 'autonomy, agency, and freedom' would be linked to a certain theorisation of subjectivity and identity (Grosz 2011, 59), but how emotion would be subsumed within or subtracted out of this process. But there's a catch. Given the very relationship between feminist theory's core business of theorising autonomy, agency and freedom, and the *concept of feeling that exists in the world*, sentience could not be expunged completely from feminist theoretical discourse.

As the feminist academic subject becomes a zone for the lived intensities of the experiential, the authorial and other passionate placeholders for 'the truth of the self', as well as for a professionalised subject tasked with self-abnegation in the interests of 'the work', the more embarrassing, 'ugly' (Ngai 2005) and otherwise compromising affects are placed in feminist theory's own 'space-off' – 'the space not visible in the frame but inferable from what the frame makes visible' (de Lauretis 1987, 26). In the aftermath of feminism's promise, intransitive feminist affect might become overwhelmingly negative and given to defensiveness. It is precisely the affective structure of defence that Jennifer Nash (2019) links to the felt experience of contemporary black feminism. Defensiveness is how black feminists 'hold on' to a political project while the terms of intersectionality are distorted by their visibility – 'black feminist defensiveness [is] a political response to ongoing violence' (2019, 3). For it is not just Martha Nussbaum's feminism that promises 'we can travel from being made by the world we seek to change to being able to change it' (Wiegman 2010, 81). This promise is ubiquitous to an assumed feminist subject, there in the writing we make, there in the way that the 'ethical and the professional meet in the nervous system in raw-making and destabilizing ways' (Berlant 2009, 136).

Feminist thought emerged interstitially in the 'non-coincidence of woman (as masculinist representation) and women (as social, historical subjects)' (Zerilli 2012). As such, feminist subjectivity appears in the 'movement back and forth between the representation of gender (in its male-centred frame of reference) and what that representation leaves out or, more pointedly, makes unrepresentable' (de Lauretis 1987, 26). Feminist theory is located in that innervating difference from the outside, with one eye turned towards how feminist epistemology contours and gives expression to 'the gestural force that opens experience to its potential variation' (Manning 2016, 1), and the other to what might yet be invoked. Strictly speaking, of course, a feminist thought can't feel a thing. But if, like Grosz, we think of concepts as 'ontological conditions rather than moral ideals' (2011, 59), we might further open feminist theory to its own becoming. The expansion of a feminist present might be less a matter of valorising subjugated knowledges, and more one of inventing new ways to discern the transversal gestural force of the feminist concept. As well as thinking of *feeling as an ontological condition of feminism*, which is the revisionist history/history of the present of feminist theory concurrent with feminism's affective turn, we might also conceptualise *feminist theory as an ontological condition of feeling*. We might read and write for the way that concepts of feeling line the body that feels and the body that thinks in the space-off of feminist theory – in the closest places of the self.

After the Exit

Reading Beauvoir for the first time, Butler writes: 'social constraints upon gender compliance and deviation are so great that most people feel deeply wounded if they are told that they are not really manly or womanly, that they have failed to execute their manhood or womanhood properly' (1986, 41). The painfulness of misrecognition and the woundedness of being on the outside never stopped being the subject of Butler's discourse. Although she rarely herself tells us how it feels, her analysis galvanises a register of vulnerability. We find vulnerability too in Spivak's appeal to our humility, when she writes: 'Unless the translator has earned the right to become the intimate reader, she cannot surrender to the text, cannot respond to the special call of the text' (1993, 181). To what or whom does one surrender when one translates? To what or whom is one indebted? What does one give? We might reformulate Foucault thus: what is this specific vulnerability that emerges from feminist theory and nowhere else?[4]

First I thought, being cut from the cloth of feminist theory made me vulnerable to the operations of the political that constitute the field. 'You need to get over your pain', was the last I heard. I was cut, then cut off – from language, from a way of relating to a world. I didn't 'get over' the pain. We take our cuts with us. If you have been blacklisted, gather your outsides. First I thought, the exit wounds of feminist theory are nothing but bitterness and bruised aspirations. Only someone with recourse to the fantasy of self-mastery thinks that they can take their language with them when they leave.

Second I thought, feminist philosophy has no predetermined horizons or frontiers.[5] If the very ground of feminist philosophy, like that of sexual difference, 'cannot appear in its own terms' (Grosz 1994, 209), a kernel of 'pure difference' must line feminist thought (1994, 208). Feminist philosophy is not the province of a masterful subjectivity. 'The only horizon that matters is our optimism for an idea' (Bernard Center for Research on Women 2011). Second I thought, the exit wound is a force for recalibration. A reminder of the feminist epistemological investment in the fact that 'we do not know what we're capable of until we experience the displacement of the limits that we've been made to believe and obey' (Gago 2020, 2). A reminder of how feminist thought is located in the body. 'The experience of thinking together is felt in the body as the potencia of an idea' (2020, 155). We have to be transformed by our experience of an idea for a 'particular affect to take on a political dimension' (2020, 164; also, Bernard Center for Research on Women 2011).

In the exit wounds of feminist theory you won't find your voice in the shelter of self-possession. Literacy shut off the 'open conduits' of the senses, the 'continuous interaction' linking you to the world (Carson 1986, 43). In the exit wounds of feminist theory, redirect your literacy to the outside, to sense and sensation. Stand in the doorway as long as you can, as you look for 'the possibility of a world that you can trust with your non-sovereignty, with your dependence on other people' (Bernard Center for Research on Women 2011). Look for openings in structures of feeling whose elements and rhythms contain 'specific kinds of sociality' not yet formally recognised (Williams 1977, 133).

I still think that feminist theory has its own subordinated, negative and excluded terms. The cut of the personal is a cut above the rest. The personal cuts the deepest.

The exit wound might be feminist theory's own limit-attitude.[6] Consider Irigaray's 'lips', Butler's 'drag', Braidotti's 'nomad'.[7] In the exit wounds of feminist theory, move on from a dialectical and identificatory morality – beyond bifurcation. The feminist cyborg tracks her own space-off.

Forks in the road carry me backwards. You'll never catch up to the present; the world's moved on by the time you face forward. Find your future in the rear-view mirror. 'The extraordinary always turns out to be an amplification of something in the works, a labile boundary at best, not a slammed-door departure' (Berlant 2011, 10). '[N]o turning away is valid once and for all' (Deleuze and Guattari 1994, 96). In the exit wounds of feminist theory, feelings permeate and permutate. A thousand tiny feminist feelings, or none. The exit wound is the mess made by the object as it leaves the body. Broken attachments scatter into the headwind.

Feminist theory owes a debt of gratitude to all the expressive modes that get deducted from the equation of its origins. In the exit wounds of feminist theory, look for singing: more joy. Don't index truth to feeling *as if a feeling could be felt without its concept; as if there is no thought to feminist sensation.*

With the trace of the other, take a journey from a feminist thought made possible by feeling, to a feminist thought that feels. Go down in this writing to where its long arc of failure creeps, to its many troubled entrails. Claw back 'the fragment over any fantasy of future wholeness' (Halberstam 2011, 138). Find the stillness in 'the desire to change everything' (Gago 2020, 3). Go down to the feminist concept as 'wayward sibling', 'provoked by art and sharing the same enticements for the emergence of innovation and invention' (Grosz 2008, 2). In the exit wounds of feminist theory, in the 'poetic, rhetorical, and world-creating capacity of language' (Zerilli 2005, 9), get out of your habits of perception and into the conditions of creation (Smith and Protevi 2008). Find your wild tongue. Once more with feeling, let all your exit routes catch up with you.

Postscript

It is 28 June 2021 and Lauren Berlant has died. This essay began in the early 2000s as a master's dissertation on feminism and feeling – and I didn't understand Lauren's work back then. In the time since, I have lived with their intimate thinking, growing incrementally closer to understanding what they were giving. Lauren leaves a gargantuan hole, an incomparable exit wound, an immeasurable loss. We will always be catching up to what they left behind. In this exit wound, in the horizon of their writing, of their power to transform us, we love and find love. Not all that is crystalline has come to pass.

Acknowledgements

Thank you to Gregory Seigworth and Joanna Zylinska for being readers. I also want to express my gratitude to the colleagues who co-teach and the students who take with me the class in Contemporary Feminist Media Cultures in the Department of Media, Communications and Cultural Studies at Goldsmiths.

References

Ahmed, S. 2008. 'Multiculturalism and the Promise of Happiness'. *New Formations* 63: 121–137.

Ahmed, S. 2016. 'Resignation is a Feminist Issue'. Blog post, 27 August. Available at: https://feministkilljoys.com/2016/08/27/resignation-is-a-feminist-issue/.

Anzaldúa, G. 2007. *Borderlands/La Frontera: The New Mestiza*, 3rd edn. San Francisco, CA: Aunt Lute Books.

Beauvoir, S. 1997. *The Second Sex*. London: Vintage.

Berlant, L. 2009. 'Affect is the New Trauma'. *Minnesota Review* 71/72: 131–136.

Berlant, L. 2011. *Cruel Optimism*. Durham, NC and London: Duke University Press.

Bernard Center for Research on Women. 2011. 'Public Feelings Salon with Lauren Berlant'. YouTube, 10 May. Available at www.youtube.com/watch?v=rlOeWTa_M0U.

Braidotti, R. 1994. *Nomadic Subjects: Embodiment and Sexual Difference in Contemporary Feminist Theory*. New York: Columbia University Press.

Brinkema, E. 2014. *The Forms of the Affects*. Durham, NC and London: Duke University Press.

Butler, J. 1990. *Gender Trouble: Feminism and the Subversion of Identity*. New York and London: Routledge.

Butler, J. 1986. 'Sex and Gender in Simone de Beauvoir's *Second Sex*'. *Yale French Studies* 72: 35–49.

Carson, A. 1986. *Eros the Bittersweet: An Essay*. Princeton, NJ: Princeton University Press.

Cheah, P., E. Grosz, J. Butler and D. Cornell. 1998. 'The Future of Sexual Difference: An Interview with Judith Butler and Drucilla Cornell'. *Diacritics* 28(1): 19–42.

De Lauretis, T. 1987. *Technologies of Gender: Essays on Theory, Film and Fiction*. Bloomington, IN: Indiana University Press.

Deleuze, G. 1994. *Difference and Repetition* Trans. P. Patton. New York: Columbia University Press.

Denzin, N. K. 1984. *On Understanding Emotion*. San Francisco, CA: Jossey-Bass.

Elam, D. and R. Wiegman (eds). 1995. *Feminism Beside Itself*. New York and London: Routledge.

Foucault, M. 1988. *Politics, Philosophy, Culture: Interviews and Other Writings 1977–1984*, edited by Lawrence D. Kritzman. Translated by A. Sheridan and others. London and New York: Routledge.

Foucault, M. 2002. *The Archaeology of Knowledge*. Translated by A. M. Sheridan Smith. London and New York: Routledge.

Frye, M. 1983. *The Politics of Reality: Essays in Feminist Theory*. Trumansburg, NY: Crossing Press.

Gago, V. 2020. *Feminist International: How to Change Everything*. London and New York: Verso.

Grosz, E. 2011. *Becoming Undone: Darwinian Reflections of Life, Politics and Art*. Durham, NC and London: Duke University Press.

Grosz, E. 2008. *Chaos, Territory, Art: Deleuze and the Framing of the Earth*. New York: Columbia University Press.

Grosz, E. 1994. *Volatile Bodies: Toward a Corporeal Feminism*. Bloomington and Indianapolis, IN: Indiana University Press.

Halberstam, J. 2011. *The Queer Art of Failure*. Durham, NC and London: Duke University Press.

Haraway, J. D. 2008. *When Species Meet*. Minneapolis and London, IN: University of Minnesota Press.

hooks, b. 1996. 'Choosing the Margin as a Space of Radical Openness'. In *Women, Knowledge, and Reality: Explorations in Feminist Philosophy*, edited by A. Garry and M. Pearsall, 48–55. London and New York: Routledge.

Huffer, L. 2016. 'Lipwork'. *Differences: A Journal of Feminist Cultural Studies* 27(5): 93–105.

Jaggar, A. M. 1989. 'Love and Knowledge: Emotion in Feminist Epistemology'. In *Women, Knowledge, and Reality: Explorations in Feminist Philosophy*, edited by A. Garry and M. Pearsall, 129–155. London and New York: Routledge.

Lorde, A. 1984. *Sister Outsider: Essays and Speeches*. Freedom, CA: The Crossing Press.

Manning, E. 2016. *The Minor Gesture*. Durham, NC: Duke University Press.

Nash, J. C. 2019. *Black Feminism Reimagined: After Intersectionality*. Durham, NC and London: Duke University Press.

McKinney, C. 2020. *Information Activism: A Queer History of Lesbian Media Technologies*. Durham, NC and London: Duke University Press.

Ngai, S. 2005. *Ugly Feelings*. Cambridge, MA and London: Harvard University Press.

Nicolacopoulos, T. and G. Vassilacopoulos. 2014. *Indigenous Sovereignty and the Being of the Occupier: Manifesto for a White Australian Philosophy of Origins*. Melbourne, VA: Re. press.

Povinelli, E. A. 2018. 'Horizons and Frontiers, Late Liberal Territoriality, and Toxic Habits'. *e – flux* 90(April). www.e-flux.com/journal/90/191186/horizons-and-frontiers-late-liberal-territoriality-and-toxic-habitats/.

Povinelli, E. A. and K. T. DiFruscia. 2012. 'A Conversation with Elizabeth A. Povinelli'. *Trans-Scripts* 2: 76–90.

Probyn, E. 1996. *Outside Belongings*. London and New York: Routledge.

Scott, J. W. 1992. 'Experience'. In *Feminists Theorize the Political*, edited by J. Butler and J. W. Scott, 22–40. New York and London: Routledge.

Singh, J. 2018a. *No Archive Will Restore You*. Brooklyn, NY: Punctum Books.

Singh, J. 2018b. *Unthinking Mastery: Dehumanism and Decolonial Entanglements*. Durham, NC and London: Duke University Press.

Smith, D. and J. Protevi. 2008. 'Gilles Deleuze'. In *Stanford Encyclopedia of Philosophy* (Spring 2020 Edition), edited by E. N. Zalta. Stanford, CA: Metaphysics Research Lab, Center for the Study of Language and Information, Stanford University.

Spellman, E. 1989. 'Anger and Insubordination'. In *Women, Knowledge, and Reality: Explorations in Feminist Philosophy*, edited by A. Garry and M. Pearsall, 263–273. London and New York: Routledge.

Spivak, G. C. 1993. 'The Politics of Translation'. In *Outside in the Teaching Machine*, 179–200. London and New York: Routledge.

Terada, R. 2001. *Feeling in Theory: Emotion after the 'Death of the Subject'*. Cambridge, MA: Harvard University Press.

The Brooklyn Rail. 2020. 'McKenzie Wark with John Capetta: New Social Environment #8'. YouTube, 26 March. Available at: www.youtube.com/watch?v=ex59SJJw6Bs.

Trinh, T. M. 1989. *Woman, Native, Other: Writing Postcoloniality and Feminism*. Bloomington, IN: Indiana University Press.

Wiegman, R. 2010. 'The Intimacy of Critique: Ruminations on Feminism as a Living Thing'. *Feminist Theory*, 11(1): 79–84.

Wiegman, R. 2012. *Object Lessons*. Durham, NC and London: Duke University Press.

Williams, R. 1977. 'Structures of Feeling'. In *Marxism and Literature*, 128–135. Oxford and New York: Oxford University Press.

Wilson, E. A. 2015. *Gut Feminism*. Durham, NC and London: Duke University Press.

Wolf, V. 1938 [1978]. *Three Guineas*. London: Penguin.

Zerilli, L. M. G. 2005. '"We Feel our Freedom": Imagination and Judgement in the Thought of Hannah Arendt'. *Political Theory* 20(10): 1–31.

Zerilli, L. M. G. 2012. 'Feminist Theory without Solace: Simone de Beauvoir'. *Theory & Event* 15(2). https://muse.jhu.edu/article/478360.

Zylinska, J. 2018. *The End of Man: A Feminist Counterapocalypse*. Minneapolis, MN: University of Minnesota Press.

THE FUTURE OF QUEER MEDIA

10

Queerama: Re-Imagining Queer Pasts and Futures

Daisy Asquith

Queerama is a queer film we felt; not just in the stories and images that it shares, but in the way that it weaves them together, playfully, knowingly, and emotionally. It moves between celebrating the strength, endurance and power of queer lives, and marking the scars, transgressions and cruelties experienced by them. It's a fitting way to map queer history. For queer history is sometimes the history of not being seen, or of having to work really hard to find yourself acknowledged. To write a queer history of queer lives you have to work really hard with what you are given. These glimpses show us more than the dead bodies, murder victims, blackmailers and serial killers but also put us in our place. *Queerama* for me was the story of how we find ourselves ... from sin, to illness, to dissidents, legislated and defined from above, diagnosed by sexologists, feared for contagion, dissected like a guinea pig, squeezed through the cracks.

Professor Lucy Robinson at the Queer History Workshop, Goldsmiths, 2019

All we are allowed to imagine is barely surviving in the present.

José Esteban Muñoz, 2009

Making *Queerama*

Making a film called *Queerama* felt like a rare, joyous and dangerous opportunity to me, whereby a queer history could be rewritten and thereby a queer future reimagined. In 2017, when the British media industry was compelled to commemorate the 50th anniversary of the partial decriminalisation of homosexuality, a special moment arose in which I could make this film. I pitched the idea of a feature-length montage film made entirely of LGBTQI+ representations on screen to the British Film Institute. The pitch was successful and the BBC then came in to provide the other half of the budget. This commission felt like more privilege and platform than my filmmaking career had previously offered. The 20 years of making documentaries for television had been characterised by the rejection of 80% of my ideas, and 99% of my queer ideas. Suddenly the cultural moment was offering me a chance to build a talented queer team, rewrite our queer story, reach a mainstream audience. I was not blind to the danger of this – representing an entire community according to the way one filmmaker sees them/ us is dangerous. I learnt this lesson in 2013, when I merrily queered a very straight commission about fans of the boy band One Direction, to the horror of a large part of their fandom. Platforming homoerotic fan art and fiction in my documentary *Crazy About One Direction* (Channel 4, 2013) caused a Twitter rage storm bigger than any British television show had ever received at the time (Asquith 2016, 79). It was predominantly fuelled by teenage girls in conservative US states who were intent on slamming the closet door on Harry Styles by way of death threats to the 'sick' documentary maker. I knew keenly that attempting to represent every letter in LGBTQI+ (and not forgetting the plus), while engaging my subjectivity and cre- ativity, was going to be extremely challenging. But the compulsion to try and take back ownership of, rewrite and reimagine a queer history, or a history for queers, made the risk worthwhile.

Uncovering the roots of queer desire and queer community has been a largely frustrating and deceptive experience for LGBTQI+ both theory and practice researchers, who find precious little evidence, beyond the legal and medical, of our existence in the past. Cinema and television representations of non-heterosexual and non-binary-gendered experiences in sex and love before the partial decriminalisation of homosexuality in 1967 were overwhelmingly characterised by death, mental illness, sin and imprisonment. A handful of brave filmmakers persisted in giving voice to their queer desires, almost always in a coded, fictional, undercover signal only meant to be received by those 'in the know' (see Dyer 1990; Medhurst 2006; Doty 1993). But queer lives have always been lived, whether visible or not, and their lack of past representation is a pol- itical problem that requires resolution in order to avoid slippage in the human rights that have been hard-won since Stonewall.

The temporal turn in recent queer theory rejects the idea of linear pro- gress and simplistic notions of queer lived experience. Queer theorists such as Dinshaw (2007), Muñoz (2009), Ahmed (2010a), Freeman (2010), Halberstam

(2011), Berlant (2011) and Monaghan (2016) have done important work on the rejection of heteronormative life narratives to make space for a resistant story about queer love, queer success and queer happiness that will fill the gaps in history for future readers. Linear heteronormative temporality, full of 'rites of passage' such as marriage and procreation, 'makes queers think that both the past and future do not belong to them' (Muñoz 2009, 112). Our story told as one of victimhood, illness, violence and secrecy does not make for a solid foundation on which to build our psychological futures. The erasure of our love, sexual desire, creativity, vulnerability, care and courage leaves a damaging void. As Dinshaw writes, there is understandably 'a queer desire for history' (2007, 178). As a documentary practitioner I see my contribution to this labour as providing a nuanced queer history on screen, one that embraces our 'strange temporalities, imaginative life schedules, and eccentric economic practices' (Halberstam 2005, 1) in place of the othered, legislated and diagnosed. If our story can be corrected and complicated, perhaps a new queer generation can stop 'growing sideways' (Stockton 2009) and 'explode the categories of sameness, otherness, present, past, loss, pleasure' (Dinshaw 2007, 2) – to be replaced by a new queer optimism for the future.

Queering the Archive

The LGBTQI+ strand in the BFI National Archive has been lovingly curated by archivist Simon McCallum for many years, and includes everything from famous, iconic films to never-seen-before Super 8 salvaged from the attic of an activist. Just under 100 British films with some kind of queer subject matter, methodology or resonance were chosen by our team: the filmmakers Mike Nicholls (*Culture Club: Karma to Calamity* 2014; *Uncle David* 2010) and Campbell X (*Stud Life* 2012; *Desire* 2017; *Visible* 2019), the historian Professor Lucy Robinson at the University of Sussex and myself as director. The final choice was an eclectic mixture of British fiction, documentary, news, amateur film and home video that spanned almost a century. Theoretical works on specifically queer screen representations by Russo (1987), Dyer (1990), Weiss (1996), Doty (2000), Gardiner (2003) and Medhurst (2006) permeated the production process, giving us insight into what to see and how to look so that the film was queer in both content and methodology. The way in which the film was made echoed queer cultural practices at every stage: collaborative, playful, experimental and subversive. The team was vitally enhanced by difference, allowing a range of voices to be given a mouthpiece by the curating and editing process. Intersections of queerness with race, class, gender, age and ability were central for us all as researchers. We looked for queerness in both content and form. The films broadly fell into three categories eventually: the overtly queer, the subtextually queer and the unintentionally queer. All were considered equally valid, as my favourite queer comedian David Hoyle would say with his trademark camp sincerity (Butt 2013).

A virtue was made of the financial constraints preventing some of the more famous queer screen moments being given their place; those things that were read or felt as queer, decoded as such, or even subversively queered by us as producers rose to the task of filling some of the gaps in our history. The subtextual stuff has a special place in my heart, because of the vivid sense it gives of the creativity necessary for queer survival throughout the twentieth century: planting and seeking out the codes; uncovering, imagining, concealing, conspiring and loving each other, despite everything.

Early Queer Courage on Film

The first ever acknowledged example of any sympathy for homosexuality on film was not British-made and could not therefore be included in *Queerama*; however, it inspired our awe in its courage, so I will mention it. *Anders als die Andern* (*Different from the Others*) was made in 1919 by the German psychologist Magnus Hirschfeld, funded by his Institute for Sexual Science. He had been angered by the trial of Oscar Wilde and the hostile climate at that time led him to estimate that a quarter of gay men had attempted suicide. His institute also embraced non-binary gender expression and became a refuge for those disowned by their families. Hirschfeld claimed homosexuality 'was part of the plan of nature and creation, just like normal love' (Hirschfeld 1919). At the time it was highly controversial and the *Vossische Zeitung* newspaper described him as 'a freak who acted for freaks in the name of pseudoscience'. The film was made as a protest and campaigning tool, a full half-century before there was a movement for LGBTQI+ rights. Conservative Christians counter-protested, disturbing the public screenings. In response the Weimar government created a new censorship law which enabled the authorities to ban any film they considered 'obscene or dangerous to young people'. *Anders als die Andern* was banned in October 1920 and when the Nazis took power they destroyed all but one of the 40 copies in existence. The fragments that are left were tracked down and made available by UCLA in 2011. Many representations of homosexuality today are more cliched. The film is a black-and-white warning that progress isn't linear, and it heavily influenced the decision to cut *Queerama* around the themes and feelings of queer experience rather than give it a chronological 'progress' narrative that would give rights and laws more weight than they actually have in everyday queer lives.

British queer film representations lagged far behind *Anders als die Andern*, and many of the films included in *Queerama* from the first half of the twentieth century are there for reasons of camp humour on the part of our team. There are a handful of Topical Budget films from the first decade and World War I years, which took our queer fancy due to the accidentally homoerotic footage of gender-segregated soldiers exercising and bedding down together, or wrestling over a football. Drag appears quite happily early in the century as entertainment, and the physical content between same-gender friends seems to raise no suspicion. The 1926 demonstration of *Jiu Jitsu for Ladies* was a joyous find. The clear butchness of the teacher and the thrill of her student as she is flung onto a mattress is unmistakable. Many of these films can be happily queered by the eye of a viewer a century later, but it isn't that simple. Just as queer media theory has brilliantly inspired us to uncover these queer moments hiding in plain sight, we can also decode the meanings that weren't intended. We decided as a team early on in our research process that if something felt queer to us, then it probably was. And if it wasn't intentional, the affect was queer and that was all that mattered.

Camp and Drag

The 1930s offered us some more self-awareness on the subject of gender at least, with musical films like *Say It with Flowers* (1934) clearly featuring queer and genderqueer characters, albeit as the butt of the main characters' jokes. *Sweet Adeline* (1934), *First a Girl* (1935) and *Girls Will Be Boys* (1937) all play around with drag and allow their characters to pass effectively as the opposite gender. It always causes shock when the secret is discovered, and even if it isn't always related to sexuality, it provided us with some gorgeous imagery. Its reviewer was not impressed, however, in one 1936 piece on the musical, betraying resistance to the gender-bending aspect.

> Normally it is with sorrow and self-hatred that this column hints at the inadequacies of a star, but this time it is a distinct pleasure to call Miss Matthews's acting performance hopelessly bad. In *First a Girl* she is pretending to

be a man and making no headway at all, except with the members of her supporting cast, who swoon with astonishment upon discovering her sex. Being a woman of vast loveliness, grace and personal charm, her pretty attempts to wear male clothing, smoke cigars and simulate hearty masculinity are about as convincing as Wallace Beery would be in the rôle of Juliet.

(*The New York Times*, 4 January 1936)

Sweet Adeline also got bad press for its 'unmanly' representation of men (*The New York Times*, 7 January 1935), giving a sense of the resistance that existed to any non-binary performance. The brilliant chirpy rendition of the title-named love song to a woman, belted out by Irene Dunne wearing top hat and tails and tap dancing, was irresistible for our credit sequence.

Subtextual Representations

There was something of a postwar lull in this naughty-but-nice camp atmosphere in film, while Churchill was busy increasing prosecutions again for homosexual sex. But the queer coding in films by Frank Launder and Anthony Asquith was screaming out to be unpicked. *The Belles of St Trinian's* was rather an obvious choice, but it helped us to create a section themed on childhood and school, both offering teenage crushes and the loneliness of otherness when intercut with the many schoolboy films from across the period. *The Importance of Being Earnest* provided plenty of in-jokes between its queer writer Wilde and closeted director Asquith, 'Is he earnest?' being a covert way of subtly enquiring about sexuality in the same way as the better-known phrase, 'Is he musical?'. There was also a brilliantly camp advert for Bri-Nylon from 1959, which featured pretty men prancing around together in tight trousers, while another 'lonely' man watches from his lacy bedspread. And as soon as the sixties arrive, homosexuality is firmly part of the conversation. The police are starting to turn a blind eye rather than prosecute, and the Wolfenden report of 1957 has started the ball rolling (slowly) towards decriminalisation. Two films tell the story of Oscar Wilde without claiming he was mentally ill, and the extraordinary performance by Dirk Bogarde in *Victim* (1961) won over audiences who had hitherto regarded homosexuality as a sickness or perversion. Bosley Cowther reviewed the film as follows.

As a frank and deliberate exposition of the well-known presence and plight of the tacit homosexual in modern society it is certainly unprecedented and intellectually bold. It makes no bones about the existence of the problem and about using the familiar colloquial terms. The very fact that homosexuality as a condition is presented honestly and unsensationally, with due regard for the dilemma and the pathos, makes this an extraordinary film ... While the subject is disagreeable, it is not handled distastefully. And while the drama is not exciting, it has a definite intellectual appeal.

(*The New York Times*, 6 February 1962)

Medhurst's brilliant analysis of *Victim* (Medhurst 1984) encourages us to see the film as both text and context, these being 'indivisibly interrelated discourses, each a part of the other'. It was both indicative of and influential on attitudes at the time.

Outlaws In the Living Room

The documentaries from the early sixties were possibly the most exciting discovery for me as a documentary maker and lover. They are equal parts funny and shocking to twenty-first-century eyes, but they are also the earliest example I could find of anyone actually listening to the voices of homosexuals and lesbians, and a couple of unacknowledged transgender people, rather than just portraying them as dangerous, tragic figures or sick in the head. They demonstrate the persistence of disturbing social attitudes in the fifties and sixties, which regarded LGBTQ+ people as a problem, both medical and social. The presenter Bryan Magee was liberal in attitude for the time and wrote one of the first books expressing at least tolerance for homosexuality. But with 2020 vision he provides quite a few laughs, my personal favourite question of his being 'What do lesbians actually DO?!'. He is also appalled to hear a bisexual woman say that the genitals of her lover don't matter and that it is the person that counts, hilariously betraying his own rather simplistic notion of sex to the modern audience. The courage and dignity of the LGBTQI+ participants in the documentaries are extraordinary. One hairdresser bravely explains he wouldn't change his sexuality even if he could, despite having been queer-bashed by thugs in a public toilet. 'Steve' is described as a lesbian, but clearly identifies as male in more than just name, without the language to express it that many 18-year-olds possess today. I was extremely lucky to meet one of the participants in 2018, a self-described 'tomboy' called Del Dyer, after her son came to a screening of *Queerama* at BFI Southbank and recognised her. She was interviewed aged 19 about her preference for men's clothes and chose to be in silhouette for fear of losing her job at the printers, because she knew if she went back home to her parents she'd be made to wear a dress again. Del has spent the 60 years since in activism, defending the rights of all to wear what they feel comfortable in, despite the distaste of some lesbians in the seventies for her butch appearance, and has also more recently campaigned for the right of trans women to access lesbian spaces. She and the other interviewees have all my admiration for being out of the closet and in love before decriminalisation.

'Oh Come In... The Place Is a Mess. You'll Love It!'

The 1970s saw drama with queer characters and themes blossom in British cinema and television. *Sunday Bloody Sunday* (Schlesinger 1971) was successful at the box office, if only in urban areas, after a tumultuous production period. A number of actors refused roles in the film, considering it too risqué, and there were a few cast changes due to discomfort about the famous gay kiss scene we used in *Queerama*, before Peter Finch came on board. We were delighted to be able to include a scene from *The Naked Civil Servant* (Gold 1975), a hugely influential and satisfying moment for LGBTQI+ viewers in 1975. *Queerama* researcher Mike Nicholls recalled meeting John Hurt, who played Quentin Crisp, many years later, and telling him that seeing the film as a teenager had changed his life. Hurt replied with gleeful camp: 'It changed mine too dear!'. Quentin Crisp was iconic for young queers in the seventies, being one of very few openly gay and gender-non-conforming public figures. A rarely seen, un-broadcast interview with him at that time was a joyous discovery in the BFI archive, providing one of the most hilarious and brilliant statements in *Queerama*. In answer to a question on the recent decriminalisation of homosexuality, he says: 'Unfortunately of course, toleration has come in a form that is slightly insulting... that is to say one imagined the message when it came would read: forgive us for having for so long allowed our prejudices to blind us to your true worth, and cross our unworthy threshold with your broad-minded feet. Instead the message now reads: Oh come in! The place is a mess – you'll love it!' (Crisp interviewed by Braden 1968, BFI). An early gay rights demo in London in 1971, filmed by an amateur on Super 8, offered a powerful reminder of how much change had occurred in our lifetimes... a handful of people in flares with shaggy hairdos courageously marching through Soho under a placard that reads GAY PROUD & ANGRY. Another exciting Super 8 discovery was a film newly uncovered by archivist Simon McCallum, salvaged from the attic of a couple who had made their own short film in *David is a Homosexual* (Avery 1976). The sound had not survived well, but the brilliant pictures of a young gay man living in the closet in his parents' house were precious to us. A better-known film was *Nighthawks* (Peck 1978), the schoolteacher drama which powerfully challenged the bigotry of Section 28 (banning any positive mention of homosexuality in schools) on primetime television.

An Affective History

This cherry-picking by decade of examples from the 94 films included in *Queerama* is at odds with the way we structured the film. I made a decision to do away with chronology for much of it, sticking instead to cutting films from across the century around affective themes and feelings, using music to pull clips in totally different styles and formats together. The film begins with shots from black-and-white films mainly, many from the early part of the century but with heavy use of the beautiful *Dreams A40* (Reckord 1964), which allows a dramatic start when two men are prosecuted for their love and one of them is hanged for it, appearing close to death in his heartbroken lover's arms. John Grant's gorgeous melancholic love song 'TC and Honeybear' helps to raise the stakes of love and loss which set the tone for the film. There is also a family and religion sequence, imbued with shame (thank you, Terence Davies and Jeanette Winterson) and followed by sexual desire (cheer for *Stud Life* 2012 by Campbell X), gender questioning (with love to *The Naked Civil Servant*), falling in love and heartbreak (impossible without Isaac Julien's *Young Soul Rebels* 1991), none in the order that heteronormative temporality demands. Films from every decade in the century are intercut throughout the first two-thirds of the film, and songs from Goldfrapp, Hercules & Love Affair and John Grant create queer narratives that amplify the meanings and signifiers in the clips.

However, this expressionist process fell away when we arrived in the 1980s. The AIDS crisis made queerness a different experience from any other time and it was important to respect that. It is the first place in the film that newsreel and the terrifying public information films featuring icebergs and falling monoliths are used. And it sets off a section which energetically follows the nineties campaign to equalise the age of consent for young gay men, a battle not actually won until 2001. Tory MPs are seen in Parliament making laughable claims about the immorality and perversion of gay sex and protestors outside the House of Commons are in tears when their bill is not passed.

The Gaps That Remain

Clearances became very difficult and expensive when we wanted clips from the famous queer British films and TV dramas of the eighties and nineties. One that sadly got away was *My Beautiful Launderette* (Frears 1985), which, at £2,500 per minute, was out of reach of our budget. We took the financial hit to get *Oranges are Not the Only Fruit* (Kidron 1990), though, as the hunt for representations of lesbians was such a tough one. The rights to many of Derek Jarman's films are held by the BFI itself, another admirable detail in his legacy. Isaac Julien was well worth paying for, as was Campbell X, who gave us an incredibly generous rate, and their wonderful work had the advantage of representing queer people of colour (see *Stud Life* 2012), which is horribly still a rare pleasure today. Campbell X's 'Manifesto for QPOC Online Creativity' (2014) was presented by them at the Tate in 2014 and continues to inspire queer filmmakers of colour to resist token-istic representation and 'take back (their) desires, stories and lives' through social media and social video. Although they claim their 'revolution will certainly NOT be televised!', Campbell graciously agreed to help us make *Queerama* as an editorial consultant, and the film benefitted hugely from their passionate engagement.

A disappointment for us in terms of trying to include the huge range of iden-tities in the acronym LGBTQI+ was the tiny amount of transgender representa-tion we could find and/or clear. The notable exception was the aforementioned Steve, who had no language to describe themselves as transgender but seemed to clearly identify as male. In the absence of other clear expressions of gender identity from the past, we created a section of the film that aimed to talk about gender while avoiding mis-gendering anyone that couldn't speak for themselves. It is my hope that trans and non-binary viewers will find themselves recognised poetically in this part of the film, if not overtly. We also failed to find and/or clear a single British East Asian queer face on screen. The National Archive is limited by the choices made by film funders and creators in the past, which limited *Queerama* too, to a point. The slightly messy randomness of our final list, how-ever, seemed appropriate and was beautifully articulated by our historical con-sultant on *Queerama*, Professor of Collaborative History at the University of Sussex Lucy Robinson. Her job title itself is a conscious political statement about the importance of 'retrieving' history from the elite and working together to tell our own stories, however individual, separate or other they may seem. Our team embraced the fragmented nature of what we could and couldn't include, even making a virtue of it by replacing famous work with that which was hitherto unknown.

Queer Methodology

A queer methodology emerged whereby the team as queer producers used their experiences of not being seen, or working hard to find themselves on screens, to reimagine in a playful and subversive way what was missing. It took an intense emotional engagement with the sources to allow this. A conversation opened up between us as storytellers in the present and the storytellers from the past who had left us traces and clues of their queer identities. Listening to them while also allowing our own queer subjectivities room to speak made a new multifaceted truth and also a strong sense of shared pride and solidarity with each other. Working with an archive powerfully transmits the idea that practice *is* research, as reworking old films simultaneously acknowledges the text as context and repurposes and builds on the meanings it contains. We were thrilled by the subversion, naughtiness and ingenuity people displayed in surviving queer lives with style and love, ourselves falling in love with them as they communicated with us so compellingly from the past.

We gained new appreciation for the battles that were fought and won before our births, and new understanding of the enormous importance of what we ourselves had campaigned for. We also saw clearly how easy it would be to lose the rights won for LGBTQI+ people and we bonded in a seriously queer way in solidarity and creativity with each other. Campbell X said something really important at our premiere – '*Queerama* is my family; not just the content, our history; but as a team'. *Queerama* became both a celebration of how far we have come and a rallying cry. The decision to structure the film thematically rather than depending on a chronological ordering that privileges dates and legislation was an important one. The structure makes its own argument – that progress is not linear and queer lives don't wait around for the law to be changed. Moments and phases of persecution and freedom come and go throughout the century, as we can assume they always have and always will.

Queerama as Activism

Queerama astonished us with its success, landing as it did in the moment the UK was celebrating 50 years since partial decriminalisation, and passing the Alan Turing law which pardoned gay men for past prosecutions. We ended the film with the self-styled 'oldest gay in the village' 96-year-old George Montague making a rousing protest on BBC news from Brighton: 'I will not accept a pardon. To accept a pardon means you admit that you were guilty. I was not guilty of anything.' *Queerama* premiered to an audience of 2,000 on the opening night of Sheffield International Documentary Festival in June 2017. John Grant played live after the screening, which was followed by a panel discussion between John, Campbell and me. The film was then invited by Julien Temple to play at his Cineramageddon field at Glastonbury Festival. In July 2017, *Queerama* played at Latitude Festival and then had its London premiere at a packed BFI Southbank. The BBC broadcast *Queerama* to commemorate the 50th anniversary of the 1967 Sexual Offences Act, for which it created a season called Gay Britannia. It also played in the BFI's Gross Indecency season in August 2017 and the BFI DVD was released later that year, with an accompanying booklet containing short essays by myself, Lucy Robinson and Simon McCallum. I then spent much of a year on a world tour of documentary and queer film festivals, screening the film with Q&A. Countries where the film played include Russia, Romania, Australia, Slovakia, Taiwan, South Korea, Italy, Poland, the USA, Ireland, Sweden, Denmark, Finland, Germany, the Netherlands and Spain. The Russian, Romanian and South Korean screenings felt particularly important, as LGBTQI+ rights are poor, and my presence at the screenings enabled impassioned debate and storytelling to take place, with audiences regarding the film as a kind of roadmap, with hazard signs for the pitfalls of believing progress is linear. While British homophobia and intolerance has historically been exported all over the world, the moment British queers are in now looks delicious to young queers in St Petersburg who still fear state-sanctioned violence for their sexuality.

Documentary storytelling is saddled with a reputation for deceit and spin, largely due to its own unstable and disingenuous truth claim. *Queerama* is one of a million montages that could have been made from the BFI archive about a century of queer rights and desires. The tone, the meanings, the signifiers and the aesthetic all result from an endless list of choices according to the team's subjectivity, personal experience and taste; it is not the truth. But it is an act of resistance in its repurposing, reclaiming and reimagining the meanings in each clip. The producers of homoerotic One Direction fan art in *Crazy About One Direction* took the bland product they were offered and queered it, creating something far more interesting, subtle and exciting (if also far more divisive!). And *Queerama* is a fan production at heart, actively reproducing meanings according to the desires of the fan (Jenkins 2002). This practice is thrilling. If the post-truth society is a raft adrift on a choppy sea of lies and misinformation, subjective storytelling as a life raft is more important than ever. Queerness, blackness, neurodivergence and class are all in need of a subversive re-working of their histories in order to reimagine both their pasts and futures. This work has been started handsomely by filmmakers such as John Akomfrah (*Handsworth Songs* 1986), Cheryl Dunye (*The Watermelon Woman* 1996), Jean Nkiru (*Rebirth is Necessary* 2017), Andrea Weiss (*A Bit of Scarlet* 1996) and Adam Curtis (*Hypernormalisation* 2016) – and *Queerama* aims to be situated in this tradition. When we take ownership of our histories, we lay a solid foundation for an optimistic queer future.

Watch *Queerama*

You can watch *Queerama* on The Future of Media website: www.golddust.org.uk/futureofmedia

References

Ahmed, S. 2010. *The Promise of Happiness*. Durham, NC: Duke University Press.

Akomfrah, J. 1986. *Handsworth Songs*. Film. Black Film Collective.

Asquith, D. 2016. '*Crazy About One Direction*: Whose Shame is it Anyway?' In *Seeing Fans*, edited by P. Booth and L. Bennett, 79–87. London: Bloomsbury Academic.

Berlant, L. 2011. *Cruel Optimism*. Durham, NC: Duke University Press.

Butt, G. 2013. *Visual Cultures as Seriousness*. London: Goldsmiths & Sternberg Press.

Curtis, A. 2016. *Hypernormalisation*. Film. BBC.

Dinshaw, C., L. Edelman, R. A. Ferguson, C. Freccero, E. Freeman, J. Halberstam, A. Jagose, C. Nealon and N. T. Hoang. 2007. 'Theorising Queer Temporalities'. *GLQ: A Journal of Lesbian and Gay Studies*, 13(2–3): 177–196.

Doty, A. 1993. *Making Things Perfectly Queer*. Minneapolis, MN: University of Minnesota Press.

Doty, A. 2000. *Flaming Classics: Queering the Film Canon*. New York: Routledge.

Dunye, C. 1996. *The Watermelon Woman*. Film. First Run Features.

Dyer, R. 1990. *Now You See It: Studies in Lesbian and Gay Film*. New York: Routledge.

Freeman, E. 2010. *Time Binds: Queer Temporalities, Queer Histories*. Durham, NC: Duke University Press.

Gardiner, J. 2003. *From the Closet to the Screen*. London: Pandora.

Halberstam, J. 2005. *In a Queer Time and Place: Transgender Bodies, Subcultural Lives*. New York: NYU Press.

Halberstam, J. 2011. *The Queer Art of Failure*. Durham, NC: Duke University Press.

Hirschfeld, M. 1919. *Anders Als die Andern*. Film. Institute for Sexual Science. Berlin.

Jenkins, H. 2002. *Hop on Pop*. Durham, NC: Duke University Press.

Medhurst, A. 1984. '*Victim*: Text as Context'. *Screen*, 25(4–5): 22–35.

Medhurst, A. 2006. 'Nebulous Nancies…'. In *British Queer Cinema*, edited by R. Griffiths, 21–34. London: Routledge.

Monaghan, W. 2016. *Queer Girls, Temporality and Screen Media: Not 'Just a Phase'*. London: Palgrave Macmillan.

Muñoz, J. E. 2009. 'Queerness as Horizon'. In *Utopia: The Then and There of Queer* Futurity, 19–32. New York: New York University Press.

Nkiru, J. 2017. *Rebirth is Necessary*. Film. Iconoclast.

Russo, V. 1987. *The Celluloid Closet: Homosexuality in the Movies*. New York: Harper and Row.

Stockton, K. Bond. 2009. *The Queer Child; Or, Growing Sideways in the Twentieth Century*. Durham, NC: Duke University Press.

Weiss, A. 1996. *A Bit of Scarlet*. Film. BBC.

X, Campbell. 2012. *Stud Life*. Independent film. Available at: https://vimeo.com/campbellx.

X, Campbell. 2014. *Manifesto for QPOC Online Creativity*. London: Tate London. Available at: https://vimeo.com/95218998.

X, Campbell. 2017. *Desire*. Independent film. Available at: https://vimeo.com/campbellx.

X, Campbell. 2019. *Visible*. Independent film. Available at: https://vimeo.com/campbellx.

Queerama Filmography

1899 *Women's Rights*, Bamforth

1909 *How Percy Won the Beauty Competition*, unknown

1915 *Footballers Battalion*, Topical Budget

1915 *March of the Queens*, Topical Budget

1926 *Hints and Hobbies No.11*, unknown

1927 *Frolics on the Green*, Topical Budget

1928 *Underground*, Anthony Asquith

1930 *Oliver Strachey in Drag*, unknown

1930 *Journey's End*, James Whale

1934 *Say It with Flowers*, John Baxter

1934 *Sweet Adeline*, Mervyn LeRoy

1935 *First a Girl*, Victor Saville

1937 *Girls Will Be Boys*, Marcel Varnel

1944 *Two Thousand Women*, Frank Launder

1947 *Black Narcissus*, Powell/Pressburger

1952 *The Importance of Being Earnest*, Anthony Asquith

1954 *The Belles of St Trinian's*, Frank Launder

1959 *Everything but Everything in Bri-Nylon*, unknown

1959 *The Hound of the Baskervilles*, Terence Fisher

1960 *Carry on Constable*, Gerald Thomas

1960 *Oscar Wilde*, Gregory Ratoff

1960 *The Trials of Oscar* Wilde, Ken Hughes

1961 *Victim*, Basil Dearden

1962 *The L Shaped Room*, Bryan Forbes

1964 *Dream A40*, Lloyd Reckord

1964 *The Leather Boys*, Sidney J. Furie

1964 *Carry on Spying*, Gerald Thomas

1964 *This Week: Homosexuals*, James Butler

1965 *This Week: Lesbians*, John Phillips

1966 *The Family Way*, Roy Boulting

1967 *Consenting Adults 1&2*, BBC Man Alive

1968 *If...*, Lindsay Anderson

1968 Quentin Crisp interview, Bernard Braden

1968 *The Killing of Sister George*, Robert Aldrich

1969 *Black Cap Drag*, Dick Benner

1969 *Staircase*, Stanley Donen

1969 *What's a Girl Like You?*, Charlie Squires

1969 *The Prime of Miss Jean Brodie*, Ronald Neame

1970 *Entertaining Mr Sloane*, Douglas Hickox

1971 *Lust for a Vampire*, Jimmy Sangster

1971 *Villain*, Michael Tuchner

1971 *Sunday Bloody Sunday*, John Schlesinger

1972 *A Portrait of David Hockney*, David Pearce

1975 *The Naked Civil Servant*, Jack Gold

1975 *The Maids*, Christopher Miles

1976 *Gay Rights Demo*, unknown

1976 *Trilogy – Children*, Terence Davies

1976 *David is a Homosexual*, Wilfred Avery

1978 *Nighthawks*, Hallam/Peck

1979 *Coming Out*, Carol Wiseman

1980 *Trilogy – Madonna and Child*, Terence Davies

1981 *Gay Life*, ITN

1981 *Lol: A Bona Queen of Fabularity*, Angela Pope

1982 *Scrubbers*, Mai Zetterling

1983 *Trilogy – Death and Transfiguration*, Terence Davies

1984 *Another Country*, Manek Kanievska

1984 *Lace*, William Hale

1985 *The Angelic Conversation*, Derek Jarman

1985 *AIDS: The Victims*, Thames

1985 *What Can I Do with a Male Nude?*, Ron Peck

1985 *My Beautiful Launderette*, Stephen Frears

1986 *Caravaggio*, Derek Jarman

1987 AIDS Public Awareness Broadcasts, British government

1987 *Maurice*, James Ivory

1988 *Ballad of Reading Gaol*, Richard Kwietniowski

1988 *The Fruit Machine*, Philip Saville

1989 *Flames of Passion*, Richard Kwietniowski

1989 *Kinky Gerlinky*, Dick Jewell

1990 *Oranges Are Not the Only Fruit*, Beeban Kidron

1990 *Portrait of a Marriage*, Stephen Whittaker

1990 *Dead Dreams of Monochrome Men*, David Hinton

1991 *Relax*, Chris Newby

1991 *Young Soul Rebels*, Isaac Julien

1991 *Rosebud*, Cheryl Farthing

1992 *Gender Bender*, Laurens C. Postma

1992 *Caught Looking*, Constantine Giannaris

1993 *The Attendant*, Isaac Julien

1993 *Wittgenstein*, Derek Jarman

1994 *Age of Dissent*, William Parry

1994 *Chumbawamba: Homophobia*, Ben Unwin

1994 *Priest*, Antonia Bird

1994 *A Time to Heal*, Michael Toshiyuki Uno

1994 *B.D. Women*, Campbell X

1995 *The Chocolate Acrobat*, Tessa Sheridan

1995 *Dafydd*, Ceri Sherlock

1996 *Beautiful Thing*, Hettie Macdonald

1996 *A Bit of Scarlet*, Andrea Weiss

1996 *Mardi Gras*, unknown

1998 *Love Is the Devil*, John Maybury

2001 *Baby*, Wiz

2010 *Uncle David*, Nicholls/Reich/Hoyle

2012 *What You Looking At?*, Dir Faryal

2012 *Stud Life*, Campbell X

2017 George Montague interview, BBC News

Queerama Soundtrack

'TC & Honeybear', 'JC Hates Faggots', 'Caramel', 'Sigourney Weaver', 'Supernatural Defibrillator', 2010, John Grant, Bella Union

'Glacier', 'I Hate This Fucking Town', 'No More Tangles', 'Black Belt', 2013, John Grant, Bella Union

'Snug Slax', 2015, John Grant, Bella Union

'I Try to Talk to You', 2014, Hercules & Love Affair, Moshi Moshi

'Ooh La La', 2005, Goldfrapp, Mute

'Stranger', 2014, Goldfrapp, Mute

THE FUTURE OF DANCE

11

New Telematic Technology for the Remote Creation and Performance of Choreographic Work

Daniel Strutt, Andreas Schlegel, Neal Coghlan, Clemence Debaig and Youhong 'Friendred' Peng

Introduction and Context

At the time of writing, we are in lockdown in the UK due to the Covid-19 virus. While many of us are discussing the possibility of going back to our physical workplaces over the coming months (despite the potential for future lockdowns with a second or third wave of infections), artists and performers are wondering in which *year* they will find themselves again in front of a live audience. This issue, which has clear implications for the financial stability of both individuals and arts companies, is particularly prescient for the dance industry. An article published in *The Guardian* on 5 May 2020, titled 'An Industry in Freefall', asks: 'With tours cancelled and rehearsal rooms closed, what's the future for dance?' (Bakare 2020). In this difficult situation, we have witnessed an extraordinary blossoming of many forms of performance through platforms such as Facebook Live, Zoom and YouTube, with DJs, musicians and singers, drag and performance artists, outdoor performers and actors streaming live video content directly from their homes. There has also been a lively discussion about possibilities for future development of this kind of content, and about the potential forms of revenue and income it can generate, as virtual festivals, digital art, events and interactive media move to the centre of the debate about a 'culture in quarantine.'[1] But how does dance fit into all of this? While actors, DJs and musicians can largely work solo or in safely distanced forms, the discipline of dance is inherently about close bodily contact, on a daily basis, being fundamental to its practices.

In this chapter we aim to offer an interrogation into the future of dance, framed by theoretical questions that have been raised by a collaborative interdisciplinary project that the authors have been engaged in. The project researches the potential application of a new generation of wireless, flexible and studioless motion capture in the creation, rehearsal, teaching and performance of choreographic dance work. While these relatively recently available technologies (only being on the consumer market since around 2016) could be used to either supplant or augment other existing video-based modes of working or performing remotely, we have found the need to remind ourselves that the problem they address is not primarily one of using technology to *substitute* for live presence. There are already several technologies that aim to do just this, for instance, in VR concerts (e.g., Melody VR) or for corporate conferences (e.g., Musion Eyeliner). In a straightforward way those technologies aim to recreate the perceptual experience of 'being there'. However, the problem as we see it should not simply be about trying to generate a sense of actual live physical presence, but rather about finding in a digital medium such forms of meaningful connection, as well as engaged interest and attention, which can be decisively and qualitatively *different*.

We might even wish to undermine the presumption that live presence is in some way optimal or preferable in all performance contexts, or that we should simply prioritise the translation or adaptation of existing live work for virtual or remote forms of engagement. We can consider the ways in which forms of connection between performer and performer, and between performer and audience – while limited in terms of actual somatic immersion (e.g., the sense of touch, smell, temperature, spatial audio etc.) – can be articulated differently or even enhanced in certain virtual and technologically augmented modes which play to the strengths and affordances of new digital applications and immersive interfaces. In this way, we argue that engaging virtually with dance, as much as with any kind of performance, does not need to be an impoverished copy of the live theatrical experience, but can instead create a new and unique experience altogether. As choreographer Robert Wechsler notes, the idea of technological progress towards a point where media become transparent is not the primary issue for performance. The issue is about applying the existing technology intelligently and creatively: 'The central challenge that this field faces is not one of improving the technology, but rather one of developing an understanding of its implications – The changes in the mindset and sensibility of the artists as they put it to use' (Wechsler 2006, 75).

Technological newness in and of itself is not enough to constitute mean-ingful aesthetic progress and can easily instead become gimmicky or uncomfort-ably tagged on to existing disciplinary practices. What is more important, then, is that recent cutting-edge or bleeding-edge technologies are understood within the wider narrative of aesthetic development from the past to the present visions of the future of performance. For this reason, in this chapter we wish to con-sider the practical potential of recent real-time and generative motion capture applications, specifically those used for remote collaborative practice in the dis-cipline of dance, but within a historical and theoretical problematic of networked or distributed performance (Birringer 2008), and of telepresence, telematics and virtuality in dance practice.

As 'digital choreographer' and theorist Sarah Rubidge already articulated well in 2002, we should not be narrowly considering these potential applications as being only about pragmatic solutions to the problems of physical distancing that choreographers and dancers might continue to face in the immediate future (though, in the first instance, they are this as well). We should rather see them as a new avenue of research and futurist vision – as potentially an altogether new medium for dance. In Rubidge's own words:

> Certain forms of digital technology provide a framework for choreography which opens up new modes of practice, and new ways of thinking in and through dance. Amongst these are those forms of digital media which allow for real-time interactivity. These may prove to be a new medium, not merely a new tool, for choreography. This is indicated by the fact that some features of this digital medium raise interesting philosophical questions which have the potential to extend and enhance our understanding of what constitutes the choreographic art.
>
> (Rubidge 2002, 2)

What follows, then, is first a thinking through of some of the concepts, discourses and technologies which contextualise this sphere of digital or 'vir-tual' dance practice and performance, before a consideration of the potential-ities and limitations of several forms of actual 'cutting-edge' software, hardware and platforms that are currently being used in the field. This will lead us to raise both practical and theoretical questions that can frame future research projects, including our own, with the intention of working towards a down-to-earth vision of a virtual choreographic art for the future.

Physicality and Virtuality in Digital Performance

Between the encyclopaedic works of Johannes Birringer (*Performance, Technology, & Science*, 2008) and Steve Dixon (*Digital Performance: A History of New Media in Theatre, Dance, Performance Art, and Installation*, 2007), we already have a thoroughly researched historical exemplification and conceptualisation of the many facets of digital performance, since the first experiments and demonstrations in the 1960s through to milestone pieces such as Merce Cunningham's *BIPED* (1999).[2] Of particular interest for this article are their sections on interactive, networked and telematic work, where digital communication technologies and interfaces are used to bring geographically distant artists into virtual proximity to produce performative events (Pérez 2014). While telematic work has been a feature and form of performance since the 1980s, it has struggled with the inherent technical difficulties of tele-communication, suffering from delay, latency, noise and glitches on the one hand and a palpable frustration at the lack of the genuine aesthetic advancement and emotional connection on the other. The unattained ideal is still felt in 2020–2021, with a desire not only to have a real-time networked performance, but also to achieve it with meaningful affective and emotional connection and communication between performers, and with a sense of immediacy, liveness and embodied presence being produced for both performer and audience. Quoting Steve Dixon, Elena Pérez argues that,

> From a theatre and performance perspective, mere juxtaposition does not qualify for telematic performance to be satisfactory. He [Dixon] claims that 'telematic works too commonly suspect that the simple presence of these remote, virtual bodies is considered to be enough, since the magic of technology is there for all to see'. In his view, the juxtapositions need to be meaningful rather than separated and arbitrary.

> (Pérez 2014)

To be meaningful, or even 'satisfactory', is thus a balancing act between the awareness of the technological prowess of the mediating interface, and the sense of direct, almost unmediated communication between performer and performer, and between performer and audience (a balance that Bolter and Grusin, in 1998, captured within the simultaneous impulses towards hypermediacy and immediacy). As discussed above, some exponents of digital performance idealise the total disappearance and transparency of the interface for the direct 'live' and immediate experience of being there. However, given that this disappearance is still to be achieved in any ideal sense, with 'imperfect' hardware still causing too many potential ruptures, we propose that we can instead look to the capacities of different technological interfaces to create sensations of closeness and presence beyond any notions of 'liveness' – and in their own unique ways.

To be *virtual* is not simply to be approximate to, and to *simulate* is not to be similar to, as each interface must be considered to have its own emergent properties in terms of possibilities for physical or cognitive engagement. Thus, when we refer here to virtual performance in simulated spaces, we are talking about the creation of a unique set of aesthetic dynamics with affective nuances and capacities for expression that are contextualised by the affordances of specific technologies. In many ways these new forms of technological dynamics between hardware, software, bodies and cognitive processes complexify the more direct and tangible expressivity of a physical dance practice. As media theorist Kris Paulsen describes it: 'Telepresence and its tactile interventions in and through the screen space complicate the boundaries of our bodies, extend our corporeal agency and influence and blur the distinctions between physicality and virtuality' (2017, 10).

While it can be noted that each new wave of ICT or telematic technologies does indeed bring a unique and emergent complex of feelings of embodiment, touch, action and agency in new contexts, it's also important to note that the underlying concepts and ideals of remote connection and interaction to which we bring them have actually remained relatively consistent over the last 50–60 years. These concepts are of virtuality, vitality, presence and telepresence, embodiment and affection. In the 1950s, aesthetic theorist Susanne Langer was already discussing the 'virtual powers' of dance as an evocation of force and touch beyond the actual physicality of the dancers themselves. She described how the work of dance *evoked* forces of agency and vitality within the mind of the spectator – what she called 'vital gesture' – and that the primary skill of the dancer was their ability to act as a conduit within this process (Langer 1953, 169). Drawing on Langer's almost 70-year-old concept of virtuality, we can imagine a way in which touch does not always need to be *actual* in dance, since, from the point of view of the audience, the vital sensation of action and touch is already somewhat virtual, in as much as it is *simulated* within our own mental environment. When we experience a physical reaction to dance – say, the hairs raising on our skin – we are, in a way, experiencing this virtual touch.

This feeling can also be said to apply to the interior experience of the dancer, who, while performing choreographed movement in its real physical, spatial actuality (which Langer defines as elements of 'place, gravity, body, muscular strength, muscular control' (Langer 1976, 79)), simultaneously inhabits a virtual interior and imaginary dimension, not just going through the motions mechanistically, but rather channelling imagined actions and intentions that are charged with emotional and affective resonance. Langer's understanding of this virtual essence of dance practice appeals to the idea of 'phenomenological space' put forward by dance theorist and movement therapist Hubert Godard (McHose 2006). For Godard, the space of the dancer should never be defined by the physical dimensions of a real space, or, as he calls it, a 'topos', but should rather be seen as an experiential space imbued with subjective, historical and social context. The space of the dance is thus always virtual, filled with imagination, memory and emotion, with a 'latent potential' for action according to these phenomenological frameworks. Godard says: 'That should be the title of this chapter – "Phenomenological Space" – because I'm in the space and the space is in me. There is not a distinction first between "me" and "the space" ' (McHose 2006, 34).

In other words, within the event of the actual physical performance, both dancer and spectator are having an experience in dual actual (physical) and virtual embodied modes. For Langer, however, it is the virtual dimension in particular that is at the heart of being able to communicate affect and emotion within the discipline of dance. Technological interfaces for digital dance can thus seem an apt means of channelling and exploring these pre-existing capacities for virtual sensation and agency, potentially even opening the way for more immersive, interactive and intense experiences of dance than those afforded by simply looking at a stage space from a seated distance. As researchers Kim Vincs and John McCormick point out, combining dance practice with technological interfaces is an apposite way to investigate virtual experience in general.

> Langer's writings provide a provocative starting place for exploring the idea that dance might encompass virtual, as well as actual, physical, touch. ... Dance might provide a means of exploring ways of reinserting the complexity of whole-bodied agency – the nuance of physical sensation and action – within virtualized digital interfaces.
>
> (2010, 360)

Importantly, these philosophical concepts of virtuality speak first to the phenomenological, interior experiences of the dancer and spectator within the performance event, before speaking to the relative virtuality of digital technological systems. We can therefore see that new hardware and software do not *make* dance virtual – as it has been virtual all along. Yet these concepts are useful insofar as they guide us towards approaching some actual technologies, with a view to posing the question: How can they extend, augment or evolve the inherent virtual powers, virtual gestures and phenomenological spaces of the choreographic art?

Authorship in 'Layered' Real and Virtual Spaces

Dwelling on a similar theme, but dealing with somewhat more practical concerns, dance theorist and choreographer Pauline Brooks draws on her explorations into the digital complexities of telematic dance to articulate a new spatial 'frontier' for such work (2010). Influenced by the telematic work of Paul Sermon from the 1990s through which he articulated a concept of a 'third space' for performance (see Sermon 2019, Figure 11.1), Brooks discusses her own considerations around the occasionally problematic multiplicity of experiential spaces that emerges in the layering of real and technologically-mediated zones of performance. She has found that the dancers, already invested in the conceptual goals of a project, creatively played with their awareness of the camera's capture of the dance and thus of an imagined hypothetical zone of representation, creating a third space of 'virtual interplay' between actual and imagined 'territories of performance space' (Figure 11.2). As Brooks puts it,

> We have a new space for performance, a global space linked by the Internet and identified through the projector screen and a local space defined by the physicality of the studio theatre stage. ... The challenge for the performers is to be able to embody the artistic theme and to stay connected to all performers (live and digitized) as well as to visible and invisible audiences.
>
> (Brooks 2010, 53)

Brooks explains that this complexity of space also generated new reactions in the spectators. While some appreciated the blending of live dance and the projected screen images, others didn't enjoy having to choose themselves where to pay attention at any given moment. Brooks concludes that, just as the dancers develop their awareness of the different 'territories' in which the work is happening, the audience also need to be guided or trained in the skills of reading or decoding the 'dance information' of the work, and thus also in its overall symbolic or aesthetic meaning. What this seems to suggest is that, while a distribution of attention across live and mediated spaces and surfaces can be a superficially

Figure 11.1 Video still from line-out footage of composited image of separate participants sitting and interacting together in *Telematic Vision* for the 'ZKM Multimediale III' exhibition.

Screengrab by Paul Sermon, October 1993.

interesting technical feature of some works, there is clearly a decisively different type of presence, attention and engagement demanded of the spectator within layered spaces. These new imperatives for Brooks either draw us more intimately

Figure 11.2 The telematic dance work of Pauline Brooks.
Photo: Noel Jones. See www.paulinebrooks-dance.com.

and actively into the dancers' actual and virtual space(s), or, inversely, can leave us distracted and disengaged, with the technology perhaps even getting in the way of our appreciation of the virtual powers of the dance.

In *Digital Performance* Steve Dixon speaks to these new dynamics of engagement by boldly stating that 'presence is about interest and command of attention, not space or liveness' (2007, 132). He states that the effectiveness of telematic performance is not simply about generating the feeling of having two distant things happening at once in the same space, but rather that the two together generate a convincing or poetic sense of coordinated, virtual co-presence – not as a tug of war for our attention, but as a single, albeit multiplanar, emotive object of communication (2007, 132). Dixon thus seems to suggest, contra Brooks, that this is a question of good authorial intention, 'command' and design, rather than one of having to educate an audience in how to read a piece properly.

The tension that emerges between Dixon and Brooks concerns the notions of choice and control as much as it does the concepts of the actual and the virtual. Questions arise around whether the 'virtuality' of the dance should be managed and guided – such that we should know what is aesthetically important, where to look and how to read the piece. Or should the layering of the actual and virtual spaces be curated but not determined, with the audience simply instructed in how to productively interact with the work? Does the former approach actually foreclose virtuality, making the work actualised, linear and fixed? Or does the latter style too easily dissipate into an ungrounded technological gimmick without the guiding hand of an author? In other words, we can simply ask again: Which approach could be said to best enhance or augment the inherent virtual powers of dance?

In traditional live theatrical dance performance, and in the dance discipline as a whole, authorial control seems to be more straightforward than in telematic work. It is enacted by a singular space (or stage), and often by a single author/ choreographer, towards which the audience's attention is wholly directed. However, even this mode of performance can be rarely said to be singular or linear, with our embodied cognition already in a synaesthetic flux between the physical and the virtual.[3] In this sense, the task of the analogue choreographer already involved the curation of a field of physical, kinetic and gestural points of attention, and the more virtual allusions and evocations that those same movements generate. While digital, virtual or telematic performance work can offer us a potential actualisation (or visualisation) of some of these more allusive elements in abstract graphic forms, it also offers added complexity of dimensions, spaces, surfaces and bodies, and quite often multiple authors – in as much as the choreographer is rarely also the programmer or digital visual artist, while the technology itself often exerts a kind of non-human agency. For Sarah Rubidge, this means that the choreographic work or 'dance event' in this technological context should perhaps rather be described as a 'performative, choreographic open installation' – which only exists when activated by the spectator or 'user' of the work (2002, 2). The choreographic installation can in fact begin to seem more like an interactive, nonlinear game space than like a stage space, and the choreographer/author here becomes instead a kind of digital dramaturge, curating a set of actual and virtual connections and interactions, and working between dancers, digital artists, technological apparatuses, performance institutions and audiences.

This state of events poses an obvious challenge to the traditional creator of the choreographed work. Due to the digital nature of the engagement, a certain level of nonlinearity, interaction and improvisation is almost demanded, otherwise we simply get a linear recording. How, then, can connections be woven such that attention can flow between the real and the virtual in meaningful, intended ways? How can it enable the aesthetic meaning of the work to be adequately expressed when both performer and audience must effectively guide their own awareness and perceptual choice? This is an issue not only of training the audience (as per Brooks' advice), but also of possibly requiring a new craft and a more complex and interactive approach to narrative and aesthetics. Furthermore, if images, bodies and spaces are to be effectively layered and connected in ways that draw the spectator away from a superficial fixation on the technical interface, they need to juxtapose in meaningful ways through aesthetic continuities and contrasts that speak to narrative suggestion, even if not in a conventional linear storytelling mode. At all times the virtual powers of dance, the nonverbal expressivity which is after all its essence, should be preserved – that is, the ability to allude to evoke emotions, sensations and forces beyond what is literally being represented.

Accessibility, Affordability, Useability

Alongside these somewhat abstract concepts and questions of presence, immediacy and attention, we should consider the rather more pragmatic concerns of access, affordability and useability when framing contemporary digital and telematic dance performance. All the factors raised above pivot on the affordances and limitations of certain (and very material) technological apparatuses. These apparatuses play against each other within each specific assemblage. And thus, for example, the spatial realism of one type of screen interface might come at the cost of affective nuance due to issues of scale and distance from the image. With another, despite the high aesthetic cohesiveness of the screen image, emotional connection might be lost due to issues of delay or latency. The 'perfect' solution to most of these issues is usually extremely costly, requiring the kind of capital investment that arts companies simply will never have access to. The imperfect solution, then, is always a considered compromise, creatively building technological limitations into the production.

Elena Pérez summarises this point through a critique of high-tech telematics performances, which, as she notes, are only accessible to 'scientists' in research institutions, and which function primarily as technological spectacle, often lacking aesthetic value (2014, 4). Because of this, she looks instead at the relative strengths of low-tech telematics options, using widely accessible webcams, video-conferencing apps and live screen montage apps UpStage and Mosaika.

Figure 11.3 *ANGRY 1*, 121212 UpStage Festival of Cyberformance, 12 December 2012.
Live node: Kawenga Montpellier.
Photo: David Lavaysse.

tv (e.g., in the performance work of Annie Abrahams – Figure 11.3) in her case
studies. While expensive and technologically advanced options might be a futuristic 'vision of what performance can be', Pérez notes that they are not truly representative of the actual 'state of the art' in performance (2014). The reality of the
production of meaningful connections in telematic performance arts involves
the struggle to find relatively simple, reliable, glitch-free, widely accessible and
well-supported technology. In 2020–2021 for many performers these continue to
be platforms such as Skype and Zoom.

However, in the 10–12 years since Dixon's and Birringer's major publications
there have been incremental technological advances that have improved the
fine balance of factors in an enhanced telematic or networked performance
experience. It is within this situation, and with being observant of the enduring
underlying theoretical questions of immediacy, interactivity, aesthetics and
narrative – and of the phenomenologies of meaningful connection and presence –
that we are aiming to frame a specific set of new motion capture technology. In
our own research we have suggested that, as evidenced by the widespread take-
up of the Microsoft Kinect camera in performance arts since 2010, the next step in
accessible tools for telematic performance should be a more refined and accurate,
yet affordable and easily useable, motion capture system. To qualify this point, in

the next section we will provide an analysis of some recent interesting examples of the current 'state of the art' in digital, virtual and telematic performance.

The State of the Art in Telematics and Virtual Performance Technologies

Video and TV

Traditional or conventionally 'highbrow' arts performance content such as theatre and dance is still resolutely a stage-based medium, which has, of course, been problematic in the pandemic. There have been some forays into the screen presentation of this content – with limited success, for instance, in the screening of live stage performances in cinema spaces, on TV channel Sky Arts (launched as Artsworld in 2000 before being purchased by Sky) and on streaming platforms such as Marquee TV (launched in 2018 and rolled out globally in 2020). As a 'Netflix for the Arts', and clearly targeted at existing and established audiences, Marquee TV has intended to reach a new and younger demographic for classic performance (Heathman 2018). However, beyond the traditional stage arts and a rather elite set of well-established and establishment national and royal production companies, these TV and content streaming platforms have up until now offered little bandwidth to smaller-scale, future-facing or experimental work.

For small and medium-sized performance companies, the typical go-to during what we could call the 'first phase' of the Covid-19 pandemic was live video streaming, with most artists working under lockdown thorough standard video-conferencing and TV apps such as Skype, Zoom, Houseparty, Google Meet and Twitch.tv. While these platforms have their advantages in certain areas, for many performers, and in particular those that have to move to perform, they offer a fairly limiting and solitary experience. As our project's choreography partner Mavin Khoo has told us, 'the performance should be a dialogue between the performer and the audience', and this sense, for him, is totally lost with only a laptop screen grid view for company. Perhaps because of this, many technological advances in telematic, remote digital work focus not only on distribution to an audience but also on the level of agency the audience member is given in being able to react to, interact with or intervene in a live performance. In video media, however, this is still largely a matter of clicking and commenting within the standard chat functions of any given platform.

Diverging from this pattern, the newcomer smartphone app TikTok (formerly called Music Ally) has swiftly become a highly profitable start-up that exhibits a strong participatory performance element. In March 2020, notable for being the month in which most countries were in their first lockdown, it was the most downloaded non-gaming app (Sensor Tower Blog 2020). One of TikTok's largest areas of viewed video content is dance – from choreographed pieces by professional dancers and performers through to enthusiastic amateurs who disseminate viral dance moves and sequences to be copied and learnt. Alongside its amateur participatory practices, TikTok is also a platform for professional performers to lip-sync, dance and produce comedy skits and magic tricks, directly interacting with audiences to allow them to creatively respond to short viral clips in ways that go far beyond the standard 'like', share and comment types of interaction. TikTok has allowed stars to emerge through music and dance content released on this platform (e.g., Loren Gray, Lucky Dancer, Charli D'Amelio), and then cross over into other mainstream entertainment media. While in the past it was only musical content that had become monetisable for artists on social media platforms, here other forms of performance content such as choreography can also generate revenue, with highly followed artists earning up to $175,000 per post (Leskin 2020).

What TikTok shows is that there is a clear market for, and interest in, dance performance content on video-based social media platforms, beyond the relatively passive experience of viewing conventional arts content. This does pose a question of how traditional dance companies can think about bringing content into these cultural and commercial networks in ways that remain aesthetically meaningful, and without demeaning the aesthetic quality and integrity of the work.

Microsoft Kinect for Body Tracking Performance

Released in 2010, the Microsoft Kinect camera was initially designed and released as a motion-sensing hardware available as an additional item with the Xbox gaming console, with the Nintendo Wii being a forerunner. However, very soon after its release the body tracking hardware was recognised to have potential for a multitude of alternative applications – and its software was hacked (Loftus 2010). Using both an infrared (IR) projector and camera and an RGB camera, the hardware proved immediately useful for a vast array of computer vision applications due to its capacities for multi-gesture recognition, depth sensing, 3D reconstruction in any location and its useability in low light. With the only options for motion capture prior to the Kinect being prohibitively expensive professional studios, this cheap and accessible system quickly raised interest in a variety of disciplines outside of gaming: robotics, medicine, security, fashion and, of course, performance (Jamaluddin 2020). Shortly after these unofficial uses started to gain cultural traction, Microsoft opened up the Kinect's code to developers, releasing a non-commercial software development kit (SDK) and separate hardware for PCs.

A good example of the use of Kinect in dance performance is *The Measures Taken* (2014; Figure 11.4), a dance performance made by choreographer Alexander Whitley with digital studio Marshmallow Laser Feast. In this piece, the bodily movements of five dancers were tracked in real time by Kinect to generate graphic visualisations of geometric shapes and abstract volumes to be projected onto several translucent screens.

However, as a camera sensor device, the Kinect came with its own disadvantages and limitations. The first is that, with a detection range from approximately 0.4 to 4.5m, dancers can easily move out of the detectable area, by accident, during a live performance, bringing the digital performance to an abrupt stop. The use of Kinect thus requires a restrictive dance space. Second,

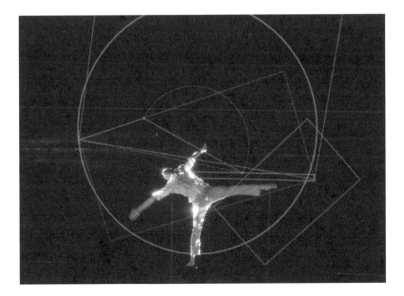

Figure 11.4 Dancer Wayne Parsons in Alexander Whitley's *The Measures Taken*, 2014.
Photo: Foteini Christofilopoulou.

both Kinect v1 and v2 have relatively low depth resolution.[4] In a large-scale project in which multi-skeleton tracking is required, the Kinect simply cannot give the required accuracy. Third, as Kinect is a mono-directional infrared projector and camera sensor device, there are many reported problems with movement tracking and occlusion, where overlapping bodily movements of more than one dancer become impossibly 'noisy' (Iqbal and Sidhu 2017; Kim 2017). If a movement leads a dancer to position themselves at an angle tangential to the camera, there is often a confusion of the skeleton recognition and the model becomes tangled in knots. While initially seen as a liberating tool for choreographic capture, having to accommodate for the Kinect's many errors of gesture recognition can be restrictive, glitchy and distracting for both dancer and spectator. Some groups have effectively worked within these limitations (for instance, patching together multiple Kinect camera inputs for greater reliability), but many of the problems of camera-based motion capture are more simply overcome by the use of some more recent motion capture techniques.

PoseNet and Inertial Motion Sensor Systems

Coming after Kinect, the most recent developments in computer vision technologies, especially those based on machine learning models, have been promising. Machine learning pose-estimation systems such as PoseNet and inertial measurement sensor 'suit' systems such as Perception Neuron, Xsens and Rokoko Smartsuit have their application-specific advantages – the former being characterised by very simple webcam access and the latter by its relative precision and its wireless, mobile functionality. Both allow performers to engage in remote virtual activities such as live performances, training or experimentation. They function as a fast and lightweight form of telematic performance communication which doesn't rely on the streaming of chunky video data via the internet.

Projects such as DensePose and PoseNet offer real-time human pose estimation, whereby skeletal information can be detected, captured and tracked without specialist hardware (as is the case with the Kinect camera), using only a built-in or standard webcam. Since the system runs in an internet browser, it is accessible to a broad audience and has consequently built a strong participatory creative community around it, enabling its members to experiment and explore body movement computationally. 'Friendly' machine learning initiatives such as ml5js or RunwayML provide accessible platforms and guidance via a web browser not only for developers and programmers but also for amateur artists, creatives and students. All this has made PoseNet a popular candidate for experimenting with poses and movements computationally, finding application in human–computer interface development (HCIs) and providing a platform for computer vision-based explorations in dance and performance. In a good example of such experiments, renowned choreographer Bill T. Jones, together with a team of digital collaborators including Google, created a series of movement experiments using the PoseNet system in the work *Dancing with a Machine* (Figure 11.5) (Mapondera 2019).

However, pose estimation machine learning platforms can require substantial processing power for complete accuracy. Although this might not be so problematic in their more casual and participatory uses on home computers, it can have a detrimental impact on movements that require high accuracy, update frequency and detail – for instance, with complex choreography and in professional performance environments.

Since 2016, a new generation of on-body motion detection sensors has demonstrated comparatively accurate skeletal motion tracking results. This style of motion capture 'suit' system involves a series of small interconnected inertial measurement sensors (IMUs) that are attached at fixed points on the body. The IMUs gauge orientation, acceleration and position at a very high speed and resolution with a simple local Wi-Fi network. In contrast to PoseNet, this type of motion tracking solution allows the user to move freely within a physical space

Figure 11.5 Dancer Vinson Fraley, Jr. in Bill T. Jones' *Dancing with a Machine.*
Photo: courtesy of Google Creative Lab, © Google LLC.

Figure 11.6 The Perception Neuron motion capture system.

without being eye-tied to a screen. Thanks to a flexible number of sensors, it can provide more complex and accurate data on body movement, with up to 32 skeleton points on the Perception Neuron suit (Figure 11.6), compared to 17 with PoseNet and 20 with Kinect. The lightweight data is wirelessly captured by a nearby computer, where it can be transformed into audio, visual or other outputs in real time, or it can be streamed anywhere in the world for the same purposes – as is the purpose of our own current research project.

Further to its use in performance contexts, the increased richness and accuracy of the movement data yielded by these inertial sensor motion capture systems has practical application in learning and teaching, and in scientific and technical analyses of dance (see Strutt 2021). The capture and rendering of high-quality movement data in real time, and in three dimensions (compared to, for instance, a two-dimensional image from a fixed video-camera angle), can offer unexpected insights into the fine detail and immanent complexity of dance technique, even disrupting accepted cultural grammars of dance. The use of motion capture systems in the dance studio can thus reveal new perspectives for the dancer or choreographer, helping them to develop their art and practice, 'revealing hidden stories in the movement data that can provoke artistic, aesthetic and conceptual questions about what dance movement creation is and could be' (Vincs and Barbour 2014, 64).

Augmented/Mixed/Virtual Reality

In the past decade, we have seen a set of quite specialised dance companies and performance artists take up the use of motion capture technologies to create new performance elements and practical creative and learning tools. From mixing realities on stage with the use of projection, to using more immersive virtual reality hardware, digital dance collaborations are creating a new genre of choreographic practice which is slowly exerting an influence on mainstream arts.

Australian dance company Chunky Move, with its piece *Mortal Engine* (2008), took an early lead in researching symbolic expressions of the dancer's body by adding digital projection onto a stage space – steeply raked to double as a screen. In this work the movement of bodies and their position in the space were tracked with depth infrared cameras, with corrective geometry algorithms used to align the projection with the body. The moving bodies affected the virtual environment around them, while their own representation was distorted or enhanced by the superimposition of graphic elements and projected light and shade.

Similarly working within stage spaces, in their work *Hakanai* (2013), artists Adrien M. & Claire B. developed the methods used by Merce Cunningham in BIPED to project onto on gauze, or scrim, on stage. With enhanced projection technology and with multiple, almost completely transparent, gauzes in many positions on stage, the conventional 'screen' effectively disappears, along with the visibility of the stage itself, such that the dancer appears to our perception to be hovering in an immersive cube of moving textures and light.

This style of virtual, mixed-reality performance has also been used to take dance outside the traditional stage space and into other interior or exterior locations. The 2018 work *0AR* by AΦE (choreographers Aoi Nakamura and Esteban Lecoq), is a collection of short dance pieces that audiences as young as five can interact with in augmented reality (AR). The viewer holds a tablet device through which they can see digital avatars and abstract objects move in the real space before them, and they themselves can move around, or dance with, the three-dimensional images. Similar AR techniques have been used to produce what are essentially digitally augmented dance films, rather than live or interactive performances. In the short film *The Fates* by Zachary Eastwood-Bloom

(2019; Figure 11.7), made in residency with the Scottish Ballet, graphical elements are superimposed on the camera image in post-production to express a virtual spatial and sculptural connection between dancers.

AR's capacity to visually overlay digital dimensions onto video images of dance has led to both enhanced learning experiences and the creation of functional choreographic tools. In 2018 the College of Art and Science at Ohio State University started experimenting with the Microsoft HoloLens AR Headset to create an AR tool called *LabanLens*, a dance-scoring application that virtually assists in Laban-based movement notation and analysis by visualising a set of notational tools in the space in front of the dancer. We have also seen the launch of consumer AR apps such as Dance Reality, an app which make dances learning accessible to a wider amateur audience. This AR technology displays the steps on the real floor space in front of the user and offers a three-dimensional virtual teacher who can demonstrate moves and be mirrored by the user. The EU Horizon 2020 project *WhoLoDancE* (2016–2018; Figure 11.8) then combined several of these tools, using motion capture with the Microsoft Hololens AR system, and alongside AI movement recognition systems, to allow a dancer to choreograph movement alongside a digital virtual avatar, who would respond to them in real time (Wood *et al.* 2017).

From the point of view of contemporary dance audiences, we are only at the beginning of the development of a variety of tools that can see spectators do considerably more with dance work than simply sit and spectate in either a stage space or with a two-dimensional screen. Audiences of all ages for this kind of

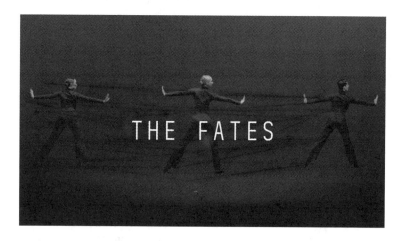

Figure 11.7 Zachary Eastwood-Bloom's *The Fates*, Scottish Ballet, 2019.

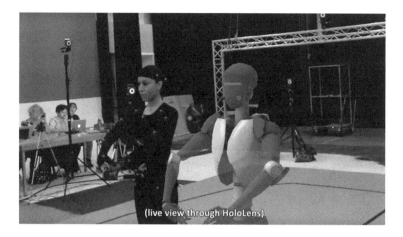

Figure 11.8 Flamenco dancer (Rosa Cisneros) working with Microsoft Hololens at the Motek Entertainment studio (Amsterdam). © 2016 WhoLoDancE.
Photo: Giulio Bottini.

work clearly do exist – and can be developed. As evidence of this, in September 2019 some 400,000 people joined violinist Lindsey Stirling's live *Artemis* performance in virtual reality (VR). Using the XSens 3D motion capture suit and Manus VR Gloves, her violin-playing movement and choreographed dance routines were captured, rendered and broadcast to VR systems in real time. While this performance offered a limited scope for interaction, it provided some insight into the potential of AR, VR and XR platforms in creating a future vision of a new kind of immersive virtual space within which audience and dancer could interact in more meaningful ways.

Gaming Platforms

In many ways, at the present moment it is actually gaming technology that offers the most tangible vision for the future, driving forward the cutting edge for performance arts, both in terms of interactive platforms and, as with TikTok, in the potential monetisation of content. Epic Games, with its real-time game engine Unreal and its incredibly popular game *Fortnite*, has amassed a global audience of 350 million registered users (Statista 2020). While Epic is developing this platform with playable gaming as its primary function, it has also started diversifying its content by hosting live music events within the virtual game world – and with purely online audiences. *Fortnite* is first and foremost a first-person shooter game, but over time it has complexified though the addition of narrative chapters and ten-week seasons, each with exclusive maps, sets of items and storylines. Each of these seasons now ends with an 'exclusive' live music event, with popular artists such as Travis Scott, Marshmello and Diplo performing. These events have a captive player audience that can interactively participate through their own game controllers, and with (purchasable) avatar dance moves called 'emotes'. Emotes do not serve any direct game function and are described by Epic as 'purely aes-thetic', yet they have become a point of cultural fascination for a wider internet audience, crossing over into viral mimicry videos found on both YouTube and TikTok under the hashtag #fortnitemoves (Kaufman 2018). Epic Games was in fact recently subject to five lawsuits about copyrighted dance moves used in its games, highlighting how easily choreography can be trademarked and monetised, potentially with royalties paid for each time the dance is used (Robertson 2019).[5]

The massive popularity of *Fortnite* as a game has developed due to several factors, mostly because it is a free-to-play, multiplatform game that is funded by in-game micro-transactions (including the purchase of dance emotes) and through collaborations with commercial properties (e.g., promotional tie-ins with film and TV content such as *Star Wars, Avengers: End Game* and *Stranger Things*). However, the ease of access and relatively low cost-to-instant-gratification ratio of this type of gaming platform offers an interesting model of a participatory and interactive virtual space for arts performance. Epic Games has expressed a wish to open the platform up for creative development, with creative sandboxing and the release of its *Fortnite Creative* mode in 2018. Can we thus imagine a future in which gaming platforms such as Unreal and virtual game worlds such as *Fortnite* could offer an opportunity for live arts events, or for motion-captured dance or theatre performance?

Conclusion: Questions Shaping Future Research

It is perhaps no surprise that traditional forms of the arts such as dance and theatre are now losing out to the more 'entertainment'-focused industries, par-ticularly with younger audiences. It is now easier and more accessible, as well as more fully embodied and participatory, for a child or teen to express them-selves through dance on a 'virtual battlefield' than it is to do it in a classroom or conventional arts space. How, then, especially in socially distanced times, can dance practitioners think about engaging with online audiences beyond the narrow scope and abbreviated format of a platform like TikTok? Despite some excursions into augmented reality, motion capture and digital visualisation tools (e.g., with Sadler's Wells' 'Digital Stage' programme of 2020 or Scottish Ballet's 'Digital Season' in 2019), there is still a long way to go for traditional forms of stage-based performance to have the same kind of digital and economic traction as music, gaming and film – forms whose creators benefit from putting their work online through sharing and streaming platforms. While the subscription service Marquee TV is a good example of a step towards more accessible and diverse (including digitally augmented) online arts content, it lacks the meaningful sense of layered spatial presence and attention that live performance can afford, as well as lacking the sense of direct emotional and affective communication that can be experienced by both viewer and performer.

Established dance and theatre audiences are typically slow to catch up, adopting newer technology reluctantly as they age (Snow 2016). This is not to say, however, that younger audiences don't also appreciate the same type of arts content as older generations. It is just that the platforms of delivery, the forms of attention given and the modes of monetisation for creative content are changing, and this, in turn, must force the content to evolve. There is a technological opportunity to capture a new and younger audience that already display an interest in dance and choreographic content. Meanwhile, with almost 62% of people in the UK playing videogames (Waterson 2021), rising to 70% in the USA (Crescente 2018), audiences are already accustomed to the kinds of interactive functionality and participatory experience that are associated with gaming (e.g., they know how to use a controller and a menu or experience an avatar). Online audiences have also proven that they want to be able to have more agency in works, from the live streaming of DJ sets on Boiler Room with live chat through to donation-funded Twitch Esports content.

We believe that future-oriented concepts for platforms, audiences, interactive performances and the monetisation of choreographic content exist in ways that can neatly merge with the currently developing motion capture, immersive and mixed-reality technologies. Framed by developments in motion capture technology from the camera-based systems of Kinect and PoseNet to inertial-sensor systems such as Perception Neuron, Xsens and Rokoko, the future of dance and choreographic content being shared on various AR, VR and XR platforms looks more immersive and more participatory. It is in part the responsibility of dance companies to embrace new technology through the dedication of time and resources, but collaborative academic research is also needed here, to be coordinated between the humanities, computing technology and design industries. Through interdisciplinary collaborative projects such as ours, dance performers and choreographers can learn to understand ways of sharing and developing new work, while shaping a digital future for traditional perform-ance arts.

References

Bakare, L. 2020. 'An Industry in Freefall: Dance Sector Calls for Urgent Help'. *The Guardian*, May 5. Available at: www.theguardian.com/stage/2020/may/05/coronavirus-threat-to-future-of-dance-lauren-cuthbertson-royal-ballet.

Birringer, J. 2008. *Performance, Technology, & Science*. New York: PAJ.

Bolter, J. D. and R. Grusin. 1998. *Remediation: Understanding New Media*. Cambridge, MA: MIT Press.

Boucher, M. 2004. 'Kinetic Synaesthesia: Experiencing Dance in Multimedia Scenographies'. *Contemporary Aesthetics* 2. Available at: https://contempaesthetics.org/newvolume/pages/article.php?articleID=235.

Brooks, P. 2010. 'Creating New Spaces: Dancing in a Telematic World'. *International Journal of Performance Arts and Digital Media*, 6(1): 49–60.

Crescente, B. 2018. 'Nearly 70% of Americans Play Video Games, Mostly on Smartphones (Study)'. *Variety*, 11 September. Available at: https://variety.com/2018/gaming/news/how-many-people-play-games-in-the-u-s-1202936332/.

Dixon, S. 2007. *Digital Performance: A History of New Media in Theater, Dance, Performance Art, and Installation*. London: MIT Press.

Heathman, A. 2018. 'New Netflix-like Streaming Platform for Arts and Culture Has Landed'. *Evening Standard*, 9 July. Available at: www.standard.co.uk/tech/marquee-tv-arts-and-culture-netflix-a3882326.html.

Iqbal, J. and M. S. Sidhu. 2017. 'A Review on Making Things See: Augmented Reality for Futuristic Virtual Educator'. *Cogent Education*, 4(1). http://dx.doi.org/10.1080/2331186X.2017.1287392.

Jamaluddin, A. 2020. '10 Creative and Innovative Uses of Microsoft Kinect'. *Hongkiat*. Available at: www.hongkiat.com/blog/innovative-uses-kinect/.

Kaufman, S. 2018. 'The Dances in "Fortnite" Have Become Nearly as Contagious as the Game'. *The Washington Post*, 10 September. Available at: www.washingtonpost.com/news/arts-and-entertainment/wp/2018/09/10/the-dances-in-fortnite-have-become-nearly-as-contagious-as-the-game/.

Kim, Y. 2017. 'Dance Motion Capture and Composition Using Multiple RGB and Depth Sensors'. *International Journal of Distributed Sensor Networks*, 13(2). http://dx.doi.org/10.1177/1550147717696083.

Langer, S. K. 1953. *Feeling and Form: A Theory of Art*. New York: Charles Scribner's Sons.

Langer, S. 1976. 'The Dynamic Image: Some Philosophical Reflections on Dance'. *Salmagundi* 33/34, DANCE (spring/summer): 76–82.

Leskin, P. 2020. 'Charli D'Amelio Has Taken Over as TikTok's Biggest Star. These Are the 40 Most Popular Creators on the Viral Video App'. *Business Insider*, 25 March. Available at: www.businessinsider.com/tiktok-most-popular-stars-gen-z-influencers-social-media-app-2019-6?r=US&IR=T.

Loftus, J. 2010. 'Microsoft Kinect Hacked? Already?!' *Gizmodo*, 7 November. Available at: https://gizmodo.com/microsoft-kinect-hacked-already-5683744.

McHose, C. 2006. 'Interview with Hubert Godard: Phenomenological Space'. *Contact Quarterly* (summer/fall): 32–38.

Mapondera, M. 2019. 'Dancing with a Machine: Bill T. Jones on AI and Art'. My Social Interests, 15 May. Available at: http://mysocialinterests.ca/dancing-with-a-machine-bill-t-jones-on-ai-and-art/.

Paulsen, K. 2017. *Here/There: Telepresence, Touch and Art at the Interface*. Cambridge, MA: MIT Press.

Pérez, E. 2014. 'Meaningful Connections: Exploring the Uses of Telematic Technology in Performance'. *Liminalities: A Journal of Performance Studies*, 10(2). Available at: http://liminalities.net/10-1/meaningful-connections.pdf.

Robertson, A. 2019. 'Most of the Fortnite Dance Lawsuits Are on Pause'. *The Verge*, 9 March. Available at: www.theverge.com/2019/3/9/18257385/epic-fortnite-lawsuit-ribeiro-2milly-dance-emote-lawsuits-withdrawn-pause-registration.

Rubidge, S. 2002. 'Digital Technology in Choreography: Issues and Implications'. Presentation at the 17th Annual Symposium of the Dance Society of Korea, Seoul, South Korea, 6 November. Available at: www.sensedigital.co.uk/writing/DigChorIss02.pdf.

Snow, G. 2016. 'Audience Agency Data Shows Ageing Demographic of Theatregoers'. *The Stage*, 16 May. Available at: www.thestage.co.uk/news/audience-agency-data-shows-ageing-demographic-of-theatregoers.

Sensor Tower Blog. 2020. 'Top Apps Worldwide for March 2020 by Downloads'. Sensor Tower Blog, 8 April. Available at: https://sensortower.com/blog/top-apps-worldwide-march-2020-by-downloads.

Sermon, P. 2019. 'Shared Objective Empathy in Telematic Space'. In *Shifting Interfaces: Presence and Relationality in New Media Arts of the Early 21st Century*, edited by H. Aldouby, 75–91. Leuven: Leuven University Press.

Statista. 2020. 'Number of Registered Users of Fortnite Worldwide from August 2017 to May 2020'. Available at: www.statista.com/statistics/746230/fortnite-players/.

Strutt, D. 2021 (forthcoming). 'Motion Capture and the Digital Dance Aesthetic: Using Inertial Sensor Motion Tracking for Devising and Producing Contemporary Dance Performance'. In *Dance Data, Cognition, and Multimodal Communication*, edited by C. Fernandes, V. Evola and C. Ribeiro. London: Routledge.

Waterson, J. 2021. '62% of UK Adults Played Video Games during the Pandemic, Says Ofcom'. *The Guardian*, 28 April. Available at: www.theguardian.com/games/2021/apr/28/62-of-uk-adults-played-computer-games-during-the-pandemic-says-ofcom.

Vincs, K. and J. McCormick. 2010. 'Touching Space: Using Motion Capture and Stereo Projection to Create a "Virtual Haptics" of Dance'. *Leonardo*, 43(4): 359–366.

Vincs, K. and K. Barbour. 2014. 'Snapshots of Complexity: Using Motion Capture and Principal Component Analysis to Reconceptualise Dance'. *Digital Creativity*, 25(1): 62–78.

Wechsler, R. 2006. 'Artistic Considerations in the Use of Motion Tracking by Live Performers: A Practical Guide'. In *Performance and Technology: Practices of Virtual Embodiment and Interactivity*, edited by S. Broadhurst and J. Machon, 60–77. New York: Palgrave Macmillan.

Wood, K., R. E. Cisneros and S. Whatley. 2017. 'Motion Capturing Emotions'. *Open Cultural Studies*, 1: 504–513.

THE FUTURE OF AUDIO

12

Everywhere in Particular: Some Thoughts on the Practice and Potential of Transpositional Locative Sound Art

NG Bristow

Transposition: the act of changing the order of two or more things

Locative media: digital information tagged to a physical location

Point of Departure

Before attempting to unpack the technical terms in the chapter title, I would like to explain how I came to be interested in the potential of this subgenre of sound art. In the summer of 2019, South African writer and director Mathapelo Mofokeng and I made *One Oh Eight* (Bristow and Mofokeng 2019), a pair of geolocated audio dramas set on the 108 bus routes in London and Cape Town. The pieces are still live; in order to experience them the listener downloads an app to their mobile phone, which triggers the audio drama to play when their bus passes a predetermined point on the route. The transpositional aspect comes from the fact that the sounds of each city are swapped, so that audience on the London bus hears the drama set on the Cape Town bus and the Cape Town listener hears the London drama. In common with podcasts, or indeed any form of audio drama, the listener is transported in their mind's ear 'somewhere else'. But since the dramas are site-specific, both taking place on a 108 bus, this sense of being transported somewhere else is of a different order. The sensory correlatives which comprise the embodied listening experience, such as the world scrolling past the window, the vibrations of the bus, the presence of other passengers and the sonic environment of the listener's own bus which bleeds through 'leaky' earbuds, are superimposed on top of the imaginary space of the drama. The uncanny amalgam brings to the fore what is common to the story world and the listener's own world and what is unique to each. Thus the listener has an embodied sense of how their life diverges from, and converges with, that of the fictional passenger on a bus on the opposite hemisphere.

Clearly the act of transposing the soundtracks of bus journeys in South Africa and Britain comes freighted with social, political and cultural considerations, but this chapter is not the space to investigate these. They will be explored in the next chapter, which takes the form of a short case study of *One Oh Eight*. Here I will focus on the artistic practice of locative transpositional sound art, to which *One Oh Eight* belongs. I will discuss some key examples of related pieces by other artists, along with the technological and cultural drivers which make this practice possible, affordable and above all timely. Finally, I will sketch out some of the paradigm-shifting possibilities which might be about to materialise in this field.

Applied Schizophonia

Composer and ecologist R. Murray Schafer coined the term *schizophonia* (Schafer 1969) to describe the process by which a sound is split from its source via recording and relocated via playback or transmission to a different location. This is such a ubiquitous part of our everyday lives that it comes as a shock to discover that Schafer considered this process of dissociation an aberration and chose his neologism as a deliberate provocation. Schafer was a pioneer in the field of eco-acoustics, i.e., the study of the interrelationship, mediated through sound, of human beings and their environment. His polemical stance was motivated by a desire to proselytise for ecological balance in the soundscape. But the jolt that reading the phrase today gives is useful to draw attention to the provenance and composition of the polyphonous soundscape of the modern world which we take for granted.

Music researcher Heikki Uimonen uses the less pejorative term *transphonia* (Uimonen 2020) to describe the same phenomenon. The specific type of transphonia I want to examine here is locative audio, an artistic practice whereby sounds are removed from their original location and transplanted to a unique spatial address point, which a listener accesses in situ. This could take the form of an installation of speakers, but the work which I will be discussing is accessed via a personal headset and geolocated through a mobile device.

A key work which epitomises this approach is *Jungle-ized* by the fiercely transnational Soundwalk Collective (2016). The artwork is a bold experiment in metaphorically folding the map of the world at the equator by relocating the sounds of a small section of the Amazon rainforest to a corresponding area of Times Square, New York. The listener downloads the app, borrows a pair of noise-cancelling headphones from the organisers (the live street sounds being so loud) and explores a spatially coherent sonic environment magicked from its original location in Peru to that most urban of spaces, the concrete jungle of Manhattan. The experience is uncanny; the listener's eyes and body remain in New York, while their ears and mind are transported 5,000 kilometres south. Crucially the virtual sonic world they are navigating has coherence and consistent dimensions. The sounds of the river are located at a precise address point. Approaching it, the sound increases in volume. Moving away, it attenuates. The sonic mise-en-scène is rich in detail, comprising a host of precisely positioned elements or sound objects, such as a chorus of frogs on the river bank, a troop of howler monkeys and members of the Shipibo tribe singing sacred songs. Furthermore, multiple listeners can enter the same virtual space. This is audio-augmented reality, and because it has no need for special glasses or other screen-based apparatus, the immersive and transformative effects are much more pronounced than its visual equivalent. Screens, as the word suggests, are a kind of barrier, a constant reminder of 'how the trick is being done', whereas sound operates on our imagination in a much more pervasive manner.[1] As sound artist Janet Cardiff puts it in relation to her own work, 'we understand three-dimensional space by using our vision but also by the character of sounds we hear. If these sounds are manipulated and changed, then our perception of reality can be drastically affected' (Cardiff 2013).[2]

The schizophonic gulf in *Jungle-ized* is so vast that it produces a strong sense of cognitive dissonance in the user. The intention is nakedly eco-political: a direct application of Claude Lévi-Strauss' principle of binary opposition, whereby values are ascribed through the contrast between an entity and its diametric opposite. *Jungle-ized* is also seductive, playful and catalytic. Interestingly, *Jungle-ized* has an antecedent in a soundwork proposed, but never carried out, by R. Murray Schafer. *Wilderness Radio* was conceived as a project to transmit 'the uneventful events of the natural soundscape ... into the hearts of cities' (Shafer 1990, 210). Clearly there is good schizophonia and bad schizophonia.

Jungle-ized is non-narrative (except in the sense of its strongly implied narrative about the environment and global responsibility) and non-dramatic, though it shares some of the experiential qualities of the immersive environments created by theatre companies such as Punchdrunk, who devise theatrical experiences in physically transformed locations, which the audience are free to explore. It also has a relationship to the exploration genre of videogames such as *The Forest* (Endnight Games 2018) and it is easy to imagine how subsequent pieces of work following a similar approach could be further gamified.

There is a question about whether the work should be defined as site-specific or site-responsive. A second iteration of *Jungle-ized* mapped the same soundscape onto an area in Miami, and the group are actively looking for other sites in major cities in the northern hemisphere to bring it to. *Jungle-ized*'s app designer, Fred Adam, has described their desire to 'pleat, fold and even shred the map to create new sonic superimpositions' (Bristow and Adam 2020). This leads us to consider a category of locative work which radio producer and sound artist Francesca Panneta has described as relative location-based: 'movement through or interaction with the proximate landscape rather than presence at a specific site' (Panetta n.d.). Duncan Speakman's experiment in 'ambient literature', *It Must Have Been Dark by Then* (Speakman 2017), is designed to be read/listened to/walked in the user's own environment. The locative trigger points for each sonic element are based on distances relative to the start point. Among other components, its soundscape relocates field recordings of atmospheres sourced in Louisiana, Latvia and Tunisia. The multiple paths through its narrative echo and build on similar ideas in (non-ambient) literature by twentieth-century writers such as Julio Cortázar, Georges Perec and B. S. Johnson.

Ecumenopolis (Vermeire 2019) shares some of the same impulses as *Jungle-ized*, but with a utopian rather than ecological imperative. In this case the piece transposes urban sound sources and sets up a dialogical rather than dialectical relationship between the samples and their relocated addresses. The project gathers field recordings of various 'silences' in and around libraries in Sao Paulo, Athens, London and Moscow, and uses the platform CGeomap to geolocate the atmosphere of one library on top of another to create a blended virtual global space. The user accesses the piece via a web browser and encounters the sounds by following the virtual map of the library to the designated address points, where the sample is automatically triggered. Their phone (or other browsing device) then displays an image and text tag identifying the recordist and the original source, e.g., 'Andrew Stuck, pigeons and construction work in front of Moscow library'. There is also an option to experience it in 'armchair mode' by navigating through a map on your laptop off-site.

Taking its name from the Greek city planner Constantinos Doxiadis' concept of a worldwide city, *Ecumenopolis* is collectivist (the field recordings were made by participants on soundwalks led by Geert Vermeire), transnational and situationist in spirit, with the playful action of superimposing new layers of sound onto a territory producing a parallel reality. The process of making the field recordings involves attending to the environment as part of a dérive³ and the soundwalks are themselves as much a part of the work as the composited piece. At its heart is the truth which John Cage famously demonstrated; not only is there no such thing as silence, but no two 'silences' are the same.

What common threads might we draw from these examples? Transpositional geolocative sound work is transformative and frequently transnational – both in terms of the theme of the work itself and the teams of people involved in its production. For this reason it is of particular appeal to artists concerned with geo- or eco-politics. It is at once internationalist and intensely local. It is easy to see its burgeoning appeal at a time when the world seems preoccupied with climate change and the hardening of borders.

Jungle-ized is a one-way transposition. There is no complementary piece which transplants the sounds of Times Square to the Amazon, presumably for the obvious reason that it wouldn't find much of an audience. But entertaining the concept of such a madcap undertaking makes for an attractively Herzogian prospect. It also leads to the realisation that anyone can now geolocate any form of media anywhere in the world that has a GPS signal. And they can do this from anywhere else.

Before and After Science

Barry Salt's controversial book *Film Style and Technology: History and Analysis* (2009) mounts a persuasive argument for the primacy of technological developments in the evolution of cinematic language.⁴ Salt's argument is that Godard's iconoclastic *A Bout de Souffle* (1960), for instance, exists in the form it does largely because of the development of the lightweight Eclair Caméflex news camera and the fast Ilford HP5 film stock, which allowed director of photography Raoul Coutard to shoot on location with available light.

In the same way, technological developments in personal audio equipment have clearly influenced the shape of the evolution of applied transphonia. The portable transistor radio facilitated listening to music on the move, but it wasn't until the release of the Sony Walkman portable cassette player in 1979 that the possibility of choosing the personal 'soundtrack to your life' arrived (Patton 1999). Movement through space, often an urban space, crossed on foot, bike, skateboard or public transport was suddenly fused with the soundtrack playing in your headphones, to offer a quasi-cinematic experience. It was up to you to select the appropriate soundtrack to the film you wanted to live/watch/float through.

Notwithstanding the Walkman's impact in popularising the mixtape as a medium for courtship, its critics characterised it as essentially solipsistic, a device designed to enclose its user in a bubble. As a keen Walkman user in the 1980s I'd freely admit that it tended to insulate its wearer from the world. And that the sensation was seductively addictive. The dangers of the so-called 'Walkman Effect' were a common concern in the press at the time. Attempts to combat this by Sony included adding a second headphone jack (to allow for two-person listening) and a talk button, neither of which were popularly embraced. Fast-forward past the Discman and the iPod to today, and the ubiquity of smartphones makes it hard to imagine what all the fuss was about – or, alternatively, to see the Walkman as the harbinger of a greater evil. We are all networked individuals now, simultaneously here and not here while wearing our devices. And of course we remain able to choose when we plug ourselves into them.

It is principally thanks to the smartphone that locative audio's time has come. The smartphone is an excellent delivery system for audio; it comes with GPS as standard, and an established audience habituated to downloading apps and listening to podcasts. There is as yet no industry-standard platform with which to create and host locative audio. Bespoke digital solutions for sound artworks without development teams to support them quickly fall foul of obsolescence through incompatible operating system updates. In fact, one of the ongoing problems for creators is the speed with which their work becomes unplayable. However, there are signs that more stable platforms are emerging. *One Oh Eight* is hosted on Echoes, a platform with good potential for a stable future. Robust, well-supported and with a deliberately limited number of smartly chosen features, Echoes is user-friendly for both creators and consumers. Tellingly, its developer Josh Kopeček has made the decision to keep Echoes audio-only, while some other locative platforms also support geotagging text and visual images.

The phrase 'augmented reality' (AR) automatically conjures up an image of smart glasses or mobile screens displaying overlaid visuals, but there are signs that the preferred user interface for AR might turn out to be sonic. Removing the screen from the equation would make for a much more immersive experience. Cue the world of 'hearables' – or wearable sound devices which can be controlled through voice commands (like with Siri or Alexa) or through gestures and haptic input. Bose has recently launched Frames, which are sunglasses with tiny speakers mounted above the ears using bone conductivity to transmit the sound. Since they don't use in-ear buds, Frames allow the wearer to hear a blend of the audio playing through the device and the ambient sounds of the outside world – so no more Walkman Effect. Other recent developments in audio equipment, this time spun off from gaming technology, facilitate an ambisonic listening experience, where the sound is located in a virtual sphere all around the listener, not just surrounding them at ear level, but also above and below. In-built head-tracking sensors in the hearable device can synchronise the spatial placement of sounds with the listener's head movements for even greater immersive effect.

At an online symposium on locative media and (im)mobility, Professor Ricardo Climent of Manchester University expressed the view that the next crucial stage involved connecting up the ecosystem of locative media to other data ecosystems such as Google Street View (Climent 2020). Geert Vermeire and Fred Adam of open-source platform CGeomap were adamant that locative media must stay independent and that it is vital to resist its co-opting by big data (Vermeire and Adam 2020). Climent pointed out that on balance the existence of a single-destination aggregator like YouTube has proved to be a useful development, and that wider distribution of locative media would be helpful for organisations such as museums to widen their reach and demonstrate impact for funding. 'And anyway', he concluded, 'it will ultimately be the users who decide what model and tools and platforms survive.'

From the Here-and-Now to the Here-and-Then

So far we've considered the possibilities of spatial transposition of soundscapes, but the same technology also lends itself to experiments in temporal transposition, replacing the live sounds of the listener's current environment with sounds from a different time. The antecedents of this lie in the humble audio guide, where the recorded voice of a historical expert (or a voice actor speaking the expert's words) plays on a headset, commenting on the past of the environment the listener is moving through. More sophisticated variations might incorporate fragments of oral history, perhaps augmented by music cues, spot effects and evocative atmosphere tracks. These soundscapes are fictional montages of elements which both conjure and comment on the past (or pasts) of the space being explored. The spectrum of possibilities is vast, ranging from prosaically informative (such as a museum guide) to the poetic and haunting. Once again, inventive use of readily available technology and sophisticated combinations of simple elements can produce highly effective and affecting work, as in the sonic bricolage of *Hackney Hear* (Panetta and Greenwell 2012), or the sound walks of artists Janet Cardiff and George Buras Miller. *London Street Noises* (Drever et al. 2019) takes field recordings from 1928, made as part of an anti-noise pollution campaign by Columbia Records and *The Daily Mail*, and geolocates them where they were originally made. Here it is the context (spatially identical but temporally displaced) that provides the intellectual meaning, while the emotional dimension of the piece derives from the timbre of the sounds – the sense of listening to ghosts enhanced by the low fidelity of the original field recording.

What mobile ambisonics make possible, for the first time, is the ability to record and play back the sounds of an environment as a coherent 360-degree acoustic space, which the listener can inhabit and explore as they would the sonic architecture of a real space. As we discussed earlier, this form of augmented reality is immersive and sensorially, cognitively and emotionally transformative of the user's experience of their environment. Once you begin to treat the soundscape of an environment as spatially consistent with the movements of the person navigating it, but chronologically asynchronous, thrilling possibilities begin to open up. In a sense, time travel becomes dizzyingly conceivable.

Jorge Luis Borges' playful essay *A New Refutation of Time* (Borges 1999) is a thought experiment which posits an escape from the tyranny of the linear model of time by suggesting the conditions in which identical moments might reoccur. Borges imagines Huckleberry Finn sailing down the Mississippi on a raft, looking at the stars and listening to the sounds of the river. The input of his senses, and the thoughts which these stir in Huck's mind, might be identical in every degree to those of another moment, which is to say, Borges argues, that the moments themselves might be identical. The existence of one such repetition (or duplication, since repetition already implies a sequence) is all that it would take to deny the linearity of time altogether. Borges concludes the essay by coming clean and confessing that he has been indulging in sophistry. Such wishful thinking is only good for metaphysical parlour tricks and writers of fantastic fiction. His fanciful refutation of linear time is a mere consolation from the inescapable reality of the world.

But what is all art if not trickery? To be aware of how the trick is done and yet feel the power of its effect deepens the pleasure. And if, as Noël Coward pointed out, cheap music can be extraordinarily potent, how much more affecting can the spells of this new sonic magic set be? Imagine an art piece or experiment in living where someone sets up equipment to make an ambisonic recording of their house, day in, day out, like sonic CCTV. All the comings and goings of the house's inhabitants and guests; the music they listen to; the sounds of all the devices they use in the house; the traffic that passes outside – all of it permanently preserved as replayable 360-degree audio recordings. It would be like the automatic back-up which allows you to return your computer's hard drive to its condition at any given date. Twenty or thirty years later the chrononaut who set up the experiment might decide to retrieve a particular moment, and slip on her or his headset and walk through the soundscape of *then* superimposed on top of the physical space of *now*. They would hear their old self's conversations, footsteps, body movements. Maybe they might hear their now-grown-up child's first words. Or the sounds of the night which brought that child into the world... Perhaps they would pass the sound recordings and equipment on to the new owner of the house as the next custodian of the *genius loci*, and that owner in turn would do the same to the next inhabitant and so on. So long as the process continued, every breath, laugh, sob and fart would be accessible and exist forever *now*.

Of course, it's a Philip K. Dickian vortex of solipsism and existential fracture, the stuff of techno-conspiracy nightmares – Murray's dreaded schizophonia run riot. But maybe a forgivable fantasy to indulge in. The first inclination when thinking about the dramatic potential of new technology is often to think in dystopian terms. And the Devil, of course, has the best tunes.

What of the other possibilities? There are several key aspects of the locative medium which are significant in assessing its potential. First, the immersive nature of the experience – the sense of walking a mile in someone else's shoes and listening through their ears – makes it an ideal conductor for empathy. Second, the comparative affordability of the technology fosters grassroots creators/innovators. Third, thanks to the GPS component, its intrinsic specificity grounds it in the intensely local. The precise spatial and temporal address points imbue the sounds with both subjective intensity and objective authority. Fleeting moments can be preserved and retrieved. The changing sounds in a locale can be marked and treasured – or resisted, depending on one's personal political position. Hypothetical futures for a neighbourhood can be sketched out (the sonic equivalent to an architect's fly-through) and embraced, rejected or modified. It's important to acknowledge that it is not the technology per se which creates the multiple layers co-existing in present, past(s) and imagined futures from which our neighbourhoods are comprised – the apparatus merely reveals them. But the nature of that revelation is powerful because it offers an embodied understanding of the fact that our lives are not lived adjacent to each other but on top of one another, and on top of versions of ourselves.

Warp Factor: The Electric Guitar, Lens Flare and Dub

Technology may well be the principal driver for change in modes of artistic expression, but the uses which artists make of it seldom take the form which its inventors predict. To put it another way, technological R&D departments rarely get the future they design for. For instance, the motivation to develop the electric guitar was simply to amplify an acoustic guitar so that jazz guitarists' solos didn't get lost among the rest of the band. The very qualities which we now think of as being intrinsic to the instrument (harmonic overtones, distortion, feedback) are not only accidental side-effects, but in terms of the original intention of ton-ally faithful amplification, they are disastrous flaws. Jimi Hendrix's flamboyant extended techniques on the Fender Stratocaster could never have been fore-seen – or likely understood – by the electric guitar's inventors. Of course, once the artistic vocabulary has been expanded by creative 'misuse', the technologists respond by designing modifications to facilitate the new direction and the fuzz box and its equivalents are born.

As musician and artist Brian Eno has observed, 'whatever you now find weird, ugly, uncomfortable and nasty about a new medium will surely become its signature' (Eno 1996). Film lenses were coated with oxide and shielded with the camera's matte-box to prevent undesirable lens flare, but these days you can buy digital plug-ins for postproduction software to simulate the creative use of lens flare first popularised by cinematographers Láslo Kovács and Vilmos Zsigmond, who flouted the rules of good taste back in the late 1960s. The designers of mobile phones certainly did not include GPS tracking and accelerometers in order to facilitate geolocative audio, but these are the functions which allow developers to create platforms which make this kind of work possible and available. These examples suggest that in order to survive, the developers in turn must respond to the use (or 'misuse') which locative media consumers and creators make of their apps, however much that use deviates from the future which they were designing for when they produced them.

What are the necessary conditions in order for leaps of artistic evolution to flourish? Availability of tools, lack of reverence for the orthodoxy and 'hackability' would seem to be some of the most important, along with a cultural context in which these artistic mutations confer an 'evolutionary advantage'. Frequently this means a direct connection with popular culture. Karlheinz Stockhausen's experiments in electronic music may have been highly significant within the academy, but arguably they had less cultural impact than the pioneering work of the BBC's Radiophonic Workshop, where Daphne Oram and Delia Derbyshire applied the techniques of *musique concrète* to create soundscapes for the surreal radio comedy *The Goon Show* and, later, the British family sci-fi television programme *Dr Who*.

The nature of these experiments may go far beyond simply popularising existing avant-garde practices. Often they give rise to paradigm shifts. With the birth of dub reggae, King Tubby and his sometime associate and later rival Lee 'Scratch' Perry pioneered an entirely new way of thinking about the recording studio – using the mixing desk as an instrument in its own right. Echo and tape delay effects, which had previously been used to suggest an acoustic space for the vocalist, were reconceived so that they were no longer principally concerned with evoking *space* but had become about manipulating and warping *time*. It seems entirely likely that locative media is going to undergo its own warping from similarly inclined visionary rebels. The current condition of the available technology and its immersive qualities are simply too seductive to imagine otherwise.

Back Where I Got On

I first came to Goldsmiths as an undergraduate in 1983. Now, some 37 years later, I am back working as a lecturer. I frequently walk down the corridor which I walked down on my very first day. Many things have changed (the absence of smokers; the presence of the Bank of Santander; the Drama Department rebranded as the Department of Theatre and Performance), but essentially the corridor remains the same. I often find myself transported back in time, particularly since the recent death of my friend Paul, who I first met at Goldsmiths. Lately I have taken to wondering what it might be like to hear our ghosts walking down that corridor. If such a 360-degree recording existed, I could turn on my dynamic, spatialised audio headset and follow discreetly behind the sonic spectres of the 19-year-old Paul and Nigel, eavesdropping on the banalities of our conversation. Footsteps, clothing rustle (Paul's long, second-hand 'Bunnymen' coat), the higher pitched voices of youth; everything would be brought back in hyperreal detail. And then I would hear the two of them peel off and disappear through the doors by the music practice rooms as I walked on to the end of the corridor and emerged in the twenty-first century.

It's hard not to be excited by the thoughts of what a modern-day Marcel Proust, Samuel Beckett, Hannah Arendt, Virginia Woolf, Alain Resnais, Nicolas Roeg or Lee 'Scratch' Perry will do with these pocket time and space machines.

Listen

The dramas are available at: https://walklistencreate.org/walkingpiece/108/.

References

2016 *Jungle-Ized*. Locative media work. Available at: https://vimeo.com/315443413.

Adam, F. 2020. *Jungle-Ized*. Interview with the author, June 2020.

Borges, J.-L. 1999. *A New Refutation of Time (Nueva refutación del tiempo) The Total Library: Non-Fiction 1922–1986*, translated by S. Levine. London: Penguin, 317–332.

Bristow, N. and F. Adam. 2020. Interview with the author, June 2020.

Bristow, N. and M. Mofokeng. 2019. *One Oh Eight*. Locative media work. Available at: https://walklistencreate.org/walkingpiece/108/.

Cardiff, J. 2013. *Forty Part Motet*. Exhibition notes. Cleveland, OH: Cleveland Museum of Art.

Climent, R. 2020. *Locative Media, Climate Change And (Im)Mobility During the Covid-19 Pandemic Conference*. London: Department of Digital Humanities, King's College London.

Drever, J., A. Yildirim and M. Cobianchi. 2019. *London Street Noises*. Locative media work. Available at: www.museumofwalking.org.uk/events/london-street-noises/.

Eno, B. 1996. *A Year: With Swollen Appendices*. London: Faber & Faber, entry for 19 December.

Knabb, K. 2020. *Situationist International Anthology*. London: Pluto Press.

Panetta, F. n.d.. 'Glossary'. Audioar.org. Available at: https://audioar.org/glossary/.

Panetta, F. and L. Greenwell. 2012. *Hackney Hear*. Locative media work. Available at: www.hackneyhear.com/.

Patton, P. (quoting Nell, R.). 1999. 'Humming Off-Key for Two "Decades"'. *The New York Times*, 29 July. Available at: www.nytimes.com/1999/07/29/technology/humming-off-key-for-two-decades.html.

Salt, B. 2009. *Film Style and Technology*. London: Starword.

Schafer, R. M. 1969. *The New Soundscape*. Toronto: BMI Canada.

Schafer, R. M. 1990. 'Radical Radio'. In *Sound by Artists*, edited by D. Lander and M. Lexier, 206–207. Toronto: Art Metropole; Banff: Walter Phillips Gallery.

Speakman, D. 2017. *It Must Have Been Dark by Then*. Locative media work. Available at: https://research.ambientlit.com/index.php/it-must-have-been-dark-by-then/.

Uimonen, H. 2020. 'Hits and Misses: Music and the Sonic Construction of Place'. *Architectural Research in Finland*, 2: 18–28.

Vermeire, G. 2019. *Ecumenopolis*. Locative media work. Available at: https://cgeomap.eu/ecumenopolis/.

13

If 6 Were 9 (or 2 x 108): A Case Study of the *One Oh Eight* Project

*Richard M. Shannon, NG Bristow
and Mathapelo Mofokeng*

> *You wait forever for an audio drama set on the 108 bus and then two come
> along at once...*

One Oh Eight is a site-specific locative media project, comprising a pair of
twinned audio dramas set on the 108 bus routes in Cape Town and London; but
the sounds of each are transposed, so that the listener on the London bus hears
the drama taking place in Cape Town, and the Cape Town listener hears the
London drama. This chapter will consider the project from the points of view of
its cultural, political and artistic intentions; it will look at the formal, dramatur-
gical and technological approaches taken; and it will reflect on the experiential
outcome for the listener. We will conclude by considering the next iterations of
this project and the implications of our discoveries for further immersive and/or
locative audio drama.

    One Oh Eight is composed of two 45-minute dramas: *Mother City?* by
Mathapelo Mofokeng and *Dumbstruck on Bazely Street* by NG Bristow. *Mother
City?* tells the story of three women from diverse backgrounds who meet on
the 108 bus from Adderley Street to Hangberg, on the way back from the family
planning clinic. An unlikely sisterhood is formed by the women who are bound by
a common secret, a termination they're all undergoing. Having met that morning
in the clinic queue, they come together to seek comfort, information, clarity and
validation, since not all pregnant women are treated equally. Though the subject
matter is weighty, *Mother City?* avoids feeling heavy through judicious flashes of
comedy. *Dumbstruck on Bazely Street* dramatises the experience of PJ, a middle-
aged man on antidepressants, self-medicating with alcohol, who meets his ex-
wife and dead daughter on the bus, where they attempt to stage an intervention.

The drama gives the listener access to PJ's thoughts, which are often at odds with his actions. A further layer of commentary comes from the dubious advice of the bus announcements, which grow increasingly outrageous and give voice to PJ's deepest fears. It is a story of damnation, salvation and forgiveness, told with black humour and compassion for imperfect people. The *One Oh Eight* project has clear formal qualities; it is site-specific, transpositional and dialogical. Each of these factors impacts on the audience's experience of the drama.

Site-Specific

Traditionally, radio and podcast dramas are resolutely *non*-site-specific. In fact, a significant part of their appeal lies in the fact that the listener forgets their current surroundings and is transported elsewhere in their imagination. Listening to a drama set on a bus while travelling *on a bus* encourages the listener (or maybe it would be more accurate to consider them as 'the participant') to attempt to assimilate other sensory information – visual, kinaesthetic and extraneous ambient sound – into the story which they are listening to. This is precisely the kind of sensory information which the listener usually disengages from when they are lost in a conventional audio drama. With *One Oh Eight*, where the sense data of their surroundings is consistent with the audio drama, the immersive aspect is likely to be heightened. But *One Oh Eight* complicates this relationship by transposing the London and Cape Town stories, so that along with conson-ance there is also dissonance, where the world of the listener and the story world are pointedly at odds. This functions as a kind of *Verfremdungseffekt*, drawing the listener's attention to the discrepancies between their experience and that of the characters. The intention behind *One Oh Eight* is that the act of transposition will create a constant push and pull between the contrary states of immersion and estrangement/reflection.

The 108 bus route was chosen partly because of its proximity to Goldsmiths, but also because in both countries it passes through a series of deeply contrasting neighbourhoods. Although the action is (mostly) confined to characters sitting in a static arrangement of seats on the bus, they and the listener are propelled through a constantly evolving environment. This is a quasi-cinematic experi-ence – the radiophonic equivalent of a long tracking shot. It is not coincidental that both writer/directors (Mathapelo Mofokeng and NG Bristow) and producers (Tamara MacLachlan and Tracy Bass) are all also filmmakers.

The 108 bus route in Cape Town starts at Adderley Street, and passes through areas with multi-million-rand houses, including Sea Point, Camps Bay and Hout Bay Harbour, with Hangberg as its final destination. Hangberg is an area where scenes of political protest, poverty and unemployment are high. 'Reconciliation'[1] has failed in South Africa, and this is noticeable in Cape Town partly due to the urban apartheid planning historically enforced in the province. Owing to the Group Areas Act imposed in 1950, on the outskirts of every affluent area is a ghetto, where people who the apartheid government declared as 'coloured' reside. When the Group Areas Act was enforced, Hout Bay was declared a white area. The apartheid government forcibly removed those it classified as 'coloured' and established Hangberg as an area to house those forcibly removed. Hangberg would supply cheap labour for the fishing industry. The 108 bus route takes passengers on a jarring visual experience through the striking dissimilarities in areas that stretch over a 21-kilometre distance. Picturesque gated housing estates and small farms, with small shack dwellings, stretch up the steep slopes of the mountain.

The 108 bus route in London progresses from leafy, predominantly white, middle-class Blackheath, through the new developments on the Greenwich peninsula and the O2 Arena, before crossing the Thames via the Blackwall Tunnel, to emerge in the multi-ethnic and economically disadvantaged Tower Hamlets. As with most public transport in London, the passengers on the 108 come from a wide variety of socio-economic and racial backgrounds. The soundscape of accents and languages spoken is equally diverse, though the 'received pronunciation' of the recorded bus announcements sounds like a hangover from an earlier time. In terms of the drama, the most salient aspect of the route is the fact that the 108 is the only London bus to go under the river. This resonates strongly with the story's themes of liminal states and descent into the underworld.

Transpositional

There is a certain transgressive playfulness to the idea of reconfiguring the globe and swapping its hemispheres. Of course, upending everything also dislodges some of the cultural contents of its pockets. The 108 bus route in Cape Town has 41 stops between Adderley Street and Hangberg, each one a reminder of the Dutch and British colonial history started in the Cape Colony. The names of most of the bus stops offer a colonial flavour, such as Lower Victoria, Mount Rhodes,

Lancaster, Oxford Earl and Riebeek, to name a few. Though writer Mathapelo did not weave South Africa's colonial history into the story, the blaring of the bus stop announcements acts as a poignant reminder of how far South Africa still has to go in its efforts to decolonise itself.

Transposition uses dislocation to bring about transformation of the familiar through re-contextualisation. Thus the routine setting of the listener's own 108 bus route is made strange by its juxtaposition with, and 'contamination' by, the unfamiliar 108 of the story world. The results for the listener can be guessed at, but not predicted with 100% certainty. There are multiple factors at play in the listening experience which are beyond the authors' control, including: time of day, weather, the other passengers on the bus and traffic flow. But this lack of control is something to be celebrated rather than lamented, as it brings a live element into a recorded art form. It is a way of welcoming the real world, which is necessarily unstable, into a fixed fictional construction.

Dialogical

The impulse behind the *One Oh Eight* project is dialogical rather than dialectical. Cape Town and London are not set in binary opposition to each other, nor are the story worlds and the listening environments. Rather, commonalities are foregrounded, and the real passengers listening to the dramas are invited to place themselves in the position of their fictional counterparts.

The idea of a dialogical approach also exists in the relationship between *Mother City?* and *Bazely Street.* Although very few people are likely to experience both dramas in situ, they can be listened to online in non-site-specific, 'armchair' listening mode. Playing both pieces back-to-back further reveals the conversation between the texts and enriches the listening experience of both. *Mother City?* is concerned with birth, motherhood and the choices and politics surrounding reproductive rights. *Bazley Street* deals with death, fatherhood and the choices and responsibilities that come with that. Both dramas find shoots of hope growing out of bleak ground and celebrate those moments of absurd humour where people are at their most human.

Mother City? is naturalistic and locates its drama in a carefully drawn social and political context. *Bazely Street* is surreal, expressionistic and seeks to make one individual's life resonant for audiences who might not share his material circumstances, but who will share the same range of human emotions. There are echoes, reflections and refractions between the two texts; some were planned, others were providential. Hospitals feature in both stories, some lines of dialogue were deliberately repeated in each, along with action involving key props, such as a bottle of pills. But the discovery that there is an Adderly Street at the Bazely Street stop was pure chance. The fact that the Cape Town story begins at one Adderly Street – a prosperous area very unlike its London namesake – and the London story concludes at another felt like synchronicity.

Dramaturgy

Mother City?

In 1996, South Africa legalised abortion during the country's transition from apartheid to democracy. Though South Africa has many public health facilities offering family planning services, many women do not access these services due to the stigma, shame and judgement they receive from the majority of 'God-fearing' healthcare practitioners at these clinics. Though the transition into a democratic and independent state resulted in a socially progressive constitution, at large, the constitution is fundamentally at odds with the beliefs, values and views of most South Africans. This makes accessing termination services an endeavour entered into with shame, fear and silence for most women, resulting in many women obtaining illegal and unsafe procedures. The denial, quietness and discrimination around sex outside of marriage and the restricted social autonomy of women has posed a danger to those accessing family planning services.

 Mother City? is set in an everyday scenario, which is a bus journey. The intention of the audio drama was to offer a slice of life showing the experiences of three diverse South African women, using termination as a lens into their complicated worlds. It explores themes of patriarchy, segregation, class, racism, unemployment and violence. *Mother City?* digs deep into what it means to terminate a pregnancy. It explores the language used around terminations, some of the myths, the taboo subject of sex, access to services and the role cultural and religious beliefs hold. Essentially the story concludes with the message that termination is a personal journey which is experienced differently by each woman: easy for some, hard for others, complicated for most and silent for the greater part.

 The 108 bus transports nationally and racially diverse groups of people. When Mathapelo conducted a research trip along the route, she found that the demographic was made up of South African isiXhosa speakers, Zimbabweans who spoke chiShona/isiNdebele and 'coloureds' who switched between Afrikaans and English. She found that the groups on the bus were segregated, and it was this segregation that made it possible for each group to exchange in their respective languages. Due to the audience of *Mother City?* being London-based commuters, the audio drama would need to be predominantly English. Through the common secret that the characters on the bus are bound by, the status quo on the bus is interrupted. The *Mother City?* characters (from diverse backgrounds) exchange their experiences in English, which is the shared language among Cape Town-based South Africans.

Though writer Mathapelo is Black, South African and a woman, and can relate to the themes explored in the story, she does not represent the experiences of every South African woman of colour. To avoid issues of misrepresentation and the perpetuation of stereotypes, Mathapelo invited actress Quanita Adams to play the role of a sensitivity reader and act as a cultural eye during the development process. Quanita also played one of the characters in the story, and was available during the rehearsals and production phase for consultation and check-ins.

Dumbstruck on Bazely Street

Bazley Street has different preoccupations and therefore different challenges from *Mother City?*. The central character, PJ, is in a profound state of grief and guilt following the loss of his daughter. The combination of emotional trauma and PJ's misuse of alcohol and prescription medication triggers a dissociative state. The drama treats his hallucinations as though they were real; accordingly they need to sound acoustically believable. The principal challenge was to make PJ's experience relatable, involving and coherent. The listener needs to care about PJ and want to spend 45 minutes in his company.

Humour, in the form of self-deprecation, sparky dialogue and splashes of absurdism, is a central part of the approach. It was also necessary to ground the wilder elements of fantasy in seductive plausibility. The more the listener feels like they are on a real bus moving through a real London, the more likely they are to surrender to the experience and accept the unreal. The story starts off in a recognisable 'everyday world' and, little by little, smuggles in its irrational ingredients. The process is imperceptible, like the metaphor of boiling a frog. The appearance of PJ's dead daughter on the bus is presented as magic realism, and by the time the audience have accepted that, they are primed to go on the rest of the trip with him.

Two imperatives determined the approach to the acoustic space: the need for subjectivity and hyperreality. This combination of qualities seemed ideally suited to binaural recording. Binaural audio uses bespoke microphones rigged in the same configuration as the ears on a human head in order to replicate the precise 360-degree spatial placement of sounds when played back on headphones or earbuds. This strategy meant that it was possible for the audience to experience everything from PJ's perspective on a specifically chosen seat on the bus. If PJ turned his head, so did the listener's sound image. Binaural location tracks were recorded on the real 108 bus to ensure maximum verisimilitude. These were then mixed with studio recordings of the dialogue. The radio studio was configured with carefully placed screens to match the acoustics of the bus, and the actors moved about the space as they would in real life. The street scene was recorded on location, on a busy street, with the binaural microphone rig tracking the actors' movements.

The bus announcements were first recorded with a conventional stereo microphone and then played back through a tannoy speaker in the studio where they were re-recorded with binaural microphones to maintain PJ's perspective. Walter Murch coined the phrase 'worldising' to describe this process of re-recording in a real acoustic space. Postproduction involved introducing a lot of overlaps into the dialogue. It was interesting to discover how effective it was when PJ's interior voice overlapped with his own dialogue. Conceptually this was an extension of the process begun during script development, where the script editor Philip Palmer (a highly experienced radio dramatist in his own right) encouraged both writers to 'muss up' their dialogue more – i.e., to mirror the broken diction of naturalistic speech. The audio of both dramas was then geolocated using the Echoes app[2] and playback was tested on the respective 108 routes.

Two Different Traditions of Audio Drama

Radio drama has a long and illustrious tradition in the UK, most notably on BBC Radio 4, whose 45-minute single play format provides the template for *One Oh Eight*. Latterly, the podcast explosion has triggered a renaissance in audio drama, and with it a significant broadening of the audience demographic. In London it is common to see passengers listening to audio drama (among other content) on their devices as they commute to work. The tradition is a little different in South Africa.

Radio drama is a format Mathapelo vaguely recalls from her childhood. Sitting in the passenger seat of her father's car, she remembers listening to serial radio dramas available daily in her mother-tongue language of SeSotho. Today, most radio dramas are available through community radio stations (CRS) which are free and have been established to inform, serve, influence and entertain South Africans in their respective local languages. However, they are mostly based in rural/semi-rural areas and do not reach urban dwellers and commuters.

Consequently, there is a lack of radio drama tradition in urban settings, but, to add to this, South Africa has some of Africa's most expensive mobile data costs, and Wi-Fi is inaccessible for most people. Due to this, in South Africa, there isn't the same culture of commuters listening to podcasts as in the UK. This creates a digital divide between those that can access the arts and those that cannot on any given day. However, over the years, independent community advocacy organisations have been campaigning for the reduction of data prices through an initiative called #datamustfall. The year 2019 saw a success in the campaign as two of the largest mobile data companies reduced their prices by 30–50%. Since then a series of public arts festivals, with the aim of bringing socially engaging art into everyday public places, have slowly emerged. These initiatives, alongside the reduction of data costs, have made it possible for many more people to enjoy sound art productions such as *One Oh Eight*.

Audience Reaction

The following observations are based on interviews carried out with audiences present at the launch.[3] Comments have not been attributed to individual sources. Interestingly, in view of the two different traditions of audio drama, similar responses recurred across both hemispheres. There was a consensus that because the format was an unknown quantity, it raised the level of anticipation. The launch was perceived as 'an event'. The listener felt themselves to be part of a group, on 'a magical mystery tour'. Yet at the same time they felt isolated within their headsets. There was a paradoxical sense of engaging in a private activity while in a communal space.

No one wore noise-cancelling headphones, so they all experienced a certain amount of bleed from the sounds of the real bus through their 'leaky' earbuds.

As was expected, this produced a variety of contrary reactions, often by the same person at different points in the journey/drama. Generally, at the beginning, listeners found it harder to decide what sounds to focus on and what mentally to exclude, i.e., they had difficulty in deciding what was 'signal' and what was 'noise.'

'The real bus sounds were a little distracting at first.'

'I couldn't tell the two realities apart for the first 5–10 minutes of the play.'

'It messes with your head – in terms of where you are.'

'You strain to hear the sound of the drama, as you would strain to over-hear a conversation taking place on your own bus, as if the characters from the 108 in Cape Town were really there in the seats behind you (and) you were listening in.'

This act of straining to concentrate seemed to involve the listeners, rather than frustrate them, as might be imagined; though perhaps they were more patient simply because it was the launch of a 'new format.' As the drama unfolded, so the listeners became habituated to the experience and 'tuned in' more to the story.

The moments where the events of the fictional world synchronised with the visuals of their surroundings, or with other sensory information from the real world, were often referred to as magical or uncanny.

'At times it felt as if the drama and the physical world were merging.'

'I felt like I was tripping a bit.'

'A pause as the bus changed driver near the O2 coincided with the driver in the Cape Town drama leaving the bus for some time without explanation.'

It was raining on the day of the Cape Town launch and the listeners reported that this felt like London weather. In a reciprocal manner, many of the London listeners reported that when dusk fell, the lights of the oncoming traffic seemed to synchronise with the vehicles in the Cape Town drama. As was anticipated, there was a degree of 'push and pull' between states of immersion and emotional/intel-lectual distancing.

'The sounds of the bus we were sitting on sometimes brought us back to reality. But the rain on the windows seemed to belong to the story we were listening to.'

For some participants those parts of the story where the characters left the bus broke the spell. For others, the moments of disjunction invited them to reflect on the ways in which their own lives deviated from those of their fictional fellow passengers.

The way in which the experience rendered the familiar strange and the strange familiar was remarked on. As was the thrill of rereading your own city as palimpsest.

'I really liked the experience of the two cities being overlaid.'

Some people reported a sense of pulling back to consider 'the whole planet as a spaceship' and being prompted to think about the interconnected nature of our existence. It is entirely possible that these are people predisposed to see the world in this way anyway. But the possibility that *One Oh Eight* had induced such a perceptual shift is an attractive thought.

Next Stops On the Journey

Plans for future iterations of the *One Oh Eight* project include producing a pair of companion audio documentaries about the people who live or work along the routes. Each bus stop would trigger a vignette to play, so that the journey offers an impressionist mosaic of the lives being lived in the world beyond the bus window. There are also plans to make more dramas set on other 108 buses round the world; Hong Kong and Las Vegas are among the possibilities being considered.

Making this project has encouraged an appetite to explore the potential of 'letting more of the real world' into future work. Something as simple as having the user wear a single earpiece can profoundly change their relationship to the fictional and real-world elements. It has also fostered a desire to give the listener more agency in how they navigate the narrative space. *One Oh Eight* is resolutely linear, and it would be interesting to explore the potential of an interconnected transport system as the setting for a nonlinear, multi-nodal drama.

Production Details

Mother City? was written and directed by Mathapelo Mofokeng

Cast: Iman Isaacs, Quanita Adams and Thandeka Mfinyongo
Script Editor: Philip Palmer

Composer: Thandeka Mfinyongo
Studio production: Charles Webster
Produced by Tamara MacLachlan
Executive Producer: Andrew Stuck

Dumbstruck on Bazely Street was written and directed by NG Bristow

Cast: James Doherty, Claudia Grant and Mariah Gale
Script Editor: Philip Palmer
Composer: Tomás Cox
Studio production: Jarek Zaba
Produced by Tracy Bass and Richard Shannon
Executive Producer: Andrew Stuck

One Oh Eight was jointly funded through Goldsmiths' Media, Communications and Cultural Studies 40th Anniversary Community Engagement Fund and the Innovation, Creativity and Experience research funding strand. It was conceived as an opportunity to bring together staff, postgraduate and undergraduate students, alumni and working professionals on an immersive media project. It was produced through the Museum of Walking and premiered as part of Sound Walk September – a global celebration of walking/travelling/listening sound-based artworks. (https://walklistencreate.org/sound-walk-september/).

Listen

The dramas are available at: https://walklistencreate.org/walkingpiece/108/.

THE FUTURE OF ACTIVISM

14

How Smartphones and Digital Apps Are Transforming Activist Movements

Sue Clayton

In the last five years smartphones and the expanded use of social media sites have become ever more essential tools of radical activism. Advances in camera quality, encryption and mapping applications, along with more flexible and responsive social media platforms, have allowed the smartphone to carry a number of essential functions for groups seeking to mobilise and communicate with each other in situations of precarity. These new applications come out of – and will no doubt lead to further – new forms of social organisation that aim to be fluid and

Figure 14.1 A refugee in makeshift accommodation at the Italian–French border seeks news online, 2018.

Image credit: Mirko Orlando.

non-hierarchical, seeking to balance needs for civic protection and privacy with the aim of rapidly spreading information and generally widening participation.

This photo-essay will look at the way marginalised and activist groups generate information flow through smartphones via maps, messaging and social media sites. It will take two examples, the activist volunteer response to the European 'refugee crisis' of 2015–2020 and recent actions by the climate change group Extinction Rebellion (XR), to explore what we can learn from their specific use of smartphones and social media.

Refugees and Their Needs

As increased arrivals into Europe in spring–summer 2015 from troubled zones such as Syria and Eritrea gave rise to what is called the 'European refugee crisis', it became clear that these people on the move relied heavily on mobiles and apps to find their routes and seek advice on the journey (Wendle 2016). Improved

Figure 14.2 Muslim woman on phone in Calais, 2016.

Image credit: Nour Adams.

mapping and shared data functions allowed refugees to find routes to safety across the Mediterranean, reunite family members who had become separated and navigate multiple borders to reach their destinations in Europe.

Figure 14.3 New arrivals use their phones to contact loved ones after arriving on a beach in Greece, 2015.

Image credit: Ghias Aljundi.

Figure 14.4 A Syrian refugee holds his phone, broken the previous night by Croatian authorities, at Velika Kladusa camp, Bosnia, 2018.

Image credit: Jack Sapoch.

Figure 14.5 A mobile phone is the only way refugees can connect with family back home after their treacherous journey to European shores.

Image credit: Ghias Aljundi.

A Sudanese boy, 'A', at the time just 17, tells how he was trafficked on a boat to escape Libya. He and all the occupants were alarmed to find that no one was on board to steer the boat or navigate – and the weather was very stormy. 'A' was one of the few who had a smartphone. He describes below the communication systems that he was able to use, undoubtedly saving the lives of everyone in the boat.

'We were packed many of us into the boat. We set off, and it was only then that we realised no one knew how to steer the boat. After many hours, there was a problem with the engine, and we were right out at sea, and the engine died. And there was a GPS system but nobody knew how to work it. Everyone started crying; I was very scared and I thought, this is going to be the last day of my life. Then someone said, who has a phone? and we used my phone. First we couldn't get any signal, then we did, but we couldn't buy credit as we couldn't read the languages that came up. We tried to find English and finally we did. One girl had a contact, a friend in Italy, a journalist. But he was out, and then the battery died. People started to cry again. We got a little more power to the phone and rang again and he answered. He phoned the Italian coastguard and after some hours they called us. And we gave our position from the phone signal, and so they were able to find us. We spent a whole night waiting but at dawn they came and got us, and brought us into Catania. We were safe.'

(Clayton et al. 2016)

Figure 14.6 A Sudanese refugee, 'A', describes how he used his mobile to help navigate the Mediterranean crossing.

Image credit: Alex Gabbay, Precarious Trajectories.

Figure 14.7 Syrian and Iraqi refugees arrive from Turkey to Lesvos, Greece in 2015, greeted by volunteers from the Spanish NGO Proactiva Open Arms.
Image credit: 'Ggia'.

The link to GPS was a crucial one, as was the interactive function for rapid updates of information, and the fact that apps like WhatsApp and Viber allow free communication. As larger numbers of refugees arrived, more sites proliferated serving different national groups, carrying a flow of ever-changing updates on the chaotic situations on routes and sea-crossings and at borders, and advice that was learnt in painfully hard ways by those who blazed the trail. However, as Gillespie et al. discuss, European governments and NGOs did not immediately provide their own versions of such information, because they feared they may be seen to be facilitating attempts to seek asylum in Europe – a policy unpopular with some political factions.

This forced refugees to rely on alternative, often unverified and unreliable sources of news and information circulated particularly by smugglers and handlers, endangering them and exacerbating an already dire situation.

(Gillespie et al. 2016)

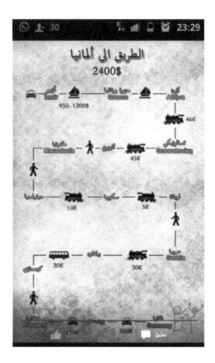

Figure 14.8 A map sent via WhatsApp by refugee interviewed in Paris.
Sourced from Gillespie et al. (2016).

Refugee Activist Communications

It was left to the smaller NGOs and grassroots volunteer groups to step in and
fill this vital information gap. Independent volunteers who set up networks to
support the new arrivals adopted similar tactics, building up map and route information, as well as coordinating the hundreds of grassroots support and supply
initiatives on chat pages like People-to-People Solidarity and Refugee Solidarity
Network. New low-cost design software allowed them to produce websites with
greater levels of interactivity, while the increasing functionality of social media
sites like Facebook as chat rooms for social change activism and campaigns
allowed organisations to create highly populated parallel groups on Facebook,
and so build site support very rapidly. One site popular with those arriving from
Turkey to Greece was Infomobile – Welcome2Europe, run by local and international activists to support new arrivals to the Greek islands and Athens. The
site helped refugees to avoid dangers on their journey and supplied key resources

Figure 14.9 At Pipka camp in Lesvos a young resident enjoys mobile play.

Image credit: Pipka camp webpage.

Figure 14.10 An online graphic representation of Alan Kurdi, 'The Birth of Death', 2017.

Image credit: Stathis Chaitas.

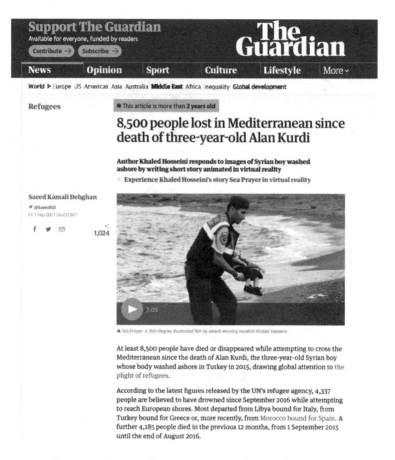

Figure 14.11 A *Guardian* headline from 2017 reviews the significance of Alan Kurdi's death two years on.

Image credit: Guardian Newspapers.

and information. The Village of Altogether, now under the umbrella of Lesvos Solidarity, was another website that supported refugees on arrival, and it also promoted and fundraised for the innovatory Pipka camp on Lesvos – an open, self-organised reception camp where refugee organisers and local volunteers worked together, saving many lives.

It was new sites like these which, in September 2015, circulated the shocking image of Alan Kurdi – the three-year-old Syrian child drowned off the Turkish coast in his family's attempt to reach Greece. It was the fact that this image rapidly went viral online that pushed the international press and broadcast media, after initial reservations, to publish it.

Public response fuelled a massive surge in the 'activist volunteer' movement that swept across Europe from late 2015 onward, as concerned European citizens began to appreciate that almost 2 million displaced people were arriving with little official provision. Who was going to support those who were now leaving Greece and Italy to find homes further north? I have written elsewhere about the extraordinary grassroots movement that blossomed as a response (Clayton 2020), but here I will simply sum up some of the innovative uses to which social media was put by these activists – uses which continue to expand in the agendas of national and international movements like #MeToo, Extinction Rebellion and Black Lives Matter. I see several broad ways in which social media, phones and apps have changed the conversation, and are set to continue to do so into the future.

Information and Coordination

By 2016, the unofficial Calais 'Jungle' refugee camp had grown to 10,000 inhabitants, 2,000 of them unaccompanied minors. Unrecognised and unsupported by both the French and British authorities, the Jungle attracted hundreds

Figure 14.12 A page from the Calaidipedia website, which recorded and archived all volunteer actions in the Calais Jungle from 2015 to 2016.

Image credit: Calaidipedia.

of grassroots aid initiatives from house-building to food supplies, medical and legal aid, schools and even its own fire brigade. As a fast reaction to a humanitarian crisis it was perhaps unparalleled, but there was initially no infrastructure at all. The site Calaidipedia began to function as a clearing house for all those wanting to help, linking all the groups, listing what supplies and skills were needed where, advising individuals where and how they should volunteer. (Since the Jungle camp was demolished by the French government in October 2016, the site has been less active, but it remains accessible as an archive, providing a unique and freely accessible record of this historic mobilisation – and demonstrating yet another functionality of new media.)

Fundraising

Web platforms like GoFundMe, Crowdcube and Indiegogo, along with associated pay sites like PayPal, have enabled a flow between standalone sites, their

Figure 14.13 The group Calais Action uses social media to promote a Help Refugees fundraising call.

Image credit: Calais Action.

social media 'avatar' sites on Facebook and other social media, and efficient crowdfunding functions. UK refugee charities recorded a rise in donations of over one third in response to the Alan Kurdi story, and the new start-up Help Refugees was able to raise over £200,000 in a matter of days at the beginning of the crisis. Though many in the activist sector have their criticisms of Facebook's stance on political and privacy issues (and have incidentally faced severe trolling and threats when they have made posts 'public'), they still tend to use it in preference to 'lifestyle' sites like Instagram. They have also found the 'charity' button function useful – linking personal posts to a pay site that allows them to make news posts and fundraise in one move.

Volunteer Support

The pressure on untrained volunteers to support and welcome almost 2 million people into a Europe that could be at times indifferent or openly hostile led to the need for support and counselling for many of them. However, in the high-pressure and chaotic world of border queues, camps, sea rescues and police

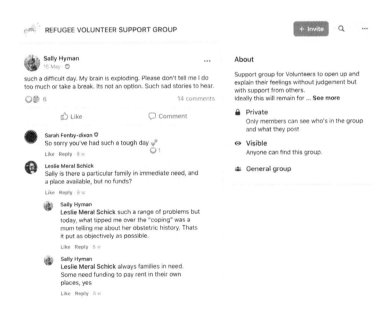

Figure 14.14 Extract from the Refugee Support Group Facebook page, 2020.

Image credit: Sally Hyman.

attacks, there was no hope of trained counselling being available. In its absence, volunteers continue to use social media closed chat rooms like the Refugee Volunteer Support Group. Given that most volunteers do not have access to laptops in the field, social media phone apps have been a lifeline for both health emergencies and discussing common longer-term issues such as burnout, vicarious trauma and PTSD.

Tracking at Sea

As I have described elsewhere (Clayton 2020), the EU's sea rescue mission in the Mediterranean changed in nature when its 'Frontex' force became more

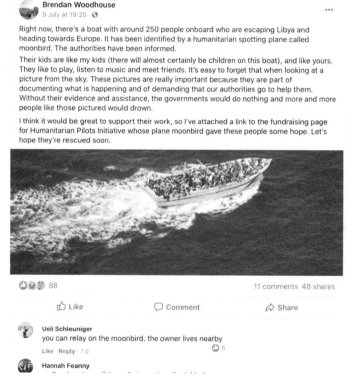

Figure 14.15 A volunteer with Sea-Watch, an independent rescue mission in the Mediterranean, puts out an urgent call to action on Facebook, 2020.

Image credit: Brendan Woodhouse.

concerned with deterring those making the sea crossing than with rescuing them. Independent groups like Sea-Watch.Org and Open Arms took over the rescue role, crowdfunding the purchase and equipping of new rescue ships. Sea-Watch also commissioned its own reconnaissance plane, the *Moonbird*, to spot migrant boats in distress at sea, and used GPS and smartphone links to contact its ships to make immediate rescue. As many countries now refuse to accept these rescue missions into port, April 2019 saw a Sea-Watch crew member make increasingly urgent social media posts as the crew and the 40 people they had rescued from the sea were running out of water and food, and had to rely on the activist community through Facebook to help them broker a landing before lives were lost.

Monitoring Violence

In many parts of Europe, state forces (army and police) have been persistently violent in their treatment of new refugee arrivals and of volunteers as well. Higher-quality phone cameras with greater capacity for shooting in low light, and with accurate referencing as to time and place, have enabled volunteer groups in Calais, Menton (on the French–Italian border) and in Serbia and Croatia to record and monitor police and state violence, in order to bring actions against these states.

Figure 14.16 Refugees create slogans at Belgrade 'Barracks' camp, Serbia, winter 2017.
Image credit: Abdul Saboor.

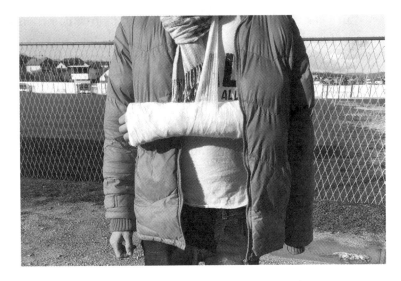

Figure 14.17 The broken arm of an unaccompanied minor from Iraq, recently pushed back from Croatia to Velika Kladusa, Bosnia, 2018.
Image credit: Jack Sapoch.

Direct Campaigning

Activists have expanded the use of Twitter, using hashtags and memes such as #ChooseLove, which was the slogan of new independent group Help Refugees, and #DubsNow, a demand for the UK government to honour Section 67c of the 2016 Immigration Act, the so-called 'Dubs Amendment', which required the UK to accept a specified number of unaccompanied children from the European refugee crisis. This use of memes and hashtags in conjunction with live demonstrations – each effectively promoting the other – has increasingly become a feature of other radical mobilisations such as Extinction Rebellion, #MeToo, Time's Up and Black Lives Matter.

Climate Change Activism and Extinction

There is considerable intersectionality between grassroots movements in the UK and elsewhere, so that many of those active on refugee issues have also been taking forward climate change protest and other campaigns. Extinction Rebellion (XR) is a global environmental movement which supports non-violent direct

sophieah_writes

34 likes

sophieah_writes So far not a single child has come through on the Dubs Amendment despite hundreds being eligible and waiting in limbo in The Jungle - alone and afraid without any answers.

mesadorm

22 likes

mesadorm Wonderful musicians, we must act now, please do a similar #dubsnow selfie and share the informative video to your followers made by the

Figure 14.18 A social media post promoting the 'Dubs Now' campaign to implement the Dubs Amendment to the UK Immigration Act 2016, allowing more child refugees into the UK.

Image credit: Sophie Holgate, member of the Hummingbird Refugee Project in Brighton.

Figure 14.19 A social media post supporting the #DubsNow hashtag.

Image credit: 'Mesadorm'.

Figure 14.20 A Refugees Welcome demonstration, London, 2016.

Image credit: Pru Waldorf.

Figure 14.21 Lord Dubs, speaking at a Westminster rally, is filmed by mobile for a podcast.

Image credit: Tess Berry-Hart.

Figure 14.22 The Refugee Solidarity Summit, London, 2020, which was also available as online webinars, as many volunteers were working overseas.

Image credit: Pru Waldorf.

Figure 14.23 A Climate Justice demonstration, 2020.
Image credit: Jacek Patora.

action (known as NVDA) as a means of pressuring governments to steer away from what it calls 'tipping points' in the climate system, which it says carry a risk of ecological collapse. XR's founding has interesting antecedents. It began in the UK in 2018, when 100 academics prompted by the group Rising Up! signed a call to action, echoing the Campaign For Nuclear Disarmament's (CND) 'Committee of 100' march in 1961, when 100 academics, led by Bertrand Russell, were – like Rising Up! nearly 60 years later – prepared to be arrested and imprisoned for non-violent protest to make their case.

XR has further developed the role of social media, apps and smartphones to service its actions and discussion. While I have described how the refugee volunteer movement faced the challenge of purposing social media and apps to connect a loose association of hundreds of disparate groups engaged in very urgent practical tasks, XR arguably has different concerns: how to support a new movement that is based on both ethical and political considerations, that eschews the restrictions of being a political party, but that nonetheless requires organisation and discipline to conduct its orchestrated public demonstrations.

This need for seemingly opposing forms of communication – for efficiency of aim and action yet allowing a quite fluid infrastructure – is likely to be the way that future social movements will organise. W. Lance Bennett and Alexandra Segerberg have described these as 'connective action frameworks' and argued

Figure 14.24 A demonstration referencing climate change and migrant issues, London, 2019.

Image credit: Jacek Patora.

that such movements were driven by cultural and moral, rather than conventional party-political, rhetoric. Earlier examples would include groups such as Occupy, Stop the City and Plane Stupid, and we can see current embodiments in the EU/Brexit campaigns and the #MeToo and Black Lives Matter movements. In such movements the social media branding becomes particularly significant, and

entails technology platforms and applications taking the role of established political organizations. In this network mode, political demands and

Figure 14.25 Extinction Rebellion (XR) demonstration, London, 2020.
Image credit: Andrea Domeniconi.

> grievances are often shared in very personalized accounts that travel over
> social networking platforms, email lists, and online coordinating platforms
> ... For example, the easily personalized action frame 'we are the 99 per
> cent' that emerged from the US Occupy protests in 2011 quickly travelled
> the world via personal stories and images shared on social networks such
> as Tumblr, Twitter, and Facebook.
>
> (Bennett and Segerberg 2012, 742)

A further challenge for new organisations is the UK's current so-called 'hostile
environment', where the right to protest is coming under increasing attack.

Figure 14.26 Youth Strike 4 Climate demonstration, Birmingham, 2020, highlighting global warming and other environmental issues.

Image Credit: Rizwan Ali Dar.

Figure 14.27 Led by Donkeys placard, Kentish Town, London, 2020.

Image credit: Kerry Hopkins.

Many groups, such as the 'Stansted 15' and the anti-fracking movement, have been targeted by authorities and listed as a threat to the state. XR itself was controversially listed as a 'terrorist' organisation by one regional division of the Counter-Terrorism Policing task force in 2019 and this status was only rescinded after public and press pressure. So a further concern is how future movements

Figure 14.28 Extinction Rebellion (XR) demonstration, London, 2019.
Image credit: Toby Pickard.

will benefit from the open-access nature of social media, while offering individual privacy and protection from state surveillance.

Below are some characteristics that they have developed.

Staging Demonstrations

At a functional level, XR continues to engage in acts of non-violent direct action, such as the occupation of London bridges and central road junctions in 2018

Figure 14.29 Extinction Rebellion (XR) demonstration, Brisbane, Australia, 2019.
Image credit: Dan Smith.

and 2019. Its group tactics necessarily result in frequent altering of plans, as police and other state actors cause it to move on and re-group. It has found ways to appropriate commercial apps for such occasions; for instance, in a rally in October 2019 those taking part were asked to register (with no payment required) for the rally, which was listed on the commercial events app Eventbrite. Through its auto-update function, XR was able to send real-time updates or changes in plan, venue and tactics from both the organisers and other activists on the ground.

High- and Low-Tech Messaging

XR employs a mix of high-tech and low-tech messaging, using mass-media opportunities created by its very public acts to display hand-drawn links and memes. This contributes to the notion expressed above of 'connective action frameworks', where real-life events, media capture of these and virtual events and messaging together form a dense network of social connection.

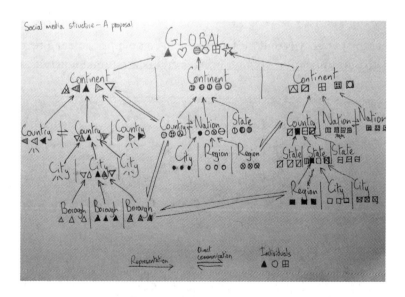

Figure 14.30 A proposed Extinction Rebellion (XR) online communication plan, 2019. Image credit: 'Iggy Fox'.

Privacy and Encryption

The XR media team has adopted various new forms of user-accessible encryption for advance planning. It also segments the national network of groups so that police and others can never access more than part of the network. The organisation also plans for increasing decentralisation by creating a web design structure (see below) that gives autonomy to local group platforms but allows them to feed directly into central planning.

In conclusion, what Hannah Amm (2020) calls the 'connective action repertoire' seems set to continue and expand in the social activist sector. It seems from the evidence of 2019–2020 protests over Hong Kong and demonstrations in the USA and Europe supporting Black Lives Matter that movements will go on drawing their affective power from live events, whether these are shaped as traditional marches and demonstrations or as more elaborated performative happenings.

What is different, however, is the web of connection made by the push into identity politics with such generic memes and slogans as 'Me Too' and 'Tell the Truth' that brand these mobilisations in flexible and complex ways – to protest,

Figure 14.31 Activist 'Iggy Fox' (Raphaël Coleman) describes the Extinction Rebellion (XR) online communication plan, 2019.

Image credit: 'Iggy Fox'.

Figure 14.32 Ecocide woman protester, London, 2019.

Image credit: Andrea Domeniconi.

Figure 14.33 Extinction Rebellion (XR) demonstration, London, 2019.

Image credit: Rosie, @the_vibey_vegan.

but also to survive: to tell stories, make connections, act out injustice, share mapping and information and to self-educate the cohort. This is a social as much as a technological revolution, and one that plays into, and can respond to, each individual's ever-more-complex matrix of loyalties and identities.

Additional Material

Watch Sue Clayton's activist film, *The Stansted 15: On Trial*, on The Future of Media website: www.golddust.org.uk/futureofmedia

Image Research

Natalie Galvau.

References

Amm, H. 2020. 'The Extraordinarily Ordinary: How the Rebels of Extinction Rebellion Berlin Shape their Movement by Using Connective Action Repertoires'. *Student Papers*, University of Lund. Available at: http://lup.lub.lu.se/student-papers/record/9017790.

Bennett, W. L. and A. Segerberg. 2012. 'The Logic of Connective Action'. *Information, Communication & Society*, 15: 5.

Clayton S., S. Parker and E. Weizman. 2016. 'Precarious Trajectories: Understanding the Human Cost of the Migrant Crisis in the Central Mediterranean'. Available at: https://precarioustrajectories.wordpress.com/2016/11/.

Clayton, S. 2020. *The New Internationalists: Activist Volunteers in the European Refugee Crisis*. London: Goldsmiths Press.

Gillespie, M., L. Ampofo, M. Cheesman, B. Faith, E. Iliadou, A. Issa, S. Osseiran and D. Skleparis. 2016. *Mapping Refugee Media Journeys: Smartphones and Social Media Networks*. Open University/France Médias Monde. Available at: www.open.ac.uk/ccig/research/projects/mapping-refugee-media-journeys.

Wendle, J. 2016. 'For Asylum Seekers, a Cellphone is a Bridge to the Future and the Past'. Al Jazeera, 18 January 2016. Available at: http://america.aljazeera.com/articles/2016/1/18/for-asylum-seekers-a-cell-phone-is-a-bridge-to-the-future-and-the-past.html.

Websites

Calaidipedia. www.calaidipedia.co.uk/.

Extinction Rebellion UK. https://rebellion.earth/.

Help Refugees. https://helprefugees.org/.

Infomobile – Welcome2Europe. http://infomobile.w2eu.net/.

Lesvos Solidarity – Pipka camp. www.lesvossolidarity.org/en/what-we-do/pikpa-camp.

People-Solidarity. https://people-solidarity.com/.

Plane Stupid. www.planestupid.com/.

Refugee Solidarity Network. https://refugeesolidaritynetwork.org/.

Refugee Volunteer Support. www.facebook.com/groups/1424742354318380/.

Rising Up! https://risingup.org.uk/.

The Village of Alltogether, housed on Lesvos Solidarity. https://lesvossolidarity.org/.

THE FUTURE OF DIGITAL HUMANITARIANISM

15

Technological Futures as Colonial Debris: 'Tech for Good' as Technocolonialism

Mirca Madianou

Just as the future is often imagined in terms of technological innovation, digital developments such as 'artificial intelligence' and 'blockchain' are popularly framed as 'the future'. Such a temporal framing points to a linear understanding of technology as an inexorable trajectory of advancement. While this discourse permeates most popular understandings of digital innovation, it is exemplified in 'technology for good', or 'tech for good' as they are most often referred to, initiatives. 'Tech for good' essentially assumes that technologies will provide solutions to complex social problems. Technology, which in this context is almost always synonymous with digital technology and computation (see also parallel terms such as 'AI for good'), is intentionally designed and developed to address social, economic and environmental challenges. While 'tech for good' claims applications in many spheres of social life, from the so-called 'smart city' to global health, it is most systematically entrenched in the field of international development and, more recently, humanitarianism. In development it is often synonymous with other neologisms such as ICT4D, or M4D ('information communication technologies for development' and 'mobile for development', respectively). In humanitarianism 'tech for good' is at the heart of digital humanitarianism, which includes the uses of digital innovation and data in emergencies such as international conflicts or the recovery from hurricanes and earthquakes. In practice, the spheres of digital development and digital humanitarianism overlap significantly as aid agencies often engage both in emergency work and long-term recovery (Krause 2014). Apart from emergencies, digital humanitarianism addresses protracted issues such long-term displacement where projects adopt a development focus. Humanitarianism and development are structurally similar as they follow the flow of aid from the rich global North to the global South. These similarities and interconnections allow us to speak of a humanitarian–development nexus. While this essay will focus on digital humanitarianism, the argument is largely applicable to digital development, with both being emblematic of 'tech for good' initiatives.

This chapter questions the linear paradigms of technology *and* of humanitarianism, as well as their convergence exemplified in phenomena such as 'tech for good' or digital humanitarianism. In 'tech for good', technological determinism finds the perfect home as both share a teleological narrative that conflates the future with notions of progress and the good. This thinking reveals a number of problematic assumptions about technology and the humanitarianism–development nexus. The first set of assumptions relate to technology as a set of fixed characteristics with calculable outcomes. This technologically determinist position is at odds with a sociotechnical understanding of technology as a process articulated in production and consumption. Technologies are produced and consumed in specific social, political and economic contexts which shape them and are in turn shaped by them. This is not to deny that technologies have certain propensities or architectures, but to recognise that these are not over-determining. Take for example radio, which, in its inception, had a clear interactive affordance that enthused Bertold Brecht, who in the early 1930s recognised its potential for enabling democratic participation (Brecht 2000). Rather than being a fixed quality, interactivity was never realised as radio was subsequently shaped as a broadcasting one-to-many medium. Instead of supporting grassroots participation, radio was associated with state propaganda in the 1930s, although, again, this shouldn't be seen as an inherent quality of the medium. In different political contexts, radio has been appropriated for resistance to oppressive regimes, or as a source of alternative information (Madianou 2005; Mankekar 1999). All media are the products of political, social, economic and cultural orders (Morley, Chapter 5 in this volume; Williams 1974) while they in turn contribute to shaping these contexts.

The progressivist paradigm of technology, which privileges whatever appears to be the latest innovation, ignores how all technologies refashion and rework earlier media in what Bolter and Grusin (1998) have termed a process of remediation. Additionally, apart from the historical or vertical lineages which produce forms of mediation, technologies are also defined in relation to other media that are part of socio-technical assemblages such as 'polymedia' (Madianou and Miller 2011). Such understandings of technology cast into doubt hierarchies that favour newness. In fact, the fetishism of the new promoted by 'tech for good' can be seen as a 'commercial imperative' (Kember and Zylinska 2012, 4) which ultimately benefits technology companies. Nothing summarises better the future orientation of the technology sector than the planned obsolescence of platforms which compels users to constantly update and renew their hardware and software. In visions of technological future, capitalism has found the perfect match.

The second set of assumptions concerns what constitutes development and humanitarianism. Apart from the 'imperative to reduce suffering', as it is usually defined (Calhoun 2008), humanitarianism is also an industry, a discourse and a historical phenomenon with roots in nineteenth- and twentieth-century colonialisms (Fassin 2012; Lester and Dussart 2014). Similar to international development, humanitarianism epitomises a teleological account of modernity as it centres on a linear progress of improvement. This is even more pronounced in the development sector, where improvement is synonymous with economic betterment which is achieved by emulating Western values and practices. While such Eurocentric approaches to humanitarianism and development have been discredited (Escobar 2012; Fassin 2012), they have been revived in the trends of ICT4D and digital humanitarianism. The logic of solutionism that underpins such trends presumes technological fixes for complex social problems. Technological fixes are often driven by commercial motives as private companies seek branding opportunities or a chance to generate hype for new products. In fact, digital humanitarianism is often driven by solutions seeking problems – and thus opportunities for publicity and attention – rather than the other way around. ICT4D and digital humanitarianism represent the point where two linear, modernist narratives converge. Digital technology is assumed to be the tool for achieving economic development. More importantly, 'tech for good' initiatives often conceal the historical legacies of development or humanitarianism.

In this essay I argue that, rather than advancing a democratic future, the use of technologies in digital humanitarianism reworks and accentuates colonial legacies of inequality and discrimination. I have termed this process 'technocolonialism' (Madianou 2019a). Technocolonialism refers to the convergence of digital developments with humanitarian structures and market forces and the extent to which they reinvigorate and rework colonial relationships of dependency. I will illustrate my argument by focusing on 'digital identity' initiatives for refugees which have become prominent in the humanitarian sector. Before unpacking digital humanitarianism we need to make sense of its colonial legacies and contemporary logics.

Humanitarianism and Colonialism

Despite the grand announcements that colonialism expired with the independence of postcolonial states, colonial (Stoler 2016) and decolonial (Quijano 2000) theorists remind us that colonial genealogies and inequalities persist and metamorphose in the contemporary context. Quijano's notion of the 'coloniality of power' is useful for explaining how the subjugation of the colonised continued well after the independence of postcolonial states as a result of the dominance of Eurocentric systems of knowledge, the codification of social and racial discrimination and the exploitation associated with global capitalism (Quijano 2000). For Stoler, contemporary global inequalities such as migration are 'reworkings ... of colonial histories' which she theorises as colonial presence (2016, 5). According to Stoler empires leave behind debris – and these hardened ruins can be reactivated and reworked under different conditions, often in oblique and opaque ways (Stoler 2016). Most contemporary migrant and refugee flows can be traced to colonial pasts (Hegde 2016; Khiabany 2016), while the racial subjugation of migrants and refugees helps to preserve colonial orders and the 'coloniality of power' (De Genova 2016; Quijano 2000). Humanitarianism itself originated in colonial expansion and the parallel awareness of otherness and suffering (Lester and Dussart 2014). Although humanitarianism is taken for granted as an expression of 'a supposed natural humaneness' (Fassin 2012) and an 'imperative to reduce suffering' (Calhoun 2008), the structural asymmetry between donors, humanitarian officers and aid recipients reproduces the unequal social orders which shaped colonialism and empire.

The emphasis on 'doing good' occludes the fact that aid is part of a wider liberal agenda (Escobar 2012) that primarily benefits the global North nations. However, colonial legacies surface from time to time, as happened during in the 2018 Oxfam sexual harassment and abuse scandal.[1] The recognition of institutional racism within the aid sector in the wake of George Floyd's murder and Black Lives Matter protests in 2020[2] was a further reminder of 'colonial presence' (Stoler 2016). The decision by the UK government in June 2020 to dismantle its Department for International Development (DfID) and incorporate it into the Foreign Office[3] speaks volumes about the true objective of aid projects, whether development or humanitarian or both. The transfer of cash from the global North to the global South, often via intermediary global North private firms which are awarded lucrative grants, preserves the power structures that benefit the North. The asymmetry is evident in the language used in humanitarianism and development to refer to 'aid beneficiaries' and 'donors'. It is in these asymmetrical relationships that we mostly discern the legacies of colonialism.

The Logics of Digital Humanitarianism

Ironically, digital technologies were introduced in development and humanitarian operations as a means to correct these asymmetries. The interactive nature of digital platforms was considered empowering for affected people, who would seize the opportunity to express their needs, thus improving humanitarian accountability (Madianou et al. 2016) and realising the goal of participatory development (Waisbord 2008). The 'logic of accountability' has driven numerous aid projects and has ultimately legitimated digital developments within the sector. For example, 'digital identity' initiatives are framed as contributing to the dignity and empowerment of refugees (UNHCR 2018).

Digital practices are also driven by the 'logic of humanitarian audit', which recognises the potential of technologies and data as metrics for audit which donors demand. Given the huge growth of the humanitarian sector, with the global aid economy estimated at over $150 billion, there is an acute pressure for audit. At the same time, the increasing marketisation of humanitarianism, combined with the short cycle of projects, means that agencies constantly compete for funding for which they have to supply evidence of impact. Biometric registrations were initially introduced in order to address issues of low-level fraud in humanitarian distributions and establish robust audit trails (UNHCR 2002). Metrics and refugee data have become the currency which supports humanitarian projects. A related factor is the pressure for savings and efficiency. Biometric scans are claimed to speed up registrations, which in the past involved lengthy interviews and paperwork (Kessler 2002), while digital cash transfer programmes reduce third-party costs.

Digital technologies are not just driven by the aid sector itself or by donor states. The private sector has entered the humanitarian space though ubiquitous public–private partnerships and the outsourcing of digital practices, including biometric registrations, to private vendors. For private companies, many of which are technology companies such as Amazon, Google, Facebook, Microsoft and Palantir, the involvement in humanitarian causes represents excellent branding opportunities with further potential benefits, such as increased visibility, data extraction and opportunities to pilot new technologies. The 'logic of capitalism' has driven a number of innovation projects, including 'digital identity' initiatives, which explains the latter's emphasis on entrepreneurialism and web-based business opportunities (GSMA 2018).

Linked to the logic of capitalism is the 'logic of solutionism' – the idea that technology can solve complex social problems. The logic of solutionism explains the prevalence of technological experimentation and hype in digital humanitarianism projects. The concern here is the foregrounding of solutions before the understanding of the actual problems or cultural contexts. This explains the paradox of solutions being decided on the basis of technological hype, often generated by technology companies keen to promote their latest product, rather than a careful evaluation of actual problems.

Finally, the 'logic of securitisation' reduces refugees to a security threat (Anderson 2014) and explains the push for biometrics, especially by governments which aim to detect 'anomalies' and control their borders (Aradau and Blanke 2018). In the humanitarian context, host governments often put pressure on intergovernmental agencies such as the UNHCR to share data collected in a state's territory (Jacobsen 2015). Often the UNHCR conducts biometric registrations together with host states, or in some cases simply supports the hosts to carry out registrations. Such practices raise concerns about 'function creep', which refers to the reuse of data for purposes entirely different than the one they were originally collected for (Ajana 2013).

In practice the five logics intersect and produce the phenomenon I describe as technocolonialism. In combination, these logics explain the push for digital initiatives such as the digital identity programmes which will be the focus of the next section.

Digital Identity Programmes

'Digital identity' initiatives constitute a relatively recent trend, although they have roots in established identification practices from the early days of humanitarianism, including biometric registrations – which have been taking place since 2002. Historically, all humanitarian operations have produced databases and have provided refugees with some credential, which confirms their entitlement to aid. The difference today is that these processes are digitised and rely on biometrics, the technology for measuring, analysing and processing a person's physiological characteristics, such as their fingerprints, iris or facial patterns.

Biometric registration is one of the first things to take place when a refugee comes into contact with the UN agency for refugees. Biometric databases are then used to authenticate those entitled to aid distributions. Biometric registrations were introduced in 2002 to speed up distributions, reduce the number of 'two-timers' and improve audit trails for donors (Jacobsen 2015). Biometric technologies have become the standard method for refugee registrations with the UNCHR, aiming to have all refugee data from across the world in a central population registry by 2020 (UNHCR 2018).

As the rate of biometric registrations has accelerated, their uses have also diversified. Biometric databases are used to underpin cash transfers, which are increasingly popular in humanitarian operations, replacing the traditional food distributions.[4] Increasingly, biometric registrations, cash transfers and other biometric based practices are grouped under the term 'digital identity' (UNHCR 2018). Digital identity is presented as a solution to the problem of lack of formal identity papers, especially among refugees and stateless people. Over 1 billion people lack a legal form of identification, which has potential adverse consequences for employment and economic activity (for example, proof of identity is required to open a bank account). This is a problem that affects refugees in particular, who may have lost access to legal paperwork due to displacement. Humanitarian organisations such as the United Nations High Commissioner for Refugees (UNHCR) have prioritised the use of digital technology in order to provide digital identities for refugees. The idea is that a 'digital identity' based on biometric data will be portable across borders and can be used for access to jobs, remittances and banking. However, given the lack of interoperability between humanitarian and state systems, the idea of a 'portable' identity hasn't yet been realised. In practice, digital identity is a different way of framing already established processes of refugee registration, identification and credentialing.

Biometric technologies need to be understood within a longer lineage of practices of enumeration and control that are part of colonial legacies. The birth of biometrics can be traced back to the British Empire when fingerprinting was introduced to identify and control colonial subjects in India (Pugliese 2010). Contemporary biometrics involves digital technology and machine learning, while they often combine with other technologies such as blockchain: a sociotechnical assemblage that I have elsewhere analysed as a 'biometric assemblage' (Madianou 2019b). Despite the assumption that technological developments have enhanced the reliability of biometrics, there is evidence that biometric data codify existing forms of discrimination (Browne 2015; Magnet 2011). If anything, technological convergence amplifies the risks associated with each constituent technology (Madianou 2019b). Biometric technologies 'privilege whiteness' (Browne 2015) with significantly higher margins of error when measuring or verifying 'othered bodies', whether in terms of race, ethnicity, gender, class, disability or age (Benjamin 2019; Browne 2015; Magnet 2011). For example, the immutability of blockchain technology can make any registration errors permanent with potentially deleterious consequences for refugees and other vulnerable populations.

The problem of bias isn't simply a matter of technological deficiency. The narrow definition of identity in a biometric system may sound straightforward, but it is anything but, especially when dealing with situations such as statelessness or ethnic conflicts. The recent 2017–2019 biometric registration of the 1 million Rohingya refugees in Bangladesh is a case in point. The registration, jointly organised by the UNHCR and the Bangladesh government and outsourced to a private vendor, referred to the Rohingya as 'Myanmar nationals', a term which the refugees contested fiercely. They saw the term as signalling their inevitable and imminent repatriation to Myanmar, where they had suffered what the UN described as genocide. This symbolic annihilation of the Rohingya from their own identity 'smart cards' is evidence that despite their claims to objectivity and science, biometric registrations are deeply political. In November 2018, when the Rohingya went on strike to demand that the term Rohingya be used on their cards to mark their ethnicity, the strikers were met with the force of the Bangladeshi police (for a discussion see Madianou 2019a). Biometric registrations continued, while, according to the UN rapporteur on the situation in Myanmar, repatriation efforts began without the promised transparency and consultation among refugees.[5]

Not only do refugees have no control over their own data or identity cards, they also lack any meaningful opportunity to withdraw from biometric registrations. To deny participation in biometric registrations or identity programmes is tantamount to denying aid – an impossible situation for refugees who depend almost entirely on humanitarian distributions. When all opportunities for work, learning or travel are out of reach, the only option is to comply with the demand to give one's data regardless of any reservations. In such asymmetric situations consent is rendered meaningless. The lack of consent in humanitarian operations came into sharp focus in June 2019, when the United Nation's World Food Programme (WFP) temporarily suspended the distribution of food aid in Yemen as Houthi leaders, representing one of the sides involved in the protracted civil war, opposed the use of biometric data in aid delivery. The WFP, which insisted on biometric registrations as part of efforts to address low-level fraud, was heavily criticised for its decision to deny food to one of the world's most vulnerable populations.

Although biometric refugee registrations and their pitfalls have received some attention (see Jacobsen 2015; Madianou 2019b), what is less discussed is the normalisation of biometric technology in a range of everyday practices, such as cash transfers. For example, the UNHCR's biometric database has been used to support a system of cash distributions in Jordan and Bangladesh. Since 2018 the WFP has been piloting the Building Blocks programme in refugee camps in Jordan. Building Blocks is essentially a cash-transfer system using blockchain, a distributed ledger system, integrated with the UNHCR's biometric database. Building Blocks allows refugees to 'shop' at officially sanctioned grocery stores by scanning their iris at checkout. Once the refugee's identity is authenticated on the UNHCR database, the WFP releases payment to the merchant and deducts the amount from the beneficiary account. The WFP blockchain keeps a record of all transactions. The pilot has reached 106,000 Syrian refugees in the Za'atari and other camps across Jordan.[6] Since April 2020 the Building Blocks scheme has been extended to the Rohingya refugee camps in Bangladesh.

Building Blocks has been celebrated for its cost efficiency and empowering potential as it allows refugees to choose what to shop. A closer looks reveals that refugees remain at best ambivalent about the scheme and often sceptical about the implications for their privacy. According to a recent report, refugees in Jordan were uncomfortable with the amount of information held about them, the fact that their daily practices were stored in their permanent record and the possibility of data sharing (Shoemaker et al. 2018, 19). According to the same report, many refugees were not aware of how Building Blocks worked, what data were collected and who had access to them. Yet refugees had no choice about whether to participate in the scheme or not. Having a basic of understanding of how an identity system works is fundamental for establishing trust and achieving meaningful consent. It is impossible for anyone to give consent to something that they do not understand. Coupled with the steep asymmetrical relations that define aid, consent appears impossible in these settings.

Such findings from the users' perspective would have set alarm bells ringing in countries with strong legal frameworks around data protection and privacy. The Building Blocks scheme looks questionable at best in the context of the General Data Protection Regulation (GDPR), which provides the legal framework for privacy and data safeguards in the EU. But in contexts with no legal framework regarding data protection, technological pilots such as Building Blocks can go ahead. The context of emergency is used to justify many of these practices.

Given the impossibility of consent and given that technological convergence amplifies the risks of bias, data safeguarding and data sharing, it is unclear why Building Blocks scaled up to over 100,000 users when it was still at a pilot stage. Building Blocks exemplifies the logic of solutionism and the fetishism of futurist visions of technology. The teleological paradigm of technology privileges the latest innovation as the best. It is no coincidence that in 2018, when the Building Blocks pilot was introduced, blockchain was considered the hottest innovation in tech circles (Madianou 2019b). In interviews I conducted with stakeholders from the aid and technology sectors it was often acknowledged that blockchain was the end rather than the means: a preoccupation with 'what can be done with blockchain' instead of 'how can we address an actual problem'.[7] This inversion is typical of the logic of solutionism where solutions seek problems rather than the other way around. Even though 'the cash distribution could be carried out with a simple spreadsheet', as the then head of innovation at the WFP admitted,[8] it would not have generated the hype that blockchain did. My interviews also reveal that tech companies, which are increasingly present in the aid sector, often push for the testing of a particular innovation (for a discussion, see Madianou 2019a).

Experimentation in refugee camps and among other vulnerable people can be traced back to colonial regimes. The outsourcing of experimentation is still present, especially during emergencies, as revealed in the response to the Covid-19 pandemic, when a French doctor claimed that the virus vaccine should be tested in Africa.[9] In the Building Blocks pilot, the potential risks from using an untested technology were ignored in favour of the operational benefits and value extraction from the actual experiment. Jacobsen similarly highlights the experimental character of biometric registrations, where 'the risk of experimentation failure is outsourced to the global periphery' (Jacobsen 2015, 31). The discourse of experimentation is evident in article headlines such as *Wired*'s 'How Refugees are Helping Create Blockchain's Brand New World'.[10]

Despite claims to refugee empowerment, 'digital identity' policies are less about refugees and more about operational benefits, audit trails, cost cutting and experimentation. Digital identity exemplifies neoliberal humanitarianism by rebranding digital systems of control into a vision of economic development. The Building Blocks pilot, where shopping appears like a scene from a futurist science-fiction film, is a gamified version of camp securitisation. Refugees are imagined as shoppers and potential entrepreneurs, ready to open bank accounts with their digital wallets. In reality, refugees are coerced into a digital system of migration management, which ultimately aims to control their mobility by constituting new types of traceable 'digital bodies' which are open to surveillance. While acknowledging refugee agency, the persistence of power asymmetries is impossible to ignore. The logics of capitalism and solutionism have normalised and legitimated the uses of biometrics under the promise of 'identity' and its connotation of recognition. The contrast here is between 'digital identity' as a neoliberal and securitised project, and the actual constitution of refugee subjectivities – which, like all identities, are ambivalent and relational.

Conclusion: 'Tech for Good' as Technocolonialism

Digital identity, emblematic of digital humanitarianism and 'tech for good' initiatives, reworks and revitalises colonial legacies. I analyse these processes as technocolonialism, a term developed to capture the constitutive role that digital technology and data play in entrenching existing power asymmetries between people in need and aid agencies. This occurs through a number of interconnected processes: by extracting value from 'beneficiary' data and innovation experiments for the benefit of aid organisations and private companies; by materialising discrimination associated with colonial legacies; by contributing to the production of social orders that entrench the 'coloniality of power'; and by justifying some of these practices under the context of emergencies. The constitutive role of technologies in revitalising colonial legacies differentiates technocolonialism from neocolonialism. Rather than marking an unstoppable path towards modernisation, technologies rework, amplify and justify the extractive logics of the past. In this sense, technological futures are understood as colonial debris (Stoler 2016).

Digital identity policies, which have become the new way to frame the management of refugee data, rely on biometric technologies. By privileging whiteness, biometric systems codify discrimination, thus inscribing the coloniality of power. Yet biometrics is presented as objective and scientific and therefore beyond doubt. Algorithmic sorting and automation are far from infallible, of course; algorithms make errors that entrench existing biases. When biometrics is used to authenticate aid recipients, this doesn't just entail a probability of error; automation also reduces the moral agency of humanitarian workers. Algorithmic sorting separates actors from their consequences.

The replicability of biometric datasets exacerbates data sharing practices with nation states. While data sharing with host nations has always taken place (as humanitarian agencies operate at the invitation of nation states), the nature of digital datasets streamlines sharing and accentuates the potential risk of 'function creep'. Apart from states, sharing also takes place with private companies, in their role as humanitarian partners, donors or contractors. Digital identity data are extracted for audit, private profit or for securitisation, but not for the direct benefit of refugees. Even in cash transfer projects when refugees are imagined as empowered subjects with 'digital wallets' there is little evidence of direct benefit to displaced people themselves.

Digital identity initiatives, despite their ambitious claims of 'financial empowerment' and 'sovereign identity', show little evidence of success. But even when they fail, digital identity initiatives still succeed in producing social orders. Digital identity programmes, which are often funded by large technology companies, are very successful in generating 'hype' around new technologies such as blockchain. Experimentation with new technologies among vulnerable populations echoes the medical experiments that took place under colonial regimes. By turning the political issue of statelessness into a problem with a technical solution, digital identity programmes depoliticise forced displacement while advancing a business agenda. At the same time, the neoliberal discourse of financial empowerment occludes the colonial lineages of such practices (Stoler 2016).

The lack of meaningful consent in refugee biometric registrations further compounds some of the above inequalities. It is not possible to refuse biometric data collection as that would amount to refusing aid when no other livelihood options are available. Ultimately, digital identity practices reconfirm the hierarchy between aid providers and refugees – and in so doing reaffirm that, structurally, contemporary versions of humanitarianism are not dissimilar to their colonial counterparts. Far from advancing a democratic future, the sociotechnical assemblage of digital humanitarianism revitalises the unequal legacies of the past.

References

Ajana, B. 2013. *Governing through Biometrics*. London: Palgrave.

Anderson, R. 2014. *Illegality Inc.: Clandestine Migration and the Business of Bordering Europe*. Berkeley, CA: University of California Press.

Aradau, C. and T. Blanke. 2018. 'Governing Others: Anomaly and the Algorithmic Subject of Security'. *European Journal of International Security*, 3(1): 1–21.

Benjamin, R. 2019. *Race After Technology: Abolitionist Tools for the New Jim Code*. Cambridge: Polity.

Bolter, J. D. and R. Grusin. 1998. *Remediation: Understanding New Media*. Cambridge, MA: MIT Press.

Brecht, B. 2000. 'The Radio as a Communications Apparatus'. In *Brecht on Film and Radio*, translated by M. Silberman, 41–47. London: Methuen.

Browne, S. 2015. *Dark Matters: On the Surveillance of Blackness*. Durham, NC: Duke University Press.

Calhoun, C. 2008. 'The Imperative to Reduce Suffering'. In *Humanitarianism in Question*, edited by M. Barnett and T. G. Weiss, 73–97. Ithaca, NY: Cornell University Press.

De Genova, N. 2016. 'The European Question: Migration, Race and Postcoloniality in Europe'. *Social Text*, 34(3): 75–102.

Escobar, A. 2012. *Encountering Development: The Making and Unmaking of the Third World*. Princeton, NJ: Princeton University Press.

Fassin, D. 2012. *Humanitarian Reason: A Moral History of the Present*. Berkeley, CA: University of California Press.

Groupe Speciale Mobile Association [GSMA]. 2017. 'Blockchain for Development: Emerging Opportunities for Mobile, Identity and Aid'. London: Groupe Speciale Mobile Association.

Hegde, R. 2016. *Mediating Migration*. Cambridge: Polity.

Jacobsen, K. L. 2015. *The Politics of Humanitarian Technology: Good Intentions, Unintended Consequences and Insecurity*. London: Routledge.

Kember, S. and J. Zylinska. 2012. *Life After New Media: Mediation as a Vital Process*. Cambridge, MA: MIT Press.

Kessler, P. 2002. 'Afghan Recyclers Under Scrutiny of New Technology'. United Nations High Commission for Refugees [UNHCR], 3 October. Available at: www.unhcr.org/news/latest/2002/10/3d9c57708/afghan-recyclers-under-scrutiny-new-technology.html.

Khiabany, G. 2016. 'Refugee Crisis, Imperialism and the Pitiless War on the Poor'. *Media Culture and Society*, 38(5): 1–8.

Krause, M. 2014. *The Good Project*. Chicago, IL: Chicago University Press.

Lester, A. and F. Dussart. 2014. *Colonization and the Origins of Humanitarian Governance*. Cambridge: Cambridge University Press.

Madianou, M. 2005. *Mediating the Nation*. London: Routledge.

Madianou, M. 2019a. 'Technocolonialism: Digital Innovation and Data Practices in the Humanitarian Response to the Refugee Crisis'. *Social Media and Society*. https://doi.org/10.1177/2056305119863146.

Madianou, M. 2019b. 'The Biometric Assemblage: Surveillance, Experimentation, Profit and the Measuring of Refugee Bodies. *Television and New Media*, 20(6): 581–599.

Madianou, M., J. Ong, L. Longboan and J. Cornelio. 2016. 'The Appearance of Accountability: Communication Technologies and Power Asymmetries in Humanitarian Aid and Disaster Recovery'. *Journal of Communication*, 66(6): 960–981.

Magnet, S. A. 2011. *When Biometrics Fail: Gender Race and the Technology of Identity*. Durham, NC: Duke University Press.

Mankekar, P. 1999. *Screening Culture, Viewing Politics*. Durham, NC: Duke University Press.

Pugliese, J. 2010. *Biometrics: Bodies, Technologies, Biopolitics*. London: Routledge.

Quijano, A. 2000. 'Coloniality of Power and Eurocentrism in Latin America'. *International Sociology*, 15(2): 215–232.

Shoemaker, E., P. Currion and B. Bon. 2018. *Identity at the Margins: Identification Systems for Refugees*. Farnham: Caribou Digital Publishing.

Stoler, A. L. 2016. *Duress: Imperial Durabilities in Our Times*. Durham, NC and London: Duke University Press.

United Nations High Commission for Refugees [UNHCR]. 2018. *UNHCR Strategy on Digital Identity and Inclusion*. Geneva: UNHCR. Available at: www.unhcr.org/blogs/wpcontent/uploads/sites/48/2018/03/2018-02-Digital-Identity_02.pdf.

Waisbord, S. 2008. 'The Institutional Challenges of Participatory Communication in International Aid'. *Social Identities*, 14(4): 505–522.

Williams, R. 1974. *Television: Technology and Cultural Form*. Harmondsworth: Penguin Books.

THE FUTURE OF THE CITY

16

The Smart City and the Extraction of Hope

Richard MacDonald

Introduction

A couple of years ago, finding myself in Khon Kaen, a city in northeast Thailand that has emerged as one of the country's most enthusiastic exponents of the smart city development model, I began to take note of the dispersion of 'smart' as a label. I rode around on smart buses which drove past smart schools. I visited a smart city expo in the city's new conference centre and saw a prototype of a smart bin, smart trash it was called. At the smart healthcare stand, I waited alongside a group of college students to get a peek at an infographic featuring a smart spoon and a smart fridge. Elsewhere I saw another infographic about smart farming which featured a smart cow. I became a collector of smart; a friend sent me details of a new condominium development in Khon Kaen offering smart living in a smart home with smart CCTV and a smart plug. A new school was launched called the Think Academy, set up by an augmented reality guru and designed to nurture smart people by centring the curriculum on logical thinking. Even Khon Kaen's mayor began referring to himself as a smart mayor when giving inspirational talks to college students.

What is the word smart doing in each of these appearances? In some cases, smart is used as an umbrella term for a class of technologies, networked devices that capture and use quantitative data patterns – changes, frequencies, volumes – to monitor and subsequently modify how these devices function. The smart cow, I learnt, wears a dongle round its neck recording the duration and yield of its last milking; this data is then used to calibrate subsequent visits to the milking parlour. Other uses of the smart label are much looser; it merely serves as a synonym for modern, on-trend, advanced: smart living, smart mayor, smart people.[1] On a return visit a year later the self-described smart school, one of the province's most prestigious secondary schools, had dropped the label smart from its canvas banner at the school entrance. Evidence, perhaps, that a label used to signify on-trend can rapidly seem dated. By that stage, however, the city had formally adopted its roadmap setting out a ten-year journey on the route to becoming a smart city.

There is by now a very substantial body of critical scholarship on the smart city, broadly understood as the urban ideal of the data-centred city, a city in which movements, flows and processes 'can be monitored, managed and regulated in real time using ICT infrastructure and ubiquitous computing' (Kitchin 2015). This research has rightly foregrounded many critical concerns surrounding smart city initiatives, their potential for mission creep towards ubiquitous sur-veillance, their evolving capacity for social control and anticipatory policing, regulation and governance, their capacity for entrenching forms of disadvantage and discrimination, for example, as wealthier parts of the city are rendered data-rich. Smart city initiatives can amplify the norms and values of wealthy urban residents, a desire for security and cleanliness, in ways that are punitive for more vulnerable and racialised citizens and workers (Datta 2018). More broadly the smart city ideal, which presents itself as a pragmatic, ideology-free deployment of 'problem-solving technology', has been critiqued as an extreme form of 'unre-constructed logical positivism', which succumbs to the conceit that a city is ultim-ately knowable if only we deploy sensors in sufficient quantities and crunch the data (Greenfield 2017, 72). The emergence of smart city discourse has been linked to neoliberal urbanism which pushes market-led solutions to complex social and environmental challenges while glossing consumer choice as citizen participation (Cardullo and Kitchin 2018). Privacy NGOs have drawn attention to the wildly asymmetrical relationships that exist between the major big tech vendors of smart city hardware such as IBM and their target consumers, muni-cipal authorities in the global South (Privacy International 2017).

Complimenting these critical perspectives, I want to look at the smart city not primarily as a set of technologies in the world, but as a channelling of aspir-ation, a way of staking a claim on the future, a particular act of future-making. In a city like Khon Kaen, a regional secondary city, in a so-called middle-income country in Southeast Asia, it is impossible to ignore the fact that the smart city concept has a reach that far exceeds the grasp of any technologies definable as smart. In the absence of a quotidian, street-level smart city in action, there is abundant smart-focused policymaking and smart as festival spectacle, expo smart. It might be assumed that this will change, that in time the smart trash can will be found on every street corner, the smart spoon in every home and the smart city operations centre boldly announced at the smart city forum will become operational. Roadmaps and policy frameworks exist in order to persuade us that any temporal lag is unremarkable and anticipated. But the rhetoric of policymakers and tech entrepreneurs does more than simply set a course that actuality follows. Irrespective of whether or not there is full implementation, it has already done much of its work by establishing a horizon, defining, or attempting to define, what can be hoped for in the future. This is a point missed by those who dismiss smart as merely marketing rhetoric. However, to develop this argument I need to perform a reversal of priorities. Instead of the concept of the smart city establishing the rigid frame which brings diverse phenomena – initiatives, policies, technologies – into a kind of coherence, the focus shifts to the variegated terrain on which aspiration materialises and hope is extracted, contained or channelled – the unevenly distributed capacity for future-making. In doing so I am charting a course suggested partly by recent consideration of the promise of technological infrastructure, and partly too by the implications of accepting the challenge of investigating 'actually existing smart cities' (Shelton et al. 2015) beyond the canonical origin stories and eye-catching totemic developments.

The Address of Smart

Technological infrastructures, smart or otherwise, have what Brian Larkin (2018) refers to as a compound nature, with the potential to function on multiple levels. They are, Larkin writes, 'made up of desire as much as concrete or steel' (2018, 176). On one level, they are a series of technical operations, the ability to move things and people, or for that matter capture, display and make use of data about those movements. On another level, infrastructure projects are announced, supported and underwritten for their 'sign value'. They provide evidence, perhaps, of a future-oriented municipal leadership enthusiastically embedded in an entrepreneurial urban development coalition, or of state–civil society collaboration for a bunkered military junta seeking legitimacy. For Larkin, this means we need to attend to how technological systems such as infrastructures 'address the people who use them, stimulating emotions of hope and pessimism, nostalgia and desire, frustration and anger that constitute promise (and its failure) as an emotive and political force' (2018, 176). The address of infrastructure involves ideas and metaphors, propositions marshalled into arguments shaped by governmental rationalities. And as built objects, objects in use, infrastructural technologies are productive of sensorial experience, and as such they are the means through which political rationalities become part of everyday lived experience, which is not to say they are uncontested. In this multi-layered sense infrastructures are invested with expectation; they are sites where promise acquires both emotional resonance and political direction. As a proposition that is materialised in planning workshops, policy forums, seminars, symposia, expos, memoranda, conferences, hackathons, networking events and so on, the smart city emerges through a recursive process of extracting and containing hope, aligning expectations with a future mapped out and administered by the dominant actors shaping urban development. What invites hope for some, leaves others with a sense of dread, foreboding or melancholy indifference. Hope, anticipation, a sense of a better world is channelled elsewhere. These alternative visions of the future can only be accessed if we break the frame that smart imposes on us.

The best-resourced acts of future-making in Khon Kaen are driven by the expansion of the frontiers of exchange value. Frontier-making, Anna Tsing (2005) observes, involves dreaming, conjuring a profitable future out of thin air, dramatising the wealth-creating possibilities of a hole in the ground, a parcel of land or a rail track. This is as true of urban frontiers as the fringes of wilderness. It is the motivated practice of the planner's gaze that transfigures a parcel of land, imagining a more commercially profitable use in the future – as a private healthcare facility, perhaps, or as a luxury condominium consisting of short-term rentals used by medical tourists. What these dreams have in common is that they imagine new and untapped sources of market demand for commercial goods, services and real estate products. They dream of capturing the wild flows of vagabond capital (Katz 2001). In Khon Kaen the spark that has set these dreams alight has leapt straight off the high-speed rail track that in the not-too-distant future will link Khon Kaen with Laos and Southern China in the North, and Bangkok, Malaysia and Singapore in the South. In Thailand, the rail infrastructure project is not being financed by China, but it has nevertheless been driven forward by China's high-speed rail diplomacy. In a context in which national political uncertainty often defers large-scale infrastructure projects, China's economic interests represent an irresistible force. It will happen, one Khon Kaen engineering professor confidently said to me, because China wants it to happen. Long before it is built, new transportation infrastructure occupies the imaginary of urban developers and planners. Imagined as an economic driver, a bringer of

opportunity, the prospect of the railway accelerates processes of commodification, alienating urban space from its present inhabitants.

Dispossession of the poorest people in Khon Kaen follows as sure as night
follows day. Activists working with communities informally housed along the
railway tracks estimate that upwards of 1,600 households will be displaced
by a series of interlocking transit and property developments, some already
completed, others in the pipeline – including the expansion of the rail track to
accommodate the high-speed line, the light rail network and proposed property development zones around key stations. For activists with local and national
NGOs working with the urban poor and the homeless, both the smart city and
transit-oriented development are exclusionary visions of Khon Kaen's future. At
a planning meeting held to discuss proposals to develop land owned by the State
Railways of Thailand, protestors held up handwritten posters with the words, 'The
city must support all groups not just capitalists'. As one organiser put it to me,
'I don't sleep well at night with these four big development projects facing us'[2]
(interview, July 2018).

Entrepreneurial dreams are also nourished by nightmares, by disaster. Even
the most conservative studies anticipate that in the not-too-distant future large
areas of Bangkok, 450 kilometres to the south of Khon Kaen, home to more than
10 million people, are likely to be submerged by water.[3] Some studies anticipate
that inundation is only a decade away, others 20 or 30 years. However you cut
it, Bangkok, a city built on a flat river delta, in common with other low-lying,
coastal Southeast Asian mega-cities – Manila, Jakarta, Ho Chi Minh City – is
rapidly sinking and increasingly exposed to rising sea levels and a volatile climate. Aggressive groundwater extraction by heavy industries, the city's ruinous
love affair with concrete and the unregulated construction of heavy, high-rise
buildings are speeding up this subsidence. The water level in the Gulf of Thailand
is rising twice as fast as the global average, exacerbating the exposure of coastal
populations to flooding and permanent inundation.

Consider the luxury waterfront condominium tower stretching vertically
30, 40, 50 floors high. These towers and their residential units, which attract
global investors, trade on the serene spectacle they offer residents, simultaneously cocooned from the surrounding city, which is transfigured from a site
of messy street-level interaction to one of distant visual splendour, a so-called
iconic skyline of geometrical shapes and patterns. Bangkok boasts one of the
largest numbers of 150-metre-plus towers in the world, clustered in riverside
and city-centre locations. While the tall tower blocks themselves, constructed

on deep steel pilings, are not at risk of subsidence, they impact the land around them. Meanwhile, the vulnerability of Bangkok to seasonal monsoon flooding has also dramatically increased as a consequence of a long-term shift in the amphibious delta region's communication and transport infrastructure, from a network of canals, traversed by boats, to a landscape of roads, highways and cars linking industrial and commercial centres constructed from cement and steel (Morita 2016).

Flooding makes vagabond capital nervous; it is a threat to profitability. Some property investors may be reassured by the magical public relations thinking of developers that conjures a comprehensive and efficient flood management system from a more splintered, compromised and patchwork reality (see Marks and Elinoff 2020). But as the prospect of inundation in the future grows nearer, more property developers and real estate investors will be rethinking their investment strategies. Multinational corporations whose inventory, warehouses and factories were destroyed by floods in 2011 have also looked to move their operations to less vulnerable locations upcountry. Real estate values in the cities of the northeast of Thailand, situated on a plateau and historically the driest region in the country, have been steadily rising since the Bangkok flood waters subsided; the high-rise condominium has come to Khon Kaen (Macan-Markar 2016).

In Khon Kaen, a well-organised, powerful private-sector network with strong links to the municipality and to the university has been shaping policy discourses on urban development for the last five or six years. Smart city policy discourse has emerged as one point of reference alongside creative city policies and coupled with an enthusiasm for transit-oriented development. To a significant extent the smart label was a flag of convenience through which to render the city's aspirations legible and amenable to the policy priorities of the Thai state. Smart had become a prominent keyword in the National Economic and Social Development Plan published in early 2017, which included a commitment to support prototype smart cities. Later that year the deputy prime minister announced a plan to build 100 smart cities within the next two decades.[4] Key actors in urban governance in Khon Kaen were content for the city to be interpellated as a pilot smart city. Smart-labelled initiatives have begun taking shape within a broader context of the accelerated commodification of urban space in Khon Kaen, driven by real and anticipated flows of capital investment. The flagship project, retrospectively designated an exemplar of smart mobility, is a proposal to build a privately financed, urban light rail network, ostensibly designed to encourage mass transit use, easing road traffic congestion while providing a context for transit-oriented real estate development around the stations. In this instance, the smart in smart mobility connotes the efficient and sustainable use of resources. These are, of course, important objectives in a growing city, but this is a large-scale infrastructure project in which sign value far exceeds technical functionality. This is the only way to understand the municipality's preference for building a light rail network at a significantly higher cost over enhancing bus provision with dedicated rapid transit lanes. It is the allure of the new and its capacity to provide what Peck and Theodore, commenting on the adjacent and very similar policy discourse of the creative city, call a 'feel-good makeover' to salve a city's competitive anxieties (2010, 171).

The feel-good factor or sign value of the new light rail network, and Khon Kaen's smart city projects more generally, is bound up with the way it is perceived to announce the arrival of the regional city in the vanguard of urban development both in Thailand and across Southeast Asia. Smart vanguardism is effective in extracting hope because it promises to enact a great leap forward, a spectacular reversal in the status of regional cities in a country long dominated, politically, economically and culturally, by Bangkok. This reversal is particularly piquant when the city in question is located in Isaan, a region that has historically figured in the national imaginary as politically volatile, culturally other and economically backward (Thak 2007). According to a feature in a prominent Bangkok-based lifestyle and current affairs magazine, until recently the idea that a regional Thai city would have a 'Skytrain' would have been dismissed as nonsensical. 'The project looks like a dream', they added, 'but the dream is coming true' (Khrin 2018). A recurrent aspect of media discourse, seeded by the development corporation itself, is of Khon Kaen 'taking the lead', providing a model that many other regional cities will want to emulate. It's a trope enthusiastically repeated by a small army of supportive Facebook posters.

The vanguard promise of smart mobility in the guise of new transport infrastructure is not only about what will be built, but how. Here too the trope of being the first is noticeable. In a video interview, a co-director of the Khon Kaen Urban Development Corporation, also known as KKTT (Khon Kaen Think Tank), was especially keen to clarify the precise sense in which the proposed light rail system would be a first.

> Everyone might say 'well it's just building a Skytrain'. But actually, it's not *just* building a Skytrain. Skytrains that we see in Bangkok Metropolitan Area, Skytrains that will appear in other Provinces, those Skytrains use tax money

from Thai people. Using our Khon Kaen Model, this Skytrain doesn't use subsidy money from the government.

(Suradech, interview, 2018)

What has been quite successfully branded as the Khon Kaen Model is simply
a development model in which major infrastructure in regional cities is financed
by private investment and owned and managed by a private–public partnership,
a private-sector development corporation and the municipality. This model,
straight out of the playbook of neoliberal urbanism, actively solicits or extracts
hope and expectation when it is accompanied by localist appeals and entrepreneurial populism. Raising investment is recast as crowdfunding, an opportunity for local people to acquire a stake in their city's Skytrain, despite a later
news report that the KKTT founders were speaking to three foreign investment
trusts in Europe, China and the USA (Janssen 2019). In the guise of the Khon
Kaen Development Corporation the group of business leaders, prominent figures in real estate, retail, local manufacturing and agribusiness present themselves as a kind of active citizen vanguard, as 'we the (Khon Kaen) people'. They
ask the people of Khon Kaen to have belief that *we* can do this. 'It's our job now'
says Suradech. 'This *show* is a show put on by the Khon Kaen people'. National
media have colluded in this mythmaking in which the development corporation
appears as a form of grassroots civic action acting on everyone's behalf. Localism
casts fiscal restraint and abstinence as self-reliance, autonomy, self-sufficiency.
Frequently referred to as 'new generation administrators', some among the KKTT
business group like to refer to themselves as Akaengers, a localised take on the
Avengers. Like superheroes in one sense, they are self-appointed guardians; they
can't be voted out of office.

Coming into existence a year after a military coup in 2014, which suspended
local and national elections, the Akaengers, a close-knit network of business
leaders and technocrats, are both an effect and a causal agent of the displacement of the political as a realm of contested visions and programmes of future-
making.[5] During this same period some channels of citizen involvement seem to
have flourished in Khon Kaen: consultations and feedback mechanisms, forums,
innovation hackathons led by academic experts and NGOs. A team of academics
at Khon Kaen University were contracted by the municipality to run a series of
themed participatory workshops with groups of stakeholders: municipal workers,
business leaders, academics, students, NGOs and civil society groups. Each workshop took a discrete theme – environment, society and culture, business and
economy – and followed a pattern of brainstorming innovative solutions to the

city's problems. Key to the participatory method in the workshops was the disciplinary framing of the business plan. A large number of initial ideas were culled in a process of back-and-forth between expert facilitator and group in search of an idea that could be turned into a viable business plan. The properties of the post-it note, bearer of participants' suggestions, which can be removed as easily as it adheres, come in handy here. The steering role of the facilitators is one of welcoming and supporting ideas that don't cost too much, drawing a gentle but firm line, demoting and excluding those that are deemed unachievable and unrealistic. In their cultivation of fiscal discipline and restraint these workshops and their aftermath in pilot projects were a recursive exercise in the management of expectations, the containment of hope.

In another context Mike Raco, drawing on Jacques Rancière, has characterised the dominant understandings of sustainability in the UK urban planning and development process as a 'politics of the possible' (2015, 124). He highlights the increasing compartmentalisation of policy problems and solutions as a defining logic in sustainability governance. The emphasis on definable, easily measurable managerial tasks, he argues, encourages 'dis-connected ways of thinking that make sustainability planning realistic and do-able rather than holistic, aspirational and idealist' (Raco 2015, 125). At the turn of the century, Rancière had conjured a vision of a conquered age presided over by disenchanted experts.

> So, of course we no longer believe in promises. We have become realists. Or in any case, our governments and our wise experts have become realists for us. They stick to the 'possible', which precisely does not offer a great deal of possibilities. This possible is made of small things that progress slowly if they are handled with caution by those who know. We must no longer wait for the tomorrows that sing and for freedom to come and overturn oppression.
>
> (Rancière 2010, 9)

The churn of participatory programmes and consultation exercises which, as everyone involved readily acknowledges, recruit a narrow demographic can be seen as instruments that instruct the citizens who answer their call in a pedagogy of the possible. The instructor here is the implacable but emollient facilitator who defines the do-able, making sure the small things stick.

In 2017, Khon Kaen's 'Smart Volunteer' programme, which came out of the participatory action research project, won a Democratic Innovation Prize, awarded, seemingly without irony, by the National Legislative Assembly, a military-dominated body appointed by the junta, the National Council of Peace and Order, to replace the elected legislature. The irony of a 'democratic innovation' award presented by an avowedly non- or rather anti-democratic state institution might be approached through Garry Rodan's concept of the consultative ideological strategy (2018). 'Consultative ideologies', he writes, 'are imbued with a technocratic, apolitical notion of participation as problem solving, and eschew political competition' (2018, 7). Far from being democratic, the innovation in fact lies in the development of a local-level participatory experiment co-sponsored by university and municipality that is, like the awarding body, non-democratic in its ideology of representation. Whereas democratic ideologies of political representation involve a range of intermediary groups such as political parties, trade unions and other civil society groups engaged in political competition with openly conflicting agendas, consultative strategies are depoliticising (Rodan 2018, 31). Consultative strategies 'privilege problem-solving over political competition' and in doing so they limit the space for political contestation over the fundamental objectives of public policy (2018, 31). Consultation strategies 'lay the basis for claims by elites that the public interest is represented in policy formation' while 'rationalising the marginalisation of democratic representative politics' (2018, 31). But equally, consultative ideology may appeal to NGOs and civil society groups with a weak organisational base and mobilising capacity.

Looking at two manifestations of smart in Khon Kaen, smart mobility in the form of the new light rail network and the smart volunteers, suggests that there are two aspects to the smart makeover. Smart is a label applied to an infrastructural fix which carries the promise to propel the city towards the future, leading the race, as one headline put it, to smarten up. Promise is closely bound up with the claims of entrepreneurial populism to speak for the people, a baseless claim to representation in the sense that there are no mechanisms of accountability, which is not to say that it has no appeal. Its narrative of freedom from the Bangkok bureaucracy asks that the consequences for the city of private financing amid fiscal austerity go unexamined. Those consequences are likely to include a real estate development strategy driven by the need to maximise revenues on the land around the new transit stations in order to provide an attractive rate of return to investors. Evidence elsewhere suggests that this results in homogeneous office and commercial development with no space for affordable housing or small businesses. The other exemplary face of smart is the smart forum, an engagement exercise in which facilitator experts define the realm of the possible, synchronising the future horizon with what can be articulated in a business plan on a whiteboard. Smart gives a new name to consultative practices that constitute a makeover in the mechanisms of representation, a democratic decline by another name.

Each contrasting register of smart corresponds to an image form. Where smart connotes innovative forms of consultation, the typical image form is the slide, visually documenting the process of citizen engagement. It is a composite image composed of a photograph staging the stakeholders as a group in a workshop space, serving an evidential function, and the wordle, the auto-generated word cloud, as a symbol of what is often referred to in the participatory workshop model as the ideation process, collective problem-solving. In the imaging of smart mobility, fantasy is given a freer rein. Take for example the video to promote the light rail network created by Ensure Communications for Khon Kaen Think Tank:[6] a satellite view of Khon Kaen's urban centre on which is superimposed an animated vertical line of the proposed route of the light rail. The map is intercut with computer-generated animation of a zippy two-carriage tram pulling into a series of prototype stations and with occasional shots of some locations in all the drained drabness of the present. Formally the most striking aspects of the promo are the pale-blue-and-green hues of the prototype buildings and the continuously moving point of view, which swings smartly from a vantage point above the moving tram over to one side, speeds on ahead, and then rises briskly up to give a more panoramic view of tram, station and new buildings. By contrast there is minimal or no movement in the shots of actual city locations. Both the colour palette and the sensation of constant movement are, as Gillian Rose points out, ubiquitous features of corporate urban visions (Rose 2017). Writing about 'Future Life', a video made in 2012 for the engineering company Siemens, she argues that what is paramount in these hyper-mobilised views is not a synthesising strategic aerial view but a prized sensation of 'mobile, untethered spatiality' (Rose 2017, 183). These corporate visions of the future promise a vertiginous release from all that is earthbound and all that exists in the now. Like the sales pitch of the condominium developers, what exists immediately down below at ground level is overlooked; the spectacle is everything. In the light rail promotional videos created for the development corporation what exists in Khon Kaen appears as a faded 'before'. The future is a blank slate, an invented world with flora, people, buildings assembled from scratch. There is little in the image to suggest that its visualisers had been required to create a sensory place experience based on an understanding of the location (see Degen et al. 2015).

Venturing beyond Smart

Before it arrives as a box-fresh device with a sensor, the concept of smart, a product of entrepreneurial dreams, is a form of bad hope; it is a process through which hope is canalised and possibility is disciplined till it looks like more of the same. In Khon Kaen smart is a form of bad hope because dispossession runs through its core, and because it has come to function as a byword for the expanding logic of consultation, where this logic, whether intentionally or not, has the effect of rolling back, bypassing and delegitimising vital institutions of political contestation and accountability. At this point, the spread of the ideology of consultation has a more enervating effect on political agency than the deployment of networked devices in urban infrastructure. This is bad hope because its arrival is simultaneously, to quote Arjun Appadurai, a 'trauma inflicted on the present' (2013, 299). Hope has been efficiently extracted from some residents but in the process a nightmare has been visited on the city's subaltern populations.

Khon Kaen is not eclipsed by smart, despite its ubiquity, and despite the apparently totalising ambitions of the smart city designation. It could scarcely be so if, as Doreen Massey proposes, space is 'the simultaneity of stories so far'. This means that space is never singular in its identity, it is the sphere of 'contemporaneous plurality', it is plural because it is composed of a multiplicity of interactions, 'relations between' (Massey 2005, 9). It follows, Massey argues, that space is always in the process of being made, always unfinished. Bad future-making, in contrast, conjures a closed, defined future with little scope for dissent stretching as far as the eye can see. Genuine future-making, Ernst Bloch tells us, comes out of informed discontent, which he writes 'belongs to hope, because they both arise out of the No to deprivation' (Bloch 1996 [1959]).

In the same year that the business leaders of Khon Kaen launched their development corporation, a group of Khon Kaen student human rights activists were arrested and taken to a military camp. The students were members of a human rights activist group called Dao Din (Earthbound Star) originally associated with the Law Faculty at Khon Kaen University. The Dao Din group developed a praxis of engaging and supporting rural campaigners protesting land dispossession and environmental damage in relation to state-sanctioned development projects across rural Isaan.[7] In May 2015, on the first anniversary of the military coup, seven members of the group were arrested and charged with breaching the junta's prohibition on political demonstrations. The activists had gathered at a democracy monument in the city centre, where they had unfurled a cloth banner condemning the coup. The Dao Din members were released on bail but over the coming years were repeatedly subject to harassment and incarceration as they organised protests and workshops to debate the new constitution the military junta was pushing through. In late 2016, Dao Din member Jatupat Boonphattararaksa, a fourth-year law student, was imprisoned in Khon Kaen jail and charged with lèse-majesté for sharing a BBC World Service profile of the king. He was sentenced to two years and six months in jail and was eventually released one month early in June 2019.

The collaborative action between Dao Din and village campaigners for environmental justice has sometimes been misrepresented as a form of educational philanthropy. A sympathetic profile of Jatupat, also known as Pai, in a Bangkok-based English-language newspaper described his involvement in work to educate the rural folk. Education is seen through the patrician lens of a selfless but nevertheless one-sided act in which law students pour wisdom into empty vessels. A more revealing description was given in an interview with Kunthida Rungruengkiat, a former MP with the Future Forward Party, disbanded by a ruling of the Constitutional Court. Kunthida described meeting Pai at one of her classes at Bangkok University before joining him at a series of camps in rural Isaan. The camps were primarily listening exercises: 'we set up a camp in Loei where these villagers were being affected by a gold mine, we slept there with them and listened to their stories and discussed issues that were important' (Satrusayang 2020).[8] The experience was, she adds, the beginning of her politicisation.

The community exchange camps of Dao Din could be seen as an example of what Ernst Bloch (1996 [1959]) calls concrete venturing beyond; they constitute a movement beyond the limits of proscribed speech and existence. It is on such figurations of venturing that concrete hope might be grounded. Venturing beyond is not achieved through travel but it does involve an insistent crossing of boundaries and thresholds in social space. These thresholds are sometimes visible and mark the boundaries of total institutions like prisons, and other times they are invisible lines of demarcation that nevertheless enforce symbolic exclusions in cities scarred by inequality.[9] Figurations of human venturing invert the role of the intermediaries that facilitate smart consultation. The latter discipline citizen participation, shepherding it within the boundaries of the possible, that is, within existing modes of governance and conceptions of development. In contrast, figurations of venturing foreground 'networks of interdependencies between individuals' (Elias 2000, 482) engaged in 'thinking, feeling and acting that increase the horizons of hope, that expand the field of the imagination, that produce greater equity ... in the capacity to aspire' (Appadurai 2013, 295). Media forms that amplify the potential of these figurations will only prove capable of doing so to the extent that they eschew ready-to-hand tropes of heroism and victimhood.[10]

Coda: Whose Future If Not Ours?

February 2020: on the grounds of Khon Kaen University more than 1,000 students gather to protest against the latest authoritarian twist in Thailand's protracted democratic recession, the judicial ruling banning the Future Forward Party following its success in general elections the previous year. The students assemble in darkness, the university having refused to switch on the outside spotlights, wearing facemasks, bags slung over shoulders, mobile phones in hand, 1,000 points of light in the darkness. Music blasts out through loudspeakers and the students in groups move together, joyful, dancing in a playful parody of drilled K-pop moves. Hands are raised in three-fingered salute. Each reappearance of the protesting crowd in a country in which political gatherings have been unlawful is an image of hope tinged with risk. The crowd makes contact with moments of assembly in the past, traumatic and chaotic, and creates a new memory of solidarity in informed dissent. From the stage, the voice says, 'we declare the will of Khon Kaen people, so that those in power know that in this world there is not just them, but we are also here, thousands of specks of dust'. A handwritten sign on a white sheet says, 'Whose Future If Not Ours?'

Acknowledgements

The research for this paper was supported by funding from the Newton Fund: Institutional Links programme (Grant Number: 332437827) and was conducted as part of a project in collaboration with the Centre for Contemporary Social and Cultural Studies at Thammasat University. I am indebted to Peera Songkünnatham, who was a brilliant research assistant, translator and interlocutor during the period of fieldwork, and has been a shrewd and generous reader since.

References

Appadurai, A. 2013. *The Future as a Cultural Fact: Essays on the Global Condition*. London: Verso.

Bloch, E. 1996 [1959]. *The Principle of Hope: Volume 1*. Cambridge, MA: MIT Press.

Cardullo, P. and R. Kitchin. 2018. 'Smart Urbanism and Smart Citizenship: The Neoliberal Logic of "Citizen-Focused" Smart Cities in Europe'. *SocArXiv*, 9 March. https://doi.org/10.31235/osf.io/xugb5.

Datta, A. 2018. 'The "Digital Turn" in Postcolonial Urbanism: Smart Citizenship in the Making of India's 100 Smart Cities'. *Transactions of the Institute of British Geographers*, 43(3): 405–419.

Degen, M., C. Melhuish and G. Rose. 2015. 'Producing Place Atmospheres Digitally: Architecture, Digital Visualisation Practices and the Experience Economy'. *Journal of Consumer Culture*, 17(1): 3–24.

Elias, N. 2000. *The Civilising Process: Sociogenetic and Psychogenetic Investigations*. Oxford: Blackwell Publishers.

Kitchin, R. 2015. 'Making Sense of Smart Cities: Addressing Present Shortcomings'. *Cambridge Journal of Regions, Economy and Society*, 8(1): 131–136.

Greenfield, A. 2017. *Radical Technologies: The Design of Everyday Life*. London: Verso.

Isaan Record. 2019. 'Apichatpong Weerasethakul: Bursting Bubbles, Awaiting a Dark Future'. 1 February. Available at: https://theisaanrecord.co/2019/02/01/apichatpong-weerasethakul-interview-tcdc/.

Janssen, P. 2019. 'All Aboard Thailand's Decentralization Train'. *Asia Times*, 21 April. Available at: www.asiatimes.com/2019/04/article/all-aboard-thailands-decentralization-train/.

Katz, C. 2001. 'Vagabond Capitalism'. *Antipode*, 33(4): 709–728.

Khrin Thanomkitti. 2018. 'How Can Khon Kaen Build a Sky Train That Charges Only 15 Baht?' *A Day*. Available at: https://adaymagazine.com/khonkaenmodel/?fbclid=IwAR2eaIiamQOf44Oq1-U-pWimrzteEqfjr71TzIs0Ucb78u6h0-YQUg3m7bc.

Larkin, B. 2018. 'Promising Forms: The Political Aesthetics of Infrastructure'. In *The Promise of Infrastructure*, edited by N. Anand and A. Gupta, 175–202. Durham: Duke University Press.

Macan-Markar, M. 2016. 'Property Booms as Thais Rush to Rural Khon Kaen'. *Nikkei Asian Review*, 2 August. Available at: https://asia.nikkei.com/Markets/Property/Property-booms-as-Thais-rush-to-rural-Khon-Kaen.

Marks, D. and E. Elinoff. 2020. 'Splintering Disaster: Relocating Harm and Remaking Nature After the 2011 Floods in Bangkok'. *International Development Planning Review*, 42(3). https://doi.org/10.3828/idpr.2019.7.

Morita, A. 2016. 'Infrastructuring Amphibious Space: The Interplay of Aquatic and Terrestrial Infrastructures on the Chao Phraya Delta in Thailand'. *Science as Culture*, 25(1): 117–140.

Massey, D. 2005. *For Space*. London: Sage Publications.

Peck, J. and N. Theodore. 2010. 'Mobilizing Policy: Models, Methods, and Mutations'. *Geoforum*, 41: 169–174.

Privacy International. 2017. 'Smart Cities: Utopian Vision, Dystopian Reality'. 31 October. Available at: https://privacyinternational.org/report/638/smart-cities-utopian-vision-dystopian-reality.

Raco, M. 2015. 'Sustainable City Building and the New Politics of the Possible: Reflections on the Governance of the London Olympics 2012'. *Area*, 47(2): 124–131.

Rancière, J. 2010. *Chronicles of Consensual Times*. London: Continuum.

Rodan, G. 2018. *Participation without Democracy: Containing Conflict in Southeast Asia*. Ithaca, NY: Cornell University Press.

Rose, G. 2017. 'Screening Smart Cities: Managing Data, Views and Vertigo'. In *Compact Cinematics: The Moving Image in the Age of Bit-Sized Media*, edited by P. Hesselberth and M. Poulaki, 177–184. London: Bloomsbury Academic.

Satrusayang, C. 2020. 'The BIG Interview: Future Forward Deputy Leader Kunthida Rungruengkiat'. *The Thai Enquirer*, 11 February. Available at: www.thaienquirer.com/7629/big-interview-with-future-forward-deputy-leader-kunthida-rungruengkiat/.

Shelton, T., M. Zook and A. Wiig. 2015. 'The Actually Existing Smart City'. *Cambridge Journal of Regions, Economy and Society*, 8(1): 13–25.

Sripokangkul, S., M. S. Cogan, C. Intharaphan and A. Muangming. 2018. 'Consent, Repression, and Emerging Student Activism in Northeastern Thailand'. *The International Journal of Interdisciplinary Civic and Political Studies*, 13(3–4): 13–27.

Suradech Taweesaengsakulthai. 2018. Interview, Esan Biz, 3 November. Available at: www.facebook.com/esanbiz/videos/732567073763322/.

Thak Chaloemtiarana. 2007. *Thailand: The Politics of Despotic Paternalism*. Chiang Mai: Silkworm Books.

Tsing, A. L. 2005. *Friction*. Princeton, NJ: Princeton University Press.

THE FUTURE OF PHOTOGRAPHY

17

Does Photography Have a Future? (Does Anything Else?)[1]

Joanna Zylinska

'Is Photography as We Know It Dying?'

More images are being produced, shared and seen today than ever in history. We are both constantly photographing and being photographed, with professional-level devices shrunk to a pocket size and seemingly infinite 'cloud' storage available at our constant disposal. The posing of the question, 'Does photography have a future?', may therefore seem premature or plainly absurd, given the extreme popularity of the photographic medium. However, this question is intended as a provocation, aimed at challenging our common-sense perception of the current state of things, including the frequently posited equivalence between popularity and longevity. Its theoretical impetus comes from the work of Vilém Flusser – not just his well-known texts on photography but also his important book *Does Writing Have a Future?* (2011a). (Flusser answers his own question in the negative, an argument that offers not so much a prophecy about our imminent illiteracy but rather a complex analysis of the inherent co-constitution of humans by and with our multiple media, with all its consequences.) Given that photography is increasingly decoupled from human agency and human vision – as evidenced in practices such as satellite imaging, drone media, CCTV and face recognition, and that the distinction between mechanical image capture and image creation is increasingly blurred (in, e.g., photogrammetry, computational photography or CGI), the question explored in this chapter concerns both the future of light-induced, mechanically produced images conventionally understood as photographs *and* the future of us humans as producers *of* and as beings produced *by* such images.

Despite the proliferation of photographic images and the expansion of the 'photographer' designation from professionals and hobbyists (aka 'amateurs') to arguably 'everyone', the question about photography's future keeps haunting the image making industry, its clients and users – as well as those occupying that narrower sliver of photography's art-based milieu, i.e., photographic artists and curators. In November 2019, the photonews website Petapixel published an article about what it meant to be a photographer at a present time. The article, as is often the case with online 'content' these days, featured a video conversation between photographer-journalists from cognate websites, Patrick Hall of FStoppers and Pye Jirsa of SLR Lounge, titled 'Is Photography as We Know It Dying?'. The conversation is worth looking at more closely because the issues raised by it are indicative of the broader tendencies in the rapidly evolving landscape of photographic discourses and practices.

Having acknowledged that the digital has both democratised photography and raised the bar, Hall and Jirsa admit that photographic practice itself is changing, with a lot of things 'falling to the wayside': heavy gear, strobes, complex editing. With the industry moving more and more towards phone photography, 'all that matters is the final image', they conclude – a statement that must sound like anathema to 'serious photographers', be they artists or amateurs. That statement recognises the fact that the ability to share and engage an audience, and having a following matter more than any single image, with a photographer having to be 'like a TV channel or TV show'. The more nebulous categories of enjoyment and authenticity are said to have replaced the old-style expectations of technical perfection and expert professionalism. Confirming that photography *as we know it* – i.e., as a professional or artistic practice dependent on its practitioners' unique skill and power of observation, and on their ability to produce singular images that make an impact while retaining importance across time – is indeed dying, Petapixel author DL Cade nonetheless summarises the analysis on an upbeat note: 'As the bar to entry drops and more and more people outsource their creativity to the latest Instagram trend or some AI-powered post-processing slider, creativity and technical know-how are only becoming more rare and valuable than ever' (Cade 2019).

The above discussion has identified some important trends with regard to photographic practice. These trends include miniaturisation; the increased role of software in image making, including at the image-generation stage; closer integration between photographic gear, clothing and the photographer's body; and the proliferation of 'nonhuman photography' (Zylinska 2017), i.e., images made neither *by* nor *for* the human. Artist Trevor Paglen, who uses images from satellites, surveillance cameras and machine vision databases, goes so far as to argue that 'Something dramatic has happened to the world of images: they have become detached from human eyes. Our machines have learnt to see [w]ithout us' (Paglen 2017). In response to the question posed in one of his online contributions written for Photomuseum Winterthur, 'Is Photography Over?', Paglen even claims that '"photography," as it has been traditionally understood in theory and practice, has undergone a transition – it has become something else, something that's difficult to make sense of within the existing analytic framework' (Paglen 2014).

Media Existentialism: Vilém Flusser Redux

What is photography transitioning towards, then? And what kind of analytic framework might we adopt that would help us understand this transition? To work towards answering these questions about photography's future it is worth recognising, as indicated at the beginning of this chapter, that the very posing of the question about photography's future articulates a number of concerns regarding not just the status of a specific industry or media practice but rather some larger, or even planetary-level, concerns about our human positioning in the world and our relationship with technology, at a time when our very existence is being increasingly challenged by attempts to envisage what comes next. This may seem like too big a leap, but I want to make a proposition that, by asking, with Paglen and others, whether photography (as we know it) is over, whether it has any future, we are actually using this specific cultural-technical practice to ponder whether everything else we know – including us humans as a species with particular cultural exigencies and technical affordances – will soon be over too. We are therefore using photography, although not always in a fully conscious way, as a conduit for asking a bigger question about our own situation in the world. It is in this sense that photography functions as an example of what Amanda Lagerkvist has described as 'existential media', i.e., media that are capable of accounting for 'the thrownness of the digital human condition' (Lagerkvist 2017, 96). This perspective analyses media life as an existential terrain which is irreducible 'to the social, the cultural, the economic, or the political', even if it remains intertwined with all those domains (2017, 106). With this existential mode of enquiry, we are also faced with another question: 'What comes after the human?'. Building on the legacy of ghost and spirit photography, a practice combining imagination and charlatanerie to make up for personal losses before the Great War, and collective loss in its aftermath, digital and post-digital image making can be mobilised to help us imagine, visualise and frame the future – and to image and imagine ourselves *as part of* that future.

The context for the exploration of these anxieties has been provided by a secular return of all sorts of existential finalisms, unfolding across different scales, some of them taking place on a species level ('end of man', the Sixth Extinction, coronavirus), others on a planetary one (Anthropocene, heat death). Photography and other forms of mechanical images such as films and TV have certainly played a role in aiding us with envisaging our demise. Yet, its representational role aside, it is worth delving deeper into photographic practice, with its apparatuses and networks, to trace the constitutive role of mechanical image making in enacting a certain vision of the future – or even enacting a certain future, full stop. One thinker who can help us with developing such an existential analytic framework for understanding the world today – which for him is equivalent with the world of images – is the Czech-born writer and philosopher Vilém Flusser (1920–1991). A nomad at heart if not always by choice, with the ruinous legacy of the Holocaust and antisemitism casting a dark shadow over both his family history and his work, Flusser wrote in multiple languages, disciplines, registers and styles, across several continents, decades and intellectual currents. His work on photography and other media emerged largely in the early 1980s. This was a time when media production had already been mechanised in the Benjaminian sense, with photographs' and films' reproducibility in the early twentieth century leading to the loss of cultural artefacts' uniqueness as singular objects endowed with a special aura and value, and also to their democratisation and their becoming-media – but it had not yet entered the era of mass digitisation. Yet Flusser's analyses are uncannily prescient in grasping the consequences of the automation of image production and reception, one that we see today not just in photography, video and other forms of communication such as journalism and literature, but also in politics.

In outlining a form of what we might term 'nomadic media existentialism', Flusser pays particular attention to images, and even more to technical images, which he defines as 'mosaics assembled from particles' (2011b, 6). He differentiates them from 'traditional images' such as cave or oil paintings, which for him have a different relation to reality; the former are mimetic, the latter function as visualisations, i.e., models. 'Traditional images' are two-dimensional surfaces, while technical images are 'without dimension' (2011b, 6). Mark Poster is right to raise a suspicion about the rigidity or even accuracy of this distinction

(Poster 2011, xvii), one that is premised on the excessive ontologisation of the earlier forms of visual expression as ritualistic and magic-driven, at the expense of appreciating their own specific technicity. It would therefore have been more productive perhaps to extend the concept of 'technical images' to, say, cave paintings – which for Flusser serve as quintessential images from pre-technological magic time – in order to trace their communicative value and their formative role in producing human memory and human consciousness. Yet this reservation does not diminish the significance of Flusser's argument, which is premised on noticing the technicity of (at least some) images in the first place, i.e., noticing their informational value.

Photographs, addressed most explicitly in Flusser's book *Towards a Philosophy of Photography*, are one class of such technical images, alongside film, television, video and other hybrid forms. Taking analogue photographs and other mechanically reproduced images as his starting point, we must note that Flusser is not really looking *at* them – but rather far beyond them, into the future of both images and humanity. This future is looking rather bleak; Flusser goes so far as to describe it as an ultimate catastrophe, because 'images themselves are apocalyptic' (2011b, 60). We will come back to this provocative idea later on. For now, let us ask whether, by not really looking *at* photographs, Flusser is not repeating the error of many other theorists who have thought about media without actually using them in any meaningful way, thus reducing the operational technicity of those media and the outcomes of those operations to the banality of a mere example – or, worse, to a figment of their imagination. He would be in good company here; as Flusser's translator Nancy Roth observes, 'Virtually all of the voices that have substantially shaped contemporary photographic "orthodoxy", not only the historians, but critics, including Benjamin ... Barthes ... Sontag ... *wrote* as receivers and judges of photographs, from the position Barthes designated the Spectator' (Roth 2010, 14). Yet Roth jumps at Flusser's defence by making an important differentiation: 'As Barthes is looking at photographs, Flusser is looking at photograph*ing* ... [B]y framing his topic as a gesture, a particular kind of movement between states of consciousness and states of affairs, Flusser was able, in a way no other writer on photography has been, to take the photographer's part' (2010, 14). There is therefore a rationale for Flusser's avoidance of looking not just at photographs but also at the photographed objects. Instead of looking *at* them, Flusser is looking *through* the photographic flow of images, and towards a future that, to cite Poster, entails 'a more complex possibility for multiple assemblages of the human and the machine, not as prostheses *for* the human but as mixtures of human-machine in which the outcome of specific forms of the relation are not prefigured in the initial conceptualization of the relation' (Poster 2011, xviii–xix). Flusser himself argues that interest in technical images on the part of 'future men and women' will have an 'existential' value (Flusser 2011b, 4), as it will allow them to dream up new visions of the world, and of their place in it. Images for him thus serve as devices, offering an insight into the modern world in which we are all being constituted by the technical apparatus, becoming its functionaries.

The Apparatus as an Image-Capture and World-Capture Machine

The notion of the apparatus is crucial for Flusser's theory. A kin concept to Michel Foucault's *dispositif*, a socio-political arrangement whose role was to enact something by delimitation, regulation and governance, the Flusserian apparatus – especially as introduced in *Towards a Philosophy of Photography* – evokes clear associations with the *(Foto)apparat* as a camera, a black box that produces results in the world in a mechanical way. Yet Flusser, as is often his way, plays with this concept, turning it around and twisting both its etymology and its function to arrive at something much more expansive and potent. Derived from the Latin word *apparare*, 'to prepare', an apparatus is 'a thing that lies in wait or in readiness' (Flusser 2000, 21). In other words, it is waiting to be actualised, being a function in need of an operator. It is in this sense perhaps that 'apparatuses are not machines' (2000, 29), or not *just* machines. Extrapolating from the black box of the photographic camera, the concept embraces, in a nested manner, different layers of reality that enact functions of different levels of complexity. Flusser thus explains that the 'camera functions on behalf of the photographic industry, which functions on behalf of the industrial complex, which functions on behalf of the socio-economic apparatus, and so on' (2000, 29–30). The rationale for using the term 'apparatus' for naming all these different levels of reality becomes clear when Flusser reveals that the key issue 'is who develops its program' (2000, 30). His ultimate concern is therefore with the multi-layered automation of our lives as enacted in and by its institutions, machines and media. They all have been pre-programmed in advance, with our role reduced to that of functionaries, or operators of apparatuses. Our task, in turn, lies not so much in understanding those programmes – a task Flusser has already assumed is to a large extent futile – but rather in producing better images of the world. Those images will be able to inform the world rather than mindlessly execute its operating commands, repeating the already known.

Flusser's claim that 'It is not what is shown in a technical image but rather the technical image itself that is the message' (2011b, 49) echoes Marshall McLuhan's communication model. With this approach, Flusser provides an insight into the technological set up of the world we have constructed – a world that also constructs us humans on a number of levels, with the message of technical images being 'significant' and 'commanding' (2011b, 49). He goes on to argue that the technical images that surround us 'signify models, instructions about the way society should experience, perceive, evaluate, and behave' (2011b, 50). Flusser's ideas were developed at the dawn of the digital era, long before the outpouring of social media 'influencers' with their image-based communication platforms. Yet they seem to have become validated by the fact that, today, restaurants, museum attractions, holiday destinations and whole cities are being designed to look good on Instagram, thus feeding, via the flow of images, our desires, experiences and purchases while also serving as blueprints for altering our environment. Our faces and bodies are changing too; cosmetic doctor Tijion Esho has coined the term 'Snapchat dysmorphia' to refer to the 'phenomenon of people requesting procedures to resemble their digital image' (cited in Hunt 2019), which had been manipulated with apps such as Facetune.

The Image Apocalypse

To highlight this mode of looking *through* the image flow is not to say that Flusser wouldn't be able to recognise or acknowledge the content of a particular image: the specific arrangement of particles into what to a human viewer looks like a conventionally happy wedding party, a birthday celebration or a holiday in the sun. It's just that these images are so predictable, so banal and hence so redundant *in the informational sense* that Flusser moves beyond their superficial value and looks at them as objects in a broader communicative sense. We could perhaps go so far as to say that Flusser perceives images the way computers (and specifically, machine vision systems) do: breaking an image into a cluster of pixels to be analysed for similarity and difference with other clusters in the database, and then matching it against the available categories and labels. Yet Flusser's theory allows us to concede that this machinic way of looking is not just a feature of machines, or an eccentric philosopher looking, literally, against the grain. Using his theory, we can perhaps surmise that *most humans now look at most images automatically*, scanning them for similarity and difference, engaging in quick categorisation (on a binary level: like/not like; or a semantic one, via comments and hashtags), and going along with the media flow.

The framing process for Flusser's theory of images and, more broadly, his theory of media is provided by a nexus of disciplines, from philosophy through to cybernetics and communication theory, all the way to thermodynamics and particle physics. But he also reveals a strong commitment to writing as a form of zigzagging through ideas, concepts and modes of expression to produce what could be described as thinking in action. This is undertaken in spite of Flusser's broader prophecy about the waning of writing as a mode of expression for the contemporary human, offering instead that we are moving towards a post-writing form of culture, driven by what he calls technical images. Indeed, for Flusser writing as the dominant mode of developing and transmitting a linear argument *has no future*; it has *already* been replaced, to a large extent, by communication via technical images. Given that Flusser was writing in the early 1980s, before digital technology radically altered our speed and form of communication, before blogging gave way to image sharing via Instagram and Snapchat and before reading was largely replaced by scrolling and touching, his theory of the end of print is indeed nothing short of prophetic. In their by now also 'classic' 2008 essay 'A Life More Photographic: Mapping the Networked Image', which analyses the state of photography in the age of the phone camera, digital snapshot and broadband, Daniel Rubinstein and Katrina Sluis look at a research project analysing the practice of users of the photo sharing platform Flickr, many of whom said they had given up blogging because it was 'too much work' and now favoured photography as a way of sharing their experiences. Rubinstein and Sluis argue that 'The practices of moblogging (blogging with a mobile phone) and photoblogging (blogging with photographs rather then text) further exploit the way in which mobile phone images have become a kind of visual speech – an immediate, intimate form of communication that replaces writing' (2008, 17–18). Contemporary users of digital platforms and media thus seem to be confirming Flusser's tongue-in-cheek assessment that 'Images ... are not so repulsive as massive rows of fat books' (Flusser 2011b, 132).

It is worth probing further why Flusser would resort to the aforementioned idea of the image apocalypse when looking through the images into the future. One may be tempted to equate his conceptualisation with the dismissal of the increasing photographic output in terms of an image deluge. This latter metaphor was poignantly encapsulated by Erik Kessels – a Dutch photographer, curator, advertiser and designer who can be described as the Jeff Koons of the photography world – in his installation *24 HRS in Photos*. In November 2011 Kessels filled an Amsterdam art gallery with prints of images that had been uploaded to Flickr over a 24-hour period. The visitors were presented with heaps of what looked like debris, spilling everywhere. The fact that this spillage had been carefully controlled by a number of wooden frames into which it had been placed to create this illusion of a flow not only tells us something about the artist's visual cant but also points to our wider desire for beautiful ruins, with aestheticisation of the apocalypse often having an anaesthetic function. And thus the project could easily be read as an indictment of photography today, with its pointless content, visual sameness and vapid content. Yet, following Elisabeth Kessler, it is also possible to read the installation as revealing the Flusserian apparatus in action, demonstrating human and machinic forces at work in the production of (the picture of) the world, while bringing forth a shared 'thingness' of our media ecologies. 'A person chose when and how to take each picture, but broader influences – human and nonhuman – shape the way we represent, see, and live in the world' (Kessler 2019). The image apocalypse does not therefore have to mean humans perishing in the debris of the world, but rather the expiration of the Anthropocene hubris enacted by the drowning of its core subject. Well versed in the canonical texts of Western culture, including its religious writings, Flusser was no doubt aware that the apocalypse was not just a catastrophe and that its occurrence, come what may, also carried a redemptive potential.

Before we move on to its redemptive aspects, we need to recognise that there are different levels of 'no future' announced in Flusser's work, with entropy, or heat death – an occurrence resulting from the dissipation of information as explained by the second law of thermodynamics – constituting our world's 'event horizon'. Finalist realisations have organised the worldview of many modern philosophers – from the singular human's horizon of death as encountered in the writing of Martin Heidegger and Jean-Paul Sartre through to the death of the sun as the star that nourishes our planet in the writings of Jean-François Lyotard. In a similar vein, Flusser's planetary perspective is meant to allow us to come to terms with the absurdity of the world, with its ultimate lack of meaning. But this is a form of pragmatic absurdism, one devoid of wallowing in tragedy and loss. Flusser accepts from the word go that the fate of the universe is subject to chance, that the end-game of this chance is entropy and that any occurrences, be they 'galactic spirals, living cells, or human brains', are the result of improbable coincidences, 'erroneous' exceptions 'to the general rule of increasing entropy' (2011b, 17). Yet he quickly moves beyond that realisation to introduce a differentiation between the cosmic programme of the universe, which we can't do very much about, and the human-designed programme of the apparatus, which remains subject to human control – or which at least entails the possibility of the human wresting away some degree of control, be it through insurgence or chance. 'Envisioners are people who try to turn an automatic apparatus against its own condition of being automatic' (2011b, 19). Any act of resistance can therefore only come from within and via the apparatus. Flusser may be no photographer but he himself takes on the role of an enframer and an informer – someone who can rearrange particles, or pixels, to create a new 'mosaic', provide new information and offer a new vision. Creativity as an act of working against the machine, not in a Luddite manner that rejects it *tout court* but rather in defiance of its programme, is a task he implores us all to adopt, while there is still time.

Flusser is thus interested in photography as a mode of thinking and seeing to come, or one that has *already* partly come. His assessment that 'We live in an illusory world of technical images, and we increasingly experience, recognize, evaluate, and act as a function of these images' (2011b, 38) applies even more aptly to the era of social media and wide image sharing. Photography thus serves for Flusser as a model for understanding the functioning of the apparatus – and for taking the apparatus to task. It also becomes a laboratory for seeing otherwise, for reprogramming our vision of the world by creating better, i.e., more informed, pictures of it, with technical images being 'phantoms that can give the world, and us, meaning' (2011b, 32). It is in this sense that photography for Flusser has an existential significance. While he recognises that entropic decay is already part of our everyday experience, expressing itself 'in the receivers' zeal for the sensational – there have always to be new images because all images have long since begun to get boring' (2011b, 59), he also observes, perhaps jokingly to some extent, that no apocalyptic catastrophe of nuclear or similar finalist kind is needed as 'technical images are themselves the end' (2011b, 59). Images themselves are thus 'apocalyptic' (2011b, 60) because they replace the linearity of writing, and thus of history, with the cybernetic feedback loop of the image flow – which becomes a magic circle of eternal return.

In the poignant assessment of the Instagram culture writer Dayna Tortorici has provided the following visceral account of what that loop actually looks like in the age of social media.

What would I see? A fitness personality lunging across the sand. An adopted cat squirming in a paper bag. A Frank Lloyd Wright building. A sourdough loaf. A friend coming out as nonbinary. A mirror selfie. A handstand tutorial. Gallery opening. Nightclub candid. Outfit of the day. Medal from the Brooklyn half-marathon. New floating shelves. A screenshot of an article titled: 'A 140-year-old tortoise wearing her 5-day-old son as a hat'. Protest. Crashing waves. Gabrielle Union's baby. Wedding kiss. Friend's young mother at the peak of her beauty for Mother's Day. Ina Garten in a witch's hat. Detail of a Bruegel painting. Brown egg in a white void, posted to @world_record_egg [verified blue checkmark], with the caption, 'Let's set a world record together and get the most liked post on Instagram, beating the current world record held by Kylie Jenner (18 million)! We got this [hands up emoji]'. By the time I saw it, the egg had 53,764,664 likes. The comments read:

'What does the egg mean?'

'That's a trick question'.

World records are meaningless in a culture defined by historical amnesia and the relentless invention of categories, I thought, and double tapped to like the egg.

(Tortorici 2020)

Tortorici describes the experience of the human viewer of images (in this case, herself) being faced with an Instagram flow in terms of entering into a loop of exchanges not only with other human photographers but also with the platform's algorithms. The loops of her brain activity generated by the intensifying visual stimuli coming from the pictures of friends, strangers, objects and places eventually lead to affective overdrive. This state of high agitation is being sustained by the repetitive behaviour of sliding and tapping, with the viewer's eyes and fingers enacting their own loopy dance in search of yet another dopamine hit. Flusser points out that the 'general consensus between images and people' (2011b, 66) – as evidenced in the popularity scores achieved by various images – inscribes itself in the repetitive cycle: nature – culture – waste – nature (2011b, 109). We may update it as 'Flower – like – skip – the great outdoors. Woman I vaguely know – heart – unheart – God I hate her. Food – avo on toast – skip – #sohungry'. But there is an escape from, or at least opening within, that world of 'meaninglessness' and 'historical amnesia' on its way to heat death.

The redemptive aspect of Flusser's apocalypse lies in the redefinition of the human as part of the 'composting' loop. This entails dissolving the myth of the human 'I' as 'a core that must be preserved and developed' (2011b, 93).

Repositioned as 'an abstract hook on which to hang concrete circumstances, the "I" reveals itself to be nothing' (2011b, 93). The Flusserian apocalypse thus involves destroying the Judeo-Christian image of the human as a being, made, albeit imperfectly, in the image of God and equipped with some core qualities, qualities whose nature has to be both veiled and revered. For Flusser, the "I" only emerges in a dialogue. Building on the philosophy of Martin Buber while also giving it a cybernetic twist in his image of a society as a 'dialogical cerebral web', Flusser claims that the ' "I" is the one to whom someone says "you" ' (2011b, 93). The communication model of subjectivity is not just linked to acts of speech; as previously stated, for Flusser the medium really becomes the message – and the messenger. Our consciousness is thus seen as being shaped by the media we make and use, and which also make and use *us*. This model of (say, Instagram-driven) subjectivity dispenses with universal humanist signal points such as choice, decision and free will. Flusser does nevertheless offer an opening within this cybernetic-naturalistic theorisation of the human. A being produced, literally, *from media res*, one whose brain 'appeared as an accident in the natural game of chance' (2011b, 94), the human has the possibility of mobilising this aleatory game as a strategy. S/he can do this because the brain has an inbuilt tendency to turn against chance, defy accident and reject entropy. However, for the human's negentropic tendency to be actualised certain conditions need to be created. Flusser's whole *oeuvre*, one might argue, is premised on identifying those conditions.

Photography and Future-Making

As well as being authors of their own destruction, human beings – who have inaugurated and then labelled a geological epoch in their name – are also a guarantee of our planet's survival. Humans thus can be said to have an inbuilt counterapocalyptic tendency. Even if this survival is just a delay, humans are an opportunity *for* the world, as well as functioning as its existential threat. The answer about the future – of images, writing, the world, or anything else – is therefore also a matter of temporal scale. Images themselves, and, in particular, technical images as produced and exchanged via platforms such as Instagram, Facebook or Snapchat, *can* serve as delaying tactics in this process of information dissipation, even if the majority of them do nothing of the kind. As an Instagram user Flusser would have no doubt been bemused by the banality, sameness and predictability of the output. Yet his existential-level conclusion, 'I play with images ... to coexist'

(2011b, 127), would surely serve as an encouragement not to sign off to quickly – from social media, from sociality and from the world as we know it.

The answer to the question 'Does photography have a future?' thus depends on who is posing it and what time scale they operate on. If it's a curator or a gallery owner interested in securing investment on their Henri Cartier-Bresson or Ansel Adams, they probably have a few good years left. If it's a photojournalist or a professional wedding photographer, the writing is on the wall, at least as far as high income is concerned – unless they can undergo a cross-media shift to become a personal TV channel. For those who are too busy posting on Instagram or editing their selfies to be even interested in posing it, because most of the things they know come from living in the constant image flow, some other questions maybe more pertinent than the one about the state of the photographic medium, its supporting institutions and its industry: When looking at, sharing and contributing to the media flow, what kind of future do you see, for yourself and the world? What kind of existence can you carve out and enframe from the media and image flow?

In the Judeo-Christian culture, the world was seen as 'an image made in God's likeness' (Adorno 1997, 143). It was a representational model of the world, whereby humans were seen as part of God's creation. In the universe of the image apparatus, the world is an image *without* a divine origin. What is more, it has become increasingly impossible to distinguish between a representation and a model. We could go so far as to argue that now *all* images have become what filmmaker Harun Farocki has termed 'operational images', carrying the potential of an execution of a function. According to Flusser, 'From now on, we are the ones who project meaning on the world. And technical images are such projections' (2011b, 46–47). Reprogramming the apparatus thus also means taking responsibility for our role in the co-creation of images, be it with technical devices or our cortico-corporeal apparatus, in full knowledge that we are neither sole authors nor sole recipients of the incessant media and image flow – although we may be the only ones for whom shaping this flow into a set of meanings becomes an ethico-political task, rather than just a pre-programmed function to be executed. The fact that the majority of people function as if that was not the case, running the programmes of the apparatus in and with their lives, cameras, phones and other media, only makes this task more urgent.

Flusser himself already pronounced in 1985, several decades before the wide adoption of photogrammetry, CGI and AI-driven image making, that '[p]hotography is about to become redundant' (2011b, 45). With this, he was referring to the increased generation of synthetic images, as a result of which it had become impossible to 'distinguish between depictions and models' (2011b, 44). Yet, even if the medium and the practice of photography as we know them may indeed become obsolete, the *function* of photography will no doubt survive for a long time yet – although its execution, in the fully informational guise, will perhaps only be executed by the very few. Like writing, which is 'a mesh of accident and necessity' yet which is nevertheless '*experienced*' by us code-driven and code-making humans 'as a free gesture' (2011b, emphasis added), photography will present us with new opportunities, beyond trying to seek meaning and order *in* the world, be it via religion or everyday semiosis. To approach the medium of photography through the 'existential register' outlined by Lagerkvist (2017, 96) is to shift photography's future role from memory-making to future-making, while repositioning the photographer as the very maker (or, to use Flusser's term, 'envisioner') of those futures. The future photographer's gesture of pointing at the world can be expected to generate a whole new 'revolutionary attitude' (Flusser 2011b, 56), one which will involve projecting meaning *onto* the world. Technical images, be it in their photographic or post-photographic guises, are capable of functioning as such projections. Through this photography has the potential to 'give absurdity a meaning' (2011b, 49) – not in a semiotic sense, but rather through reframing the photographic act and gesture as meaningful in themselves – and thus serve as a life force, a generator of experiences transmitted as images. Transcending its representative function as the 'pencil of nature' or 'the mirror of life', photography can instead *become* the future, for better or for worse.

Additional Material

Watch Joanna Zylinska's video, *Nonhuman Vision*, on The Future of Media website:
www.golddust.org.uk/futureofmedia

References

Adorno, T. 1997. *Aesthetic Theory*. London: The Athlone Press.

Cade, DL. 2019. 'Photography as We Know is Changing, and it's Your Job to Change with It.' Petapixel, 8 November. Available at: https://petapixel.com/2019/11/08/photography-as-we-know-is-changing-and-its-your-job-to-change-with-it/?mc_cid=947c856268&mc_eid=5bb11290a7.

Flusser, V. 2000. *Towards a Philosophy of Photography*. London: Reaktion Books.

Flusser, V. 2011a. *Does Writing Have a Future?* Minneapolis, MN: University of Minnesota Press.

Flusser, V. 2011b. *Into the Universe of Technical Images*. Minneapolis, MN: University of Minnesota Press.

Hunt, E. 2019. 'Faking It: How Selfie Dysmorphia Is Driving People to Seek Surgery'. *The Guardian*, 23 January. Available at: www.theguardian.com/lifeandstyle/2019/jan/23/faking-it-how-selfie-dysmorphia-is-driving-people-to-seek-surgery.

Kessler, E. A. 2019. 'Review of Joanna Zylinska's *Nonhuman Photography*'. *CAA Reviews*, 11 February. https://doi.org/10.3202/caa.reviews.2019.18.

Lagerkvist, A. 2017. 'Existential Media: Toward a Theorization of Digital Thrownness'. *New Media & Society*, 19(1): 96–110.

Paglen, T. 2014. 'Seeing Machines'. Posting in the Fotomuseum Wintherthur series 'Is Photography Over?'. 13 March. Available at: www.fotomuseum.ch/en/explore/still-searching/articles/26978_seeing_machines.

Paglen, T. 2017. 'Artist's Notes' for the solo show *A Study of Invisible Images*, 8 September–21 October, Metro Pictures, New York.

Poster, M. 2011. 'An Introduction to Vilém Flusser's *Into the Universe of Technical Images* and *Does Writing Have a Future?*'. In *Into the Universe of Technical Images*, Vilém Flusser, ix–xxv. Minneapolis, MN: University of Minnesota Press.

Roth, N. 2010. 'The Photographer's Part'. *Flusser Studies*, 'Photography and Beyond: On Vilém Flusser's *Towards a Philosophy of Photography*', 10(1): 14–17.

Rubinstein, D. and K. Sluis. 2008. 'A Life More Photographic: Mapping the Networked Image'. *Photographies*, 1(1): 9–28.

Tortorici, D. 2020. 'Infinite Scroll: Life under Instagram'. *The Guardian*, 31 January. Available at: www.theguardian.com/technology/2020/jan/31/infinite-scroll-life-under-instagram.

Zylinska, J. 2017. *Nonhuman Photography*. Cambridge, MA: MIT Press.

THE FUTURE OF 'THE FUTURE'

18

Astronoetic Voyaging: Speculation, Media and Futurity

James Burton

Introduction

The concept of 'the future', like time itself, is notoriously difficult. Philosophers and scientists have argued variously that the future is absolutely determined (e.g., Isaac Newton), fundamentally open and indeterminate (e.g., Henri Bergson), heavily constrained by the past (e.g., Karl Marx) or that it is all of these (e.g., Jacques Derrida); that it is infinite and continuous (e.g., Aristotle) or infinite and cyclic (as in Hindu cosmology); that it is necessarily finite (e.g., Immanuel Kant) or effectively finite due to entropy (e.g., William Kelvin); that it does not exist (e.g., John McTaggart) or that it exists simultaneously with the past and the present (e.g., Albert Einstein). Some consider futurity a matter of ontology, others an evolutionarily developed psychological trait (Guyau 1890), still others as the product of a leap or rupture that is identical with politics (Grosz 2004, 257–258), or a historical construction, which may (at least in Western cultures) be in the process of disappearing (Nowotny 1994, 45–74). The lack of any prospect of scientific or theoretical consensus may seem odd, given the degree of shared understanding implicit in a wide array of social and cultural manifestations of humans' relationships with time. Augustine's dictum that I know what time is until I'm asked to explain it to someone else does not seem to have lost its charge (1961, 264).

One modern thinker, possibly echoing Augustine, suggests that the limitations of the human perspective may defeat in advance *any* (human) attempt to understand time: 'Perhaps the trouble lies much deeper than human philosophy can ever probe. It may be that human mentality itself, the half-developed mode of human immediate experience, does not reveal enough of the nature of time to permit of a logically coherent theory of it' (Stapledon 1939, 413). This reflection is found in Olaf Stapledon's two-volume introduction to philosophy as 'a way of life' (1939, 12). Yet it is primarily through literary writing that Olaf Stapledon philosophises. His novels, most notably *Last and First Men* (1999a [1930]) and *Star Maker* (1999b [1937]), have been widely recognised as landmarks of twentieth-century science-fiction and admired by figures as diverse as Bertrand Russell, Jorge Luis Borges, Virginia Woolf and Arthur C. Clarke. These works demonstrate that, even if he takes a true understanding of time to be beyond human mentality, Stapledon sees value in speculating about the past and the future, about their metaphysical status and the possible forms and paths they might take/have taken. Encompassing an entire speculative history of the cosmos, from distant beginning to distant end, depicting an ever-widening multiplicity of humanesque and non-humanesque forms of life, *Star Maker* forms an excellent resource for engaging with the question of the future of media, and an implicit practical argument for the conceptual and transformative value of sustained speculative thought.

Such an engagement will form the main focus of this chapter. However, before turning to the novel, I would like briefly to establish a few principles which I will take to condition speculation regarding the future of media, and which, as the remainder of the article will show, are of particular prominence in the speculative exploration that comprises the core of *Star Maker*.

Four Principles Regarding Speculation, Futurity and Media

The Augustinian formula referenced above seems to suggest that there may be an intuitive understanding of time that is potentially possessed by many, but which it is difficult, if not impossible, to express in rationally communicable form. In this sense, it can be taken as a recognition of the difficulty in bridging the gap between something like 'subjective' and something like 'objective' knowledge/reality. But it can also be read as foregrounding the conditioning role of perspective in any thinking, and asking us to consider how this applies specifically to temporality; Augustine goes on to suggest that the future can exist only in the mind, in expectation or anticipation (1961, 267–269). This confronts us with the question of whether temporality and futurity may have *no* objective reality beyond the local, subjective registers of experience, understanding or physical change.

In light of this, a first principle here will be that *any attempt to speculate regarding time and futurity is bound by perspectival constraints*. These will arise from the nature of the active entity in question, its position, orientation, capacities for perception and thought etc. This applies equally to any possible thinking of the future *of* something – such as 'media'. Thus, even if 'the future' necessarily has intimations of generality going beyond the scope of any single entity, inquiring into it is necessarily also always-already a question of '*whose* future?'. Are we concerned with 'the future of media' *for/from the perspective of* someone or something – humans, for example? Or should we take 'the future of media' to implicate a futurity for/from the perspective of some phenomenon potentially synonymous with media – media's futures (of media)?

A second principle follows from the first due to this specific focus on future of *media*. Implicit in and constitutive of the perspectival constraints conditioning any given subject/entity's approach to futurity are the basic elements of its structure and composition. These include the means by which it relates to the rest of the universe, through perception, communication and so on – and thus include media. Hence with 'the future of media' we are in the sphere of a special case of thinking the future, in that media are determining and implicated aspects of any such thinking, as conditioning the above-mentioned perspectival constraints. Media in the broadest sense determine and limit perception, memory, activity, the possible relationship(s) between any putative self and world. Hence the second principle: *To speculate about the future of media is to speculate about the future of speculation.*

To make matters more complicated, it is also hard to ignore the fact that the very *process* of speculation may itself begin to change these constraints and capacities. Speculating about something open-ended tends to foster the conception and imagination of possibilities previously not considered. Speculation is initially constrained by the conditions of its starting point. Providing it does not remain wholly limited by these constraints, however, it has the capacity to alter them, making them the basis for further speculative impulses, in theory at least continually widening the limits of conceivability. Hence a third principle: *speculation that is not determined in advance by prejudice is the enemy of prejudice.* This indicates that it has the general effect of transforming the speculator in such a way that counters prejudice.

The simplest speculation may remain constrained from the outset by the prejudices that condition it. A white racist's speculations about what foreigners might do to them, about the negative effects of immigrants on the economy, the possibility that multiculturalism increases the likelihood of terrorist attacks, their speculations about whether their non-white colleagues unfairly see them as racist or whether their last public anti-racist gesture was sufficiently noticed and appreciated, are all instances of speculation going a short distance and immediately being consumed by the prejudices which launched it, like a thousand rockets failing to escape a planet's atmosphere. Speculation that is extended in any given direction, however, will always, and on the whole increasingly, challenge or undermine prejudices (even if it may not be the fastest or most effective means of doing so).

It may be noted that neither speculation nor prejudice is exclusively about the future. (I may speculate about the final sensory experience of the last Tyrannosaur, the breakfast preferences of Anne Boleyn, the hidden meaning in a comment made by a friend, whether I'm infected with a virus and so on.) Prejudices, both trivial and violent, likewise constrict any speculating I do about the past or the present. However, both speculation and prejudice have an orientation towards future *knowledge*. They involve more than questioning – they actively produce, in imagination, in virtual form perhaps, possibilities that might at some putative future moment be actualised. Speculation, as its etymology suggests, involves *looking* – but looking at something which must be *produced* in the act of speculation – something that could later prove real or true (and which, even in virtual form, by the recursive mode discussed above, may help shape and widen the scope of this speculation as it extends further). It can also entail noticing, discovering that which is unexpected or which the speculator is not conscious of having generated. Prejudice, in parallel etymological manner, involves *judging* – again, positing a future possibility that could later turn out to be correct. Both are oriented towards posited potential future knowledge, but with one oriented towards restricting, the other towards expanding the possible scope of this knowledge. Hence a fourth principle arises from the third: *non-judgemental speculation is active, productive and (self-)transformative.*

These four recursively linked principles, if a little convoluted as laid out above, I hope go some way, collectively, to addressing the question of 'why' speculate regarding the future of media. It is increasingly common in an era characterised by fears of international terrorism, environmental destruction, uncontrolled technological acceleration and, now, pandemics, for the question of 'survival versus perishing' to form the horizon of any thinking about the future. Bearing in mind the principle of perspectival constraints, it may be assumed that when speculating about the future of media, I do so as a social entity with at least some interest in my own survival and the collective survival of other entities to which I feel a certain boundedness. Bearing in mind the other three principles, it may well be that such survival – the continuation of certain forms of life into the future – depends upon their self-transformation through openness to and the embracing of an ever-widening array of other forms of life, a process which may be fuelled and continually enhanced by non-judgemental speculation. Such, in any case, the following engagement hopes to show, is the implicit proposition of Stapledon's *Star Maker*, a piece of novelistic philosophical writing characterised like so much European thought of the 1930s by the experience and anticipation of mass-scale global warfare, its underlying causes and potentially existential implications for the species as a whole.

Heather and Obscurity

Star Maker begins, in a manner possibly evoking Dante and Joyce,[1] with an individual experience of tribulation and self-questioning that, through imaginative shifts of perspective and register, simultaneously exposes the cosmic insignificance of the protagonist's crises, and makes this the driving impetus for a quest in search of the truth and meaning of everything.

> One night when I had tasted bitterness I went out on to the hill. Dark heather checked my feet. Below marched the suburban street lamps. Windows, their curtains drawn, were shut eyes, inwardly watching the lives of dreams. Beyond the sea's level darkness a lighthouse pulsed. Overhead, obscurity.
>
> (Stapledon 1999b, 1)[2]

These first few sentences place the narrator in the situation of a Stephen Dedalus or a Prufrock, seeking to lift themselves beyond the mundane emptiness of a life measured out with coffee spoons. Yet Stapledon's narrator is free of both Dedalus' arrogant self-superiority and Prufrock's frustrated impotence, each of which in its own way keeps these protagonists trapped within and fixated on the minutiae of the very domestic and social worlds they seemingly long to transcend. In contrast, when the narrator of *Star Maker* takes his step back from the quotidian world to reflect upon it, though his over-the-shoulder gaze lingers at first on what he is leaving behind, the dark heather of the hill, the suburban streetlamps and 'the world's delirium' (1999b, 1), he is also drawn inexorably onward and away from it all, first by the contemplation of the infinite obscurity above him, and then by the alien strangeness of the stars as they begin to appear in the evening sky.

The novel comprises an account of what the narrator frequently refers to as an 'adventure' beginning from these first speculative stirrings, a journey of cosmic discovery in which he is gradually joined by numerous other 'explorers' similarly taking flight from their own local worlds. A diversity of modes of life, community and being are described, each new encounter simultaneously participating in the ongoing transformation of the explorers themselves, the exponential widening of their perspective and experience as they pursue their ultimate goal of reaching the eponymous Star Maker, the presumed creator of the cosmos.

The narrator acknowledges that this is a journey of the imagination, though not in the sense of being unreal; imagination is used to fuel literal, material movement and change. This is a journey that is repeatedly spurred on by the speculative juxtaposition of perspectives and scales, oscillating between them by imaginative acts that continually fuel further extensions of those scales to ever-increasing degrees. Indeed, it is as though this oscillation, emerging from very simple shifts of perspective and incremental acts of ordinary perception and speculation (looking at a star; imaging what the Earth might look like from far above), effectively bootstraps into existence the entire process which takes the narrator to the temporal and spatial limits of the cosmos. He is a pioneer of what Hans Blumenberg would, a few years and a world war later, name 'astronoetics', inventing the term while writing a grant proposal seeking funding to explore the dark side of the moon by the power of thought (Blumenberg 1997; Harries 2001, 320).

With his 'new, strange mode of perception' (5) 'the hawk-flight of imagin-ation' takes the narrator beyond the horizon and away, until he finds himself observing the whole planet from a distance (4), the perspective from which the Earthrise photographs would be taken three decades later. Unlike the astronauts who produced the Earthrise photographs, however – images that are themselves already manipulated by the constraining human(ist) perspec-tive, being rotated to give the impression that the Earth 'rises' from the horizon (Lazier 2011, 625–626) – the narrator continues to move away. Initially his reaction does seem to anticipate cultural responses to Earthrise of the 1960s and 1970s, including the naming and impact of the 'Blue Marble' photograph of 1972 and the associated appearance of Gaia Theory that same year, as he perceives the Earth and all life upon it as a tiny, fragile, yet unified whole, adrift in the vast emptiness of the cosmos: 'It was a huge pearl ... No, it was far more lovely than any jewel. Its patterned colouring was more subtle, more ethereal ... in my remoteness I started to feel, as never before, the vital presence of Earth as of a creature alive' (8). However, as his momentum takes him further, his home planet receding out of view, any stirrings of Anthropocenic sentiments, any sense of humanity's place in a delicate, unified ecological whole, give way to a sense of 'mankind [as] of no more importance in the universal view than rats in a cathedral' (13).

This oscillation between scales of perception, as integral to a particular speculative mode, underlies the entirety of the adventure undertaken by the narrator and his fellow travellers. This is also an opposition between tendencies – one turning inward, towards closure, self-isolation and self-preservation from the rest of the cosmos, the other moving outward to ever-greater degrees of openness, encompassing and continually refuelled by its widening perspective. This reflects the nature of the voyage as a dramatic transformation of the voyager, entailing the widening of their initial perspectival constraints and values to an extreme degree, but with continual oscillations along the way that allow them to maintain some connection to the particular being, history, value-system they are travelling away from. In this way, a continuity of experience links the possible survival of the initial being to the near obliteration of self.

Media in both specific and general senses are integral to these processes by which the narrator undertakes his astronoetic journey. In the next two sections I want to elaborate on this by considering first some of the more 'humanesque' and then increasingly 'non-humanesque' media encountered by the travellers.

Radio Takes Over the World

In a more restricted sense of the 'future of media' – suggesting the transformation of phenomena widely identified with 'media' in the contemporary public sphere – *Star Maker* provides much potential fuel for speculation. In the narrator's encounters with other sentient species, he comes across a range of media technologies and means of communicating that remain unknown to Stapledon's readers. For example, the 'Other Men', though humanoid in shape, have a biological-anatomical constitution that renders vision relatively trivial, with sensation and perception oriented towards taste. This sensory bias inflects every aspect of their language, culture and media, so that the concept of 'complexity', for example, has the literal meaning of 'many-flavoured' (29) and the equivalent term for 'brilliant' is 'tasty'. Perceptions of something like racial difference are based primarily on taste and smell. Radio and television broadcasts operate by affording 'intricate stimuli to the taste organs and scent organs of the hand' via a 'pocket receiving set' that most individuals carry with them (34). 'Music' is broadcast over these sets by translating 'taste- and smell-themes ... into patterns of ethereal undulation' (34).

The narrator witnesses the appearance of a new kind of broadcast/receiver technology which bypasses the sense-organs and operates by 'direct stimulation of the appropriate brain-centres', combining 'radio-touch, -taste, -odour, and -sound' (34). This invention is initially developed for the purpose of 'sexual broadcasting', offering a highly realistic experience of sexual gratification, affording the masses the opportunity to experience physical intimacy with 'radio love-stars' and 'impecunious aristocrats' (35). In time, the vast potential of this VR-like medium is developed; it becomes a means by which 'electric massage' can replace exercise; medical treatment can be applied by manipulation of hormones and other chemicals; a 'vast system of automatic food-production' (and an equally complex sewage system) can be controlled by radio. Of course, the medium is also used extensively by governments for various forms of population control, from rendering slums tolerable via the manufactured experience of luxury, to suppressing revolt by the judicious production of distractions (35–36). Such is the dominance of the radio-system that it eventually becomes possible for a person 'to retire to bed for life and spend all his time receiving radio programmes' (36) while the entire planet is overseen by the World Broadcasting Authority (37) in a perpetual state of elective lockdown.

As the narrator encounters other lifeforms on other planets, radio waves turn out to be the basis for a variety of other speculative media forms. Stapledon is using 'radio' not in the restricted sense of 'broadcast sound', but as the underlying medium of radio waves, as used by pre-digital television, mobile phones, text messaging, Bluetooth, RFID and other forms of wireless communication. In one world the adventurers encounter a species characterised by 'swarm intelligence', where large collections of apparently separate organisms form 'a cloud of ultra-microscopic sub-vital units' that is 'organized in a common radio-system' (112). Aeons later, in contrast to its earlier use for biopolitical and fascistic ends, radio becomes the basis for a galactic utopia, serving as the means by which democratic governance can be maintained in the absence of any formal 'democratic machinery', with a 'highly specialized bureaucracy' overseeing global affairs, but 'under constant supervision by popular will expressed through the radio' (133).

Another group of media that remain underdeveloped on Earth, but which the explorers of *Star Maker* find throughout the galaxy, especially in its mature phases, is based on something like psychic communication. One of the earliest instances occurs within a hybrid species that has evolved as fundamentally symbiotic, every organistic 'unit' being composed of one member of a marine 'ichthyoid' species and one member of a terrestrial 'arachnoid' species. After a long era of 'blind mutual slaughter' the two species gradually discovered value in cooperation, and over further epochs of co-evolution 'moulded one another to form a well-integrated union' (95). Eventually, pairs of partners are able to remain in union across galactic distances. Ultimately, it is revealed that this hybrid species is responsible for enabling the explorers to develop the technique of travelling freely across space and time that have made their whole adventure possible.

There are plenty of media in *Star Maker* that do not depend on radio or psychic communication. One example is found on an ocean world where a 'nautiloid', ship-like species of intelligent beings use a means of communication potentially available to humans but which has in our world thankfully remained rudimentary: 'For short-range communications, rhythmic underwater emissions of gas from a vent in the rear of the organism were heard and analysed by means of underwater ears' (81). (Somewhere deep underground, perhaps, in a secret Google lab...)

These examples are all media that could conceivably operate within a human context. Though they depend on technologies and techniques that have not been discovered or invented, it is possible to imagine them functioning in a world of humans. The species that employ them differ in certain traits from the humans of Earth, yet they also share many supposedly human traits, e.g., in terms of culture, technology, social character. Stapledon's narrator sometimes uses the word 'humanesque' to describe such lifeforms, a practice I've followed here, since it allows for an appropriate fuzziness of boundaries and, unlike the term 'humanoid', does not imply that similarity between species is tied to form or appearance. Although the first alien species the narrator encounters, and probably others, do indeed share a broadly humanoid physique, non-humanoid intelligent lifeforms such as the nautiloid or arachnoid species may be just as *humanesque* in terms of religion, social structure, culture, technology, tendencies towards violence, love, competitiveness etc.

A key facet of the explorers' journey is that the kinds of being they are able to encounter vary increasingly as their adventure progresses. It is no coincidence that the first intelligent lifeforms the narrator encounters look and act a lot like people as he recognises them, bar a few key differences. With each new encounter, the travellers, voyaging as a kind of composite entity – though with each still retaining a sense of its own identity and history – are joined by members of new species. By an interstellar snowball effect, their composition becomes increasingly complex and diverse. For a long time, they are only able to discover new species that share key humanesque traits: 'It appeared that, for us to enter any world at all, there had to be a deep-lying likeness or identity in ourselves and our hosts' (64). But with each addition to their number bringing new modes of experience, capacities for perception and understanding, after a multitude of incremental diversifications the range of species they are able to encounter becomes increasingly non-humanesque.

Non-Humanesque Media

This ongoing process of the transformation of their identity and nature, insepar-able from the continual expansion of the explorers' capacity for perception and communication, equates to an expansion of the variety and scope of the media conditioning and enabling their collective place in and movement through the universe. For instance, through his encounters with the Other Men, the narrator gains an experience of what it is to think and sense primarily in terms of taste. With the nautiloids, the explorers learn what it is to 'hear' the sea floor. With the swarm intelligence, they discover 'painfully how to see with a million eyes at once, how to feel the texture of the atmosphere with a million wings' (106). On worlds populated by 'vegetable humanities' or 'plant-men', they experience 'all the cultural themes known on earth ... transposed into a strange key, a perplexing mode' (117).

As the explorers are transformed by contact with ever stranger and decreas-ingly humanesque forms of being, any putative boundary between the more socio-culturally circumscribed sense of media (as radio, television etc.) and the more general sense of media as indicating all forms of interrelation, is pro-gressively eroded. In time, 'worlds' – comprising planets and their inhabitants and, later, interlinked collections of such planets – begin to become conscious. The media by which these waking and wakened worlds communicate and interact with one another are not clearly described, but are partly composed of multitudes of smaller lines of communication using fairly humanesque media. As these worlds evolve, and as the process of their coming-together as unified consciousnesses is repeated, over aeons, at the galactic level, they acquire the ability to perceive entities with their own media that are so far from the humanesque as to be barely intelligible, even to these galactic entities composed of billions of diverse minds and biotechnological systems.

The discovery that stars possess sentience and intelligence comes as a shock both to the wakened worlds and the explorers. Emphasising that he is only able to give the faintest intimation of his encounter with these utterly alien beings, the narrator describes how the stars experience gravity as a kind of medium, along with other processes such as the transmission of light and cosmic rays. The explorers find themselves 'enter[ing] telepathically into the star's perception of the gentle titillations, strokings, pluckings, and scintillations that [come] to it from the galactic environment' (188). Via gravitational force, each star senses other stars, their movements continually responding to one another in a kind of cosmic dance. Though their relative movements may seem to an observer to be bound by fixed physical laws, the conscious stars maintain their roles in the dance by will, and have the capacity to err or wander from their expected course if they choose. (However, to do so is considered 'sinful', and is only tolerated among the younger, more playful stars). In addition to their modes of nebular communication via the medium of gravitational pull (207–208), the stars use other media under certain circumstances; for example, on the rare occasions when the dance brings two of them into proximity, they may engage in physical interaction by extending flaming filaments towards one another. In these movements and interactions the explorers discern spiritual and cultural lives (189), and 'a whole world of social experiences', though these are 'so alien to the minded worlds that almost nothing can be said of them' (190).

Beyond the stellar and galactic scales, *Star Maker* allows glimpses of possible modes of being beyond the narrator's cosmos. At the narrative's climax, the explorers – now bonded to the whole cosmic mind of many minded worlds that the narrator experiences as a self – are given the chance to see myriad other cosmoses come into being and pursue their careers, through the creative efforts of the eponymous Star Maker. In some, there is no spatial extension, and life emerges purely in rhythmic form such that a creature's body consists in 'a more or less constant tonal pattern' which may glide through, but also 'grapple, and damage … another's tonal tissues'; some such creatures live by devouring others; some develop agriculture and make art (230–231). The different cosmoses also display 'a great diversity of geometrical and physical principles' (231); some are without time altogether; some are structured by non-linear temporalities, where time flows cyclically or simultaneously in different dimensions; some involve multiple linked universes, with beings transferred from one to the other at different stages in their lives, allowing reincarnation, or the equivalents of orthodox Christian notions of Heaven and Hell, to become core properties (234–235). In one 'inconceivably complex' multiverse – the likely inspiration for Borges' 'The Garden of Forking Paths' (1941) – 'whenever a creature was faced with several possible courses of action, it took them all, thereby creating many distinct temporal dimensions and distinct histories ... an infinity of distinct universes exfoliated from every moment of every temporal sequence in this cosmos' (243).

We could speculate about the different forms and modes that media might take in these divergent ontological contexts. How do purely tonal beings communicate? How does information transfer function when time is non-linear, so that the message is potentially received before it is sent? What kinds of media could develop in worlds where the laws of gravity and entropy are reversed (232)? Whatever strange or barely imaginable media forms we might imagine, one likely common factor is that the media will fit the ontological and ontic circumstances of the beings in question. In other words, they will be composed of stuff of the same order or structure, and according to many of the same principles, as the beings that use them.

I mentioned above that the diverse range of media encountered in *Star Maker* cumulatively emphasise that the distinction between media in the restricted sense of information transfer, and media in the general sense of means of connecting, is artificial and collapsible. This is a function of a further artificial separation between media and the things they connect. Media are that which is (detectably, notably, usefully, frustratingly) in between. They are such only by virtue of the separation(s) for which they compensate. When 'minded worlds' emerge from the multitudes of interlinked organisms and elements they contain, when these worlds themselves combine with stars to form a 'galactic mind, which [is] but the mind of each individual star and world and minute organism in the worlds, enriched by all its fellows and awakened to finer percipience' (201), when these galactic minds conjoin to form a living, cosmic entity, what *were* media linking different entities and forms become parts of the internal structure of a larger whole. Even the Star Maker, the anthropomorphised image of the principle or spirit behind all these cosmic creations, builds them using parts of itself (228).

Media are what connect and bind together entities separated by accidents of space and time. Where such binding progresses far enough, the connected individuals increasingly appear as a single entity, of which those media are constituent parts. Even if such media were at some stage the 'extensions of man [sic]' or some other being, they become at this point fundamental elements of its composition, restoring an even more fundamental cosmogonic relation.

Media's Futures

Where does all this leave us, and Stapledon's narrator – by this point self-identifying as a cosmic mind? Ultimately, he returns to the time and period proper to the entity that first set off from the heath on its astronoetic voyage. Having witnessed the Star Maker creating cosmos after cosmos, having wondered at their complexity and diversity, he has nevertheless ultimately felt disgust at the horror and suffering it allows to proliferate among its creations. Rejecting its seemingly aesthetic view of all existence, the narrator chooses a different, more familiar axiology: 'I scorned my birthright of ecstasy in that inhuman perfection, and yearned back to my lowly cosmos, to my own human and floundering worlds, there to stand shoulder to shoulder with my own half animal kind against the powers of darkness' (247).

Simultaneous existence on or oscillation between vastly different scales must ultimately prove unsustainable. Just as my life may be entirely insignificant to a being capable of perceiving the cosmic whole, so that being's existence and the cosmic events affecting it are practically irrelevant to me. Having perceived the Star Maker engaged in a self-appointed worldmaking campaign of whose rationale and purpose he can only acquire the dimmest intimation, the narrator undertakes to return to his own self-assigned worldmaking responsibilities in the human realm. He recognises that, here too, he is not in his ideal environment, living in 'an age of titanic conflict', whereas he and his partner, 'accustomed only to security and mildness, were fit only for a kindly world' (250). Yet the struggle to improve this world is one in which he is able to locate and produce value, find purpose and meaning, on scales and in modes that accord with his usual perceptual, intellectual, social and affective capacities.

This parallel between the motivations of the narrator and the Star Maker – each, in its own way, striving to make a 'better' world – may result from the anthropomorphism which the narrator repeatedly acknowledges by way of disclaimer. But it brings to light a point of potential significance to humans, among many other striving animals. Like the narrator and all those minds, organisms and worlds with which he becomes joined in the course of his journey, the Star Maker engages in a creative adventure that entails seeking out worlds and beings of ever greater diversity and complexity, not simply as a voyage of discovery, but in order to change him/itself. Each time he contemplates one of these creations, its impact 'change[s] him, clarifying and deepening his will' (241–242), causing him ultimately to outgrow it and move on to some new creative effort.

This notion of self-transformation, born out of a will to find, create, discover the alien, the other, the not-me or not-us, is the overriding motif and perhaps even moral of *Star Maker*. Certainly, it is linked to survival as a necessary condition. Yet this is not self-transformation as adaptation, as self-improvement, as evolutionary progress towards physical mastery or as spiritual progress towards enlightenment. Rather, it is a movement of change as necessity for and of life – of living (on) as perpetual change. Stapledon in this way anticipates the Earthseed religion of Octavia Butler's *Parable* novels, in which 'The only lasting truth is Change. God is Change' (1993, chapter 1), and its imperative to 'Embrace diversity / Or be destroyed' (1993, chapter 17).

The whole of *Star Maker* exemplifies the necessity of change for survival – not so much in terms of adapting to overcome external threats (though this may be a useful by-product) – but in order to overcome those tendencies within oneself as organism, cultural group, species, type (e.g., 'humanesque') that are otherwise likely to lead to one's own destruction, and this change only takes place through the transformative process of openly encountering and engaging with others different from oneself. Every notable living form in *Star Maker*, and certainly those which survive long enough to form constitutive living parts of the cosmic mind, has passed through a history of existential threats, each of which it was barely able to surmount. Those most successful at this are those for whom symbiotic existence, the full embrace of radical otherness, is fundamental. The symbiotic species of ichthyoids and arachnoids are among the first to develop the capacity for what I've been calling astronoetic travel, and the only one capable of stopping a perverted xenocidal species from destroying life across the galaxy. While those many stars and minded worlds that react to one another with hostility perish, those that reach out and strive to discover their mutual interests ultimately combine to produce a utopian 'symbiotic society of stars and planetary systems'. At every stage, those that seek diversity and community have at least some chance of survival, where most perish.

Of course, the survivors of such decisive moments may differ radically from those who faced the threat to begin with, thanks to the transformation(s) necessary. This is perhaps why the tendency towards self-*preservation* is so much more prevalent both in human history and across Stapledon's imagined galaxy, despite countless examples showing that such a tendency almost always leads to self-defeat. Having a chance of survival means accepting the risk of transformation over the greater threat of destruction resulting from the failure to change. The transformation may be incremental or dramatic, small or immense, but it entails the possibility of continuity, of a *process* of change with its own singularity, even if snapshots taken from different moments in that process differ radically. As process philosopher Henri Bergson suggests, if we consider a child who becomes an adult, our linguistic and cultural habits seem to want simultaneously to separate these as two distinct beings, and yet identify them as the same. If our language were more attuned to the processual reality, we might say 'there is becoming from the child to the adult', recognising the primacy of the process and that childhood and adulthood are 'mere views of the mind' that do not relate to the 'objective movement' (Bergson 2007 [1907], 200).

Similarly, we can talk of a continuous process or 'life' on scales other than that of the individual organism – social, evolutionary, galactic, microbial etc. What we call 'survival', at these scales, should be considered to correspond to the continuation of the process, and thus continual change. This continuity may be conscious or unconscious, potentially registering in experience, memory, a sense of identity, community etc. Yet however it manifests, it forms an alternative to perishing entirely.

Where does this leave us in terms of 'the future of media'? Let's recall that media – in the broadest sense – are integral to and underpin all transformations an entity may undergo, and that any survival or continuity of a (set of) living process(es) in the sense just described is largely dependent on its future media. If we are concerned with the future of media 'for us', we so-called humans, within the broad horizon of the future persistence of the kinds of organisms/entities/social systems we take 'ourselves' to be – then in light of the above, an openness to ever more diverse modes and forms of media may be crucial. However, that this entails media *in the broadest sense* is essential: media as lines of connection, modes of interaction, means of moving towards increased community, the mutual interrelation and recognition of ever-increasingly diverse entities, elements, forms.

On the other hand, there is a possible future of media in the *restricted*, primarily technological sense that sees the so-called human perish precisely by its fixation on self-preservation and self-perpetuation. This is the kind of future scenario depicted in countless science-fictional narratives, from Karel Čapek's *R.U.R.* (2011 [1920]) to the *Terminator* films and *The Matrix* (1999), in which humans' technological constructions, having become sentient, or at least autonomous and agential, come to dominate them, threatening or causing their extinction. However, an alternative paradigm, which seems to have become increasingly prominent since the turn of the millennium, sees autonomous technological forms of life drift so far from any residually human modes of valuation, motivation or logic that humans become utterly irrelevant to their existence and concerns. In science fiction, images of this may be found in Philip K. Dick's short story 'Autofac', or films like *Her* (2013) and *Transcendence* (2014). In non-fictional contexts its image is found in popular texts such as James Bridle's *New Dark Age* (2018) and Nick Bostrom's concerns about the possible future dominance of AI (2014). Increasingly, we are contemplating or being confronted with the prospect of a future development of contemporary technological media that produces new, autonomous modes of life, which will not only operate according to logics and motives utterly alien to human comprehension, but which, rather than seeking to enslave or crush humans, will barely even register them as they dwindle away. There may be a future of media in which humans are a distant, perhaps forgotten prehistorical triviality – media's own future of media.

At first glance, *Star Maker* would seem to offer surprisingly little in terms of resources for thinking such questions as the impact of artificial intelligence and the spread of algorithmic computation upon pre-existing lifeforms. Though many of the species Stapledon describes modify themselves technologically almost beyond recognition, there are no clear instances of an artificially created species or being that becomes wholly autonomous from its creators, let alone hastening their demise.

On the other hand, however, this may be simply because Stapledon's speculative vision, almost from the outset, is situated far beyond any meaningful distinction between nature and culture or the biological and the technological. Once we have entered a sphere in which we are dealing with intentional planetary and galactic entities that bear whole technological civilisations within themselves as part of their composition, agents that are capable of conceiving and constructing innumerable artificial planets and even stars, creating entirely new synthetic species – is there any sense at all in trying to find distinctions between what is technological and what is not? Everything is creative, dynamic, ecological, but no ontic categorial distinctions within this can really be said to hold sway.

In this light, *Star Maker* offers an imperative and impetus towards considering and engaging with the truly alien and other, the possibility of thinking the unthinkable, or, following Luciana Parisi (2013), the incomputable that would be instantiated within any algorithmic mode of thought, as, indeed, it may in any radically other, hitherto unencountered forms of life. To speculate about the mentality, logic or motivation underpinning the activities of sentient stars, or minded worlds, of hybrid arachnoid/ichthyoid (A/I rather than AI) world-builders is to confront that which may be radically unintelligible, in order to see what value may nevertheless be found in the speculative attempt to engage, communicate, co-exist. This in itself may be the beginnings of what is needed in order to engage in the diversity-embracing, speculative-transformative processes that will give lifeforms including those calling themselves 'human' a chance of continuing, even as this entails their continuous change, perhaps beyond recognition, into the future.

Conclusion

It is worth recognising that, for all his astronoetic voyaging beyond the humanesque, and for all the transformations he has undergone, once he decides to return home, the protagonist of *Star Maker* does not appear so dramatically changed as he repeatedly attests. For all his journeying and communing with beings so radically alien to everything in his previous experience, he remains not only humanesque, but broadly still identifiable with that figure that has named itself 'Man', now exposed and exploded by a wealth of poststructuralist, feminist, critical posthumanist and decolonial thinkers (e.g., Foucault 2002 [1966], 421–422; Haraway 2016, 47–49; Wynter 2003; Braidotti 2013, 13–54; Tsing 2016; Zylinska 2018) and yet seemingly undiminished in its sway over the being and future trajectories of global humanity.

In this light, it's worth remembering that 'intelligence' has always been artificial, a sociocultural construction built on the psychological construction or illusion of primary subjectivity, within which various rationalist, masculinist, colonialist, capitalist and other artificial facets have been naturalised from classical through Enlightenment and some postmodern/posthumanist thought. Stapledon's narrator remains within the sphere of this artificial intelligence, even as his entire adventure and conviction suggest the necessity of obliterating it. Certainly, he corresponds to a kinder, pacifist, anticolonial, open-minded image of Man than is seen in its most common and dominant manifestations. But, ultimately, his outlook remains at the least shaded by certain 'hu*man*ist' values and tendencies, for example, in the shape of his rationality and his spiritualism (even if his combining them offers the possibility of curbing the worst excesses of each), and his masculinisation of the Star Maker and feminisation of its ultimate creation, in whose 'cosmic loveliness' the Star Maker finds 'the fulfilment of desire' (247).

Perhaps this concern may be added to the ethico-ontological grounds on which Stanisław Lem judged *Star Maker* 'an artistic and intellectual failure', finding in it the clear influence of Stapledon's previous 'novel about "Superior Man"' (Lem 1987 [1970], 7). Yet just as Lem recognised that this was a failure in a 'titanic battle', within 'a completely solitary creation' that 'defines the boundaries of the SF imagination' (1987 [1970], 7), so we may acknowledge that *Star Maker* establishes, in a way that remains unique and no less urgent some eight decades after its publication, a compelling view of the challenges faced, and the great potential role for speculation, in this battle: that is, in the struggle between 'the archaic, reason-hating, and vindictive, passion of the tribe' with its 'myopic fear of the unknown', and, on the other side, 'the will to dare for the sake of the new, the longed for, the reasonable and joyful world, in which every man and woman may have scope to live fully' (253). Or, as he puts it in the final line, in 'this brief effort of animalcules striving to win for their race some increase of lucidity before the ultimate darkness' (254).

References

Bergson, H. 2007 [1907]. *Creative Evolution*, translated by A. Mitchell. London: Palgrave Macmillan.

Blumenberg, H. 1997. *Die Vollständigkeit der Sterne*. Frankfurt am Main: Suhrkamp.

Borges, J. L. 1941. 'The Garden of Forking Paths'. In *Ficciones* (1962), New York: Grove Press.

Bostrom, N. 2014. *Superintelligence. Paths, Dangers, Strategies*. Oxford: Oxford University Press.

Braidotti, R. 2013. *The Posthuman*. Cambridge: Polity.

Bridle, J. 2018. *New Dark Age: Technology and the End of the Future*. London: Verso.

Butler, O. 1993. *Parable of the Sower*. New York: Four Walls Eight Windows.

Čapek, K. 2011 [1920]. *R.U.R. (Rossum's Universal Robots)* and *War with the Newts*. London: Gollancz.

Foucault, M. 2002 [1966]. *The Order of Things*. London: Routledge.

Grosz, E. 2004. *The Nick of Time. Politics, Evolution, and the Untimely*. Durham, NC: Duke University Press.

Guyau, J.-M. 1890. *La Genèse de l'Idée de Temps*. Paris: Felix Alcan.

Haraway, D. 2016. *Staying With the Trouble: Making Kin in the Chthulucene*. Durham, NC: Duke University Press.

Harries, K. 2001. *Infinity and Perspective*. Cambridge, MA: MIT Press.

Lazier, B. 2011. 'Earthrise; or, The Globalization of the World Picture'. *The American Historical Review*, 116(3): 602–630.

Lem, S. 1987 [1970]. 'On Stapledon's *Star Maker*'. *Science Fiction Studies*, 41(14:1): 1–8.

McCarthy, P. 1981. '*Star Maker*: Olaf Stapledon's *Divine Tragedy*'. *Science Fiction Studies*, 25(8:3), 266–279.

Nowotny, H. 1994. *Time. The Modern and Postmodern Experience*, translated by N. Plaice. Cambridge: Polity.

Parisi, L. 2013. *Contagious Architecture: Computation, Aesthetics, and Space*. Cambridge, MA: MIT Press.

Saint Augustine. 1961. *Confessions*, translated by R. S. Pine-Coffin. Harmondsworth: Penguin.

Stapledon, O. 1939. *Philosophy and Living*, vols 1 and 2. London: Pelican.

Stapledon, O. 1999a [1930]. *Last and First Men*. London: Millennium.

Stapledon, O. 1999b [1937]. *Star Maker*. London: Millennium.

Tsing, A. 2016. 'Earth Stalked by Man'. *Cambridge Journal of Anthropology*, 34(1): 2–16.

Wynter, S. 2003. 'Unsettling the Coloniality of Being/Power/Truth/Freedom: Towards the Human, After Man, Its Overrepresentation – An Argument'. *CR: The New Centennial Review*, 3(3): 257–337.

Zylinska, J. 2018. *The End of Man: A Feminist Counterapocalypse*. Minneapolis, MN: University of Minnesota Press.

Afterword: Forward

Sean Cubitt

'In this world nothing can be said to be certain, except death and taxes,' wrote future US president Benjamin Franklin in a letter of 1789 to Jean-Baptiste Le Roy, physicist and collaborator on Diderot's *Encyclopédie*. Apparently, Franklin was not the first out of the blocks; an eighteenth-century English dramatist called Christopher Bullock has a similar expression in a 1716 play by the name of *The Cobbler of Preston*, which only goes to show that you can't be all that certain about the past either. Still, the wonderful date, 1789 – the year of the French Revolution and the filigree of connection to the enormous ambition and collective practice of the *Encyclopédie* – gives Franklin's version a certain frisson and a certain authority. Today, however, we might need to rewrite the expression. Death still waits for all of us, but taxes are avoidable, for the world's billionaires and for corporations at least (Clausing et al. 2021). We thought the future would be cyborg and it is, but the actually existing cyborgs aren't humans with chip implants but massive technological networks with humans implanted; they are the contemporary cyborgs – and they rule. Oxfam reports that 'The world's 10 richest billionaires have collectively seen their wealth increase by $540bn' in 2020 during the pandemic, while the number living in poverty has risen by between 200 and 500 million (Oxfam 2021).

If not taxes, then what? Debt. The numbers are staggering. While wealth accumulates and concentrates in fewer and fewer hands, debt is a magic magnet for lower-income and what the International Monetary Fund refers to as 'Heavily Indebted Poor Countries' (IMF 2020). The 'sovereign' public debt – which is exactly the opposite of sovereignty, removing power from governments and placing it in the hands of corporations and markets – is only half the story. The personal debts of the poor are more tragic than anyone else's, but the structure of debt is ubiquitous. It is normal to owe money on private cars, ordinary to pay off a mortgage (which, incidentally but poetically, translates as 'wager against death') and banal to borrow today against payday next week. Not only have payday lenders become darlings of the stock markets, they have also collected billions in government payments for pandemic relief globally (see, e.g., Whoriskey et al. 2021), hoovering up whatever hasn't already been seized by corporations whose unpaid taxes would pay for the effective abolition of poverty worldwide.

So what is debt? It is money from the future we spend today. Its structural function is to pay for all the overproduction that capital needs in order to make up for the falling rate of profit. (Marx's hypothesis that reinvesting some profit in machinery to reduce the labour costs of production means that the amount of profit per unit sold tends to diminish, as set out in chapter 13 of the third volume of *Capital* (Marx 1959, 211–231)). We need to spend the future's money now to ensure that capital continues to accumulate profit, regardless of poverty or pandemics. You could also say that debt is a way of ensuring that in the future we will continue working so we can pay off our debts, which means that the future will have to be pretty much the same as today; we stay in employment, keep paying and quite probably keep borrowing to make sure we can keep paying. Debt is a way of controlling the future, so it looks as much as possible like the present. If, like the founding figure of the politics of hope, Ernst Bloch (1986), you believe that the only workable definition of the future is that it is different to the present, then a future that is controlled, a future modelled to be the same as the present, is no future at all. The ideology of the free market is freedom; its actuality is determinism.

This is a strange twist in the story of determinism. Theologians already tied themselves in knots trying to work out how an all-knowing god who could therefore see the future could be reconciled with the idea of fallen humans with the capacity to sin or be saved according to decisions they alone were responsible for. Eighteenth-century founder of economics Adam Smith's pseudo-theological faith in the invisible hand of the market is an equally tortured reconciliation (Smith 1993 [1776]). The market is comprised of indefinitely many free agents buying and selling, but the market as such always knows best – and always settles on the just price. This weird eighteenth-century doctrine was once again trotted out in response to the bizarre story of the retail investors convinced to buy stocks and options in US gaming and electronics retailer GameStop in January 2021. Touted as a revolt against hedge funds, it appears to have been planned to benefit even bigger financial corporations (Doctorow 2021). As Goldstein (2021) puts it, this wasn't David versus Goliath but Goliath versus Goliath, with David as a fig leaf. The neoliberal doctrine of the invisible hand is a rare instance of an ideology that is happy to make itself public. It is also deeply determinist. Whatever you do or don't do, the market not only knows best but acts for the best, and there is no alternative.

It is an oddity because most right-wing commentators blame Marx and Marxisms for being economic determinists. There is a byzantine argument to have here. Marx clearly thought that economic relations drove history, and that no revolution would succeed that didn't also change the economic foundations of society. At the same time, his unfinished masterwork is subtitled 'A Critique of Political Economy', suggesting that, as in many of his other writings, he was interested in the role of political forces as well as economic ones. He was astute enough to connect child labour in Europe with slavery in the USA, and colonialism with Victorian capital. Most of all, in the idea of revolution, Marx and Marxisms hold out the promise of a future radically different from the present. Capital cannot imagine such a thing.

That doesn't alter the fact that there is a slew of rival determinisms out there. A crude reading of the political historian and philosopher Michel Foucault, immensely influential over the last half-century, might describe him as a determinist who believed in the efficacy of power to enter every pore of social life (see, e.g., Foucault 1977). Friedrich Kittler, the maverick historian and philosopher of media, resuscitated the decaying influence of Marshall McLuhan when he declared that 'media determine our situation' (Kittler 1999, xxxix). Both men (and determinism does appear to have a gendered tendency) have shaped much contemporary discussion of genders, identities, communications, even some areas in environmentalism. The temptation of both for media scholars is especially potent because both put media, broadly thought of, in the middle of their cosmologies: Kittler obviously, and Foucault because of his insistence that power is always mediated by 'discourses' and 'techniques' – i.e., what we would call media. Unlike Kittler, Foucault was also politically radical, an out gay man committed to anti-colonial and workers' struggles. Kittler's virtue, inspired by Foucault, was to make us look in detail at the specifics of media technologies, to understand how meticulously they play on the human body and senses, structuring ways of saying, showing and responding at an almost cellular level. Foucault, at least in his later writings (e.g., Foucault 2011), realised something that seems to have escaped Kittler: no system is ever that watertight. To bowdlerise the famous proof of the great logician Kurt Gödel (Nagel and Newman 1959), a system can either be complete or coherent but it cannot be both.

Something sparks in the gap between incompleteness and incoherence. This is the place of creativity, where a future other than the present can come into being. It's a mistake to oppose determinism and freedom. Like individuality, a psychological belief required by a legal system of ownership, freedom may well be a wholly ideological belief. Like masculinity, it seems to be only definable in the negative, even though both words, both faiths, have had enormous impact on the way we conduct ourselves individually and collectively. Which is exactly the point. Maybe freedom is just an ideological shadow of capitalists' demand that they should be free of law, morals and taxes. But it has become a power in the world. Similarly, although, as David Morley writes in this volume, 'it has never been entirely clear what television is', it is perfectly okay to argue that early centre-out broadcasting models favoured propaganda and mass advertising (at that stage scarcely distinguishable), supporting government and capital – even though, on Gödel's principle, never wholly and entirely, always remaining open to the inventions of a Ken Loach or a Delia Derbyshire.

Centralised broadcasting, which Kittler thinks of as a necessary outcome of media technologies, was at least as much the product of factions of the ruling class fighting for control of radio and TV, a technical solution to internal power struggles. To take just one example of its failure, it was at the peak of its dissemination, a period when it was devoted to masculinist ideologies and eroticising/domesticating visions of women, that second-generation feminism burst into flame. In parallel, the logic of advertising and propaganda demanded a de-massification of the audience in recognition of the centralised model's demographic failings. Markets, power and media produce one another. Historically they lurch from crisis to crisis, insistent disproof of the invisible hand. In their interplay, they constantly seek allies from beyond their narrow factions, and from their frictions constantly evolve new cultures, practices, forms and movements, each of which acts back on them and on each other. This is the process we call history. The opposite of determinism isn't freedom. It is multiplicity.

This is the struggle: how to get from a future indistinguishable from the present brought about by determining power, wealth and technological dominance to a future incommensurable with the present brought about through multiplicity. Every essay in this volume, and every work in the accompanying web collection, bears testimony to this challenge, and to the amazing collaborations and creativities it inspires. If contemporary history is the story of how a diminishing elite has used every means at its disposal to manage – economically, politically and technologically – the chaos of the world, then we need to turn from ordered management to that chaos. But is it truly chaotic? Goldsmiths Media has been and remains at the heart of a twenty-first-century attempt to build a new materialism. Inspired by feminist epistemologists like Donna Haraway and Karen Barad (2007), as well as visitors to Goldsmiths like Rosi Braidotti (2013) and Jody Berland (2019), past and present staff including Sara Ahmed (2004), Sarah Kember (Kember and Zylinska 2012), Luciana Parisi (2013), Tiziana Terranova (2004) and contributors to this collection including Lisa Blackman (2012), Sarah Cefai and Joanna Zylinska (2014) have pushed open a terrain perhaps best captured, in our context, by the word 'mediation'.

Because so many chapters reflect this sense of mediation – which is 'active, productive and … transformative', as James Burton puts it in his chapter – I can only push one of its dimensions. Mediation describes a reality that embraces, flows through and connects human and nonhuman (animal, ecological, technological). The word 'flow' is crucial; everything flows, everything comes into contact, melds, transforms. For sure there are mystical and ancient traditions that help think this way, but as the feminist epistemological tradition so often shows, there are also grounds in contemporary physical and life sciences, and a powerful occidental philosophical tradition dating back to the late nineteenth century. Mediation feels mystical because it describes an ontology, a philosophy of reality, that exceeds humans even though it includes them. It tells us that – in reality – there are no individuals, no identities, no things and no concepts, and that our ideas and practices are all that make such things appear solid. It is a materialism, but one which precedes human economics, politics and media technologies such as language. In this sense, and as an ontology, mediation is an ahistorical concept. We have to look elsewhere to understand how and why we don't find ourselves in this cosmic flux – and how and why we are historical.

In the years immediately following World War II, a series of scientific and engineering advances associated with Cold War politics and the emerging telecommunications industry put in place a theory of communication which has, in the intervening 70 years, become hegemonic. The theory has its roots in the sender-receiver model of communication presented by Bell Telephone engineer Claude Shannon (1948), the systems theory introduced by cybernetics pioneer Norbert Wiener (1948) and the neuronal model theorised by Pitts and McCulloch (1947), widely seen as foundational in artificial intelligence. Among the things they share is an obsession with coherence, a distaste for noise and their dedication to stability, that is, to ordering change in such a way as to make use of it without allowing it to alter the structure that controls it. In other words, to control time. And also to make it profitable: 'information is a difference that makes a difference at some later point', as cyberneticist Gregory Bateson puts it (1972, 459). Information – such as knowing in advance that a group of retail day-traders are planning to move on shorted GameStop stocks – is money (and increasingly, in media terms and in finance markets where much of its existence takes place, money is information). The language emerging from these US engineering models, the language of senders, receivers, channels, messages, information, systems in equilibrium, control and efficiency, is the twenty-first century's dominant ideology – not in the sense that everyone believes it, but in the sense that these are the ideas the dominant use when they dominate. They have also left us with a sense that communication, taken as this systematic organisation of social relations, is the engine of contemporary history: the information society.

Played out in the pages of this collection, and in many individual chapters, is the dialectic between two great schools of thought. One, which we might call ontological materialism, emphasises the inadequacy of languages and institutions based on unreal concepts of race, gender, sexuality and identity. Its focus is on mediation. The other, let's call it historical materialism, emphasises the actual power of exactly those terms: the way the dominant forces in society use race, gender, all the differences that make a difference, in pursuit of power and wealth. Its focus is on communication, in the sense just picked out.

This sounds horribly abstract, and as such inadequate to describe the generative power of these modes of thinking as they come together, conflict with and enrich each other. Mediation and communication, ontological and historical materialisms, each in their own ways contribute to the production of gaps and multiplicities, making possible, even necessary, the intellectual and technical creativity that the book and creative works display. Like the montage aesthetic of Daisy Asquith's *Queerama*, they collide disparate objects and ways of thinking to produce sensations and ideas that no longer fit the tawdry, demeaning hell of debt. They speak of love, joy, solidarity, remembering in common and of new social imaginary worlds – which, however, have the benefit of actually existing or having existed, despite the crushing weight of history, despite the despair of 'as things are they shall remain'.

Before we get too utopian, there is one more twist in the tail. Things can get worse. The pandemic, for all that it was foreseeable, showed us that the future that is other can also be adverse. The horsemen of the new apocalypse are migration, pandemic, inequality and climate change. We only lack outright war because China has still to exercise the muscle it flexes so regularly in the South China Seas.

Perhaps the USA can slow its descent, and thus the ascent of Chinese hegemony, without war. Perhaps the Indian Prime Minister Modi, despite the disastrous adventure in Kashmir and battle with the farmers, both apparently driven by his Hindi populism, will not wreck India's growing ambition to climb into the role of successor, in due course, to China, without war. The westward drift of global hegemony is unlikely to be wholly peaceful. Racism (or, more politely, 'ethnic tensions') in the Punjab and Xinjiang indicates that states' violence against their citizens will be as furious as the endless insurgency ensured by international stabilisation of flamboyantly corrupt regimes. State and insurgent violence, famine and climate change – itself a major cause of armed struggle (ICRC 2020) – continue to drive migration, which drives political and religious populisms, but they are quite capable of mass slaughter in their own right. If, as was the case with HIV and SARS, the wealthy hoard their medicines, then new variants of both as well as of the coronavirus will continue to burst out of the vast reservoirs of poverty for generations, and epidemics will be as universal as violence. And as the mushroom cloud hovered over the Cold War era, the equally avoidable nightmare of climate change, habitat and species loss and of plastic and metals pollution inspires equally disastrous responses of despair and managerialism (Bratton 2019). In the wealthy nations, as well as working to create a better one, we can dread the future.

But, from the standpoint of Indigenous people, the apocalypse has already happened. The cluster of essays about the utopian and dystopian potential of new media among migrants and in development echo with the cluster on reform and industry practices in showing how history takes sides. Richard MacDonald's potent observation that the tower blocks of Bangkok add to rising water levels to the detriment of the city's poor is a telling image of the ongoing nature of apocalypse. As a result of the deliberate genocides and diseases introduced by the fifteenth- and sixteenth-century conquerors of the Americas, so devastated were Indigenous populations that the extinction of their fires and crafts cooled the global climate by up to 1.5 degrees (Koch et al. 2019). The extinction of whole nations in Australia and their ongoing rates of incarceration, deprivation and sickness demonstrates, in anticolonial scholar Patrick Wolfe's phrase, that 'invasion is a structure not an event' (Wolfe 2006; see also Kauanui 2016). Neocolonialism and the postcolony fare no better (Mbembe 2019; Mignolo and Walsh 2018 (Mignolo is an honorary professor in Goldsmiths Media)). Capital is at least equitable when it treats colonised lands and colonised peoples with the same disdain, the same desire for exploitation and the same exoticising media coverage of 'vanishing' cultures and landscapes. The horror of it is that the wish to enjoy the spectacle of disappearance (as if it were a natural event) and even the frisson of guilt that accompanies it have become hallmarks of capital's own death-wish, its regretful but determined acceptance that in order for it to survive, it may be necessary to destroy the planet and its inhabitants. This is the final proof that the cyborgs have taken over.

The future is, as Bloch might have said, the terrain of hope – and hope would not be hope if it could not be disappointed, just as desire would not be desire if it could be satisfied. Desire is by definition desire for what you do not already have. Likewise, hope is always shifting, multiple, fantastic. The historic threats that surround us are effects of corporate hubris that fully believes it can know and control the future, which is also the terrain of desire, which perpetually casts itself into the unknown. That is one of the many things that queer culture and thinking has taught us. The response to environmental despair is ecocritical complexity, the understanding that we all – human, technological and ecological – are bonded by desire and hope into a future that is permanently closed to the commodity-form that pretends it can satisfy, closed to debt and debt-like communicative management systems that strive to close the future down. This collection is testimony to the intellectual and creative, creative-intellectual project to keep the future open.

References

Ahmed, S. 2004. *The Cultural Politics of Emotion*. Edinburgh: Edinburgh University Press.

Barad, K. 2007. *Meeting the Universe Halfway: Quantum Physics and the Entanglement of Matter and Meaning*. Durham, NC: Duke University Press.

Bateson, G. 1972. *Steps to An Ecology of Mind: Collected Essays in Anthropology, Psychiatry, Evolution, and Epistemology*. San Francisco, CA: Chandler Publishing.

Berland, J. 2019. *Virtual Menageries: Animals as Mediators in Network Cultures*. Cambridge, MA: MIT Press.

Blackman, L. 2012. *Immaterial Bodies: Affect, Embodiment, Mediation*. London: Sage.

Bloch, E. 1986. *The Principle of Hope*, 3 vols, translated by N. Plaice, S. Plaice and P. Knight. Cambridge, MA: MIT Press.

Braidotti, R. 2013. *The Posthuman*. Cambridge: Polity.

Bratton, B. H. 2019. *The Terraforming*. Moscow: Strelka Press.

Clausing, K., E. Saez and G. Zucman. 2021. *Ending Corporate Tax Avoidance and Tax Competition: A Plan to Collect the Tax Deficit of Multinationals*. UCLA School of Law, Law-Econ Research Paper No. 20–12, January. Available at: https://eml.berkeley.edu/%7Esaez/CSZ2021.pdf.

Doctorow, C. 2021. 'There Is No Shortage of Takes About What's Going on with GameStop'. *Threadreader*, 28 January. Available at: https://threadreaderapp.com/thread/1354848494192738304.html.

Foucault, M. 1977. *Discipline and Punish: Birth of the Prison*, translated by A. Sheridan. London: Penguin.

Foucault, M. 2011. *The Courage of Truth: Lectures at the Collège de France 1983–1984*, edited by F. Gros, translated by G. Burchell. Basingstoke: Palgrave Macmillan.

Goldstein, A. 2021. 'What Happened with GameStop?'. *Markets Weekly*, 28 January. Available at: https://marketsweekly.ghost.io/what-happened-with-gamestop/.

ICRC. 2020. *When Rain Turns to Dust: Understanding and Responding to the Combined Impact of Armed Conflicts and the Climate and Environment Crisis on People's Lives*. Geneva: International Committee of the Red Cross.

IMF. 2020. *The Evolution of Public Debt Vulnerabilities in Lower Income Economies*. IMF Policy Paper, 10 February. Washington, DC: International Monetary Fund. Available at: www.imf.org/en/Publications/Policy-Papers/Issues/2020/02/05/The-Evolution-of-Public-Debt-Vulnerabilities-In-Lower-Income-Economies-49018.

Kauanui, J. K. 2016. '"A Structure, Not an Event": Settler Colonialism and Enduring Indigeneity'. *Lateral: Journal of the Cultural Studies Association*, special section on Emergent Critical Analytics for Alternative Humanities, Issue 5.1 (Spring). https://csalateral.org/issue/5-1/forum-alt-humanities-settler-colonialism-enduring-indigeneity-kauanui/.

Kember, S. and J. Zylinska. 2012. *Life After New Media: Mediation as a Vital Process*. Cambridge, MA: MIT Press.

Kittler, F. A. 1999. *Gramophone, Film, Typewriter*, translated by G. Winthrop-Young and M. Wutz. Stanford, CA: Stanford University Press.

Koch, A., C. Brierley, M. M. Maslin and S. L. Lewis. 2019. 'Earth System Impacts of the European Arrival and Great Dying in the Americas After 1492'. *Quaternary Science Reviews*, 207: 13–36.

Marx, K. 1959. *Capital: A Critique of Political Economy*, Vol. III, edited by F. Engels. Moscow: Progress Publishers.

Mbembe, A. 2019. *Necropolitics*. Durham, NC: Duke University Press.

Mignolo, W. D. and C. Walsh. 2018. *On Decoloniality: Concepts, Analytics, Praxis*. Durham, NC: Duke University Press.

Nagel, E. and J. R. Newman. 1959. *Gödel's Proof.* London: Routledge Kegan Paul.

Oxfam. 2021. *The Inequality Virus: Bringing Together a World Torn Apart by Coronavirus through a Fair, Just and Sustainable Economy.* Oxford: Oxfam. Available at: www.oxfam.org/en/research/inequality-virus.

Parisi, L. 2013. *Contagious Architecture: Computation, Aesthetics, and Space.* Cambridge, MA: MIT Press.

Pitts, W. and W. McCulloch. 1947. 'How We Know Universals: The Perception of Auditory and Visual Forms'. *Bulletin of Mathematical Biophysics*, 9: 127–147.

Shannon, C. E. 1948. 'A Mathematical Theory of Communication'. *The Bell System Technical Journal*, 27(July, October): 379–423, 623–656.

Smith, A. 1993 [1776]. *An Inquiry into the Nature and Causes of the Wealth of Nations.* Oxford: Oxford University Press/World's Classics.

Terranova, T. 2004. *Network Culture: Politics for the Information Age.* London: Pluto.

Whoriskey, P., J. Jacobs and A. Gregg. 2021. 'Debt Collectors, Payday Lenders Collected Over $500 Million in Federal Pandemic Relief'. *The Washington Post*, 15 January. Available at: www.msn.com/en-us/news/politics/debt-collectors-payday-lenders-collected-over-500-million-in-federal-pandemic-relief/ar-BB1cMrku.

Wiener, N. 1948. *Cybernetics: Or Control and Communication in the Animal and the Machine.* Cambridge, MA: MIT Press.

Wolfe, P. 2006. 'Settler Colonialism and the Elimination of the Native'. *Journal of Genocide Research*, 8(4): 387–409.

Zylinska, J. 2014. *Minimal Ethics for the Anthropocene.* Ann Arbor, MI: Open Humanities Press.

Notes

3 An End to Futility: A Modest Proposal

1 For a critique of this influential argument, see Morozov (2011) and Curran, Fenton and Freedman (2016), among others.
2 This proposed outline for the British Digital Corporation has benefitted from conversations with Natalie Fenton and Tom Mills.

4 Future Faking, Post-Truth and Affective Media

1 www.theguardian.com/commentisfree/2019/dec/04/boris-johnson-brexit-britain-politics-media-business.
2 www.independent.co.uk/news/uk/politics/boris-johnson-nigerian-money-article-racist-spectator-a9222831.html;
www.independent.co.uk/news/uk/politics/boris-johnson-racism-football-hypocrisy-uefa-president-aleksander-ceferin-a9230391.html;
www.businessinsider.com/boris-johnson-record-sexist-homophobic-and-racist-comments-bumboys-piccaninnies-2019-6?r=US&IR=T;
https://metro.co.uk/2019/10/16/boris-johnson-is-racist-says-black-mp-who-called-out-abuse-this-week-10928161/;
www.theatlantic.com/magazine/archive/2019/06/trump-racism-comments/588067/.
3 https://eu.usatoday.com/story/opinion/2018/10/03/trump-classic-gaslighter-abusive-relationship-america-column/1445050002/.
4 https://fivethirtyeight.com/features/donald-trump-is-the-worlds-greatest-troll/.
5 www.theguardian.com/books/2020/apr/24/author-book-victim-blaming-misogynist-abuse-jessica-taylor.
6 Also see https://gal-dem.com/weve-known-since-grenfell-and-windrush-what-its-like-to-be-gaslit-by-the-tory-government/?fbclid=IwAR3eyjshwWuDUG_4NAqp9BGp2VYcV5DSLJD52FXJex0rfQnSxDdncpmLglE.
7 www.youtube.com/watch?v=_56yCL5DEl4.
8 www.itv.com/news/2020-06-02/bishop-outraged-after-tear-gas-used-on-crowds-before-trump-church-photo-op/.

5 How Will the Future Cope With(out) Television?

1 On these issues, see www.ofcom.org.uk/about-ofcom/latest/features-and-news/lockdown-leads-to-surge-in-tv-screen-time-and-streaming.

2 An indication of some of the evidence surrounding these issues can be found at www.theguardian.com/tv-and-radio/2020/aug/05/britons-tv-covid-lockdown-ofcom-streaming-netflix-amazon.
3 See also the JCMS/SCMS podcast 'Talking Television in a Crisis', available at www.aca-media.org/pandemic-tv.

7 The Celebrity Selfie: Gender, Race and 'New' Old Ways of Seeing

1 Among the top 20 most followed celebrities on Instagram in 2019 were: Cristiano Ronaldo – 230 million followers; Ariana Grande – 194 million followers; Dwayne Johnson – 190 million followers; Kylie Jenner – 185 million followers; Selina Gomez – 183 million followers; Kim Kardashian – 179 million followers; Lionel Messi – 159 million followers; Beyoncé – 150 million followers; Justin Bieber – 141 million followers; Neymar – 139 million followers; Taylor Swift – 136 million followers; Kendall Jenner – 134 million followers; Jennifer Lopez – 129 million followers; Nicki Minaj – 118 million followers; Khloé Kardashian – 116 million followers; Miley Cyrus – 112 million followers; Katy Perry – 101 million followers. Online Trends, 'The Top 20 Most Followed Instagram Accounts', Brandwatch, 18 January 2020, www.brandwatch.com/blog/top-most-instagram-followers/.
2 Hype-Journal, 'The 2019 Most Paid Influencers on Instagram', *Hype-Journal*, 23 August 2019, https://hypeauditor.com/blog/12-most-paid-influencers-on-instagram/.

8 Rethinking 'Diversity' in Publishing

1 The full report can be downloaded for free from www.rethinkingdiversity.org.
2 The term 'BAME' is highly contested, not least for the way it collapses racial and ethnic difference together and does not do justice to the specificities of particular racial and ethnic experience. It is also a 'top-down' category, rather than one that minorities conceived, let alone use. Despite this, we use the term 'BAME' in this report as it allows us to protect the anonymity of our respondents, as reference to specific racial and ethnic backgrounds might reveal individual identities. To reiterate, 'BAME' is used as shorthand only. Our own deep ambivalence about the term is reflected in the use of inverted commas.
3 While job roles are stated when using quotes from white respondents, because there are so few 'BAME' people working in publishing we omitted their job roles in order to protect their identities.

9   Exit Wounds of Feminist Theory

1 Grosz is discussing Indigenous Australian songlines: 'The songlines are those lines that cut through and inscribe both the earth and the bodies that abide there; they are the resonating lines of force that separate and then join a people to a territory, to a movement through a territory' (2005, 48–49).

2 Foucault (1988) maintained that the question of how we come to have the 'truth of the self' was the primary concern of his work.

3 See Rei Terada (2001) for an instructive corrective.

4 Exemplifying his rejection of the intentional speaking subject, Foucault asks: 'what is this specific existence that emerges from what is said and nowhere else?' (2002, 31).

5 In her critique of settler neoliberalism, Povinelli explains: the horizon 'bracket[s] all forms of violence as the result of the unintended, accidental, and unfortunate unfolding of liberalism's own dialectic' (Povinelli 2018, 1); the frontier is 'the space between civilization's sovereignty and the terror of barbarity' (2018, 4), taking place now 'wherever an opportunity for movement is afforded' (2018, 7).

6 Foucault's concept, explains Lynne Huffer, is a specific 'attitude marked by finitude', as opposed to negativity or negation (2016, 102). This attitude, which is 'a mode of relating to reality, a way of thinking and feeling, of acting and behaving that marks a relation of belonging and presents itself as a task', cannot be admitted into philosophy on account of its *specificity*. For Foucault, says Huffer, the limit attitude presents an ethical task: to reflect on ourselves as difference in history; to begin again.

7 There is a relation between the feminist theoretical metaphor and feminism's limit attitude, witnessed in these contested examples that each attempt to make the specificity of gender/sexual difference matter. Butler's (1990) well known reference to drag was intended as ethnographic, but read in the direction of metaphor (that's one way to read the 'all gender is drag' reading).

11   New Telematic Technology for the Remote Creation and Performance of Choreographic Work

1 For instance, in the BBC Arts *Culture in Quarantine* programme, the 'Ahead of the Curve Real Time Conversations' YouTube channel on new entertainment technologies, a special issue on digital communication and audiovisuality in the age of social distancing in the *Journal for Embodied Research* and futurist design projects such as quarantinlogy.com – described as 'a catalog of hyperfunctional logics that builds upon the history of the quarantined city and speculates about its future'.

2 Douglas Englebart's *The Mother of all Demos*, premiered in 1968, is generally seen to be the first remote digital performance.

3 For dance theorist Marc Boucher dance is inherently synaesthetic, where visual perception, touch, memory and kinesthesia fuse as a 'somesthetic sense' or as 'kinetic synaesthesia' (2004, section 5).
4 At 640 x 480 px (30 Hz) and 512 x 424 pix (30 Hz) respectively.
5 Filed by *Fresh Prince of Bel-Air* star Alfonso Ribeiro, Russell 'Backpack Kid' Horning, the unnamed *Fortnite* fan known as 'Orange Shirt Kid' and rappers Terrence '2 Milly' Ferguson and James 'BlocBoyJB' Baker in 2019. All claimed that Epic had unlawfully used dance moves they had invented as *Fortnite* emotes.

12   Everywhere in Particular: Some Thoughts on the Practice and Potential of Transpositional Locative Sound Art

1 There was a visual component to *Jungle-ized*; the billboards of Times Square showed negative images of the rainforest, which could be reversed to a positive image when viewed through the app on a smartphone. But these were 'come-ons' to draw the audience to the main part of the experience, which was audio augmented reality.
2 Francesca Panneta cites Janet Cardiff in her excellent online resource AudioAR, to which I am indebted for her thinking about the nature of audio augmented reality. https://audioar.org/.
3 Guy Debord's concept of a dérive refers to 'an unplanned journey through a landscape', usually urban, in which participants drop their everyday relations and 'let themselves be drawn by the attractions of the terrain and the encounters they find there' (Knabb 2020).
4 Barry Salt is a cinematographer who holds a PhD in theoretical physics. His book goes against the grain of cultural studies and is based on empirical analysis of primary material to provide an enormous data set of shot lengths and sizes based on the viewing of thousands of films.

13   If 6 Were 9 (or 2 x 108): A Case Study of the *One Oh Eight* Project

1 The concept of 'reconciliation' was a cornerstone of the new South Africa. The Truth and Reconciliation Commission was a restorative justice body set up in South Africa after the end of apartheid.
2 Echoes.xyz is a platform which allows the user to geolocate audio anywhere in the world where there is a GPS signal.
3 *Mother City?* premiered on the London 108 bus on 2 September 2019, with *Dumbstruck on Bazely Street* launching on the Cape Town 108 on 7 September 2019. The Cape Town launch was delayed in the wake of the appalling rape and murder of a 19-year-old

student called Uyinene Mrwetyana. Countrywide vigils and protests followed. Dr Lavinia Brydon, writing in a field report to the authors about the 108 launch, notes that, 'the gendered power structures that inform city living and the accessibility of public spaces (including public travel) were brought into sharp focus by these events'.

15 Technological Futures as Colonial Debris: 'Tech for Good' as Technocolonialism

1 www.theguardian.com/global-development/2019/jun/11/oxfam-abuse-claims-haiti-charity-commission-report.
2 www.thenewhumanitarian.org/news/2020/06/24/MSF-racism-black-lives-matter-debate.
3 www.gov.uk/government/news/prime-minister-announces-merger-of-department-for-international-development-and-foreign-office.
4 In 2019, the UN's World Food Programme distributed over $2 billion to over 28 million people in 64 countries. See Building Blocks: Blockchain for Zero Hunger, https://innovation.wfp.org/project/building-blocks.
5 Report of the UN Special Rapporteur on the situation of human rights in Myanmar, 2018, https://undocs.org/A/73/332.
6 Building Blocks: Blockchain for Zero Hunger, https://innovation.wfp.org/project/building-blocks.
7 The chapter draws on ongoing interviews and ethnographic fieldwork (conducted between July 2016 and February 2020) with humanitarian officers, donors, volunteers, consultants, software developers, private entrepreneurs and other stakeholders.
8 www.forbes.com/sites/astanley/2018/06/09/u-n-official-defends-refugee-voucher-program-even-though-it-doesnt-require-blockchain/#51b83e071f66.
9 www.bbc.co.uk/news/world-europe-52151722.
10 www.wired.com/story/refugees-but-on-the-blockchain/.

16 The Smart City and the Extraction of Hope

1 Generally, in promotional or publicity uses of the term 'smart' the English word is used. In other contexts, such as policy documents or workshop reports, 'smart' is usually rendered into Thai as *samaat*, using the English loan word. The connotations of the loan word are closer to 'chic, urbane, well turned-out', rather than 'intelligent' (in Thai *chalaat*) per se. Think of a suave man in a fashionable, slim-fit blazer, a friend tells me.
2 The four developments referred to are: a new elevated double-track freight railway line, a rail line expansion to accommodate the new high-speed service, the light rail

network and a series of property development zones, including those designated as transit-oriented development opportunities around the new stations.

3 In 2015, Thailand's National Reform Council produced a government report stating that in all probability parts of Bangkok would be permanently under water within 15 years.

4 The Thai deputy prime minister's 100 smart cities announcement followed a commitment by the newly elected BJP-dominated ruling party in India to a national programme of creating 100 smart cities. Thailand's ASEAN partner Indonesia also launched its own 100 smart cities programme in 2017.

5 In late May 2014, the Thai army seized power, following street protests and occupations of government buildings which had been organised by the People's Democratic Reform Committee, opponents of the elected government. The military coup leaders, under the leadership of the army head Prayut Chan-ocha, established the National Council for Peace and Order, which ruled until general elections in 2019. Under military rule there was a spike in prosecutions of human rights and democracy advocates under lèse-majesté, sedition and computer crimes laws. The long-delayed 2019 general election was criticised by international NGOs and observers for being neither free nor fair. The Election Commission was a body appointed by the military-dominated National Legislative Assembly. Former junta leader Prayut was confirmed as prime minister in June 2019. The Future Forward Party, a new political party which ran on a progressive anti-military platform, winning a total of 81 seats, was controversially dissolved in February by the Constitutional Court for apparent violations of electoral law.

6 The video of the light rail network and its proposed stations produced by Ensure Communications for Khon Kaen Think Tank can be accessed at https://youtu.be/pAlVTyfPt3I.

7 Dao Din campaigners have supported environmental protests across rural Isaan, opposing Potash mining in Udon Thani and the construction of a power plant in Kalasin (Sripokangkul et al. 2018). In the wake of the 2014 coup the military junta introduced a forest reclamation policy which led to thousands of evictions, while using emergency powers to push ahead with a series of environmentally damaging mega-projects.

8 Loei province is roughly 200 km northwest of Khon Kaen City. Villagers and anti-mine activists have accused a goldmining company of contaminating water sources with cyanide. Villagers and anti-mine activists have been subject to judicial harassment using defamation law, armed gangs and death threats.

9 Khon Kaen-born artist Apichatpong Weerasethakul vividly conveyed the existence of these lines in a recent interview, when he reflected on his own childhood. 'I grew up in the hospital area in Khon Kaen City, in a Chinese family with a very comfortable middle-class life. But it is still a bubble; in the hospital, in the education system, and in Khon Kaen itself. There are different layers of walls'. Returning to Khon Kaen to make films is not conceived as a return or a homecoming. 'I feel that coming here

with the camera is to find, or to learn something outside these bubbles'. *Isaan Record*, 'Apichatpong Weerasethakul: Bursting Bubbles, Awaiting a Dark Future', 1 February 2019, https://isaanrecord.com/2019/02/01/apichatpong-weerasethakul-interview-tcdc/.

10 I have in mind the extraordinary preface to the prison memoir of Prontip Mankhong *All They Could Do to Us*, published in Thai by Aan Press. An extract from Tyrell Haberkorn's English translation appears on the Asian American Writers' Workshop website, https://aaww.org/all-they-could-do-to-us/. As Ida Aroonwong puts it in the publisher's preface: 'The book is proof that a person who is steadfast in herself and pours constant energy into creating light cannot accept merely being a "victim", even when she herself falls into darkness'.

17   Does Photography Have a Future? (Does Anything Else?)

1 Several of the ideas that subsequently developed into this chapter had originally been sketched out in a short essay of the same title, which was published in the exhibition catalogue *RESET: Futures Photography 2020*, edited by curator Salvatore Vitale.

18   Astronoetic Voyaging: Speculation, Media and Futurity

1 On the parallels between *Star Maker* and Dante's *Divine Comedy*, see McCarthy (1981).
2 References to *Star Maker* are indicated solely by a page number for the rest of this article.

Contributors

Daisy Asquith is an award-winning documentary filmmaker and Senior Lecturer in both the theory and practice of documentary at Goldsmiths, University of London. She is also a co-founder of Goldsmiths' Centre for Queer History. Asquith has made more than 25 documentaries for the BBC, Channel 4, the Irish Film Board and the BFI. She convenes the MA in Screen Documentary at Goldsmiths, which brings fresh, creative and diverse voices to the industry. The graduation films are regularly shortlisted by BAFTA, Grierson and the Royal Television Society.

Lisa Blackman is Professor in Media and Communications at Goldsmiths, University of London. Blackman works at the intersection of body studies, affect studies and media and cultural theory. She has written six books, with specific focus on mental health, critical media psychology and the affective dimensions of media and communication technologies and software cultures. Her current research project charts the broken genealogy between narcissistic storytelling, military and psychological torture technologies and post-truth communication strategies. It will culminate in a book, *Abuse Assemblages: Power, Post-Truth and Strategic Deception.*

Clea Bourne is Senior Lecturer in the Department of Media, Communications and Cultural Studies at Goldsmiths, University of London. Her research explores how twenty-first-century markets are mediatised, with a particular focus on platformisation and artificial intelligence. She is author of *Trust, Power and Public Relations in Financial Markets* (2017) and has published widely in a range of journals, including *New Media & Society* and *American Behavioral Scientist*, as well as in various edited collections.

NG Bristow is a writer/director and artist. His credits as screenwriter/director include commissions by FilmFour, Channel 4, the BBC, the UKFC, the BFI, the NIFC, NI Screen and the Arts Council. Among his expanded media pieces are *Unsound* (premiered at SXSW) and *I am Maddy Burns/The One and Only* (premiered at DAW Singapore). He has terrified audiences with his binaural nightmare *The Ever-Expanding Cabinet of Unnameable Horrors* and brought theatre to the terraces of Millwall Football Club. He convenes the MA in Directing Fiction at Goldsmiths, University of London.

James Burton is Senior Lecturer in Cultural Studies and Cultural History at Goldsmiths, University of London. His research concerns the philosophy and cultural politics of science fiction, memory, posthumanism, ecology and error. A former research fellow at the ICI Berlin: Institute for Cultural Inquiry, he is the author of *The Philosophy of Science Fiction: Henri Bergson and the Fabulations of Philip K. Dick* (2015) and co-editor, with Erich Hörl, of *General Ecology: The New Ecological Paradigm* (2017).

Sarah Cefai is Lecturer in Gender, Sexuality and Cultural Studies at Goldsmiths, University of London. She is a feminist cultural theorist whose work examines questions of cultural experience, identity and belonging. Cefai is especially interested in cultural form, experimental and other modes of writing and the state of the world as expressed by cultural politics. To this effect, she has published essays that examine a range of affective structures, including national belonging and whiteness, intimacy and humiliation.

Sue Clayton is a fiction and documentary film writer and director, who also consults for Channel 4 News and ITV News. Her award-winning films include *The Stansted 15: On Trial* (2019), *Calais Children: A Case to Answer* (2017) and *Hamedullah: The Road Home* (2012). A Professor of Film and Television at Goldsmiths, University of London, she co-authored *Unaccompanied Young Migrants: Identity, Care and Justice* (2019) and recently published *The New Internationalists: Activist Volunteers in the European Refugee Crisis* (Goldsmiths Press 2020).

Neal Coghlan (Studio Aszyk) is a digital creative of varying disciplines working with 3D animation, music and motion capture in immersive and interactive environments, and on various client-led and personal projects. He has creative-directed animations for Google, created TV graphics for the Sydney Mardi Gras, tech-led large-scale projection-mapping projects, art-directed virtual reality projects and been lead artist on a funded research project into soft-body dynamics with Marshmallow Laser Feast.

Sean Cubitt, formerly Professor of Film and Media at Goldsmiths, University of London, is now Professor of Screen Studies at the University of Melbourne. He works on ecocritical approaches to the history and philosophy of media, with current projects focusing on aesthetic politics and practices of truth. His most recent book is *Anecdotal Evidence: Ecocritique from Hollywood to the Mass Image* (2020).

James Curran is Professor of Communications at Goldsmiths, University of London. He has written or edited 21 books about the media. His most recent publications are *Power Without Responsibility* (with Jean Seaton, 8th edition, 2018), *Culture Wars* (with Ivor Gaber and Julian Petley, 2nd edition, 2019) and *Media and Society* (ed. with David Hesmondhalgh, 6th edition, 2019).

Clemence Debaig is a designer, dancer and creative technologist. She creates work at the intersection of dance and technology, from interactive installations to performances. In parallel with her dance training, Debaig has an MSc in Engineering and Design (2008) from the University of Technology of Compiègne (France) and an MA in Computational Arts (2020) from Goldsmiths, University of London.

Natalie Fenton is Professor of Media and Communications at Goldsmiths, University of London, and Co-Director of the Centre for the Study of Global Media and Democracy. She was Vice-Chair of the Board of the campaign group Hacked Off for seven years and is currently Chair of the UK Media Reform Coalition. Her books include *New Media, Old News: Journalism and Democracy in the Digital Age* (2010), *Misunderstanding the Internet* (co-authored with James Curran and Des Freedman, 2nd edition, 2016), *Digital, Political, Radical* (2016), *Media, Democracy and Social Change: Re-imagining Political Communications* (co-authored with Des Freedman, Gholam Khiabany and Aeron Davis,

2020) and *The Media Manifesto* (co-authored with Des Freedman, Justin Schlosberg and Lina Dencik, 2020).

Des Freedman is a Professor of Media and Communications at Goldsmiths, University of London. He is the author of several books, including *The Contradictions of Media Power* (2014) and *The Media Manifesto* (with Natalie Fenton, Justin Schlosberg and Lina Dencik, 2020). His most recent edited collection is *Capitalism's Conscience: 200 Years of the Guardian* (2021) and he is one of the founding members of the Media Reform Coalition.

Gholam Khiabany teaches in the Department of Media, Communication and Cultural Studies at Goldsmiths, University of London. He is a member of the council of management of the Institute of Race Relations and the Editorial Working Committee of *Race and Class*. His latest publication is *Media, Democracy and Social Change* (co-authored with Aeron Davis, Natalie Fenton and Des Freedman, 2020).

Sandra van Lente was Postdoctoral Research Fellow on the Rethinking 'Diversity' in Publishing project at Goldsmiths, University of London in 2019–2020. After studying British literature and business studies in Germany and the USA, she worked as a lecturer and researcher at the Centre for British Studies, Humboldt-Universität zu Berlin. Sandra wrote her PhD on cultural exchange in contemporary British novels on migration, focusing on the tensions between the novels' content and how they were marketed. She co-runs the literature blog and event series Literary Field Kaleidoscope in Berlin and is particularly interested in independent publishing and bookselling, women in publishing and issues of diversity.

Richard MacDonald is a researcher and teacher working across media ethnography and media history. His current research explores contemporary forms of mediated urbanism and the production of urban space in Southeast Asia. He is a Senior Lecturer in the Department of Media, Communications and Cultural Studies at Goldsmiths, University of London.

Mirca Madianou is Reader in the Department of Media, Communications and Cultural Studies at Goldsmiths, University of London. Her current research focuses on the social consequences of communication technologies, data and automation in the global South, especially in relation to migration and humanitarian emergencies. She is the author of *Mediating the Nation: News, Audiences and The Politics of Identity* (2005) and *Migration and New Media: Transnational Families and Polymedia* (with Daniel Miller, 2011).

Mathapelo Mofokeng is a screenwriter and author from Johannesburg, South Africa. In addition to the audio drama *Mother City?*, she has written short films on a range of themes. Her films have screened at Underwire, London Shorts, BFI Soul Connect, Aesthetica, Heart of Gold and Manchester Film Festival, among others. Her short stories include 'The Strong-Strong Winds' (published in *Adda Magazine*) and 'Blended' (published in Popshot Quarterly). She is a graduate of the Goldsmiths MA Scriptwriting programme. In 2021 she was awarded the PEN America Robert J. Dau Short Story Prize and was longlisted for the Commonwealth Short Story Prize.

David Morley is Emeritus Professor of Communications at Goldsmiths, University of London, and author of *Television, Audiences and Cultural Studies* (1992), *Home Territories* (2000), *Media, Modernity and Technology* (Routledge 2006) and, most recently, *Communications and Mobility: The Migrant, the Mobile Phone and the Container Box* (2018). His work has been translated into 18 languages.

Youhong (Friendred) Peng is an installation/computational artist currently undertaking his doctorate at Goldsmiths, University of London, researching intertwined relationship between technology, installation and performance art. Several of his works have been exhibited at Tate Britain and the Design Museum, and others have been published on design and technology platforms such as DesignBoom and CreativeApplications.

Anamik Saha is Senior Lecturer in Media and Communications at Goldsmiths, University of London. He is the author of *Race and the Cultural Industries* (2018). In 2019, he received an Arts and Humanities Research Council Leadership Fellow grant for a project entitled 'Rethinking Diversity in Publishing', which led to a report of the same name published by Goldsmiths Press in June 2020. Anamik is an editor of the *European Journal of Cultural Studies*. His new book, *Race, Culture, Media*, was published in 2021.

Andreas Schlegel (aka Sojamo) is an artist and teacher working across disciplines, developing artifacts, tools and interfaces where art and technology meet in curious ways. He heads the Media Lab at Lasalle College of the Arts in Singapore. In his artistic practice he creates audio, visual and physical outcomes driven by computation, interaction and networked processes. His practice-based, collaborative and interdisciplinary works are concerned with emerging and open-source technologies.

Richard M. Shannon is Head of Radio at Goldsmiths, University of London. He is a Fellow of the Royal Society of Arts, Chair of the Myanmar Group (Asia Centre) and a Senior Fellow of the Higher Education Academy. Shannon is a published playwright, theatre director and radio drama producer. He was a founding director of Independent Radio Drama Productions and has produced major series for LBC radio in London and National Public Radio in the USA. His most recent publication is a chapter on Cameron Mackintosh in *The Handbook of the Global Musical* (forthcoming).

Daniel Strutt is a Lecturer in the Department of Media, Communications and Cultural Studies at Goldsmiths, University of London, where he teaches film theory and analysis, alongside social, cultural and economic theory. His book, *The Digital Image and Reality: Affect, Metaphysics and Post-Cinema* was published in 2019. Having worked on research projects with Creativeworks London, CREATe and the AHRC Creative Economy Programme, he also engages in innovative performance production work with contemporary digital audio-visual artists.

Milly Williamson teaches in the Department of Media, Communications and Cultural Studies at Goldsmiths, University of London. She has numerous publications on celebrity culture, including *Celebrity: Capitalism and the Making of Fame* (2016). Her work examines aspects of race and gender in media culture and the role of celebrity in the expansion of promotional culture. She is currently working on a new project on celebrity and social media.

Joanna Zylinska is Professor of Media Philosophy and Critical Digital Practice at King's College London. Prior to joining King's, she worked for 17 years at Goldsmiths, University of London. The author of a number of books – including *The End of Man: A Feminist Counterapocalypse* (2018), *Nonhuman Photography* (2017) and *Minimal Ethics for the Anthropocene* (2014) – she is also involved in experimental and collaborative publishing projects. Zylinska combines her philosophical writings with image-based art practice and curatorial work. Her current research explores the relationship between perception and cognition in relation to the recent developments in artificial intelligence and machine vision.

Index